CORTINA DICTIONARIES

TRAVELER'S
FRENCH
DICTIONARY

ENGLISH-FRENCH / FRENCH-ENGLISH

by
Teresa Nutting
Licenciée ès Lettres
Aix-en-Provence
and
Michel Marcy
Certifié de Lettres Classiques
Asst. Professor of French
St. Mary's College, Notre Dame, Indiana

•

SERIES GENERAL EDITORS
Dilaver Berberi, Ph.D.
Edel A. Winje, Ed.D.

CORTINA LEARNING INTERNATIONAL, INC.
Publishers • WESTPORT, CT 06880

Library of Congress Cataloging-in-Publication Data

Nutting, Teresa.
  Cortina traveler's French dictionary: English-French, French-
  English / by Teresa Nutting and Michel Marcy.
      p.   cm.
  Rev. ed. of: Cortina/Grosset basic French dictionary. 1975.
  ISBN 0-8327-0722-8 (paper): $6.95
    1. English language—Dictionaries—French. 2. French language
  —Dictionaries—English. I. Marcy, Michel. II. Nutting, Teresa.
  Cortina/Grosset basic French dictionary. III. Title IV. Title:
  Traveler's French dictionary.
  PC2640.N85   1993   93-3672
  443'.21—dc20   CIP

Printed in the United States of America

HH Editions 9 8 7 6 5 4 3 2 1   9307-16

Contents

CONTENTS

How to Use This Dictionary

Here is a handy, pocket-sized Dictionary that will put French at your fingertips. Whether you are a beginner or already have a working knowledge of French, whether you are a student, a businessperson, or a tourist—this Dictionary will give you what you need to get along in French.

The entries are the heart of the Dictionary; they number almost 11,000 (5000-plus in the English-French section, 5000-plus in the French-English section). On the English side, entries were chosen for their usefulness and applicability to common everyday situations. French entries were selected from words that occur most frequently in the course of everyday life in French-speaking countries. Thus, you will find here the words you will actually hear and speak when using French, whether at home or abroad. In addition, this Dictionary is unique in providing the pronunciation of the French words *on both sides,* so that whenever you encounter them you can immediately pronounce them.

Additional Special Features

In addition to the entries themselves, this Dictionary includes the following extra features to enable you to actually use the French language in a variety of different situations.

Guide to Pronunciation. The pronunciation of each French entry is given in simple English alphabet transcriptions. Thus, the user can pronounce a new word immediately, just by following the simple guide which appears with each entry. The "Key to French Pronunciation," found on page viii, explains French sounds and gives examples of each one, and shows how they compare with English.

Phrases for Use Abroad (page 311). Everyday expressions, requests, statements, questions and answers for specific situations—each with its pronunciation—let you communicate easily.

Menu Reader (page 328). A comprehensive list of food and drink, complete with pronunciation, takes the mystery out of French menus.

Concise French Grammar (page 336). For the user who wishes a quick overview of French grammar, or who wants an explanation of how verbs are conjugated or noun plurals formed, this grammar section is an invaluable aid. It is divided into sections treating nouns, verbs, adjectives, adverbs, sentence formation, etc., for easy reference and use.

Helpful Notes for the Reader

1. *All verbs* are marked *v.*, and irregular verbs are marked *irreg*. There are tables of irregular verbs showing their conjugation at the end of the Dictionary, and the "Concise Grammar" explains the conjugation of regular forms.

2. *Reflexive verbs* are those preceded by *se* or *s'*. These are always used with the reflexive pronoun. See the "Concise Grammar" for an explanation of the use of these verbs.

3. *All French nouns* have a designated gender, and adjectives must agree in gender with the nouns they modify.

4. *Parts of speech* of entries (except verbs) are not marked unless the translation does not indicate the part

of speech or if the word appears more than once as different parts of speech.

5. *Many common or idiomatic expressions* are included in the Dictionary, along with their pronunciation, so that the reader can use them correctly.

Using this Dictionary is sure to make your contact with French-speaking people and their language much more pleasurable and satisfying, whether at home or abroad.

Key to French Pronunciation

Vowels

Note that English vowels are often diphthongs (c*a*ke, for example, is k*a-ee*k), whereas French vowels are not. When an English diphthong is the closest equivalent to a French vowel, be careful to pronounce only the first half of the diphthong.

French spelling	Phonetic symbol	Sound description & Examples
a, â	ah	pronounced like *a* in f*a*ther. *Ex.*: **bal** [*bahl*] dance
e, eu, oeu	uh	pronounced like *a* in *a*bout or like *e* in unstressed th*e*. *Ex.*: **le** [*luh*] the; **feu** [*fuh*] fire; **soeur** [*suhr*] sister
è, ê	e	pronounced like *e* in l*e*t. *Ex.*: **père** [*per*] father; **tête** [*tet*] head
é, er	eh	pronounced like *e* in th*e*y or like *a* in c*a*ke, but not diphthongized. *Ex.*: **parler** [*pahr-leh*] speak; **été** [*eh-teh*] summer
i, y	ee	pronounced like *i* in mach*i*ne or like *ee* in f*ee*t. *Ex.*: **pipe** [*peep*] pipe; **Yves** [*eev*] Yves
i	y	before a vowel, pronounced like *y* in *y*es. *Ex.*: **vieux** [*vyuh*] old
o, au eau	oh	pronounced like *o* in s*o*, but not diphthongized. *Ex.*: **chose** [*shohz*] thing; **bateau** [*bah-toh*] boat
o	o	pronounced like *o* in f*o*r or b*o*y. *Ex.*: **col** [*kol*] collar
ou	oo	pronounced like *oo* in s*oo*n. *Ex.*: **vous** [*voo*] you

| u | ü | no equivalent in English. Pronounce *ee*, then round your lips. *Ex.*: **vu** [*vu*] seen |
| oi | wah | pronounced like *wa* in *wa*ter. *Ex.*: **loi** [*lwah*] law |

Certain vowels in French are nasalized before an *n* or an *m*. Do not pronounce the *n* (or *m*), but pronounce the vowel in your nose:

on	õ	pronounced like *o* in do*n*'t. *Ex.*: **bon** [*bõ*] good
un, in	ẽ	pronounced like *a* in *gra*nt. *Ex.*: **un** [*ẽ*] one; **vin** [*vẽ*] wine
an, en	ã	pronounced like *a* in British c*a*n't. *Ex.*: **blanc** [*blã*] white; **en** [*ã*] in

Glides—combinations of vowels resulting in *w* — are:

| oui, ui | wee | pronounced like *wee* in *wee*k. *Ex.*: **Louis** [*lwee*] Louis; **lui** [*lwee*] him |

Consonants

French consonants are basically similar to English ones. Final consonants are very often silent (not pronounced), and in such cases won't be marked at all in the transcription. The final consonants most commonly pronounced are *c*, *r*, *f*, and *l*.

H is never pronounced. *R* is pronounced in the back of the mouth, as in gargling. *L* is always pronounced as the first *l* in *li*ttle, never as the second one. The combination *il* is often pronounced *y* (**travail** [*trah-vahy*] work).

Some consonants will be transcribed by others to show how they are always pronounced in French, or how they are pronounced in certain combinations:

ch is always pronounced *sh*, as in *sh*irt: **chat** [*shah*] cat

j is always pronounced *zh*, as in vi*si*on: **jardin** [*zhahr-dẽ*] garden

gn is always pronounced *ny*, as in ca*ny*on: **ignorant** [*ee-nyo-rã*] ignorant. When this combination occurs at the end of a word, it is marked *ñ* to avoid confusion: **campagne** [*kã-pahñ*] country *qu* is generally pronounced *k*: **quand** [*kã*] when

c is pronounced as *s* before vowels *e* and *i*: **ceci** [*suh-see*] this. When written ç, it is also pronounced *s*: **ça** [*sah*] that. Otherwise it is pronounced *k*: **car** [*kahr*] for; **sac** [*sahk*] purse

g is pronounced *zh*, as in vi*s*ion, before *e* and *i*: **géologie** [*zheh-oh-loh-zhee*] geology. Elsewhere it is *g* as in *g*o: **glace** [*glahs*] ice cream. When a "hard" g is followed by *e* or *i*, the transcription is *gh*: **guerre** [*gher*] war

s is generally pronounced like English *s*: **six** [*sees*] six. But between vowels it is pronounced *z*: **magasin** [*mah-gah-zẽ*] store. When linking words (see below), it is also *z*: **les amis** [*leh-zah-mee*] the friends

y in the transcription is always pronounced as in *y*ellow, never as in happ*y*. Be careful at the end of words: **travail** [*trah-vahy*] work; **reveil** [*reh-vey*] alarm clock

Parentheses around a symbol mean that the sound is sometimes pronounced and sometimes not. This can occur for two reasons. If the symbol is *uh* it represents an *e* which frequently disappears in normal speech. *Fenêtre* is often pronounced *fnetre*, and so the transcription reads: [*f(uh)-netr*]. Some *e*'s disappear so often that they haven't been indicated in the transcription at all: *devenir* is transcribed [*duhv-neer*].

If the symbol in parentheses is a consonant, it means that the final consonant is pronounced in the feminine form of the adjective. Final consonants are normally not pronounced, but when you add an *e* to make the adjective feminine, the consonant is no longer final and is pronounced: *vert* (masculine) is pronounced [*ver*]; *verte* (feminine) is pronounced [*vert*], and so the transcription reads [*ver(t)*].

Linking

In French, words that go together (noun and article or adjective, or subject and verb) are usually linked in speech if the second word begins with a vowel sound. This frequently means that a final consonant, normally not pronounced, *will* be pronounced in order to link with the following word. Examples:

    les autos [*leh-zoh-otoh*] the cars
    ils ont [*eel-zõ*] they have
    de beaux habits [*duh-boh-zah-bee*] beautiful clothes
    un petit éléphant [*ẽ-ptee-teh-leh-fã*] a little elephant
    parlent-ils [*pahrl-teel*] are they speaking
    répond-il [*reh-po-teel*] does he answer

    When linking, *s* and *x* are pronounced as *z*, and *d* is pronounced as *t*.

    The letter *h* is never pronounced, but in some words its presence is "felt" enough so that the word beginning with *h* cannot be linked to the word preceding it. For example, *les haches* (the axes) must be pronounced [*leh-ahsh*], not [*leh-zahsh*]. But *les hotels* (the hotels) must be pronounced [*leh-zoh-tel*]. *H*'s that make linking impossible are marked with an asterisk.

General Considerations

In this Dictionary no accents are marked in the pronunciations because all syllables receive more or less equal stress. Some vowels are dropped at times in spoken French, as shown in the transcriptions. Since the natural tendency in English is to stress the beginning of the word, you may want to give slightly stronger emphasis to the last syllable in French. If you do this, and try to speak in the front, rather than the back of your mouth, moving your lips more than you would in English, you will be well on your way to speaking good French.

Abbreviations Used in This Dictionary

adj.	adjective	*irreg.*	irregular
adv.	adverb	*m.*	masc.
anat.	anatomy	*naut.*	nautical
arch.	architecture	*n.*	noun
art.	article	*obj.*	object
Aux.	auxiliary verb	*pers.*	person, personal
conj.	conjunction	*pl.*	plural
dem.	demonstrative	*prep.*	preposition
eccl.	ecclesiastic	*pron.*	pronoun
f.	feminine	*rel.*	relative
interj.	interjection	*sing.*	singular
interr.	interrogative	*subj.*	subject
invar.	invariable	*v.*	verb

English/French

A

a, un, une [ĕ, ün]
abandon *v.,* abandonner [ah-bã-do-neh]
ability, capacité (f) [kah-pah-see-teh]
able *adj.,* capable (de) [kah-pahbl (duh)]
  be able *v.,* pouvoir (irreg) [poo-vwahr]
aboard, à bord (de) [ah bor (duh)]
  All aboard [train], En voiture [ã vwah-tür]
abolish *v.,* abolir [ah-bo-leer]
about *adv.,* environ [ã-vee-rõ]
about *prep.,* au sujet de [oh sü-zheh duh]
above, au-dessus (de) [oh-tsü (duh)]
abroad, à l'étranger [ah leh-trã-zheh]
absence, absence (f) [ahp-sãs]
absent *adj.,* absent [ahp-sã(t)]
absent-minded, distrait [dees-tre(t)]
absolutely, absolument [ahp-so-lü-mã]
absorb *v.,* absorber [ahp-sor-beh]
abstract *adj.,* abstrait [ahp-stre(t)]
absurd, absurde [ahp-sürd]
academy, académie (f) [ah-kah-deh-mee]
accelerator, accélérateur (m) [ahk-seh-leh-rah-tuhr]
accent *n.,* accent (m) [ahk-sã]
accent *v.,* accentuer [ahk-sã-tweh]
accept *v.,* accepter [ahk-sep-teh]
accessible, accessible [ahk-se-seebl]
accident, accident (m) [ahk-see-dã]
accidental, accidentel, -clle [ahk-see-dã-tel]
accommodations *pl.,* logement (m) [lozh-mã]
accompany *v.,* accompagner [ah-kõ-pah-nyeh]
accomplish *v.,* accomplir [ah-kõ-pleer]
according to, selon [suh-lõ]
accordingly, donc, en conséquence [dõk, ã kõ-seh-kãs]

1

account n., compte (m) [kõt]
   bank account, compte (m) en banque [kõt-ã-bãk]
   accounts [of a business], comptabilité (f) [kõ-tah-bee-lee-teh]
   on account of, à cause de [ah kohz duh]
account for v., rendre compte de [rãdr kõt duh]
accountant, comptable (m) [kõ-tahbl]
accurate, exact, juste [ehg-zah(kt), zhüst]
accusation, accusation (f) [ah-kü-zah-syõ]
accuse v., accuser [ah-kü-seh]
accustomed to, habitué à [ah-bee-tweh ah]
ace, as (m) [ahs]
ache v., faire mal [fer mahl]
ache n., douleur (f), mal (m) [doo-luhr, mahl]
   I have a . . . ache, J'ai mal à . . . . [zheh mahl ah]
   headache, mal à la tête [mahl ah lah tet]
   My head aches! Ma tête me fait mal! [mah tet muh feh mahl]
achieve v., accomplir [ah-kõ-pleer]
acid, acide (f) [ah-seed]
acknowledge v., admettre (irreg) [ahd-metr]
   acknowledge receipt of, accuser réception de [ah-kü-zeh reh-sep-syõ duh]
acquaintance, connaissance (f) [ko-ne-sãs]
acquit v., acquitter [ah-kee-teh]
acre, demi-hectare (m) [duh-mee ehk-tahr]
across, à travers [ah trah-ver]
   across the street, en face (de) [ã fahs (duh)]
act n., acte (m) [ahkt]
act [do] v., agir [ah-zheer]
act [represent] v., jouer [zhoo-eh]
action, action (f) [ahk-syõ]
active, actif, -ive [ahk-teef, ahk-teev]
activity, activité (f) [ahk-tee-vee-teh]
actor, acteur (m) [ahk-tuhr]
actress, actrice (f) [ahk-trees]
actual, réel, -elle [reh-el]
actually, réellement, effectivement [reh-el-mã, eh-fek-teev-mã]

adapt *v.*, adapter [*ah-dahp-teh*]
add *v.*, ajouter, additionner [*ah-zhoo-teh, ah-dee-syo-neh*]
addition, addition (f) [*ah-dee-syõ*]
additional, additionnel, -elle; supplémentaire [*ah-dee-syo-nel, sü-pleh-mã-ter*]
address *n.*, adresse (f) [*ah-dres*]
address *v.*, adresser [*ah-dre-seh*]
addressee, destinataire (m) [*des-tee-nah-ter*]
adequate, adéquat [*ah-deh-kwah(t)*]
adhesive tape, sparadrap (m) [*spah-rah-drah*]
adjective, adjectif (m) [*ahd-zhek-teef*]
adjust *v.*, ajuster [*ah-zhüs-teh*]
adjustment, ajustement (m) [*ah-zhüs-tuh-mã*]
administer *v.*, administrer [*ahd-mee-nees-treh*]
administration, administration (f) [*ahd-mee-nees-trah-syõ*]
admirable, admirable [*ahd-mee-rahbl*]
admiral, amiral (m), -aux (pl) [*ah-mee-rahl, ah-mee-roh*]
admiration, admiration (f) [*ahd-mee-rah-syõ*]
admire *v.*, admirer [*ahd-mee-reh*]
admirer *n.*, admirateur, -trice [*ahd-mee-rah-tuhr, ahd-mee-rah-trees*]
admission [entry], entrée (f) [*ã-treh*]
admit [let in] *v.*, admettre (irreg), laisser entrer [*ahd-metr, leh-seh ã-treh*]
admittance, entrée (f), accès (m) [*ã-treh, ahk-se*]
   no admittance, défense d'entrer [*deh-fãs dã-treh*]
adopt *v.*, adopter [*ah-dop-teh*]
adore *v.*, adorer [*ah-do-reh*]
adult, adulte [*ah-dült*]
advance *n.*, avance (f) [*ah-vãs*]
   in advance, en avance [*ã-nah-vãs*]
advance *v.*, avancer [*ah-vã-seh*]
advantage, avantage (m) [*ah-vã-tahzh*]
adventure, aventure (f) [*ah-vã-tür*]
adverb, adverbe (m) [*ahd-verb*]
advertise *v.*, annoncer, faire de la réclame [*ah-nõ-seh, fer dlah reh-klahm*]
advertisement, annonce (f), publicité (f), réclame (f) [*ah-*

    nõs, püb-lee-see-teh, reh-klahm]

advice, conseil(s) (m) [*kõ-sey*]

  Take my advice, Suivez mes conseils [*swee-veh meh kõ-sey*]

  a piece of advice, un conseil [*ẽ kõ-sey*]

advise *v.,* conseiller [*kõ-seh-yeh*]

affair, affaire (f) [*ah-fer*]

affect *v.,* affecter [*ah-fek-teh*]

affection, affection (f) [*ah-fek-syõ*]

affectionate, affectueux, -tueuse [*ah-fek-twuh, ah-fek-twuhz*]

affirmative, affirmatif, -tive [*ah-feer-mah-teef, ah-feer-mah-teev*]

afraid: be afraid, avoir peur [*ah-vwahr puhr*]

Africa, Afrique (f) [*ah-freek*]

African, africain [*ah-freek-ẽ, ah-freek-en*]

after *prep. & adv.,* après [*ah-pre*]

afternoon, après-midi (m, f) [*ah-pre-mee-dee*]

afterwards, ensuite, après [*ã-sweet, ah-pre*]

again, encore [*ã-kor*]

against, contre [*kõtr*]

age, âge (m) [*ahzh*]

agency, agence (f) [*ah-zhãs*]

  travel agency, agence de voyages [*ah-zãs duh vwah-yahzh*]

agent, agent (m) [*ah-zhã*]

aggravate *v.,* aggraver [*ah-grah-veh*]

aggression, agression (f) [*ah-gre-syõ*]

aggressive, agressif, -sive [*ah-gre-seef, ah-gre-seev*]

ago, il y a [*eel yah*]

  three weeks ago, il y a trois semaines [*eel yah trwah smen*]

  How long ago . . . ? Il y a combien de temps (que)? [*eel yah kõ-byẽ duh tã (kuh)*]

agree *v.,* être d'accord [*etr dah-kor*]

agreed, entendu, d'accord [*ã-tã-dü, dah-kor*]

agreement, accord (m) [*ah-kor*]

agriculture, agriculture (f) [*ah-gree-kül-tür*]

ahead, en avant [*ã-nah-vã*]

  Go ahead! Allez-y! [*ah-leh-zee*]

aid *n.,* aide [*ed*]

first aid, premiers soins (m) [*pruh-myeh swē*]
aid *v.,* aider [*eh-deh*]
aim *v.,* viser [*vee-zeh*]
air, air (m) [*er*]
airline, compagnie (f) aérienne [*kō-pah-nee ah-ehr-yen*]
airmail, par avion [*pahr ah-vyō*]
airplane, avion (m) [*ah-vyō*]
airport, aéroport (m) [*ah-eh-roh-por*]
aisle, allée (f) [*ah-leh*]
alarm *n.,* alarme (f), alerte (f) [*ah-lahrm, ah-lert*]
alarm clock, réveil (m) [*reh-vey*]
alcohol, alcool (m) [*ahl-kol*]
alert *adj.,* alerte [*ah-lert*]
alike *adj.,* pareil, -eille; semblable [*pah-rey, sã-blahbl*]
alive, vivant [*vee-vã(t)*]
all *adj.,* tout le, toute la, tous les, toutes les [*too(t)*]
  all right, d'accord [*dah-kor*]
  not at all, pas du tout [*pah dü too*]
  That's all, C'est tout [*seh-too*]
allow *v.,* permettre (irreg) [*per-metr*]
  Allow me! Permettez-moi! [*per-meh-teh-mwah*]
ally *n.,* allié, -ée [*ahl-yeh*]
almond, amande (f) [*ah-mãd*]
almost, presque [*presk*]
alone, seul [*suhl*]
  Leave me alone! Laissez-moi tranquille! [*leh-seh-mwah trã-keel*]
along, le long de [*luh lō duh*]
aloud, à haute voix [*ah oht vwah*]
Alps, Alpes (f, pl) [*ahlp*]
already, déjà [*deh-zhah*]
Alsace, Alsace (f) [*ahl-zahs*]
also, aussi [*oh-see*]
altar, autel (m) [*oh-tel*]
alteration, retouche (f) [*ruh-toosh*]
although, bien que [*byē kuh*]
altitude, altitude (f) [*ahl-tee-tüd*]
altogether, tout à fait, entièrement [*too-tah fe, ã-tyer-mã*]

always, toujours [*too-zhoor*]

am: I am, je suis [*zhuh-swee*]

ambassador, ambassadeur, -drice [*ã-bah-sah-duhr, ã-bah-sah-drees*]

ambition, ambition (f) [*ã-bee-syõ*]

ambitious, ambitieux, -euse [*ã-bee-syuh, ã-bee-syuhz*]

ambulance, ambulance (f) [*ã-bü-lãs*]

America, Amérique (f) [*ah-meh-reek*]

   North America, Amérique du Nord [*ah-meh-reek dü nor*]

   South America, Amérique du Sud [*ah-meh-reek dü süd*]

American, américain, -caine [*ah-meh-ree-kẽ, ah-meh-ree-ken*]

among, parmi, entre [*pahr-mee, ãtr*]

amount *n.*, quantité (f) [*kã-tee-teh*]

amount to [total] *v.*, s'élever (à) [*sehl-veh (ah)*]

   It amounts to the same thing, Cela revient au même [*suh-lah ruh-vyẽ-toh mem*]

amuse *v.*, amuser [*ah-mü-zeh*]

an, un, une [*ẽ, ün*]

analysis, analyse (f) [*ah-nah-leez*]

ancestor, ancêtre (m, f) [*ã-setr*]

anchor, ancre (f) [*ãkr*]

anchovy, anchois (m) [*ã-shwah*]

ancient, ancien, -ne; antique [*ã-syẽ, ã-syen; ã-teek*]

and, et [*eh*]

angel, ange (m) [*ãzh*]

anger, colère (f) [*ko-ler*]

angle, angle (m) [*ãgl*]

angry, en colère, fâché [*ã ko-ler, fah-sheh*]

   get angry *v.*, se fâcher [*suh fah-sheh*]

animal, animal (m), -aux (pl) [*ah-nee-mahl, ah-nee-moh*]

ankle, cheville (f) [*shuh-veey*]

anniversary, anniversaire (m) [*ah-nee-ver-ser*]

announce *v.*, annoncer [*ah-nõ-seh*]

announcement, annonce (f) [*ah-nõs*]

annoy *v.*, ennuyer, gêner [*ã-nwee-yeh, zheh-neh*]

annoying, ennuyeux, -euse [*ã-nwee-yuh, ã-nwee-yuhz*]

annual, annuel, -elle [*ah-nwel*]

anonymous, anonyme [*ah-no-neem*]
another, un autre, une autre [*ĕ-nohtr, ü-nohtr*]
answer *n.*, réponse (f) [*reh-pŏs*]
answer *v.*, répondre [*reh-pŏdr*]
ant, fourmi (f) [*foor-mee*]
antique *n.*, objet (m) ancien [*ob-zheh ã-syĕ*]
antique dealer, antiquaire (m, f) [*ã-tee-ker*]
anxious, inquiet, -ète [*ĕ-kyeh, ĕ-kyet*]
any *adj.*, du, de la, des [*dü, duh lah, deh*]
   No, I don't want any, Non, je n'en veux pas [*nŏ, zhnã-vuh pah*]
any [no matter which], n'importe quel [*nĕ-port-kel*]
anybody, quelqu'un [*kel-kĕ*]
anyhow, en tout cas [*ã too kah*]
anything, quelque chose, n'importe quoi [*kel-kuh shoz, nĕ-port kwah*]
anyway, de toute façon [*duh toot fah-sŏ*]
anywhere, n'importe où [*nĕ-port oo*]
apartment, appartement (m) [*ah-pahr-tuh-mã*]
apartment house, immeuble (m) [*ee-muhbl*]
apiece, chacun, chacune [*shah-kĕ, shah-kün*]
apologize, s'excuser [*sek-skü-zeh*]
appear [seem] *v.*, paraître (irreg), sembler [*pah-retr, sã-bleh*]
appearance, apparance (f) [*ah-pah-rãs*]
appendicitis, appendicite (f) [*ah-pĕ-dee-seet*]
appetite, appétit (m) [*ah-peh-tee*]
appetizer, apéritif (m) [*ah-peh-ree-teef*]
applaud *v.*, applaudir [*ah-ploh-deer*]
applause, applaudissements (m, pl) [*ah-ploh-dees-mã*]
apple, pomme (f) [*pom*]
application, demande (f) [*duh-mãd*]
apply *v.*, appliquer [*ah-plee-keh*]
appoint *v.*, nommer [*no-meh*]
appointment [date], rendez-vous (m) [*rã-deh-voo*]
appreciate *v.*, apprécier [*ah-preh-syeh*]
apprentice, apprenti, -e [*ah-prã-tee*]
approach *v.*, approcher [*ah-pro-sheh*]
appropriate *adj.*, approprié [*ah-pro-pree-yeh*]

approval, approbation (f) [*ah-pro-bah-syõ*]
approve v., approuver [*ah-proo-veh*]
approximately, environ [*ã-vee-rõ*]
apricot, abricot (m) [*ah-bree-koh*]
April, avril (m) [*ah-vreel*]
apron, tablier (m) [*tah-blee-yeh*]
Arab n. & adj., Arabe (m, f) [*ah-rahb*]
Arabia, Arabie (f) [*ah-rah-bee*]
arbitrary, arbitraire [*ahr-bee-trer*]
arch, voûte (f), arc (m) [*voot, ahrk*]
architect, architecte (m) [*ahr-shee-tekt*]
architecture, architecture (f) [*ahr-shee-tek-tür*]
are: there are, il y a [*eel yah*]
argue v., se disputer [*suh dees-pü-teh*]
argument, argument (m) [*ahr-gü-mã*]
arise v., s'élever [*sehl-veh*]
aristocrat, aristocrate (m, f) [*ah-rees-toh-kraht*]
aristocratic, aristocratique [*ah-rees-toh-krah-teek*]
arm n., bras (m) [*brah*]
armchair, fauteuil (m) [*foh-tuhy*]
army, armée (f) [*ahr-meh*]
around prep., autour de [*oh-toor duh*]
around adv., autour [*oh-toor*]
arrange v., arranger [*ah-rã-zheh*]
arrest v., arrêter [*ah-re-teh*]
arrival, arrivée (f) [*ah-ree-veh*]
arrive v., arriver (*Aux:* ÊTRE) [*ah-ree-veh*]
art, art (m) [*ahr*]
artery, artère (f) [*ahr-ter*]
artichoke, artichaut (m) [*ahr-tee-shoh*]
article, article (m) [*ahr-teekl*]
artificial, artificiel, -elle [*ahr-tee-fee-syel*]
artist, artiste (m, f) [*ahr-teest*]
as, comme [*kom*]
   as . . . as, aussi . . . que [*oh-see . . . kuh*]
   not so . . . as, pas si . . . que [*pah see . . . kuh*]
   as for, quant à [*kã-tah*]
   as much as, autant que [*oh-tã kuh*]

as soon as, aussitôt que [*oh-see-toh kuh*]

ash, cendre (f) [*sãdr*]

ashamed: to be ashamed, avoir honte (f) [*ah-vwahr õt*]

ashore, à terre [*ah ter*]

ashtray, cendrier (m) [*sã-dree-yeh*]

Asia, Asie (f) [*ah-zee*]

aside, de côté, à part [*duh koh-teh, ah pahr*]

ask (for) *v.*, demander [*duh-mã-deh*]

    ask a question, poser une question [*poh-zeh ün kes-tyõ*]

asleep, endormi [*ã-dor-mee*]

    fall asleep *v.*, s'endormir (irreg) [*sã-dor-meer*]

asparagus, asperge (f) [*ah-sperzh*]

aspirin, aspirine (f) [*ah-spee-reen*]

assembly, assemblée (f) [*ah-sã-bleh*]

assistance, aide (f) [*ed*]

assistant *n.*, assistant, -e [*ah-sees-tã, ah-sees-tãt*]

associate *n.*, associé [*ah-so-syeh*]

associate *v.*, s'associer [*sah-so-syeh*]

assume [think] *v.*, supposer [*sü-poh-zeh*]

assumption, supposition (f), hypothèse (f) [*sü-poh-zee-syõ, ee-po-tez*]

assurance, assurance (f) [*ah-sü-rãs*]

assure *v.*, assurer [*ah-sü-reh*]

astonish *v.*, étonner [*eh-to-neh*]

    be astonished, s'étonner [*seh-to-neh*]

astonishing, étonnant [*eh-to-nã(t)*]

at, à [*ah*]

    at first, d'abord [*dah-bor*]

    at last, enfin [*ã-fẽ*]

    at once, tout de suite [*toot sweet*]

    at six o'clock, à six heures [*ah-see-zuhr*]

    at the same time, en même temps [*ã mem tã*]

athletic, athlétique; sportif, -ive [*aht-leh-teek; spor-teef, spor-teev*]

Atlantic, Atlantique (m) [*aht-lã-teek*]

atmosphere [air], atmosphère (f) [*aht-mos-fer*]

atmosphere [surroundings], ambiance (f) [*ã-byãs*]

atomic, atomique [*ah-to-meek*]

attach *v.*, attacher [*ah-tah-sheh*]
attack *v.*, attaquer [*ah-tah-keh*]
attempt *v.*, essayer [*eh-se-yeh*]
attend *v.*, assister (à) [*ah-sees-teh (ah)*]
attendant, employé, -ée [*ã-plwah-yeh*]
attention, attention (f) [*ah-tã-syõ*]
attentive, attentif, -ive [*ah-tã-teef, ah-tã-teev*]
attic, grenier (m) [*gruh-nyeh*]
attitude, attitude (f) [*ah-tee-tüd*]
attorney, avocat (m) [*ah-vo-kah*]
attract *v.*, attirer [*ah-tee-reh*]
attractive, joli [*zho-lee*]
auction *n.*, vente (f) aux enchères [*vãt oh-zã-sher*]
audience, public (m) [*püb-leek*]
August, août (m) [*oo(t)*]
aunt, tante (f) [*tãt*]
Australia, Australie (f) [*oh-strah-lee*]
Australian, australien, -enne [*oh-strah-lyẽ, oh-strah-lyen*]
Austria, Autriche (f) [*oh-treesh*]
Austrian, autrichien, -enne [*oh-tree-shyẽ, oh-tree-shyen*]
author, auteur (m) [*oh-tuhr*]
authority, autorité (f) [*oh-to-ree-teh*]
authorize *v.*, autoriser [*oh-to-ree-zeh*]
automatic, automatique [*oh-to-mah-teek*]
automobile, automobile (f), voiture (f) [*oh-toh-mo-beel,*
    vwah-tür]
autumn, automne (m) [*oh-ton*]
available, disponible [*dees-po-neebl*]
avalanche, avalanche (f) [*ah-vah-lãsh*]
avenue, avenue (f) [*ahv-nü*]
average *adj.*, moyen, -enne [*mwah-yẽ, mwah-yen*]
average *n.*, moyenne (f) [*mwah-yen*]
  on the average, en moyenne [*ã mwah-yen*]
avoid *v.*, éviter [*eh-vee-teh*]
awake *adj.*, réveillé [*reh-veh-yeh*]
awaken *v.*, réveiller, se réveiller [*reh-veh-yeh, suh reh-veh-yeh*]
aware, conscient [*kõ-syã(t)*]
away, absent, au loin [*ah-psã(t), oh lwẽ*]

go away v., partir (irreg; *Aux:* ÊTRE), s'en aller (irreg)
    [*pahr-teer, sã-nah-leh*]
  Go away! Allez-vous en! [*ah-leh-voo-zã*]
awful, terrible [*te-reebl*]
awkward, maladroit [*mah-lah-drwah(t)*]
axe, *hache (f) [*ahsh*]
axle, essieu (m) [*eh-syuh*]

B

baby, bébé (m) [*beh-beh*]
bachelor, célibataire (m, f) [*seh-lee-bah-ter*]
back [anat.], n., dos (m) [*doh*]
back [support] v., soutenir (irreg) [*soot-neer*]
back adv., en arrière [*ã-nahr-yer*]
  be back v., être de retour [*etr duh r(uh)-toor*]
  come back v., revenir (irreg; *Aux:* ÊTRE) [*ruh-v(uh)-neer*]
back adj., arrière, de derrière [*ahr-yer, duh der-yer*]
backwards, en arrière [*ã-nahr-yer*]
bacon, lard (m), poitrine fumée (f) [*lahr, pwah-treen fü-meh*]
bad adj., mauvais [*mo-ve(z)*]
  Too bad! Dommage! [*do-mahzh*]
badly adv., mal [*mahl*]
bad-tempered, de mauvais caractère [*duh mo-ve kah-rahk-ter*]
baggage, bagages (m, pl) [*bah-gazh*]
bait n., appât (m) [*ah-pah*]
bake v., faire cuire (irreg) au four [*fer kweer oh foor*]
bakery, boulangerie (f) [*boo-lãzh-ree*]
balance n., équilibre (m) [*eh-kee-leebr*]
balance v., équilibrer, s'équilibrer [*eh-kee-lee-breh, seh-kee-lee-breh*]
balcony, balcon (m) [*bahl-kō*]
bald, chauve [*shohv*]
ball, balle (f) [*bahl*]

ball [dance], bal (m) [*bahl*]
ballet, ballet (m) [*bah-leh*]
balloon, ballon (m) [*bah-lõ*]
band, orchestre (m) [*or-kestr*]
bandage *n.*, pansement (m) [*pãs-mã*]
bandaid, tricostéril (m) [*tree-ko-steh-reel*]
bank *adj.*, bancaire [*bã-ker*]
bank *n.*, banque (f) [*bãk*]
banknote, billet (m) de banque [*bee-yehd-bãk*]
baptism, baptême (m) [*bah-tem*]
bar [for drinks], bar (m) [*bahr*]
barber, coiffeur (m) [*kwah-fuhr*]
bare *adj.*, nu [*nü*]
barefoot, pieds nus [*pyeh-nü*]
bargain *n.*, occasion (f) [*o-kah-zyõ*]
bargain *v.*, marchander [*mahr-shã-deh*]
bark [of tree] *n.*, écorce (f) [*eh-kors*]
bark *v.*, aboyer [*ah-bwah-yeh*]
barn, grange (f) [*grãzh*]
barracks, caserne (f) [*kah-zern*]
barrel [cask], tonneau (m), -eaux (pl) [*to-noh*]
barricade, barricade (f) [*bah-ree-kahd*]
base *n.*, base (f) [*bahz*]
basement, sous-sol (m) [*soo-sol*]
basic, fondamental, -aux (m, pl) [*fõ-dah-mã-tal, fõ-dah-mã-toh*]
basin, cuvette (f) [*kü-vet*]
basket, panier (m) [*pah-nyeh*]
bath, bain (m) [*bẽ*]
   take a bath *v.*, prendre un bain [*prã-drẽ-bẽ*]
bathe *v.*, baigner, se baigner [*beh-nyeh, suh beh-nyeh*]
bathing suit, maillot (m) de bain [*mah-yohd-bẽ*]
bathroom, salle (f) de bain [*sahl duh bẽ*]
bathtub, baignoire (f) [*behn-wahr*]
battery [car], batterie (f) [*bah-tree*]
battery [flashlight], pile (f) [*peel*]
battle *n.*, bataille (f) [*bah-tahy*]
bay *n.*, baie (f) [*be*]

be *v.*, être (irreg) [*etr*]
beach, plage (f) [*plahzh*]
bean, *haricot (m) [*ah-ree-koh*]
bear, ours (m) [*oors*]
bear [carry] *v.*, porter [*por-teh*]
bear [give birth] *v.*, donner naissance [*do-neh ne-sãs*]
bear [endure] *v.*, supporter [*sü-por-teh*]
beard, barbe (f) [*bahrb*]
beast, bête (f) [*bet*]
beat *n.*, battement (m) [*baht-mã*]
beat *v.*, battre (irreg) [*bahtr*]
beautiful, beau (bel), belle; beaux, belles [*boh, bel*]
beauty, beauté (f) [*boh-teh*]
beauty parlor, salon (m) de coiffure [*sah-lõd kwah-für*]
because, parce que [*pahrs kuh*]
   because of, à cause de [*ah kohz duh*]
become, devenir (irreg) [*duh-v(uh)-neer*]
bed, lit (m) [*lee*]
bedroom, chambre (f) à coucher [*shãbr ah koo-sheh*]
bee, abeille (f) [*ah-bey*]
beef, boeuf (m) [*buhf*]
beer, bière (f) [*byer*]
before [place], devant [*duh-vã*]
before [time], avant [*ah-vã*]
   before leaving, avant de partir [*ah-vãd pahr-teer*]
beg *v.*, mendier [*mã-dyeh*]
beggar *n.*, mendiant, -te [*mã-dyã, mã-dyãt*]
begin *v.*, commencer [*ko-mã-seh*]
   begin again, recommencer [*ruh-ko-mã-seh*]
beginning, commencement (m) [*ko-mãs-mã*]
behave *v.*, se conduire, se comporter [*suh kõ-dweer, suh kõ-por-teh*]
behavior, comportement (m) [*kõ-por-t(uh)-mã*]
behind, derrière [*der-yer*]
Belgian, belge [*belzh*]
Belgium, Belgique (f) [*bel-zheek*]
belief, croyance (f) [*krwah-yãs*]
believe *v.*, croire (irreg) [*krwahr*]

bell, cloche (f) [*klosh*]

bellboy, chasseur (m) [*shah-suhr*]

belong (to) v., appartenir (à) (irreg) [*ah-pahr-tuh-neer (ah)*]

belongings, affaires (f, pl) [*ah-fer*]

below *adv.*, en-dessous [*ã-tsoo*]

below *prep.*, en dessous de [*ã tsoo duh*]

belt, ceinture (f) [*sẽ-tür*]

bench, banc (m) [*bã*]

bend, plier [*plee-yeh*]

beneath, dessous [*duh-soo*]

benefit, bénéfice (m) [*beh-neh-fees*]

berth, couchette (f) [*koo-shet*]

beside, à côté (de) [*ah koh-teh (duh)*]

besides, de plus, d'ailleurs [*duh plü(s), dah-yuhr*]

best *adv.*, le mieux [*luh myuh*]

best *adj.*, le meilleur, la meilleure [*luh meh-yuhr, lah meh-yuhr*]

bet *n.*, pari (m) [*pah-ree*]

bet *v.*, parier [*pah-ryeh*]

better *adj.*, meilleur [*meh-yuhr*]

better *adv.*, mieux [*myuh*]

between, entre [*ãtr*]

Beware! Attention! [*ah-tã-syõ*]

beyond, au delà (de) [*oh dlah (duh)*]

Bible, Bible (f) [*bee-bl*]

bicycle, bicyclette (f), vélo (m) [*bee-see-klet, veh-loh*]

bid *n.*, offre (f) [*ofr*]

bid *v.*, faire une offre [*fer ün ofr*]

bill *n.*, addition (f) [*ah-dee-syõ*]

billion, milliard (m) [*meel-yahr*]

bird, oiseau (m), -eaux (pl) [*wah-zoh*]

birth, naissance (f) [*ne-sãs*]

birthday, anniversaire (m) [*ah-nee-ver-ser*]

   Happy birthday, Bon anniversaire, [*bo-nah-nee-ver-ser*]

bishop, évêque (m) [*eh-vek*]

bit: a bit, un peu [*ẽ-puh*]

bite *v.*, mordre (irreg) [*mordr*]

bitter, amer, amère [*ah-mer*]

bitterness, amertume (f) [*ah-mer-tüm*]
black, noir [*nwahr*]
blackboard, tableau noir (m) [*tah-bloh nwahr*]
blade, lame (f) [*lahm*]
blame *n.,* blâme (m) [*blahm*]
blame *v.,* blâmer [*blah-meh*]
blanket, couverture (f) [*koo-ver-tür*]
bleach *n.,* eau (f) de javel [*ohd-zhah-vel*]
bleed *v.,* saigner [*seh-nyeh*]
bless *v.,* bénir [*beh-neer*]
blessing, bénédiction (f) [*beh-neh-deek-syõ*]
blind, aveugle [*ah-vuhgl*]
   color-blind, daltonien, -enne [*dahl-to-nyĕ, dahl-to-nyen*]
blister *n.,* ampoule (f) [*ã-pool*]
block *n.,* bloc (m), cube (m) [*blok, küb*]
   two blocks from here, à deux rues d'ici [*ah duh rü dee-see*]
blond, blonde, blond, blonde [*blõ, blõd*]
blood, sang (m) [*sã*]
blossom *n.,* fleur (f) [*fluhr*]
blossom *v.,* fleurir [*fluh-reer*]
blouse, corsage (m), chemisier (m) [*kor-sahzh, shuh-mee-zyeh*]
blow *n.,* coup (m) [*koo*]
blow *v.,* souffler [*soo-fleh*]
blow-out [flat tire], crevaison (f) [*kruh-ve-zõ*]
blue, bleu [*bluh*]
board, planche (f) [*plãsh*]
boarder, pensionnaire (m, f) [*pã-syo-ner*]
boarding house, pension (f) [*pã-syõ*]
boat, bateau (m), -eaux (pl) [*bah-toh*]
body, corps (m) [*kor*]
boil *v.,* bouillir (irreg) [*boo-yeer*]
bold, audacieux, -euse [*oh-dah-syuh, oh-dah-syuhz*]
bomb, bombe (f) [*bõb*]
bond [financial], obligation (f) [*oh-blee-gah-syõ*]
bone, os (m) [*os*]
   fishbone, arête (f) [*ah-ret*]
book, livre (m) [*leevr*]

bookstore, librairie (f) [*lee-bre-ree*]

boot, botte (f) [*bot*]

border [frontier], frontière (f) [*frō-tyer*]

bore *v.*, ennuyer [*ã-nwee-yeh*]

boring, ennuyeux, -euse [*ã-nwee-yuh, ã-nwee-yuhz*]

born: be born, naître (irreg) *Aux:* ÊTRE) [*netr*]

borne, porté [*por-teh*]

borrow *v.*, emprunter [*ã-prē-teh*]

boss *n.*, patron (m) [*pah-trō*]

both, les deux [*leh duh*]

bother *v.*, ennuyer, gêner, déranger [*ã-nwee-yeh, zhe-neh, deh-rã-zheh*]

   Don't bother, Ne vous dérangez pas [*nuh voo deh-rã-zheh pah*]

bottle, bouteille (f) [*boo-tey*]

   baby bottle, biberon (m) [*bee-brō*]

bottom, fond (m) [*fō*]

bow [ribbon] *n.*, noeud (m) [*nuh*]

bow *v.*, saluer [*sa-lweh*]

box, boîte (f) [*bwaht*]

boxing, boxe (f) [*boks*]

box-office, bureau (m) de location [*bü-rohd lo-kah-syō*]

boy, garçon (m) [*gahr-sō*]

bracelet, bracelet (m) [*brahs-leh*]

brag *v.*, se vanter [*suh vã-teh*]

braid, natte (f) [*naht*]

brain, cerveau (m), -eaux (pl) [*ser-voh*]

brake *n.*, frein (m) [*frē*]

brake *v.*, freiner [*fre-neh*]

branch, branche (f) [*brãsh*]

brand *n.*, marque (f) [*mahrk*]

brand-new, tout neuf, toute neuve [*too nuhf, toot nuhv*]

brandy, cognac (m) [*ko-nyahk*]

brass, cuivre (m) [*kweevr*]

brassiere, soutien-gorge (m) [*soo-tyē-gorzh*]

brave, courageux, -euse [*koo-rah-zhuh, koo-rah-zhuhz*]

bread, pain (m) [*pē*]

break *v.*, casser [*kah-seh*]

breakdown, panne (f) [*pahn*]
breakfast, petit déjeuner (m) [*p(uh)-tee deh-zhuh-neh*]
  have breakfast v., déjeuner [*deh-zhuh-neh*]
breast [anat.], poitrine (f) [*pwah-treen*]
breast [bosom], sein (m) [*sĕ*]
breath, souffle (m) [*soofl*]
  out of breath, à bout de souffle [*ah boot soofl*]
breathe v., respirer [*res-pee-reh*]
breeze, brise (f) [*breez*]
Breton, breton, -onne [*bruh-tõ, bruh-ton*]
brick, brique (f) [*breek*]
bride, mariée (f) [*mahr-yeh*]
bridegroom, marié (m) [*mahr-yeh*]
bridesmaid, demoiselle (f) d'honneur [*duh-mwah-zel do-nuhr*]
bridge n., pont (m) [*põ*]
bright, brillant [*bree-yã(t)*]
brilliant, brillant [*bree-yã(t)*]
bring [something] v., apporter [*ah-por-teh*]
bring [persons] v., amener [*ahm-neh*]
  bring about, entraîner [*ã-tre-neh*]
  bring together, réunir [*reh-ü-neer*]
  bring up [rear], élever [*ehl-veh*]
Britain, Grande Bretagne (f) [*grãd bruh-tahñ*]
British, britannique, anglais [*bree-ta-neek, ã-gle(z)*]
Brittany, Bretagne (f) [*bruh-tañ*]
broad, large [*lahrzh*]
broadcast n., émission (f) [*eh-mee-syõ*]
broil v., griller [*gree-yeh*]
broiled, grillé [*gree-yeh*]
bronze, bronze [*brõz*]
brook n., ruisseau (m), -eaux (pl) [*rwee-soh*]
broom, balai (m) [*bah-le*]
broth, bouillon (m) [*boo-yõ*]
brother, frère (m) [*frer*]
brother-in-law, beau-frère (m) [*boh-frer*]
brown, marron; brun, brune [*mah-rõ; brĕ, brün*]
bruise n., bleu (m) [*bluh*]

brunette, brune (f) [*brün*]
brush [hair], brosse (f) [*bros*]
  paint brush, pinceau (m), -eaux (pl) [*pē-soh*]
  toothbrush, brosse à dents [*bro-sah dã*]
brush *v.,* brosser [*bro-seh*]
bucket, seau (m), seaux (pl) [*soh*]
buckle, boucle (f) [*bookl*]
budget *n.,* budget (m) [*büd-zheh*]
bug, insecte (m) [*ē-sekt*]
build *v.,* construire (irreg) [*kõ-strweer*]
building, bâtiment (m) [*bah-tee-mã*]
bulb [light], ampoule (f) [*ã-pool*]
Bulgaria, Bulgarie (f) [*bül-gah-ree*]
Bulgarian, bulgare [*bül-gahr*]
bulky, volumineux, -euse [*vo-lü-mee-nuh, vo-lü-mee-nuhz*]
bull, taureau (m), -eaux (pl) [*toh-roh*]
bulletin, bulletin (m) [*bül-tē*]
bulletin board, tableau (m) d'affichage [*tah-bloh dah-fee-shahzh*]
bumper, pare-choc (m) [*pahr-shok*]
bundle, paquet (m) [*pah-keh*]
burden *n.,* fardeau (m), -eaux (pl) [*fahr-doh*]
burden *v.,* charger [*shahr-zheh*]
burglar, cambrioleur (m) [*kã-bree-yo-luhr*]
Burgundy, Bourgogne (f) [*boor-goñ*]
burial, enterrement (m) [*ã-ter-mã*]
burn *v.,* brûler [*brü-leh*]
bury *v.,* enterrer [*ã-teh-reh*]
bus, autobus (m) [*oh-toh-büs*]
bush, buisson (m) [*bwee-sõ*]
business, les affaires (pl) [*leh-zah-fer*]
businessman, homme (m) d'affaires [*om-dah-fer*]
busy *adj.,* occupé [*o-kü-peh*]
but, mais [*me*]
butcher, boucher (m) [*boo-sheh*]
butcher shop, boucherie (f) [*boo-shree*]
butter, beurre (m) [*buhr*]
button, bouton (m) [*boo-tõ*]

buy *v.*, acheter [*ahsh-teh*]
buyer, acheteur, -teuse [*ahsh-tuhr, ahsh-tuhz*]
by [near] à côté de [*ah koh-teh duh*]
by [means], par [*pahr*]
  by chance, par *hasard [*pahr ah-zahr*]
bypass, bretelle (f), route (f) de déviation [*bruh-tel, root duh deh-vyah-syõ*]

C

cab, taxi (m) [*tahk-see*]
cabbage, chou (m), choux (pl) [*shoo*]
cabin, cabane (f) [*kah-bahn*]
cabinet [government], conseil (m) de ministres [*kõ-sey duh mee-neestr*]
cable *v.*, envoyer un télégramme international [*ã-vwah-yeh ẽ teh-leh-gram ẽ-ter-nah-syo-nahl*]
cable *n.*, cable (m), télégramme (m) international [*kahbl, teh-leh-grahm ẽ-ter-nah-syo-nahl*]
café, café (m) [*kah-feh*]
cage, cage (f) [*kahzh*]
cake, gâteau (m), -eaux (pl) [*gah-toh*]
calendar, calendrier (m) [*kah-lã-dree-yeh*]
calf, veau (m), -eaux (pl) [*voh*]
call *n.*, appel (m) [*ah-pel*]
  telephone call, coup de téléphone [*koot teh-leh-fon*]
call *v.*, appeler, crier [*ahp-leh, kree-yeh*]
  call off, décommander [*deh-ko-mã-deh*]
calm, calme [*kahlm*]
camera, appareil photographique (m) [*ah-pah-rey foh-toh-grah-feek*]
  movie camera, caméra (m) [*kah-meh-rah*]
camp *n.*, camp (m) [*kã*]
can [container] *n.*, boîte (f) de conserve [*bwaht duh kõ-serv*]
can [be able] *v.*, pouvoir (irreg) [*poov-wahr*]

Canada, Canada (m) [*kah-nah-dah*]

Canadian, canadien, -enne [*kah-nah-dyĕ, kah-nah-dyen*]

cancel *v.*, annuler [*ah-nü-leh*]

candle, bougie (f), chandelle (f) [*boo-zhee, shã-del*]

candlestick, chandelier (m), bougeoir (m) [*shã-duh-lyeh, boo-zhwahr*]

candy, bonbon (m) [*bõ-bõ*]

cane, canne (f) [*kahn*]

can opener, ouvre-boîte (m) [*oov-ruh-bwaht*]

cap [headgear], casquette (f) [*kahs-ket*]

capable, capable [*kah-pahbl*]

capacity, capacité (f) [*kah-pah-see-teh*]

capital [city], capitale (f) [*kah-pee-tahl*]

capital [money], capital (m), -aux [*kah-pee-tahl, kah-pee-toh*]

captain, capitaine (m) [*kah-pee-ten*]

car, voiture (f) [*vwah-tür*]

   streetcar, tramway (m) [*trahm-weh*]

card, carte (f) [*kahrt*]

   calling card, carte de visite [*kahrt duh vee-zeet*]

   playing cards, cartes à jouer [*kahr-tah zhweh*]

cardboard, carton (m) [*kar-tõ*]

cardinal, cardinal (m), -aux (pl) [*kahr-dee-nahl, kahr-dee-noh*]

care [worry] *n.*, souci (m) [*soo-see*]

care [attention] *n.*, soin (m) [*swĕ*]

care *v.*, se soucier (de), s'intéresser (à) [*suh soo-syeh (duh), sĕ-teh-re-seh (ah)*]

   care for, soigner, aimer [*swah-nyeh, eh-meh*]

   I don't care, Ça m'est égal [*sah me-teh-gahl*]

career, carrière (f) [*kah-ryer*]

careful, soigneux, -euse [*swah-nyuh, swah-nyuhz*]

   Be careful! Faites attention! [*fe-tah-tã-syõ*]

carefully, soigneusement [*swah-nyuhz-mã*]

careless, négligent [*neh-glee-zhã(t)*]

cargo, chargement (m) d'un bateau [*shahr-zhuh-mã dĕ-bah-toh*]

carnival, carnaval (m), -als (pl) [*kahr-nah-vahl*]

carpenter, menuisier (m) [*muh-nwee-zyeh*]

carpet, tapis (m) [*tah-pee*]

carry v., porter [*por-teh*]
  carry away, emporter [*ã-por-teh*]
carve v., découper [*deh-koo-peh*]
case [box], caisse (f) [*kes*]
case [situation], cas (m) [*kah*]
  in any case, en tout cas [*ã too-kah*]
  in that case, dans ce cas [*dãs-kah*]
cash n., argent liquide (m) [*ahr-zhã lee-keed*]
  pay cash v., payer comptant [*peh-yeh kõ-tã*]
cash v., toucher [*too-sheh*]
cashier, caissier, -ière [*ke-syeh, ke-syehr*]
  Pay the cashier, Payez à la caisse [*peh-yeh-zah lah kes*]
castle, château (m), -eaux (pl) [*shah-toh*]
casual, simple [*sẽpl*]
cat, chat (m) [*shah*]
catalog, catalogue (m) [*kah-tah-log*]
catch v., attraper [*ah-trah-peh*]
  catch cold, prendre (irreg) froid [*prãdr frwah*]
cathedral, cathédrale (f) [*kah-teh-drahl*]
Catholic, catholique [*kah-to-leek*]
cattle, bétail (m) [*beh-tahy*]
cauliflower, chou-fleur (m) [*shoo-fluhr*]
cause n., cause (f) [*kohz*]
cause v., causer [*koh-zeh*]
caution n., précaution (f) [*preh-koh-syõ*]
cave, grotte (f) [*grot*]
cavity [teeth], carie (f) [*kah-ree*]
cease v., cesser [*seh-seh*]
ceiling, plafond (m) [*plah-fõ*]
celebrate v., fêter [*fe-teh*]
celebration, fête (f) [*fet*]
celery, céleri (m) [*sel-ree*]
cellar, cave (f) [*kahv*]
cement n., ciment (m) [*see-mã*]
cemetery, cimetière (m) [*seem-tyer*]
center, centre (m) [*sãtr*]
central, central, -aux (m, pl) [*sã-trahl, sã-troh*]
central heating, chauffage (m) central [*shoh-fahzh sã-trahl*]

century, siècle (m) [*syekl*]
cereal, céréale (f) [*seh-reh-ahl*]
  baby cereal, bouillie (f) [*boo-yee*]
ceremony, cérémonie (f) [*seh-reh-mo-nee*]
certain, certain [*ser-tĕ, ser-ten*]
certainly, certainement [*ser-ten-mã*]
certificate, certificat (m) [*ser-tee-fee-kah*]
chain, chaîne (f) [*shen*]
chair, chaise (f) [*shez*]
  deck chair, transat (m) [*trã-saht*]
chalk, craie (f) [*kre*]
champagne, champagne (m) [*shã-pañ*]
champion n., champion, -onne, [*shã-pyõ, shã-pyon*]
chance n., chance (f), *hasard (m) [*shãs, ah-zahr*]
  by chance, par hasard [*pahr ah-zahr*]
  game of chance, jeu (m) de hasard [*zhuh duh ah-zahr*]
  take a chance v., risquer [*rees-keh*]
change n., changement (m) [*shãzh-mã*]
change [coins] n., monnaie (f) [*mo-neh*]
change v., changer [*shã-zheh*]
  change clothes, se changer [*suh shã-zheh*]
change purse, porte-monnaie (m) [*port-mo-neh*]
chapel, chapelle (f) [*shah-pel*]
character, caractère (m) [*kah-rahk-ter*]
character [in literature], personnage (m) [*pehr-soh-nahzh*]
charcoal, charbon (m) de bois [*shahr-bõ duh bwah*]
charge [a battery] v., charger [*shahr-zheh*]
charge [a purchase] v., mettre (irreg) sur le compte [*metr
    sür luh kõt*]
charity, charité (f) [*shah-ree-teh*]
charm, charme (m) [*shahrm*]
charming, charmant [*shahr-mã(t)*]
chase v., chasser [*shah-seh*]
chat v., bavarder [*bah-vahr-deh*]
chauffeur, chauffeur (m) [*shoh-fuhr*]
cheap, bon marché [*bõ mar-sheh*]
cheat v., tricher [*tree-sheh*]
check [verification] n., contrôle (m) [*kõ-trohl*]

bank check, chèque (m) [*shek*]
baggage check, bulletin (m) [*bül-tē*]
restaurant check, addition (f) [*ah-dee-syõ*]
traveler's check, cheque (m) de voyage [*shek duh vwah-yahzh*]
check *v.*, contrôler, vérifier [*kõ-troh-leh, veh-ree-fyeh*]
checking account, compte courant (m) [*kõt-koo-rã*]
checkroom, vestiaire (m) [*ves-tyer*]
cheek, joue (f) [*zhoo*]
cheerful, joyeux, -euse [*zhwah-yuh, zhwah-yuhz*]
cheese, fromage (m) [*fro-mahzh*]
chemical *adj.*, chimique [*shee-meek*]
cherry, cerise (f) [*suh-reez*]
chest [anat.], poitrine (f) [*pwah-treen*]
chest [furniture], coffre (m) [*kofr*]
chest of drawers, commode (f) [*ko-mod*]
chestnut, marron (m) [*mah-rõ*]
chew *v.*, mâcher [*mah-sheh*]
chicken, poulet (m) [*poo-leh*]
chief *n.*, chef (m) [*shef*]
chief *adj.*, principal, -aux (m, pl) [*prĕ-see-pahl, prĕ-see-poh*]
child, enfant (m) [*ã-fã*]
childbirth, accouchement (m) [*ah-koosh-mã*]
childhood, enfance (f) [*ã-fãs*]
children, enfants [*ã-fã*]
chilly, frais, fraîche [*fre, fresh*]
chimney, cheminée (f) [*shmee-neh*]
chin, menton (m) [*mã-tõ*]
China, Chine (f) [*sheen*]
china [porcelain], porcelaine (f) [*pors-len*]
Chinese, chinois [*sheen-wah(z)*]
chocolate, chocolat (m) [*shoh-koh-lah*]
choice, choix (m) [*shwah*]
choke [auto], starter (m) [*stahr-tuhr*]
choose *v.*, choisir [*shwah-zeer*]
chop [cut of meat] *n.*, côtelette (f) [*koht-let*]
Christian, chrétien, -enne [*kre-tyẽ, kre-tyen*]
Christmas, Noël (m) [*noh-el*]

Merry Christmas, Joyeux Noël [*zhwah-yuh noh-el*]
church, église (f) [*eh-gleez*]
cider, cidre (m) [*seedr*]
cigar, cigare (f) [*see-gahr*]
cigarette, cigarette (f) [*see-gah-ret*]
circle n., cercle (m) [*serkl*]
circulation, circulation (f) [*seer-kü-lah-syõ*]
circumstance, circonstance (f) [*seer-kõ-stãs*]
circus, cirque (m) [*seerk*]
citizen, citoyen, -enne [*see-twah-yẽ, see-twah-yen*]
citizenship, nationalité (f) [*nah-syo-nah-lee-teh*]
city, ville (f) [*veel*]
city hall, hôtel (m) de ville [*oh-tel duh veel*]
civilian, civil, -le [*see-veel*]
civilization, civilisation (f) [*see-vee-lee-zah-syõ*]
claim n., réclamation (f) [*reh-klah-mah-syõ*]
claim v., réclamer [*reh-klah-meh*]
clam, palourde (f) [*pah-loord*]
class n., classe (f) [*klahs*]
classic, classique [*klah-seek*]
classmate, camarade (m, f) de classe [*kah-mah-rad duh klahs*]
classroom, salle (f) de classe [*sahl duh klahs*]
clean adj., propre [*propr*]
clean v., nettoyer [*neh-twah-yeh*]
cleaner's [shop], teinturerie (f) [*tẽ-tür-ree*]
cleaning, nettoyage (m) [*neh-twah-yahzh*]
cleaning woman, femme (f) de ménage [*fahm duh meh-nahzh*]
clear, clair, net [*kler, net*]
clergy, clergé (m) [*kler-zheh*]
clerk, employé, -ée [*ã-plwa-yeh*]
clever, habile [*ah-beel*]
client, client, -te [*klee-yã(t)*]
climate, climat (m) [*klee-mah*]
climb v., monter (*Aux:* ÊTRE) [*mõ-teh*]
cloak-room, vestiaire (m) [*vest-yer*]
clock, horloge (m) [*or-lozh*]
  It's ten o'clock, Il est dix heures [*ee-le-dee-zuhr*]
close v., fermer [*fer-meh*]

close [near], près (de) [*pre (duh)*]
closed, fermé [*fer-meh*]
closet, armoire (f), placard (m) [*ahr-mwahr, plah-kahr*]
cloth, tissu (m) [*tee-sü*]
   tablecloth, nappe (f) [*nahp*]
clothes, vêtements (m, pl) [*vet-mã*]
cloud *n.*, nuage (m) [*nü-ahzh*]
cloudy, nuageux, -euse [*nü-ah-zhuh, nü-ah-zhuhz*]
club [association], club (m) [*kluhb*]
clutch [auto], embrayage (m) [*ã-bre-yahzh*]
coach [sports], entraîneur (m) [*ã-tre-nuhr*]
coal, charbon (m) [*shahr-bõ*]
coarse, grossier, -ière [*groh-syeh, groh-syer*]
coast, côte (f) [*koht*]
coat [overcoat], manteau (m), -eaux (pl) [*mã-toh*]
coat [suitcoat], veste (f), veston (m) [*vest, ves-tõ*]
cocktail, cocktail (m) [*kok-tel*]
cocoa, cacao (m) [*kah-kah-oh*]
coconut, noix (f) de coco [*nwaht koh-koh*]
coffee, café (m) [*kah-feh*]
coffin, cercueil (m) [*ser-kuhy*]
coin, pièce (f) (de monnaie) [*pyes (duh mo-neh)*]
coincidence, coïncidence (f) [*ko-ẽ-see-dãs*]
cold *adj.*, froid [*frwah(d)*]
   be cold *v.*, avoir froid [*ahv-wahr frwah*]
cold *n.*, rhume (m) [*rüm*]
   catch a cold *v.*, s'enrhumer [*sã-rü-meh*]
collar, col (m) [*kol*]
collect *v.*, assembler, collectionner [*a-sã-bleh, ko-lek-syo-neh*]
collection, collection (f) [*ko-lek-syõ*]
college, université (f) [*ü-nee-ver-see-teh*]
colonel, colonel (m) [*ko-lo-nel*]
colony, colonie (f) [*ko-lo-nee*]
color *n.*, couleur (f) [*koo-luhr*]
color *v.*, colorer [*ko-lo-reh*]
column, colonne (f) [*ko-lon*]
comb *n.*, peigne (m) [*peñ*]
comb *v.*, peigner [*peh-nyeh*]

combination, combinaison (f) [*kõ-bee-neh-zõ*]

come *v.*, venir (irreg; *Aux:* ÊTRE), arriver (*Aux:* ÊTRE)
  [*v(uh)-neer, ah-ree-veh*]

  come back, come again, revenir (irreg; *Aux:* ÊTRE) [*ruh-
    vneer*]

  come by, passer (par) (*Aux:* ÊTRE) [*pah-seh (pahr)*]

  come down, descendre (*Aux:* ÊTRE) [*deh-sãdr*]

  come forward, s'avancer [*sah-vã-seh*]

  come in, entrer (dans) (*Aux:* ÊTRE) [*ã-treh (dã)*]

  come out, sortir (irreg; *Aux:* ÊTRE) [*sor-teer*]

  Here he comes!, Le voilà! [*luh vwah-lah*]

comedy, comédie (f) [*ko-meh-dee*]

comfort *n.*, confort (m) [*kõ-for*]

comfort *v.*, consoler [*kõ-so-leh*]

comfortable, confortable [*kõ-for-tahbl*]

  Are you comfortable?, Etes-vous à l'aise?, Etes-vous bien?
    [*et-voo-zah-lez, et-voo-byẽ*]

comma, virgule (f) [*veer-gül*]

command *n.*, ordre (m) [*ordr*]

command *v.*, commander [*ko-mã-deh*]

comment *n.*, commentaire (m) [*ko-mã-ter*]

commercial, commercial, -aux (m, pl) [*ko-mer-syahl, ko-mer-
  syoh*]

commission *n.*, commission (f) [*ko-mee-syõ*]

committee, comité (m) [*ko-mee-teh*]

common, commun, ordinaire [*ko-mẽ, ko-mün; or-dee-ner*]

communicate *v.*, communiquer [*ko-mü-nee-keh*]

communication, communication (f) [*ko-mü-nee-kah-syõ*]

communist *n. & adj.*, communiste (m, f) [*ko-mü-neest*]

community, communauté (f) [*ko-mü-noh-teh*]

companion, compagnon (m) [*kõ-pah-nyõ*]

company [firm], compagnie (f) [*kõ-pah-nee*]

company [guest], invité [*ẽ-vee-teh*]

compare *v.*, comparer [*kõ-pah-reh*]

comparison, comparaison (f) [*kõ-pah-re-zõ*]

compartment, compartiment (m) [*kõ-pahr-tee-mã*]

compensation, compensation (f) [*kõ-pã-sah-syõ*]

competent, compétent [*kõ-peh-tã(t)*]

competition [business], concurrence (f) [kõ-kü-rãs]
competition [sports], compétition (f) [kõ-peh-tee-syõ]
complain v., se plaindre (irreg) [suh plẽdr]
complaint, plainte (f) [plẽt]
complete adj., complet, -ète [kõ-pleh, kõ-plet]
complete v., compléter [kõ-pleh-teh]
completely, complètement [kõ-plet-mã]
complexion, teint (m) [tẽ]
complicate v., compliquer [kõ-plee-keh]
complicated, compliqué [kõ-plee-keh]
compliment n., compliment (m) [kõ-plee-mã]
compose v., composer [kõ-poh-zeh]
composer, compositeur (m) [kõ-poh-zee-tuhr]
compound adj., composé [kõ-poh-zeh]
compromise n., compromis (m) [kõ-pro-mee]
conceal v., cacher [kah-sheh]
conceited, vaniteux, -euse [vah-nee-tuh, vah-nee-tuhz]
conceive v., concevoir (irreg) [kõ-suh-vwahr]
concentrate v., concentrer, se concentrer [kõ-sã-treh, skõ-
    sã-treh]
concept, concept (m) [kõ-sept]
concerning, concernant, au sujet de [kõ-ser-nã, oh sü-zheh
    duh]
concert, concert (m) [kõ-ser]
conclusion, conclusion (f) [kõ-klü-zyõ]
condemn v., condamner [kõ-dah-neh]
condense v., condenser [kõ-dã-seh]
condition, condition (f), état (m) [kõ-dee-syõ, eh-tah]
conditional, conditionnel, -elle [kõ-dee-syo-nel]
conduct n., conduite (f) [kõ-dweet]
conduct v., mener [muh-neh]
conductor [of train], contrôleur (m) [kõ-troh-luhr]
conductor [of orchestra], chef (m) d'orchestre [shef dor-kestr]
conference, consultation (f), congrès (m) [kõ-sül-tah-syõ,
    kõ-gre]
confess v., avouer [ahv-weh]
confession, confession (f) [kõ-fe-syõ]
confident, confiant, sûr [kõ-fyã(t), sür]

confidential, confidentiel, -elle [*kŏ-fee-dã-syel*]
confirm *v.*, confirmer [*kŏ-feer-meh*]
conflict *n.*, conflit (m) [*kŏ-flee*]
confusion, confusion (f) [*kŏ-fü-zyŏ*]
congratulate *v.*, féliciter [*feh-lee-see-teh*]
congratulations, félicitations [*feh-lee-see-tah-syŏ*]
congress, congrès (m) [*kŏ-gre*]
connection [link], relation (f) [*ruh-lah-syŏ*]
connection [transfer], correspondance (f) [*ko-res-pŏ-dâs*]
conquer *v.*, conquérir (irreg) [*kŏ-keh-reer*]
conscience, conscience (f) [*kŏ-syãs*]
conscientious, consciencieux, -euse [*kŏ-syã-syuh, kŏ-syã-syuhz*]
conscious, conscient [*kŏ-syã(t)*]
consent *n.*, consentement (m) [*kŏ-sãt-mã*]
consent *v.*, consentir (irreg) [*kŏ-sã-teer*]
consequence, conséquence (f) [*kŏ-seh-kãs*]
conservative, conservateur, -trice [*kŏ-ser-vah-tuhr, kŏ-ser-vah-trees*]
consider *v.*, considérer [*kŏ-see-deh-reh*]
considerable, considérable [*kŏ-see-deh-rahbl*]
consist (of) *v.*, consister (dans, en) [*kŏ-sees-teh (dã, ã)*]
consistent, conséquent, logique [*kŏ-seh-kã(t), lo-zheek*]
conspicuous, évident [*eh-vee-dã(t)*]
constant, constant [*kŏ-stã(t)*]
constitute *v.*, constituer [*kŏ-stee-tweh*]
constitution, constitution (f) [*kŏ-stee-tü-syŏ*]
construct *v.*, construire (irreg) [*kŏ-strweer*]
construction, construction (f) [*kŏ-strük-syŏ*]
consul, consul (m) [*kŏ-sül*]
consulate, consulat (m) [*kŏ-sü-lah*]
consult *v.*, consulter [*kŏ-sül-teh*]
consume *v.*, consommer [*kŏ-so-meh*]
consumer, consommateur (m) [*kŏ-so-mah-tuhr*]
contact *n.*, contact (m) [*kŏ-tahkt*]
contagious, contagieux, -euse [*kŏ-tah-zhyuh, kŏ-tah-zhyuhz*]
contain *v.*, contenir (irreg) [*kŏt-neer*]
container, récipient (m) [*reh-see-pyã*]

contemporary, contemporain [kŏ-tă-po-rĕ, kŏ-tă-po-ren]
contempt, mépris (m) [meh-pree]
contents pl., contenu (m) [kŏt-nü]
contest n., concours (m) [kŏ-koor]
continent n., continent (m) [kŏ-tee-nă]
continue v., continuer [kŏ-tee-nweh]
contract, contrat (m) [kŏ-trah]
contractor, entrepreneur (m) [ă-truh-pruh-nuhr]
contradiction, contradiction (f) [kŏ-trah-deek-syŏ]
contrary, contraire [kŏ-trer]
  on the contrary, au contraire [oh kŏ-trer]
contrast n., contraste (m) [kŏ-trahst]
contribute v., contribuer [kŏ-tree-bweh]
control n., autorité (f), maîtrise (f) [o-to-ree-teh, me-treez]
control v., diriger [dee-ree-zheh]
controversy, controverse (f) [kŏ-troh-vers]
convenient, commode [ko-mod]
convent, couvent (m) [koo-vă]
conversation, conversation (f) [kŏ-ver-sah-syŏ]
convert v., convertir [kŏ-ver-teer]
convict n., forçat, (m) [for-sah]
convict v., convaincre (irreg) [kŏ-vĕkr]
convince v., convaincre (irreg) [kŏ-vĕkr]
cook n., cuisinier, -ière [kwee-zee-nyeh, kwee-zee-nyehr]
cook v., faire la cuisine [fer lah kwee-zeen]
cooking, cuisine (f) [kwee-zeen]
cool adj., frais, fraîche [fre, fresh]
cool v., rafraîchir [rah-fre-sheer]
cooperation, coopération (f) [koh-oh-peh-rah-syŏ]
copper, cuivre (m) [kweevr]
copy n., copie (f) [ko-pee]
copy v., copier, reproduire (irreg) [ko-pyeh, ruh-pro-dweer]
cord, corde (f) [kord]
cordial, cordial, -iaux (m, pl) [kor-dyahl, kor-dyoh]
cork, buchon (m) [boo-shŏ]
corkscrew, tire-bouchon (m) [teer-boo-shŏ]
corn, maïs (m) [mah-ees]
corner, coin (m) [kwĕ]

corporation, société anonyme (f) [*so-syeh-teh ah-no-neem*]

correct *adj.*, correct [*ko-rekt*]

correct *v.*, corriger [*ko-ree-zheh*]

correction, correction (f) [*ko-rek-syõ*]

correspondence, correspondance (f) [*ko-res-põ-dãs*]

corridor, couloir (m), corridor (m) [*kool-wahr, ko-ree-dor*]

corruption, corruption (f) [*ko-rüp-syõ*]

cosmetics *pl.*, produits (m, pl) de beauté [*pro-dweed boh-teh*]

cost *n.*, coût (f), frais (m, pl) [*koo, fre*]

   cost of living, coût de la vie [*koo dlah vee*]

cost *v.*, coûter [*koo-teh*]

cot, lit (m) pliant [*lee plee-yã*]

cottage, petite maison de vacances [*p(uh)-teet me-zõd vah-kãs*]

cotton, coton (m) [*ko-tõ*]

couch, canapé (m), divan (m) [*kah-na-peh, dee-vã*]

cough *n.*, toux (f) [*too*]

cough *v.*, tousser [*too-seh*]

council, conseil (m) [*kõ-sey*]

count [title], comte (m) [*kõt*]

count *v.*, compter [*kõ-teh*]

countess, comtesse (f) [*kõ-tes*]

country [nation], pays (m) [*peh-ee*]

country [rural area], campagne (f) [*kã-pañ*]

couple *n.*, couple (m) [*koopl*]

courage, courage (m) [*koo-rahzh*]

courageous, courageux, -euse [*koo-rah-zhuh, koo-rah-zhuhz*]

course [way], cours (m) [*koor*]

   of course, bien entendu [*bye-nã-tã-dü*]

course [of a meal], plat (m) [*plah*]

court *n.*, cour (f) [*koor*]

   tennis court, court (m) [*koor*]

court *v.*, faire la cour [*fer lah koor*]

courteous, courtois, poli [*koor-twah(z), po-lee*]

courtyard, cour (f) [*koor*]

cousin, cousin, -ine [*koo-zẽ, koo-zeen*]

   first cousin, cousin germain [*koo-zẽ zher-mẽ*]

cover *v.*, couvrir (irreg) [*koo-vreer*]

cover *n.*, couverture (f) [*koo-ver-tür*]
cover charge, couvert (m) [*koo-ver*]
cow, vache (f) [*vahsh*]
coward, lâche (m, f) [*lahsh*]
crab, crabe (m) [*krahb*]
crack *n.*, fissure (f) [*fee-sür*]
cracker, biscuit (m) salé [*bees-kwee sah-leh*]
cradle *n.*, berceau (m), -eaux (pl) [*ber-soh*]
craftsman, artisan (m) [*ahr-tee-zã*]
crank *n.*, manivelle (f) [*mah-nee-vel*]
crash *n.*, collision (f) [*ko-lee-zyõ*]
crash *v.*, s'écraser [*seh-krah-zeh*]
crawl *v.*, ramper [*rã-peh*]
crayfish, écrevisse (f) [*eh-kruh-vees*]
crazy, fou, folle [*foo, fol*]
cream, crème (f) [*krem*]
create *v.*, créer [*kreh-eh*]
creation, création (f) [*kreh-ah-syõ*]
creature, créature (f) [*kreh-ah-tür*]
credit *n.*, crédit (m) [*kreh-dee*]
creditor, créancier (m) [*kreh-ã-syeh*]
crew, équipage (m) [*eh-kee-pahzh*]
crib, lit (m) d'enfant [*lee-dã-fã*]
crime, crime (m) [*kreem*]
criminal *adj. & n.*, criminel, -elle [*kree-mee-nel*]
crisis, crise (f) [*kreez*]
critic *n.*, critique (m) [*kree-teek*]
critical, critique [*kree-teek*]
criticism, critique (f) [*kree-teek*]
criticize *v.*, critiquer [*kree-tee-keh*]
crook [thief], escroc (m) [*es-kroh*]
crooked, tordu [*tor-dü*]
crop *n.*, récolte (f), culture (f) [*reh-kolt, kül-tür*]
cross *n.*, croix (f) [*krwah*]
cross *v.*, traverser [*trah-ver-seh*]
crossing [by sea], traversée (f) [*trah-ver-seh*]
crossroads, carrefour (m) [*kahr-foor*]
crow, corbeau (m), -eaux (pl) [*kor-boh*]

crowd *n.*, foule (f) [*fool*]
crown, couronne (f) [*koo-ron*]
cruel, cruel, cruelle [*krü-el*]
cruelty, cruauté (f) [*krü-oh-teh*]
cruise *n.*, croisière (f) [*krwah-zyer*]
crumb, miette (f) [*myet*]
crush *v.*, écraser [*eh-krah-zeh*]
cry *n.*, cri (m) [*kree*]
cry *v.*, pleurer [*pluh-reh*]
crystal *n.*, cristal (m), -aux (pl) [*krees-tahl, krees-toh*]
Cuba, Cuba (m) [*kü-bah*]
Cuban, cubain [*kü-bẽ, kü-ben*]
cube, cube (m) [*küb*]
cucumber, concombre (m) [*kõ-kõbr*]
cuff, manchette (f) [*mã-shet*]
cuff links, bouton (m) de manchette [*boo-tõd mã-shet*]
culture, culture (f) [*kül-tür*]
cup, tasse (f) [*tahs*]
cupboard, placard (m) [*plah-kahr*]
cure *n.*, guérison (f) [*gheh-ree-zõ*]
cure *v.*, guérir [*gheh-reer*]
curiosity, curiosité (f) [*kür-yo-zee-teh*]
curious, curieux, -euse [*kür-yuh, kür-yuhz*]
curl *n.*, boucle (f) [*bookl*]
curl *v.*, boucler [*book-leh*]
currency, monnaie (f) [*mo-neh*]
current *adj.*, courant, actuel [*koo-rã(t), ahk-twel*]
curse *v.*, jurer [*zhü-reh*]
curtain, rideau (m), -eaux (pl) [*ree-doh*]
curve [arc], courbe (f) [*koorb*]
curve [of road], virage (m) [*vee-rahzh*]
   dangerous curve, virage dangereux [*vee-rahzh dãzh-ruh*]
cushion, coussin (m) [*koo-sẽ*]
custard, flan (m) [*flã*]
custom *n.*, coutume (f) [*koo-tüm*]
custom made, sur mesure [*sür muh-zür*]
customary, habituel, -cllc [*ah-bee-twel*]
customer, client, -te [*klee-yã, klee-yãt*]

customs, douane (f) [*dwahn*]
   customs duty, droit (m) de douane [*drwah duh dwahn*]
   customs officer, douanier (m) [*dwah-nyeh*]
cut [wound] *n.*, coupure (f) [*koo-pür*]
cut [pattern] *n.*, coupe (f) [*koop*]
cut *v.*, couper [*koo-peh*]
cylinder, cylindre (m) [*see-lēdr*]

D

daily *adj.*, quotidien, -enne [*ko-tee-dyē, ko-tee-dyen*]
daily *adv.*, tous les jours [*too leh zhoor*]
dairy, laiterie (f) [*le-tree*]
daisy, marguerite (f) [*mahr-guh-reet*]
dam, barrage (m) [*bah-rahzh*]
damage *n.*, dommage (m) [*do-mahzh*]
damage *v.*, endommager [*ã-doh-mah-zheh*]
damaged, endommagé [*ã-doh-mah-zheh*]
damp, humide [*ü-meed*]
dance *n.*, danse (f) [*dãs*]
dance *v.*, danser [*dã-seh*]
dancer, danseur, -euse [*dã-suhr, dã-suhz*]
danger, danger (m) [*dã-zheh*]
dangerous, dangereux, -euse [*dã-zhruh, dã-zhruhz*]
dare *v.*, oser [*oh-zeh*]
daring [brave], téméraire [*teh-meh-rer*]
daring [manner], osé [*oh-zeh*]
dark *adj.*, sombre [*sōbr*]
dark [color] *adj.*, foncé [*fō-seh*]
darkness, obscurité (f) [*ops-kü-ree-teh*]
date [day], date (f) [*daht*]
date [fruit], datte (f) [*daht*]
date [appointment], rendez-vous (m) [*rã-deh-voo*]
daughter, fille, (f) [*feey*]
daughter-in-law, belle-fille [*bel-feey*]

dawn, aube (f) [*ohb*]
day, jour (m) [*zhoor*]
  every day, tous les jours [*too leh zhoor*]
  the next day, le lendemain [*luh lãd-me*]
  day after tomorrow, après-demain [*ah-pred-mē*]
  day before yesterday, avant-hier [*ah-vã-tyer*]
day [duration], journée [*zhoor-neh*]
  all day long, toute la journée [*toot lah zhoor-neh*]
daydream n., rêverie (f) [*rev-ree*]
dead, mort [*mor(t)*]
deadly, mortel, -elle [*mor-tel*]
deaf, sourd [*soor(d)*]
deal n., affaire (f) [*ah-fer*]
  a good deal, beaucoup [*boh-koo*]
deal [cards] v., donner, distribuer [*do-neh, dees-tree-bweh*]
deal (with) v., traiter (avec) [*tre-teh (ah-vek)*]
dealer, marchand (m), négociant (m) [*mahr-shã, neh-go-syã*]
dear, cher, chère [*sher*]
death, mort (f) [*mor*]
debt, dette (f) [*det*]
decanter, carafe (f) [*kah-rahf*]
deceased, défunt, décédé [*deh-fẽ(t), deh-seh-deh*]
deceive v., tromper [*trõ-peh*]
December, décembre (m) [*deh-sãbr*]
decency, décence (f) [*deh-sãs*]
decent, décent [*deh-sã(t)*]
deception, tromperie (f) [*trõ-pree*]
decide v., décider [*deh-see-deh*]
decision, décision (f) [*deh-see-zyõ*]
deck [ship], pont (m) [*põ*]
deck [of cards], jeu (m) [*zhuh*]
declaration, déclaration (f) [*deh-klah-rah-syõ*]
declare v., déclarer [*deh-klah-reh*]
decline [refuse] v., refuser [*ruh-fü-zeh*]
decorate v., décorer [*deh-ko-reh*]
decoration, décoration (f) [*deh-ko-rah-syõ*]
decrease v., diminuer [*dee-mee-nweh*]
decree n., décret (m) [*deh-kre*]

deed [act], action (f) [*ahk-syõ*]
deed [legal], act notarié (m) [*ahkt no-tar-yeh*]
deep, profond [*pro-fõ(d)*]
defeat *n.*, défaite (f) [*deh-fet*]
defeat *v.*, battre (irreg) [*bahtr*]
defective, défectueux, -euse [*deh-fek-twuh, deh-fek-twuhz*]
defend *v.*, défendre [*deh-fãdr*]
define *v.*, définir [*deh-fee-neer*]
definite, bien déterminé [*byẽ deh-ter-mee-neh*]
definition, définition (f) [*deh-fee-nee-syõ*]
degree, degré (m) [*duh-greh*]
delay, délai (m), retard (m) [*deh-le, r(uh)-tahr*]
deliberate, délibéré [*deh-lee-beh-reh*]
delicate, délicat [*deh-lee-kah(t)*]
delicious, délicieux, -euse [*deh-lee-syuh, deh-lee-syuhz*]
delight *n.*, joie (f) [*zhwah*]
delight *v.*, enchanter [*ã-shã-teh*]
deliver [from] *v.*, délivrer [*deh-lee-vreh*]
deliver [to] *v.*, livrer [*lee-vreh*]
demand *n.*, demande (f) [*d(uh)-mãd*]
demand [labor] *n.*, revendication (f) [*ruh-vã-dee-kah-syõ*]
demand [require] *v.*, exiger [*ehg-zee-zheh*]
demand [request] *v.*, demander [*d(uh)-mã-deh*]
democracy, démocratie (f) [*deh-mok-rah-see*]
demonstrate [show] *v.*, démontrer [*deh-mõ-treh*]
demonstrate [politically] *v.*, manifester [*mah-nee-fes-teh*]
demonstration, démonstration (f) [*deh-mõ-strah-syõ*]
demonstration [political], manifestation (f) [*mah-nee-fes-tah-syõ*]
denial, refus (m) [*r(uh)-fü*]
density, densité (f) [*dã-see-teh*]
dentist, dentiste (m) [*dã-teest*]
deny *v.*, nier, démentir [*nee-yeh, deh-mã-teer*]
depart *v.*, partir (irreg; *Aux:* ÊTRE) [*pahr-teer*]
department, département (m) [*deh-pahr-tuh-mã*]
department [in a store], rayon (m) [*re-yõ*]
departure, départ (m) [*deh-pahr*]
depend (on) *v.*, dépendre (de) [*deh-pãdr (duh)*]

That depends, Ça dépend [*sah deh-pã*]

dependent *n.*, personne (f) à charge [*per-son ah shahrzh*]

deposit *v.*, déposer [*deh-poh-zeh*]

  make a deposit, verser un accompte (m) [*ver-seh ē-nah-kõt*]

deprive *v.*, priver [*pree-veh*]

depth, profondeur (f) [*pro-fõ-duhr*]

deputy, adjoint (m) [*ahd-zhwē*]

descend *v.*, descendre (*Aux:* ÊTRE) [*deh-sãdr*]

descent, descente (f) [*deh-sãt*]

describe *v.*, décrire (irreg) [*deh-kreer*]

description, description (f) [*des-kreep-syõ*]

desert *n.*, désert (m) [*deh-zer*]

desert *v.*, déserter [*deh-zer-teh*]

deserve *v.*, mériter [*meh-ree-teh*]

desirable, désirable [*deh-zee-rahbl*]

desire *n.*, désir (m) [*deh-zeer*]

desire *v.*, désirer [*deh-zee-reh*]

desk, bureau (m), -eaux (pl) [*bü-roh*]

despair *n.*, désespoir (m) [*deh-zeh-spwahr*]

despair *v.*, désespérer [*deh-zehs-peh-reh*]

desperate, désespéré [*deh-zehs-peh-reh*]

despite, malgré [*mahl-greh*]

dessert, dessert (m) [*deh-ser*]

destiny, destin (m) [*des-tē*]

destroy *v.*, détruire (irreg) [*deh-trweer*]

destruction, destruction (f) [*des-trük-syõ*]

detail, détail (m) [*deh-tahy*]

detective, détective (m) [*deh-tek-teev*]

determine *v.*, déterminer [*deh-ter-mee-neh*]

detour, détour (m), déviation (f) [*deh-toor, deh-vyah-syõ*]

develop *v.*, développer [*dehv-lo-peh*]

development, développement (m) [*dehv-lop-mã*]

device, moyen (m), truc (m) [*mwah-yē, trük*]

devil, diable (m) [*dyahbl*]

devoted, dévoué [*deh-vweh*]

devotion, dévotion (f) [*deh-voh-syõ*]

dew, rosée (f) [*roh-zeh*]

diagnosis, diagnostique (m) [*dyahg-nos-teek*]

dial *n.*, cadran (m) [*kah-drã*]

dial [phone number] *v.*, composer (le numéro) [*kõ-poh-zeh (luh nü-meh-roh)*]

dialogue, dialogue (m) [*dyah-log*]

diamond, diamant (m) [*dyah-mã*]

diaper, couche (f) [*koosh*]

diary, journal (m), -aux (pl) [*zhoor-nahl, zhoor-noh*]

dictate *v.*, dicter [*deek-teh*]

dice [gambling] *n. pl.*, dés (m, pl) [*deh*]

dictation, dictée (f) [*deek-teh*]

dictionary, dictionnaire (m) [*deek-syo-ner*]

die *v.*, mourir (irreg; *Aux* ÊTRE) [*moo-reer*]

diet, régime (m) [*reh-zheem*]
   be on a diet *v.*, suivre (irreg) un régime [*swee-vrē-reh-zheem*]

difference, différence (f) [*dee-feh-rãs*]

different, différent [*dee-feh-rã(t)*]

difficult, difficile [*dee-fee-seel*]

difficulty, difficulté (f) [*dee-fee-kül-teh*]

dig *v.*, creuser [*kruh-zeh*]

digestion, digestion (f) [*dee-zhes-tyõ*]

dignity, dignité (f) [*dee-nyee-teh*]

dim *adj.*, faible, incertain [*febl; ē-ser-tē, ē-ser-ten*]

dimension, dimension (f) [*dee-mã-syõ*]

diminish *v.*, diminuer [*dee-mee-nweh*]

dine *v.*, dîner [*dee-neh*]

dining car, wagon-restaurant (m) [*vah-gõ-res-to-rã*]

dining room, salle (f) à manger [*sahl ah mã-zheh*]

dinner, dîner (m) [*dee-neh*]

dinner jacket, smoking (m) [*smo-keen*]

diploma, diplôme (m) [*dee-plohm*]

diplomat, diplomate (m) [*dee-ploh-maht*]

diplomatic, diplomate [*dee-ploh-maht*]

direct *adj.*, direct [*dee-rekt*]

direct *v.*, diriger [*dee-ree-zheh*]

directly, directement [*dee-rek-tuh-mã*]

dirt, saleté (f) [*sahl-teh*]

dirty, sale [*sahl*]

disabled, invalide, multilé [*ē-vah-leed, mü-tee-leh*]

disadvantage, désavantage (m) [*deh-zah-vã-tahzh*]

disagree v., n'être pas d'accord [*netr pah dah-kor*]
  I disagree, Je ne suis pas d'accord [*zhuhn swee pah dah-kor*]

disagreeable, désagréable [*deh-zah-greh-ahbl*]

disagreement, différence (f) [*dee-feh-rãs*]

disappear v., disparaître (irreg) [*dee-spah-retr*]

disappoint v., décevoir (irreg) [*deh-suh-vwahr*]

disappointed, déçu [*deh-sü*]

disapprove v., désapprouver [*deh-zah-proo-veh*]

disaster, désastre (m) [*deh-zahstr*]

discharge [an employee] v., renvoyer [*rã-vwah-yeh*]

discipline n., discipline (f) [*dee-see-pleen*]

disclose v., révéler [*reh-veh-leh*]

discomfort, manque (m) de confort [*mãk duh kõ-for*]

discontinue v., discontinuer, cesser [*dees-kõ-tee-nweh, seh-seh*]

discount [bank] n., escompte (m) [*es-kõt*]

discount [store] n., remise [*ruh-meez*]

discourage v., décourager [*deh-koo-rah-zheh*]

discover v., découvrir (irreg) [*deh-koov-reer*]

discovery, découverte (f) [*deh-koo-vert*]

discuss v., discuter [*dees-kü-teh*]

discussion, discussion (f) [*dees-kü-syõ*]

disease, maladie (f) [*mah-lah-dee*]

disembark v., débarquer [*deh-bahr-keh*]

disgrace n., disgrâce (f) [*dees-grahs*]

disguise n., déguisement (m) [*deh-gheez-mã*]

disgusted, dégoûté [*deh-goo-teh*]

dish, plat (m) [*plah*]

dishes, vaisselle (f, sing) [*ve-sel*]
  do the dishes v., faire la vaisselle [*fer lah ve-sel*]

dishonest, malhonnête [*mah-lo-net*]

dislike v., ne pas aimer [*nuh pah-ze-meh*]
  I dislike that, Je n'aime pas cela (ça) [*zhnem pah slah (sah)*]

dismiss v., renvoyer [rã-vwah-yeh]
disobey v., désobéir (à) [deh-zo-beh-eer (ah)]
disorder, désordre (m) [deh-zordr]
display n., étalage (m) [eh-tah-lahzh]
display v., étaler [eh-tah-leh]
dispute n., dispute (f) [dees-püt]
dissolve v., dissoudre (irreg) [dee-soodr]
distance, distance (f) [dees-tãs]
distant, distant [dees-tã(t)]
distinct, distinct [dees-tẽ(kt)]
distinguish v., distinguer [dees-tẽ-gheh]
distinguished, distingué [dees-tẽ-gheh]
distress, détresse (f) [deh-tres]
distribute v., distribuer [dees-tree-bweh]
distribution, distribution (f), répartition (f) [dees-tree-bü-syõ, reh-pahr-tee-syõ]
district, région (f) [reh-zhyõ]
district [for an election], circonscription (f) [seer-kõ-skreep-syõ]
distrust n., méfiance (f) [meh-fyãs]
distrust [someone] v., se méfier [smeh-fyeh]
disturb v., déranger [deh-rã-zheh]
disturbance, trouble (m) [troobl]
ditch, fossé (m) [foh-seh]
dive v., plonger [plõ-zheh]
divide v., diviser [dee-vee-zeh]
divine, divin [dee-vẽ, dee-veen]
division, division (f) [dee-vee-zyõ]
divorce, n., divorce (m) [dee-vors]
divorce v., divorcer [dee-vor-seh]
dizziness, vertige (m) [ver-teezh]
  feel dizzy v., avoir le vertige [ah-vwahr luh ver-teezh]
do v., faire (irreg) [fer]
  How do you do?, Comment allez-vous? [ko-mã-tah-leh-voo]
  What can I do for you?, Que puis-je faire pour vous? [kuh pweezh fer poor voo]
  do without, se passer de [spah-seh duh]
dock n., quai (m) [keh]

dock v., entrer au port (*Aux:* ÊTRE) [*ã-treh oh por*]
doctor, médecin (m) [*met-sẽ*]
   Doctor . . . [title], docteur . . . [*dok-tuhr*]
document n., document (m) [*do-kü-mã*]
dog, chien (m) [*shyẽ*]
doll, poupée (f) [*poo-peh*]
dollar, dollar (m) [*do-lahr*]
dome, dôme (m) [*dohm*]
domestic, domestique [*do-mes-teek*]
done, fait [*fe*]
   well-done, bien cuit [*byẽ kwee(t)*]
donkey, âne (m) [*ahn*]
door, porte (f) [*port*]
   car door, portière (f) [*por-tyer*]
dormitory, dortoir (m) [*dor-twahr*]
   college dormitory, résidence (f) universitaire [*reh-zee-dãs
     ü-nee-ver-see-ter*]
dose n., dose (f) [*dohz*]
double, double [*doobl*]
doubt n., doute (m) [*doot*]
doubt v., douter (de) [*doo-teh (duh)*]
   I doubt it, J'en doute [*zhã-doot*]
doubtful, douteux, -euse [*doo-tuh, doo-tuhz*]
down, en bas [*ã bah*]
   Down with . . . , À bas . . . [*ah bah*]
   go down, come down v., descendre (*Aux:* ÊTRE) [*deh-sãdr*]
   sit down v., s'asseoir (irreg) [*sah-swahr*]
   lie down v., se coucher [*skoo-sheh*]
downstairs, en bas [*ã bah*]
downtown, au centre de la ville [*oh sãtr duh lah veel*]
dowry, dot (f) [*dot*]
doze v., somnoler [*som-no-leh*]
dozen, douzaine (f) [*doo-zen*]
draft [bank], traite (f) [*tret*]
draft [air], courant (m) d'air [*koo-rã der*]
drag v., traîner [*tre-neh*]
drain n., tuyau (m) de vidange [*twee-yoh dvee-dãzh*]
drain v., faire écouler, égoutter [*fer eh-koo-leh, eh-goo-teh*]

drama, drame (m) [*drahm*]
dramatic, dramatique [*drah-mah-teek*]
draw [sketch] *v.*, dessiner [*deh-see-neh*]
draw (out) *v.*, tirer [*tee-reh*]
drawer, tiroir (m) [*teer-wahr*]
dream *n.*, rêve (m) [*rev*]
dream *v.*, rêver [*re-veh*]
dress *n.*, robe (f) [*rob*]
  evening dress, robe du soir [*rob dii swahr*]
dress *v.*, habiller, s'habiller [*ah-bee-yeh, sah-bee-yeh*]
dresser, commode (f) [*ko-mod*]
dressmaker, couturière (f) [*koo-tür-yer*]
drink *n.*, boisson (f) [*bwah-sõ*]
drink *v.*, boire (irreg) [*bwahr*]
drip *v.*, tomber (*Aux:* ÊTRE) goutte à goutte [*tõ-beh goo-tah goot*]
drive *v.*, conduire (irreg) [*kõ-dweer*]
driver, chauffeur (m) [*shoh-fuhr*]
driver's license, permis (m) de conduire [*per-meet kõ-dweer*]
drop *n.*, goutte (f) [*goot*]
drop *v.*, laisser tomber [*leh-seh tõ-beh*]
drown *v.*, noyer, se noyer [*nwah-yeh, snwah-yeh*]
drug *n.*, drogue (f) [*drog*]
drugstore, pharmacie (f) [*fahr-mah-see*]
drum, tambour (m) [*tã-boor*]
dry *adj.*, sec, sèche [*sek, sesh*]
dry *v.*, sécher [*seh-sheh*]
dry-clean *v.*, nettoyer à sec [*neh-twa-yeh ah sek*]
duchess, duchesse (f) [*dü-shes*]
duck, canard (m) [*kah-nahr*]
due, dû [*dü*]
  due to, à cause de [*ah kohz duh*]
  fall due *v.*, être dû [*etr dü*]
duke, duc (m) [*dük*]
dull [boring], ennuyeux, -euse [*ã-nwee-yuh, ã-nwee-yuhz*]
dumb [mute], muet, muette [*mü-eh, mü-et*]
dungeon, cachot (m) [*kah-shoh*]

durable, durable [*dü-rahbl*]
during, pendant [*pã-dã*]
dusk, crépuscule (m) [*kreh-püs-kül*]
dust, poussière (f) [*poo-syer*]
dusty, poussiéreux, -euse [*poo-sye-ruh, poo-sye-ruhz*]
Dutch, hollandais [*oh-lã-de(z)*]
duty, devoir (m) [*duh-vwahr*]
   be on duty v., être de service [*etr duh ser-vees*]
duty-free, en franchise [*ã frã-sheez*]
dye n., teinture (f) [*tẽ-tür*]
dye v., teindre (irreg) [*tẽdr*]
dynamite, dynamite (f) [*dee-nah-meet*]

E

each, chaque [*shahk*]
   each one, chacun, -une [*shah-kẽ, shah-kün*]
   each other, l'un l'autre, les uns les autres [*lẽ lohtr, leh-zẽ
   leh-zohtr*]
eager, impatient [*ẽ-pah-syã(t)*]
ear, oreille (f) [*o-rey*]
early adv., tôt, de bonne heure [*toh, duh bo-nuhr*]
earn v., gagner [*gah-nyeh*]
earring, boucle (f) d'oreille [*bookl do-rey*]
earth, terre (f) [*ter*]
earthquake, tremblement (m) de terre [*trã-bluh-mãt ter*]
ease [comfort], aise (f) [*ez*]
ease [competence], facilité (f) [*fah-see-lee-teh*]
easily, facilement [*fah-seel-mã*]
east, est (m) [*est*]
   Near East, Proche Orient (m) [*pro-shor-yã*]
   Middle East, Moyen Orient (m) [*mwah-ye-nor-yã*]
   Far East, Extrême Orient [*ehk-stre-mor-yã*]
Easter, Pâques (m, pl) [*pahk*]
eastern, oriental, -aux (m, pl) [*or-yã-tahl, or-yã-toh*]

easy, facile [*fah-seel*]
   Take it easy! Ne vous en faites pas! [*nuh voo-zã fet pah*]
eat *v.*, manger [*mã-zheh*]
echo *n.*, écho (m) [*eh-koh*]
economical, économique [*eh-ko-no-meek*]
edge *n.*, bord (m) [*bor*]
edible, mangeable [*mã-zhahbl*]
edition, édition (f) [*eh-dee-syõ*]
editor, éditeur, -trice [*eh-dee-tuhr, eh-dee-trees*]
education, instruction (f), enseignement (m) [*ẽ-strük-syõ, ã-se-nyuh-mã*]
effect *n.*, effet (m) [*e-fe*]
effective, efficace [*e-fee-kahs*]
efficient, efficace [*e-fee-kahs*]
effort, effort (m) [*e-for*]
egg, oeuf (m) [*uhf*]
   fried egg, oeuf au plat [*uhf oh plah*]
   hard-boiled egg, oeuf dur [*uhf dür*]
   scrambled eggs, oeufs brouillés [*uh broo-yeh*]
   soft-boiled egg, oeuf à la coque [*uh-fah lah kok*]
Egypt, Egypte (f) [*eh-zheept*]
Egyptian, égyptien, -enne [*eh-zheep-syẽ, eh-zheep-syen*]
eight, huit [*weet*]
eighteen, dix-huit [*dee-zweet*]
eighth, huitième [*wee-tyem*]
eighty, quatre-vingts [*kah-truh-vẽ*]
either . . . or, ou . . . ou [*oo . . . oo*]
elastic, élastique [*eh-lahs-teek*]
elated, ravi [*rah-vee*]
elbow, coude (m) [*kood*]
elderly, agé [*ah-zheh*]
elect *v.*, élire (irreg) [*eh-leer*]
election, élection (f) [*eh-lek-syõ*]
electric, électrique [*eh-lek-treek*]
electricity, électricité (f) [*eh-lek-tree-see-teh*]
elegance, élégance (f) [*eh-leh-gãs*]
elegant, élégant [*eh-leh-gã(t)*]
element, élément (m) [*eh-leh-mã*]

elementary, élémentaire [*eh-leh-mã-ter*]

elephant, éléphant (m) [*eh-leh-fã*]

elevator, ascenseur (m) [*ah-sã-suhr*]

eleven, onze [*õz*]

eliminate *v.,* éliminer [*eh-lee-mee-neh*]

else, autre, d'autre [*ohtr, dohtr*]

    nothing else, rien d'autre [*ryẽ dohtr*]

    someone else, quelqu'un d'autre [*kel-kẽ dohtr*]

    What else? Quoi d'autre? [*kwah dohtr*]

embargo *n.,* embargo (m) [*ã-bahr-go*]

embark *v.,* s'embarquer [*sã-bahr-keh*]

embarrass *v.,* embarrasser [*ã-bah-rah-seh*]

embarrassed, confus, gêné [*kõ-fü(z), zhe-neh*]

embassy, ambassade (f) [*ã-bah-sahd*]

embroidery, broderie (f) [*brod-ree*]

emerald, émeraude (f) [*em-rohd*]

emergency, cas (m) urgent [*kah ür-zhã*]

    in case of emergency, en cas d'urgence [*ã kah dür-zhãs*]

emigrant, émigrant, -e [*eh-mee-grã(t)*]

emigration, émigration (f) [*eh-mee-grah-syõ*]

emotion, émotion (f) [*eh-moh-syõ*]

emphasis, insistance (f) [*ẽ-sees-tãs*]

emphasize *v.,* accentuer [*ah-ksã-tweh*]

employee, employé, -ée [*ã-plwah-yeh*]

employer, employeur (m) [*ã-plwah-yuhr*]

employment, emploi (m) [*ã-plwah*]

employment agency, bureau (m) de placement [*bü-roht-plahs-mã*]

empty, vide [*veed*]

enclose [surround] *v.,* clôturer [*kloh-tü-reh*]

enclose [in letter] *v.,* joindre (irreg) [*zhwẽdr*]

encourage *v.,* encourager [*ã-koo-rah-zheh*]

encouragement, encouragement (m) [*ã-koo-rahzh-mã*]

end [ending] *n.,* fin (f), bout (m) [*fẽ, boo*]

    at the end of the road, au bout du chemin [*oh boo dü shmẽ*]

end [aim] *n.,* but (m) [*bü(t)*]

end *v.,* finir [*fee-neer*]

endless, sans fin [sã-fẽ]
endorse v., endosser [ã-doh-seh]
endure v., supporter [sü-por-teh]
enemy, ennemi (m) [en-mee]
energetic, énergique [eh-ner-zheek]
energy, énergie (f) [eh-ner-zhee]
engaged, fiancé [fyã-seh]
engagement [betrothal], fiançailles (f, pl) [fyã-sahy]
engagement [appointment], engagement (m) [ã-gahzh-mã]
engine, moteur (m) [moh-tuhr]
engine [train], locomotive (f) [lo-koh-moh-teev]
engineer, ingénieur (m) [ẽ-zheh-nyuhr]
engineer [train], mécanicien (m) [meh-kah-nee-syẽ]
England, Angleterre (f) [ã-gluh-ter]
English, anglais [ã-gle(z)]
enjoy v., aimer [eh-meh]
  enjoy oneself, s'amuser [sah-mü-zeh]
  Enjoy yourself! Amusez-vous bien! [ah-mü-zeh-voo byẽ]
enormous, énorme [eh-norm]
enough, assez [ah-seh]
enroll v., s'inscrire (irreg) [sẽ-skreer]
enter v., entrer (Aux: ÊTRE) [ã-treh]
  Do not enter! N'entrez pas! [nã-treh pah]
enterprise, entreprise (f) [ã-truh-preez]
entertain [guests] v., recevoir (irreg) [ruh-suh-vwahr]
entertain [amuse] v., amuser [ah-mü-zeh]
entertaining, amusant [ah-mü-zã(t)]
entertainment, divertissement (m) [dee-ver-tees-mã]
enthusiasm, enthousiasme (m) [ã-too-zyahzm]
entire, entier, -tière [ã-tyeh, ã-tyer]
entirely, entièrement [ã-tyer-mã]
entrance, entrée (f) [ã-treh]
envelope, n., enveloppe (f) [ã-vlop]
environment, milieu (m), environnement (m) [meel-yuh,
  ã-vee-ron-mã]
envy v., envier [ã-vyeh]
equal, égal, -aux (m, pl) [eh-gahl, eh-goh]
equality, égalité (f) [eh-gah-lee-teh]

EQ _____46

equipment, équipement (m) [*eh-keep-mã*]

erase v., effacer [*eh-fah-seh*]

eraser, gomme (f) [*gom*]

errand, course (f) [*koors*]

error, erreur (f) [*eh-ruhr*]

escape v., s'échapper [*seh-shah-peh*]

especially, spécialement [*speh-syahl-mã*]

essential, essentiel, -elle [*eh-sã-syel*]

establish v., établir [*eh-tah-bleer*]

establishment, établissement (m) [*eh-tah-blees-mã*]

estate [land], propriété (f) [*pro-pree-yeh-teh*]

estate [inheritance], succession (f) [*sük-ses-syõ*]

esteem v., estimer [*es-tee-meh*]

estimate n., devis (m) [*duh-vee*]

estimate v., estimer [*es-tee-meh*]

eternal, éternel, -elle [*eh-ter-nel*]

Europe, Europe (f) [*uh-rop*]

European, européen, -enne [*uh-ro-peh-ẽ, uh-ro-peh-en*]

eve, veille (f) [*vey*]

   Christmas Eve, la veille de Noël [*lah vey duh noh-el*]

even adv., même [*mem*]

   even so, quand même [*kã mem*]

   even then, même à cette époque [*mem ah se-teh-pok*]

   even though, bien que, même si [*byẽ k(uh), mem see*]

even [number], nombre (m) pair [*nõ-bruh per*]

evening, soir (m), soirée (f) [*swahr, swah-reh*]

   Good evening! Bonsoir! [*bõ-swahr*]

   in the evening, le soir [*luh swahr*]

event, événement (m) [*eh-ven-mã*]

   in the event of, au cas où [*oh kah oo*]

eventually, finalement [*fee-nahl-mã*]

ever, jamais [*zhah-meh*]

   as ever, comme toujours [*kom too-zhoor*]

every, chaque [*shahk*]

   every day, tous les jours [*too leh zhoor*]

everybody, tout le monde [*tool mõd*]

everything, tout [*too*]

everywhere, partout [*pahr-too*]

evidence, preuves (f, pl) [*pruhv*]
evident, évident [*eh-vee-dã(t)*]
evidently, évidemment [*eh-vee-dah-mã*]
evil *adj.,* mauvais [*mo-ve(z)*]
exact, exact [*eg-zah, eg-zahkt*]
exactly, exactement [*eg-zahk-tuh-mã*]
exaggerate *v.,* exagérer [*eg-zah-zheh-reh*]
examination, examen (m) [*eg-zah-mẽ*]
examine *v.,* examiner [*eg-zah-mee-neh*]
example, exemple (m) [*eg-zãpl*]
exceed *v.,* dépasser [*deh-pah-seh*]
excellent, excellent [*ek-se-lã(t)*]
except, excepté, sauf [*ek-sep-teh, sohf*]
exception, exception (f) [*ek-sep-syõ*]
excess, excédent (m) [*ek-seh-dã*]
exchange *n.,* échange (m) [*eh-shãzh*]
exchange [money] *n.,* change (m) [*shãzh*]
   rate of exchange, taux (m) de change, cours (m) [*toht
    shãzh, koor*]
exchange *v.,* échanger [*eh-shã-zheh*]
excited, agité [*ah-zhee-teh*]
excursion, excursion (f) [*eks-kür-syõ*]
excuse *v.,* excuser [*ek-skü-zeh*]
   Excuse me! Excusez-moi!, Pardon! [*ek-skü-zeh-mwah,
    pahr-dõ*]
exercise *n.,* exercice (m) [*eg-zer-sees*]
exhausted, épuisé [*eh-pwee-zeh*]
exhibit *v.,* exposer [*ek-spoh-zeh*]
exhibition, exposition (f) [*eks-poh-zee-syõ*]
exile, exil (m) [*eg-zeel*]
exist *v.,* exister [*eg-zees-teh*]
existence, existence (f) [*eg-zees-tãs*]
exit *n.,* sortie (f) [*sor-tee*]
expect *v.,* s'attendre (à) [*sah-tã-dr(ah)*]
expedition, expédition (f) [*ek-speh-dee-syõ*]
expense, dépense (f) [*deh-pãs*]
expensive, cher, chère [*sher*]
experience *n.,* expérience (f) [*eks-per-yãs*]

experiment *n.*, expérience (f) [*eks-per-yãs*]
expert, expert [*eks-per(t)*]
explain *v.*, expliquer [*eks-plee-keh*]
explanation, explication (f) [*eks-plee-kah-syõ*]
explore *v.*, explorer [*eks-plo-reh*]
explosion, explosion (f) [*eks-ploh-zyõ*]
export *v.*, exporter [*eks-por-teh*]
express [train], express (m); rapide (m) [*eks-pres, rah-peed*]
express *v.*, exprimer [*eks-pree-meh*]
expression, expression (f) [*eks-pre-syõ*]
extent, étendue (f) [*eh-tã-dü*]
   to a certain extent, jusqu'à un certain point [*zhüs-kah ẽ ser-tẽ pwẽ*]
exterior, extérieur (m) [*eks-ter-yuhr*]
external, extérieur [*eks-ter-yuhr*]
extinguish *v.*, éteindre (irreg) [*eh-tẽdr*]
extra, supplémentaire [*sü-pleh-mã-ter*]
extract *v.*, extraire (irreg) [*ek-strer*]
extraction, extraction (f) [*ek-strahk-syõ*]
extraordinary, extraordinaire [*ek-strah-or-dee-ner*]
extreme, extrême [*ek-strem*]
extremely, extrêmement [*ek-strem-mã*]
eye, oeil (m), yeux (pl) [*uhy, yuh*]
eyebrow, sourcil (m) [*soor-see*]
eye doctor, oculiste (m) [*o-kü-leest*]
eyelash, cil (m) [*seel*]
eyelid, paupière (f) [*poh-pyer*]
eyesight, vue (f) [*vü*]

F

face *n.*, visage (m) [*vee-zahzh*]
face *v.*, faire face à [*fer fahs ah*]
fact, fait (m) [*fe*]
   in fact, en fait [*ã fe(t)*]

factory, usine (f) [*ü-zeen*]

faculty [ability], faculté [*fah-kül-teh*]

faculty [of college], corps professoral (m) [*kor pro-feh-so-rahl*]

fade *v.,* déteindre (irreg) [*deh-tēdr*]

fail *v.,* échouer [*eh-shweh*]

failure, échec (m) [*eh-shek*]

faint *v.,* s'évanouir [*seh-vah-nweer*]

fair [just] *adj.,* juste [*zhüst*]

fair [light] *adj.,* clair [*kler*]

fair [pretty] *adj.,* joli [*zho-lee*]

fair *n.,* foire (f) [*fwahr*]

faith, foi (f) [*fwah*]

faithful, fidèle [*fee-del*]

fall [descent] *n.,* chute (f) [*shüt*]

fall [season] *n.,* automne (m) [*oh-ton*]

fall *v.,* tomber (*Aux:* ÊTRE) [*tō-beh*]

    fall in love (with), tomber amoureux (de) [*tō-beh ah-moo-ruh (duh)*]

false, faux, fausse [*foh, fohs*]

fame, renommée (f) [*ruh-no-meh*]

familiar, bien connu; familier, -ière [*byē ko-nü; fah-meel-yeh, fah-meel-yer*]

family, famille (f) [*fah-meey*]

famous, célèbre [*seh-lebr*]

fan [hand], éventail (m) [*eh-vã-tahy*]

fan [electric], ventilateur (m) [*vã-tee-lah-tuhr*]

far, loin [*lwē*]

    How far? À quelle distance? [*ah kel dees-tãs*]

fare [transportation], prix (m) [*pree*]

farewell, adieu (m), -ieux (pl) [*ah-dyuh*]

farm *n.,* ferme (f) [*ferm*]

farmer, agriculteur (m) [*ah-gree-kül-tuhr*]

farmyard, basse-cour (f) [*bahs-koor*]

farther, plus loin [*plü lwē*]

farthest, le plus loin [*luh plü lwē*]

fascinating, fascinant [*fah-see-nã(t)*]

fashion *n.,* mode (f) [*mod*]

fashionable, à la mode [*ah lah mod*]
fast *adj.*, rapide [*rah-peed*]
fast *adv.*, vite [*veet*]
fasten *v.*, attacher [*ah-tah-sheh*]
fat [person] *adj.*, gros, grosse [*groh, grohs*]
fat [animal] *adj.*, gras, grasse [*grah, grahs*]
fat [cooking] *n.*, graisse (f) [*gres*]
fate, destin (m) [*des-tẽ*]
father, père (m) [*per*]
father-in-law, beau-père (m) [*boh-per*]
fatigue, fatigue (f) [*fah-teeg*]
faucet, robinet (m) [*ro-bee-neh*]
fault *n.*, faute (f) [*foht*]
favor *n.*, faveur (f) [*fah-vuhr*]
  Will you do me a favor? Voulez-vous me faire plaisir?
  [*voo-leh-voom fer ple-zeer*]
favorite, préféré [*preh-feh-reh*]
fear *n.*, peur (f), crainte (f) [*puhr, krẽt*]
fear *v.*, craindre (irreg) [*krẽdr*]
fearful [afraid], peureux, -euse [*puh-ruh, puh-ruhz*]
fearless, sans crainte [*sã krẽt*]
feast *n.*, fête (f) [*fet*]
feather, plume (f) [*plüm*]
feature [of face] *n.*, trait (m) [*tre*]
February, février (m) [*feh-vree-yeh*]
federal, fédéral, -aux (m, pl) [*feh-deh-rahl, feh-deh-roh*]
fee, honoraires (m, pl) [*o-no-rer*]
feed *v.*, nourrir [*noo-reer*]
feel *v.*, sentir (irreg), se sentir (irreg) [*sã-teer, suh sã-teer*]
feeling, sentiment (m) [*sã-tee-mã*]
feet, pieds (m, pl) [*pyeh*]
fellow, collègue (m) [*ko-leg*]
  He's a good fellow! C'est un brave type! [*se-tẽ brahv teep*]
female, femelle (f) [*fuh-mel*]
feminine, féminin [*feh-mee-nẽ, feh-mee-neen*]
fence, barrière (f) [*bah-ryer*]
fencing, escrime (f) [*es-kreem*]
fender, aile (f) [*el*]

ferryboat, bac (m) [*bahk*]
festival, festival (m), -aux (pl) [*fes-tee-vahl, fes-tee-voh*]
fever, fièvre (f) [*fyevr*]
few, peu (de) [*puh (duh)*]
   a few, quelques [*kelk*]
fewer, moins (de) [*mwē (duh)*]
fiancé, fiancé [*fyã-seh*]
fiancée, fiancée [*fyã-seh*]
field, champ (m) [*shã*]
field glasses, jumelles (f, pl) [*zhü-mel*]
fierce, féroce [*feh-ros*]
fifteen, quinze [*kēz*]
fifth, cinquième [*sē-kyem*]
fifty, cinquante [*sē-kãt*]
fig, figue (f) [*feeg*]
fight *n.*, combat (m) [*kõ-bah*]
fight *v.*, se battre (irreg) [*s(uh) bahtr*]
figure [number], chiffre (m) [*sheefr*]
figure [form], silhouette (f) [*seel-wet*]
file [tool] *n.*, lime (f) [*leem*]
file [record] *n.*, dossier (m) [*doh-syeh*]
fill *v.*, remplir [*rã-pleer*]
   Fill up with regular (super), Le plein normal (super) [*luh plē nor-mahl (sü-per)*]
filling [tooth], plombage (m) [*plõ-bahzh*]
film, pellicule (f) [*peh-lee-kül*]
filter, filtre (m) [*feeltr*]
filthy, très sale [*tre sahl*]
final, final, -aux (m, pl) [*fee-nahl, fee-noh*]
finally, finalement [*fee-nahl-mã*]
financial, financier, -ière [*fee-nã-syeh, fee-nã-syer*]
find *v.*, trouver [*troo-veh*]
fine [small] *adj.*, fin [*fē, feen*]
fine [good] *adj.*, excellent [*ek-se-lã(t)*]
fine *n.*, amende (f) [*ah-mãd*]
finger, doigt (m) [*dwah*]
finish *v.*, finir [*fee-neer*]
fire, feu (m), incendie (m) [*fuh, ē-sã-dee*]

Fire! Au feu! [*oh fuh*]

fireman, pompier (m) [*pŏ-pyeh*]

fireplace, cheminée (f) [*shmee-neh*]

firm *n.*, firme (f), entreprise (f) [*feerm, ā-truh-preez*]

firm *adj.*, ferme [*ferm*]

first, premier, -ière [*pruh-myeh, pruh-myer*]

at first, d'abord [*dah-bor*]

first aid, premiers secours (m) [*pruh-myeh skoor*]

first name, prénom (m) [*preh-nŏ*]

fish *n.*, poisson (m) [*pwah-sŏ*]

fish *v.*, pêcher [*pe-sheh*]

fisherman, pêcheur (m) [*pe-shuhr*]

fishing, pêche (f) [*pesh*]

fist, poing (m) [*pwĕ*]

fit *v.*, aller (irreg) bien [*ah-leh byĕ*]

fitting *n.*, essayage (m) [*eh-se-yazh*]

five, cinq [*sĕ(k)*]

fix [attach] *v.*, attacher [*ah-tah-sheh*]

fix [repair] *v.*, réparer, arranger [*reh-pah-reh, ah-rā-zheh*]

fixed price, prix fixe (m) [*pree feeks*]

flag, drapeau (m), -eaux (pl) [*drah-poh*]

flame, flamme (f) [*flahm*]

flat, plat [*plah(t)*]

flatter *v.*, flatter [*flah-teh*]

flatterer, flatteur, -euse [*flah-tuhr, flah-tuhz*]

flavor [taste] *n.*, saveur (f) [*sah-vuhr*]

flavor *v.*, assaisonner [*ah-se-zo-neh*]

flea, puce (f) [*püs*]

flea market, marché (m) aux puces [*mahr-sheh oh püs*]

flee, fuir (irreg) [*fweer*]

fleet [ships] *n.*, flotte (f) [*flot*]

flesh, chair (f) [*sher*]

flexible, souple [*soopl*]

flight, vol (m) [*vol*]

flirt *v.*, flirter [*fluhr-teh*]

float *v.*, flotter [*flo-teh*]

flood, inondation (f) [*ee-nŏ-dah-syŏ*]

floor, plancher (m) [*plā-sheh*]

flour, farine (f) [*fah-reen*]

flow *v.*, couler [*koo-leh*]

flower, fleur (f) [*fluhr*]

florist, fleuriste (m) [*fluh-reest*]

fluently, couramment [*koo-rah-mã*]

flush [the toilet] *v.*, tirer la chasse [*tee-reh lah shahs*]

flute, flute (f) [*flüt*]

fly *n.*, mouche (f) [*moosh*]

fly *v.*, voler [*vo-leh*]

foam [waves] *n.*, écume (f) [*eh-küm*]

foam [of beverage] *n.*, mousse (f) [*moos*]

foe, adversaire (m) [*ahd-ver-ser*]

fog *n.*, brouillard (m) [*broo-yahr*]

   It's foggy, Il fait du brouillard [*eel fe dü broo-yahr*]

fold *v.*, plier [*plee-yeh*]

follow *v.*, suivre (irreg) [*sweevr*]

fond: to be fond of, aimer [*e-meh*]

food, nourriture (f) [*noo-ree-tür*]

fool *n.*, imbécile (m) [*ẽ-beh-seel*]

foolish, fou, folle; sot, sotte [*foo, fol; soh, sot*]

foot [anat.], pied (m) [*pyeh*]

foot [measure], trente centimètres [*trãt sã-tee-metr*]

football [game], rugby (m) [*rüg-bee*]

football [ball], ballon (m) de rugby [*bah-lõ duh rüg-bee*]

for *prep.*, pour [*poor*]

   for example, par exemple [*pahr eg-zãpl*]

for [time], depuis, pendant [*duh-pwee, pã-dã*]

   I have been here for three hours, Je suis ici depuis trois
     heures [*shswee-zee-see duh-pwee trwah-zuhr*]

   I was there for three days, J'étais là pendant trois jours
     [*zheh-te lah pã-dã trwah zhoor*]

for [because] *conj.*, car [*kahr*]

forbid *v.*, interdire (irreg) [*ẽ-ter-deer*]

force *n.*, force (f) [*fors*]

force *v.*, forcer [*for-seh*]

forehead, front (m) [*frõ*]

foreign, étranger, -ère [*eh-trã-zheh, eh-trã-zher*]

foreign minister, ministre des affaires étrangères [*mee-*

    neestr deh-zah-fer eh-trã-zher]

foreign office, ministère des affaires étrangères [*mee-nees-ter deh-zah-fer eh-trã-zher*]

foreign policy, politique internationale (f) [*po-lee-teek ē-ter-nah-syo-nahl*]

foreigner, étranger, -ère [*eh-trã-zheh, eh-trã-zher*]

forest, forêt (f) [*fo-re*]

forever, pour toujours [*poor too-zhoor*]

forget *v.,* oublier [*oo-blee-yeh*]

forgive *v.,* pardonner [*pahr-do-neh*]

forgotten, oublié [*oo-blee-yeh*]

fork, fourchette (f) [*foor-shet*]

form [shape] *n.,* forme, (f) [*form*]

form [questionnaire] *n.,* imprimé (m) [*ē-pree-meh*]

form *v.,* former [*for-meh*]

formal, formel, -elle [*for-mel*]

formality, formalité (f) [*for-mah-lee-teh*]

former, ancien, -enne [*ã-syē, ã-syen*]

formerly, avant, précédemment [*ah-vã, preh-seh-dah-mã*]

formula, formule (f) [*for-mül*]

fort, fort (m), forteresse (f) [*for, for-tuh-res*]

fortunate, heureux, -euse; fortuné [*uh-ruh, uh-ruhz; for-tü-neh*]

  be fortunate *v.,* avoir de la chance [*ah-vwahr dlah shãs*]

fortunately, heureusement [*uh-ruhz-mã*]

fortune, fortune (f) [*for-tün*]

forty, quarante [*kah-rãt*]

forward, en avant [*ã-nah-vã*]

foundation, fondation (f) [*fõ-dah-syõ*]

fountain, fontaine (f) [*fõ-ten*]

fountain pen, stylo (m) [*stee-loh*]

four, quatre [*kahtr*]

fourteen, quatorze [*kah-torz*]

fourth, quatrième [*kah-tree-yem*]

fracture *n.,* fracture (f) [*frahk-tür*]

fragile, fragile [*frah-zheel*]

fragrance, parfum (m) [*pahr-fē*]

frame *n.,* cadre (m) [*kahdr*]

France, France (f) [*frãs*]
frank, franc, franche [*frã, frãsh*]
fraud, fraude [*frohd*]
free [not bound] *adj.*, libre [*leebr*]
free [at no cost] *adj.*, gratuit [*grah-twee(t)*]
free *v.*, libérer [*lee-beh-reh*]
freedom, liberté (f) [*lee-ber-teh*]
freeze *v.*, geler [*zhuh-leh*]
freight, frêt (m) [*fre*]
French, français [*frã-se(z)*]
Frenchman, -woman, Français, -se [*frã-se(z)*]
frequent, fréquent [*freh-kã(t)*]
frequently, souvent [*soo-vã*]
fresh, frais, fraiche [*fre, fresh*]
Friday, vendredi (m) [*vã-druh-dee*]
fried, frit [*free(t)*]
friend, ami, amie [*ah-mee*]
friendship, amitié (f) [*ah-mee-tyeh*]
frighten *v.*, faire peur à [*fer puhr ah*]
frog, grenouille (f) [*gruh-nooy*]
from, de [*duh*]
   from now on, désormais [*deh-zor-me*]
front, devant (m) [*duh-vã*]
frost, gelée (f) [*zhuh-leh*]
frown *v.*, froncer les sourcils [*frõ-seh leh soor-see*]
fruit, fruit (m) [*frwee*]
fry *v.*, faire frire (irreg) [*fer freer*]
frying pan, poêle (f) [*pwahl*]
full, plein [*plẽ, plen*]
fun, amusement (m) [*ah-müz-mã*]
   Have fun! Amusez-vous bien! [*ah-mü-zeh-voo byẽ*]
function, fonction (f) [*fõk-syõ*]
funds *pl.*, fonds (m, pl) [*fõ*]
funeral, enterrement (m) [*ã-ter-mã*]
funnel *n.*, entonnoir (m) [*ã-ton-wahr*]
funny, drôle [*drohl*]
fur, fourrure (f) [*foo-rür*]
furious, furieux, -euse [*für-yuh, für-yuhz*]

furnish [provide] *v.*, fournir [*foor-neer*]
furnish [put furniture into] *v.*, meubler [*muh-bleh*]
furnished room, chambre (f) meublée [*shãbr muh-bleh*]
furniture, meubles (m, pl) [*muhbl*]
further *adj.*, ultérieur [*ül-tehr-yuhr*]
furthermore, de plus [*duh plü*]
future, futur (m) [*fü-tür*]
  in the future, à l'avenir [*ah lahv-neer*]

G

gadget, truc (m), appareil (m) [*trük, ah-pah-rey*]
gain *v.*, gagner [*gah-nyeh*]
gallon, gallon (m), quatre litres (m) [*gah-lõ, kahtr leetr*]
gamble *v.*, jouer [*zhweh*]
gambling, jeu (de hasard) (m) [*zhuh (duh ah-zahr)*]
game, jeu (m) [*zhuh*]
gangplank, passerelle (f) [*pahs-rel*]
garage, garage (m) [*gah-rahzh*]
garbage, ordures (f, pl) [*or-dür*]
garden, jardin (m) [*zhahr-dẽ*]
gardener, jardinier (m) [*zhahr-dee-nyeh*]
garlic, ail (m) [*ahy*]
garment, vêtement (m) [*vet-mã*]
garter, jarretière (f) [*zhahr-tyer*]
gas, gaz (m) [*gahz*]
gasoline, essence (f) [*eh-sãs*]
  be out of gas *v.*, être en panne d'essence [*e-trã pahn deh-sãs*]
gasoline station, station service (f), poste à essence (m)
    [*stah-syõ ser-vees, post ah e-sãs*]
gas tank, réservoir à essence (m) [*re-zer-vwahr ah eh-sãs*]
gate, portail (m) [*por-tahy*]
gather *v.*, ramasser [*rah-mah-seh*]
gauge *n.*, jauge (f) [*zhohzh*]
gay, gai [*ghe*]

gear [auto] *n.*, vitesse (f) [*vee-tes*]
  put in gear *v.*, embrayer [*ã-bre-yeh*]
  change gear *v.*, changer de vitesse [*shã-zhehd vee-tes*]
gender, genre (m) [*zhãr*]
general *n.*, général (m), -aux (pl) [*zheh-neh-rahl, zheh-neh-roh*]
general *adj.*, général, -aux (m, pl) [*zhe-neh-rahl, zheh-neh-roh*]
  in general, en général [*ã zheh-neh-rahl*]
general delivery, poste restante (f) [*post res-tãt*]
generation, génération (f)]*zheh-neh-rah-syõ*]
generous, généreux, -euse [*zheh-neh-ruh, zheh-neh-ruhz*]
gentle, doux, douce [*doo, doos*]
gentleman, gentlemen, monsieur, messieurs [*muh-syuh,*
  meh-syuh]
genuine, véritable [*veh-ree-tahbl*]
geography, géographie (f) [*zheh-oh-grah-fee*]
geometry, géométrie (f) [*zheh-oh-meh-tree*]
germ, microbe (m) [*mee-krob*]
German, allemand [*ahl-mã(d)*]
Germany, Allemagne (f) [*ahl-mañ*]
get [become] *v.*, devenir (irreg; Aux: ÊTRE) [*duh-vneer*]
get [obtain] *v.*, obtenir (irreg) [*op-tuh-neer*]
get [receive] *v.*, recevoir (irreg) [*ruh-suh-vwar*]
  get down, descendre (Aux: ÊTRE) [*deh-sãdr*]
  get in, entrer (Aux: ÊTRE) [*ã-treh*]
  get married, se marier [*smah-ryeh*]
  get off, descendre (irreg; Aux: ÊTRE) [*deh-sãdr*]
  get up, se lever [*sluh-veh*]
ghost, fantôme (m) [*fã-tohm*]
gift, cadeau (m), -eaux (pl) [*kah-doh*]
gifted, doué [*doo-eh*]
gin, gin (m) [*jeen*]
girdle, gaine (f) [*ghen*]
girl, fille (f) [*feey*]
give *v.*, donner [*do-neh*]
  give back, rendre [*rãdr*]
  give in, céder [*seh-deh*]
glad, content [*kõ-tã(t)*]
glance *n.*, coup d'oeil (m) [*koo duhy*]

glance *v.*, jeter un coup d'oeil [*zh(uh)-teh ẽ koo duhy*]
glass, verre (m) [*ver*]
glasses [eye], lunettes (f, pl) [*lü-net*]
glory, gloire (f) [*glwahr*]
glove, gant (m) [*gã*]
glue, colle (f) [*kol*]
go *v.*, aller (irreg; *Aux:* ÊTRE) [*ah-leh*]
  go across, traverser [*trah-ver-seh*]
  go away, s'en aller (irreg; *Aux:* ÊTRE), partir (irreg; *Aux:* ÊTRE) [*sã-nah-leh, pahr-teer*]
  go back, retourner (*Aux:* ÊTRE) [*ruh-toor-neh*]
  go down, descendre (*Aux:* ÊTRE) [*deh-sãdr*]
  go in, entrer (*Aux:* ÊTRE) [*ã-treh*]
  go on, continuer [*kõ-tee-nweh*]
  go out, sortir (irreg; *Aux:* ÊTRE) [*sor-teer*]
  go to bed, se coucher [*skoo-sheh*]
  go up, monter (*Aux:* ÊTRE) [*mõ-teh*]
  go without, se passer de [*spah-seh duh*]
goal, but (m) [*bü(t)*]
god, dieu (m), -eux (pl) [*dyuh*]
goddaughter, filleule (f) [*fee-yuhl*]
godfather, parrain (m) [*pah-rẽ*]
godmother, marraine (f) [*mah-ren*]
godson, filleul (m) [*fee-yuhl*]
gold, or (m) [*or*]
golden, d'or [*dor*]
golf, golf (m) [*golf*]
good, bon, bonne [*bõ, bon*]
good afternoon, bonjour [*bõ-zhoor*]
good-bye, au revoir [*ohr-vwahr*]
good evening, bonsoir [*bõ-swahr*]
Good luck, Bonne chance [*bon shãs*]
good morning, bonjour [*bõ-zhoor*]
goodness, bonté (f) [*bõ-teh*]
good night, bonne nuit [*bon nwee*]
goods *pl.*, biens (m, pl), marchandise (f) [*byẽ, mahr-shã-deez*]
gorgeous, magnifique [*mah-nyee-feek*]
Gothic, gothique [*goh-teek*]

government, gouvernement (m) [*goo-ver-nuh-mã*]

governor, gouverneur (m) [*goo-ver-nuhr*]

grace, grâce (f) [*grahs*]

graceful, grâcieux, -cieuse [*grah-syuh, grah-syuhz*]

grade [class] *n.,* classe (f) [*klahs*]

grade [mark] *n.,* note (f) [*not*]

gradually, peu à peu [*puh ah puh*]

graduate *n.,* diplômé, -ée [*dee-ploh-meh*]

graduate *v.,* recevoir (irreg) son diplôme [*ruh-suh-vwahr sõ dee-plohm*]

grain, grain (m) [*grẽ*]

grammar, grammaire (f) [*grah-mer*]

grandchildren, petits-enfants (m, pl) [*ptee-zã-fã*]

granddaughter, petite fille (f) [*pteet-feey*]

grandfather, grandpère (m) [*grã-per*]

grandmother, grandmère (f) [*grã-mer*]

grandparents, grands parents (m, pl) [*grã pah-rã*]

grandson, petit fils (m) [*ptee fees*]

grant *v.,* accorder [*ah-kor-deh*]

grape, raisin (m) [*re-zẽ*]

grapefruit, pamplemousse (f) [*pã-pluh-moos*]

grass, herbe (f) [*erb*]

grateful, reconnaissant [*ruh-ko-ne-sã(t)*]

gratitude, reconnaissance (f) [*ruh-ko-ne-sãs*]

grave, *n.,* tombe (f) [*tõb*]

gravy, sauce (f) [*sohs*]

gray, gris [*gree(z)*]

grease *n.,* graisse (f) [*gres*]

great, grand [*grã(d)*]

   a great deal, a great many, beaucoup (de) [*boh-koo (duh)*]

Great Britain, Grande Bretagne (f) [*grãd bruh-tahñ*]

Greece, Grèce (f) [*gres*]

Greek, grec, grecque [*grek*]

green, vert [*ver(t)*]

greet *v.,* saluer [*sahl-weh*]

greetings, salutations (f, pl) [*sah-lü-tah-syõ*]

grief, douleur (f) [*doo-luhr*]

grind *v.,* moudre (irreg) [*moodr*]

groan *n.*, gémissement (m) [*zheh-mees-mã*]
groan *v.*, gémir [*zheh-meer*]
grocery, épicerie (f) [*eh-pees-ree*]
ground [earth] *n.*, terre (f) [*ter*]
  on the ground, par terre [*pahr ter*]
ground floor, rez-de-chaussée (m) [*ret-shoh-seh*]
group, groupe (m) [*groop*]
grow [cultivate] *v.*, cultiver [*kül-tee-veh*]
grow [increase] *v.*, croître (irreg) [*krwahtr*]
grow [mature] *v.*, grandir [*grã-deer*]
grudge *n.*, rancune (f) [*rã-kün*]
guarantee *n.*, garantie (f) [*gah-rã-tee*]
guarantee *v.*, garantir [*gah-rã-teer*]
guard *n.*, gardien (m) [*gahr-dyē*]
guard [military] *n.*, garde (f) [*gahrd*]
guard *v.*, protéger [*pro-teh-zheh*]
guess *v.*, deviner [*d(uh)-vee-neh*]
guest, invité, -ée [*ē-vee-teh*]
guide *n.*, guide (m) [*gheed*]
guilty, coupable [*koo-pahbl*]
guitar, guitare (f) [*ghee-tahr*]
gum [anat.], gencive (f) [*zhã-seev*]
gum [chewing], chewing-gum (m) [*shween-gom*]
gun, fusil (m) [*fü-zee*]
gutter [street], ruisseau (m), -eaux (pl) [*rwee-soh*]
gutter [roof], gouttière (f) [*goo-tyer*]
gymnasium, gymnase (m) [*zheem-nahz*]
gypsy, gitan, gitane [*zhee-tã, zhee-tahn*]

H

habit [custom] *n.*, habitude (f) [*ah-bee-tüd*]
hail *n.*, grêle (f) [*grel*]
hair, cheveux (m, pl) [*shvuh*]
haircut, coupe (f) de cheveux [*koop duh shvuh*]

hairdresser, coiffeur, -euse [*kwah-fuhr, kwah-fuhz*]
half *n.*, moitié (f) [*mwah-tyeh*]
half *adj.*, demi [*dmee*]
   three and a half, trois et demi [*trwah ehd-mee*]
   half past two, deux heures et demie [*duh-zuhr ehd-mee*]
halfway, à mi-chemin [*ah mee-shmẽ*]
hall [corridor], couloir (m) [*kool-wahr*]
hall [auditorium], salle (f) [*sahl*]
ham, jambon (m) [*zhã-bõ*]
hammer, marteau (m), -eaux (pl) [*mahr-toh*]
hand, main (f) [*mẽ*]
   on the other hand, d'autre part [*doh-truh pahr*]
handbag, sac (m) à main [*sah-kah mẽ*]
handkerchief, mouchoir (m) [*moo-shwahr*]
handle *n.*, poignée (f) [*pwah-nyeh*]
handmade, fait main [*fe mẽ*]
handsome, beau (bel), belle; beaux, belles [*boh, bel*]
hang *v.*, pendre [*pãdr*]
   hang up [telephone], raccrocher [*rah-kro-sheh*]
   Don't hang up, Ne quittez pas [*nuh kee-teh pah*]
happen *v.*, arriver (*Aux:* ÊTRE) [*ah-ree-veh*]
   What's happening? Qu'est-ce qui se passe? [*kes kees pahs*]
   What happened? Qu'est-ce qui est arrivé? [*kes kye-tah-ree-veh*]
happiness, bonheur (m) [*bo-nuhr*]
happy, heureux, -euse; content [*uh-ruh, uh-ruhz; kõ-tã(t)*]
   Happy Birthday! Bon anniversaire! [*bon-nah-nee-ver-ser*]
   Happy New Year! Bonne Année! [*bo-nah-neh*]
harbor *n.*, port (m) [*por*]
hard [difficult], difficile [*dee-fee-seel*]
hard [solid], dur [*dür*]
hardly, à peine [*ah pen*]
harm *v.*, faire du mal (à) [*fer dü mahl (ah)*]
harmful, nuisible [*nwee-zeebl*]
harp, *harpe (f) [*ahrp*]
harvest, moisson (f) [*mwah-sõ*]
haste, *hâte (f) [*aht*]

hat, chapeau (m), -eaux (pl) [*shah-poh*]

hate *n.,* *haine (f) [*en*]

hate *v.,* *haïr (irreg) [*ah-eer*]

have *v.,* avoir (irreg) [*ah-vwahr*]

   have to [must], devoir [plus infinitive] (irreg) [*duh-vwahr*]

he, il, lui [*eel, lwee*]

head, tête (f) [*tet*]

headache, mal de tête (m) [*mahl duh tet*]

headlight, phare (m) [*fahr*]

headquarters [military], quartier général (m) [*kahr-tyeh zheh-neh-rahl*]

headquarters [business], siège (m) [*syezh*]

health, santé (f) [*sã-teh*]

   in good health, en bonne santé [*ã bon sã-teh*]

healthy, sain [*sẽ, sen*]

hear *v.,* entendre [*ã-tãdr*]

   hear of [about], entendre parler de [*ã-tãdr pahr-leh duh*]

   hear that, entendre dire que [*ã-tãdr deer kuh*]

heart, coeur (m) [*kuhr*]

   by heart, par coeur [*pahr kuhr*]

heart attack, crise cardiaque, infarctus [*kreez kahr-dyahk, ẽ-fahrk-tüs*]

heat *n.,* chaleur (f) [*shah-luhr*]

heat *v.,* chauffer [*shoh-feh*]

heating, chauffage (m) [*shoh-fahzh*]

heaven, ciel (m), cieux (pl) [*syel, syuh*]

heavy, lourd [*loor(d)*]

Hebrew, hébreu [*eh-bruh*]

heel, talon (m) [*tah-lõ*]

height [of person], taille (f) [*tahy*]

height [elevation], *hauteur (f) [*oh-tuhr*]

heir, héritier (m) [*eh-ree-tyeh*]

heiress, héritière (f) [*eh-ree-tyer*]

hell, enfer (m) [*ã-fer*]

hello, bonjour [*bõ-zhoor*]

hello [telephone], allo! [*ah-loh*]

help *n.,* secours (m) [*skoor*]

   Help! Au secours! [*ohs-koor*]

help v., aider [*e-deh*]
   I can't help doing it, Je ne peux pas m'empêcher de le
      faire [*zhuhn puh pah mã-peh-shehd luh fer*]
helpful, utile [*ü-teel*]
her pron., elle, la, lui [*el, lah, lwee*]
her poss. adj., son, sa, ses [*sõ, sah, seh*]
here, ici [*ee-see*]
   Here it is, Le (la) voilà [*luh (lah) vwah-lah*]
hers, le sien, la sienne; les siens, les siennes [*luh syẽ, lah
     syen; leh syẽ, leh syen*]
herself, elle-même [*el-mem*]
hesitate v., hésiter [*eh-zee-teh*]
hide v., cacher, se cacher [*kah-sheh, skah-sheh*]
high, *haut [*oh(t)*]
high school, école secondaire (f) [*eh-kol suh-gõ-der*]
hill, collinc (f) [*ko-leen*]
him, le, lui [*luh, lwee*]
himself, lui-même [*lwee-mem*]
hinge n., charnière (f) [*shahr-nyer*]
hip, *hanche (f) [*ãsh*]
hire v., engager [*ã-gah-zheh*]
his adj., son, sa, ses [*sõ, sah, seh*]
his pron., le sien, la sienne; les siens, les siennes [*luh syẽ,
     lah syen; leh syẽ, leh syen*]
historical, historique [*ees-to-reek*]
history, histoire (f) [*ees-twahr*]
hit v., frapper [*frah-peh*]
hitchhiking, auto-stop (m) [*oh-toh-stop*]
hold v., tenir (irreg) [*t(uh)-neer*]
hole, trou (m) [*troo*]
holiday [religious], fête (f) [*fet*]
holiday [legal], jour férié (m) [*zhoor fehr-yeh*]
Holland, *Hollande (f) [*oh-lãd*]
holy, saint [*sẽ(t)*]
home, chez-soi (m, invar); maison (f) [*sheh-swah, meh-zõ*]
   at home, à la maison; chez soi (lui, elle) [*ah lah meh-zõ;
     sheh-swah (sheh-lwee, sheh-zel)*]
   Make yourself at home, Faites comme chez vous [*fet*

kom sheh voo]

honest, honnête [*o-net*]

honey, miel (m) [*myel*]

honeymoon, lune (f) de miel [*lün duh myel*]

honor n., honneur (m) [*o-nuhr*]

honor v., honorer [*o-no-reh*]

hook n., crochet (m) [*kro-sheh*]

hope n., espoir (m) [*es-pwahr*]

hope v., espérer [*es-peh-reh*]

hopeful, plein d'espoir [*plē (plen) des-pwahr*]

hopeless, sans espoir [*sã-zes-pwahr*]

horn [animal or shape], corne (f) [*korn*]

horn [auto], klaxon (m) [*klah-ksõ*]

horrible, horrible [*o-reebl*]

horse, cheval (m), -aux (pl) [*shvahl, shvoh*]

hospital, hôpital (m), -aux (pl) [*oh-pee-tahl, oh-pee-toh*]

hospitality, hospitalité (f) [*os-pee-tah-lee-teh*]

host, hôte (m) [*oht*]

hostess, hôtesse (f) [*oh-tes*]

hostile, hostile [*os-teel*]

hot, chaud [*shoh(d)*]

hotel, hôtel (m) [*oh-tel*]

hotel room, chambre d'hôtel (f) [*shãbr doh-tel*]

hour, heure (f) [*uhr*]

hourly, toutes les heures [*toot leh-zuhr*]

house, maison (f) [*me-zõ*]

housekeeper, ménagère (f) [*meh-nah-zher*]

housewife, maîtresse (f) de maison [*me-tres duh meh-zõ*]

how, comment [*ko-mã*]

   How do you do? Comment allez-vous? [*ko-mã-tah-leh-voo*]

   How many?, How much? Combien (de)? [*kõ-byē (duh)*]

however, cependant [*spã-dã*]

human, humain [*ü-mē, ü-men*]

humble, humble [*ēbl*]

humid, humide [*ü-meed*]

humidity, humidité (f) [*ü-mee-dee-teh*]

humorous, humoristique [*ü-mo-rees-teek*]

hundred, cent [*sã*]

Hungarian, *hongrois [õ-grwah(z)]
Hungary, *Hongrie (f) [õ-gree]
hunger, faim (f) [fẽ]
hungry: to be hungry, avoir faim [ah-vwahr fẽ]
hunt v., chasser [shah-seh]
hunter, chasseur (m) [shah-suhr]
hunting, chasse (f) [shahs]
hurry v., se dépêcher [sdeh-pe-sheh]
  be in a hurry v., être pressé [etr pre-seh]
  Hurry up! Dépêchez-vous! [deh-pe-sheh-voo]
hurt v., faire mal [fer mahl]
husband, mari (m) [mah-ree]

I

I, je [zhuh]
ice, glace (f) [glahs]
ice cream, glace (f) [glahs]
idea, idée (f) [ee-deh]
ideal, idéal, -aux (m, pl) [ee-deh-ahl, ee-deh-oh]
identical, identique [ee-dã-teek]
identification card, carte (f) d'identité [kahrt dee-dã-tee-teh]
identify v., identifier [ee-dã-tee-fyeh]
identity, identité (f) [ee-dã-tee-teh]
idiot, idiot [ee-dyoh, e-dyot]
if, si [see]
  even if, même si [mem see]
ignition, allumage (m) [ah-lü-mahzh]
ignorant, ignorant [ee-nyo-rã(t)]
ill, malade [mah-lahd]
illegal, illégal, -aux (m, pl) [ee-leh-gahl, ee-leh-goh]
illness, maladie (f) [mah-lah-dee]
image, image (f) [ee-mahzh]
imagination, imagination (f) [ee-mah-zhee-nah-syõ]
imagine v., imaginer [ee-mah-zhee-neh]

imitate v., imiter [*ee-mee-teh*]
imitation, imitation (f) [*ee-mee-tah-syō*]
immediate, immédiat [*ee-meh-dyah(t)*]
immediately, immédiatement [*ee-meh-dyaht-mã*]
immense, immense [*ee-mãs*]
immigration, immigration (f) [*ee-mee-grah-syō*]
immoral, immoral, -aux (m, pl) [*ee-mo-rahl, ee-mo-roh*]
impartial, impartial, -aux (m, pl) [*ē-pahr-syahl, ē-pahr-syoh*]
impatient, impatient [*ē-pah-syã(t)*]
imperfect, imparfait [*ē-pahr-fe(t)*]
imperialism, impérialisme (m) [*ē-pehr-yah-leesm*]
impolite, impoli [*ē-po-lee*]
import v., importer [*ē-por-teh*]
importance, importance (f) [*ē-por-tãs*]
important, important [*ē-por-tã(t)*]
imported, importé [*ē-por-teh*]
impossible, impossible [*ē-po-seebl*]
impression, impression (f) [*ē-pre-syō*]
impressive, impressionnant [*ē-pre-syo-nã(t)*]
improbable, improbable [*ē-pro-bahbl*]
improve v., améliorer, s'améliorer [*ah-meh-lyo-reh, sah-
    meh-lyo-reh*]
improvement, amélioration (f) [*ah-meh-lyo-rah-syō*]
in, dans, en, à [*dã, ã, ah*]
    in back of, derrière [*der-yer*]
    in front of, devant [*duh-vã*]
    in spite of, malgré [*mahl-greh*]
    Mrs. Smith isn't in, Mme. Smith n'est pas ici [*mah-dahm
        smith ne pah-zee-see*]
inability, incapacité (f) [*ē-kah-pah-see-teh*]
inch, pouce (m) [*poos*]
incident, incident (m) [*ē-see-dã*]
inclination, tendance (f) [*tã-dãs*]
include v., inclure (irreg) [*ē-klür*]
included, inclus [*ē-klü(z)*]
income, revenu (m) [*ruhv-nü*]
income tax, impôt (m) sur le revenu [*ē-poh sür luh ruhv-nü*]
incomparable, incomparable [*ē-kō-pah-rahbl*]

incomplete, incomplet, -ète [ē-kõ-pleh, ē-kõ-plet]
inconvenience, dérangement (m) [deh-rãzh-mã]
incorrect, incorrect [ē-ko-rekt]
increase n., augmentation (f) [ohg-mã-tah-syõ]
increase v., augmenter [ohg-mã-teh]
incredible, incroyable [ē-krwah-yahbl]
indecent, indécent [ē-deh-sã(t)]
indeed, en effet [ã-neh-fe]
indefinite, indéfini [ē-deh-fee-nee]
independence, indépendance (f) [ē-deh-pã-dãs]
independent, indépendent [ē-deh-pã-dã(t)]
India, Inde (f) [ēd]
Indian, indien, -enne [ē-dyē, ē-dyen]
indicate v., indiquer [ē-dee-keh]
indifferent, indifférent [ē-dee-feh-rã(t)]
indigestion, indigestion (f) [ē-dee-zhes-tyõ]
indignant, indigné [ē-dee-nyeh]
indirect, indirect [ē-dee-rekt]
indiscreet, indiscret, -ète [ē-dees-kreh, ē-dees-kret]
individual, individuel, -elle; particulier, -ère [ē-dee-vee-dwel;
   pahr-tee-kü-lyeh, pahr-tee-kü-lyer]
indoors, dans la maison, dedans [dã lah me-zõ, duh-dã]
industrial, industriel, -elle [ē-düs-tree-yel]
industry, industrie (f) [ē-düs-tree]
inefficient, inefficace [ee-ne-fee-kahs]
inexpensive, bon marché [bõ mahr-sheh]
infant, bébé (m) [beh-beh]
infection, infection (f) [ē-fek-syõ]
inferior, inférieur [ē-fehr-yuhr]
infinitive, infinitif (m) [ē-fee-nee-teef]
influence n., influence (f) [ē-flü-ãs]
influence v., influencer [ē-flü-ã-seh]
inform v., informer, renseigner [ē-for-meh, rã-se-nyeh]
information, information (f), renseignement (m) [ē-for-mah-
   syõ, rã-se-nyuh-mã]
infrequent, infréquent [ē-freh-kã(t)]
inherit v., hériter [eh-ree-teh]
inheritance, héritage (m) [eh-ree-tahzh]

initial, initial, -aux (m, pl) [*ee-nee-syahl, ee-nee-syoh*]

injure v., blesser [*ble-seh*]

injury, blessure (f) [*ble-süür*]

injustice, injustice (f) [*ē-zhüs-tees*]

ink, encre (f) [*ãkr*]

innkeeper, hôtelier (m) [*oh-tuh-lyeh*]

innocent, innocent [*ee-no-sã(t)*]

innumerable, innombrable [*ee-nõ-brahbl*]

inquire v., demander [*dmã-deh*]

insane, fou, folle [*foo, fol*]

inside prep. & adv., dedans [*duh-dã*]

inside n., intérieur (m) [*ē-tehr-yuhr*]
   inside out, à l'envers [*ah lã-ver*]

insist v., insister [*ē-sees-teh*]

inspect v., inspecter [*ē-spek-teh*]

inspection, inspection (f) [*ē-spek-syõ*]

inspector, inspecteur, -trice [*ē-spek-tuhr, ē-spek-trees*]

inspiration, inspiration (f) [*ē-spee-rah-syõ*]

install v., installer [*ē-stah-leh*]

instance, exemple (m), cas (m) [*ehg-zãpl, kah*]
   for instance, par exemple [*pah-reg-zãpl*]

instead, à la place [*ah lah plahs*]
   instead of, au lieu de [*oh lyuh duh*]

instinct, instinct (m) [*ē-stē*]

institution, institution (f), établissement (m) [*ē-stee-tü-syõ, eh-tah-blees-mã*]

instruct v., instruire (irreg) [*ē-strweer*]

instruction, instruction (f) [*ē-strük-syõ*]

instructor, instructeur, -trice [*ē-strük-tuhr, ē-strük-trees*]

instrument, instrument (m) [*ē-strü-mã*]

insufficient, insuffisant [*ē-sü-fee-zã(t)*]

insult n., insulte (f) [*ē-sült*]

insult v., insulter [*ē-sül-teh*]

insurance, assurance (f) [*ah-sü-rãs*]

insurance company, compagnie (f) d'assurances [*kõ-pah-nee dah-sü-rãs*]

insurance policy, police (f) d'assurance [*po-lees dah-sü-rãs*]

insure v., assurer [*ah-sü-reh*]

intact, intact [ĕ-tah(kt)]
intellectual, intellectuel, -elle [ĕ-teh-lehk-twel]
intelligent, intelligent [ĕ-teh-lee-zhã(t)]
intend v., avoir l'intention de [ah-vwahr lĕ-tã-syŏ duh]
intense, intense [ĕ-tãs]
intention, intention (f) [ĕ-tã-syŏ]
interest [concern] n., intérêt (m) [ĕ-teh-re]
interest [financial] n., des intérêts [deh-zĕ-teh-re]
interest v., intéresser [ĕ-teh-re-seh]
  be interested in v., s'intéresser à [sĕ-teh-re-seh ah]
interesting, intéressant [ĕ-teh-re-sã(t)]
interfere v., intervenir (irreg) [ĕ-ter-vuh-neer]
interior, intérieur (m) [ĕ-tehr-yuhr]
intermission, entr'acte (m) [ã-trahkt]
internal, interne [ĕ-tern]
international, international, -aux (m, pl) [ĕ-ter-nah-syo-nahl, ĕ-ter-nah-syo-noh]
interpreter, interprète (m) [ĕ-ter-pret]
intersection, carrefour (m) [kahr-foor]
interval, intervalle (m) [ĕ-ter-vahl]
interview n., entrevue (f) [ã-truh-vü]
intimate adj., intime [ĕ-teem]
into, dans, en [dã, ã]
introduce v., présenter [preh-zã-teh]
introduction, introduction (f), présentation (f) [ĕ-troh-dük-syŏ, preh-zã-tah-syŏ]
intuition, intuition (f) [ĕ-twee-syŏ]
invalid, invalide (m, f) [ĕ-vah-leed]
invasion, invasion (f) [ĕ-vah-zyŏ]
invention, invention (f) [ĕ-vã-syŏ]
inventor, inventeur (m) [ĕ-vã-tuhr]
invest [install] v., investir [ĕ-ves-teer]
invest [money] v., placer [plah-seh]
invisible, invisible [ĕ-vee-zeebl]
invitation, invitation (f) [ĕ-vee-tah-syŏ]
invite v., inviter [ĕ-vee-teh]
invoice, facture (f) [fahk-tür]
involuntary, involontaire [ĕ-vo-lŏ-ter]

Ireland, Irlande (f) [*eer-lãd*]
Irish, irlandais [*eer-lã-de(z)*]
iron [metal] *n.*, fer (m) [*fer*]
iron [for ironing] *n.*, fer à repasser [*fer ahr-pah-seh*]
iron [clothes] *v.*, repasser [*ruh-pah-seh*]
irregular, irrégulier, -ière [*ee-re-gü-lyeh, ee-re-gü-lyer*]
irritate *v.*, irriter [*ee-ree-teh*]
irritation, irritation (f) [*ee-ree-tah-syõ*]
island, île (f) [*eel*]
it, il, elle; le, la [*eel, el; luh, lah*]
Italian, italien, -ienne [*ee-tal-yē, ee-tal-yen*]
Italy, Italie (f) [*ee-tah-lee*]
itch *n.*, démangeaison (f) [*deh-mã-zheh-zõ*]
itinerary, itinéraire (m) [*ee-tee-neh-rer*]
its, son, sa, ses [*sõ, sah, seh*]
itself, lui-même, elle-même [*lwee-mem, el-mem*]

J

jack, cric (m) [*kreek*]
jacket, veste (f) [*vest*]
jail, prison (f) [*pree-zõ*]
jam, confiture (f) [*kõ-fee-tür*]
January, janvier (m) [*zhã-vyeh*]
Japan, Japon (m) [*zhah-põ*]
Japanese, japonais [*zhah-po-ne(z)*]
jar [container], bocal (m), -aux (pl) [*bo-kahl, bo-koh*]
jaw, mâchoire (f) [*mah-shwahr*]
jazz *n.*, jazz (m) [*dzhahz*]
jealous, jaloux, -ouse [*zhah-loo, zhah-looz*]
jelly, gelée (f) [*zh(uh)-leh*]
jet plane, avion (m) à réaction [*ah-vyõ ah reh-ahk-syõ*]
Jew, Juif, Juive [*zhweef, zhweev*]
jewel, bijou (m), -oux (pl) [*bee-zhoo*]
jewelry, bijouterie (f) [*bee-zhoo-tree*]

Jewish, juif, juive [*zhweef, zhweev*]
job, travail (m), -aux (pl) [*trah-vahy, trah-voh*]
join v., se joindre à, adhérer à [*suh zhwēdr ah, ah-deh-reh ah*]
joke n., plaisanterie (f) [*ple-zã-tree*]
joke v., plaisanter [*ple-zã-teh*]
jockey, jockey (m) [*zho-ke*]
journal, journal (m), -aux (pl) [*zhoor-nahl, zhoor-noh*]
journalist, journaliste [*zhoor-nah-leest*]
journey, voyage (m) [*vwah-yahzh*]
joy, joie (f) [*zhwah*]
joyful, joyeux, -euse [*zhwah-yuh, zhwah-yuhz*]
judge n., juge (m) [*zhüzh*]
judge v., juger [*zhü-zheh*]
judgment, jugement (m) [*zhüzh-mã*]
juice, jus (m) [*zhü*]
July, juillet (m) [*zhwee-yeh*]
jump n., saut (m) [*soh*]
jump v., sauter [*soh-teh*]
June, juin (m) [*zhwē*]
jungle, jungle (f) [*zhēgl*]
jury, jury (m) [*zhü-ree*]
just adj. & adv., juste [*zhüst*]
   to have just done v., venir de faire [*vuh-neer duh fer*]
justice, justice (f) [*zhüs-tees*]
justify v., justifier [*zhüs-tee-fyeh*]

K

keep v., garder [*gahr-deh*]
   Keep out! Défense d'entrer! [*deh-fãs dã-treh*]
   Keep quiet! Restez tranquille! [*res-teh trã-keel*]
   keep doing, continuer à faire [*kõ-tee-nweh ah fer*]
   keep from doing, s'empêcher de faire [*sã-peh-sheh tfer*]
kettle, bouilloire (f) [*booy-wahr*]
key n., clef (f) [*kleh*]

kick *n.*, coup de pied (m) [*koot pyeh*]
kid [animal] *n.*, chevreau (m), -eaux (pl) [*shuh-vroh*]
kid [child] *n.*, gosse (m) [*gos*]
kidney [food], rognon (m) [*ro-nyõ*]
kidney [anat.], rein (m) [*rẽ*]
kill *v.*, tuer [*tü-eh*]
kilogram, kilo (m) [*kee-loh*]
kilometer, kilomètre (m) [*kee-lo-metr*]
kind *n.*, sorte (f) [*sort*]
kind *adj.*, bon, bonne [*bõ, bon*]
kindness, bonté (f) [*bõ-teh*]
king, roi (m) [*rwah*]
kingdom, royaume (m) [*rwah-yohm*]
kiss *n.*, baiser (m) [*beh-zeh*]
kiss *v.*, embrasser [*ã-brah-seh*]
kitchen, cuisine (f) [*kwee-zeen*]
kite, cerf-volant [*ser-vo-lã*]
knee, genou (m), -oux (pl) [*zhnoo*]
kneel *v.*, se mettre (irreg) à genoux [*sme-trah zhnoo*]
knife, couteau (m), -eaux (pl) [*koo-toh*]
knock *v.*, frapper [*frah-peh*]
knot *n.*, noeud (m) [*nuh*]
know [something] *v.*, savoir (irreg) [*sah-vwahr*]
know [someone] *v.*, connaître (irreg) [*ko-netr*]
knowledge, connaissance (f) [*ko-ne-sãs*]

L

label, étiquette (f) [*eh-tee-ket*]
labor *n.*, travail (m), -aux (pl) [*trah-vahy, trah-voh*]
laboratory, laboratoire (m) [*lah-bo-rah-twahr*]
lace, dentelle (f) [*dã-tel*]
lack *n.*, manque (m) [*mãk*]
lack [something] *v.*, manquer (de) [*mã-keh (duh)*]
   . . . **is lacking**, il manque . . . [*eel mãk*]

ladder, échelle (f) [*eh-shel*]
ladies' room, toilette pour dames (f) [*twah-let poor dahm*]
lady, dame (f) [*dahm*]
lake, lac (m) [*lahk*]
lamb, agneau (m), -eaux (pl) [*ah-nyoh*]
lame *adj.,* boîteux, -euse [*bwah-tuh, bwah-tuhz*]
lamp, lampe (f) [*lãp*]
land *n.,* terre (f) [*ter*]
land *v.,* atterir [*ah-te-reer*]
landing, atterissage (m) [*ah-te-ree-sahzh*]
landlord, landlady, propriétaire (m, f) [*pro-pree-yeh-ter*]
landscape, paysage (m) [*peh-ee-zahzh*]
language, language (m), langue (f) [*lã-gahzh, lãg*]
large, grand [*grã(d)*]
last *adj.,* dernier, -ière [*der-nyeh, der-nyer*]
  at last, enfin [*ã-fẽ*]
  last night, hier soir [*yer swahr*]
last *v.,* durer [*dü-reh*]
late, tard [*tahr*]
  It's late, Il est tard [*ee-le tar*]
  I'm late, Je suis en retard [*zhuh swee-zãr-tahr*]
lately, dernièrement [*der-nyer-mã*]
later, latest, tardif, -ive [*tahr-deef, tahr-deev*]
latest, dernier, -ière [*der-nyeh, der-nyer*]
latter, dernier, -ière; celui-ci, celle-ci [*der-nyeh, der-nyer; suh-lwee-see, sel-see*]
laugh, laughter *n.,* rire (m) [*reer*]
laugh *v.,* rire (irreg) [*reer*]
laundry, blanchisserie (f) [*blã-shees-ree*]
law, loi (f) [*lwah*]
law [body of knowledge], droit (m) [*drwah*]
lawful, légal, -aux (m, pl) [*leh-gahl, leh-goh*]
lawn, pelouse (f) [*plooz*]
lawyer, avocat (m) [*ah-vo-kah*]
lay *v.,* poser [*poh-zeh*]
lazy, paresseux, -euse [*pah-re-suh, pah-re-suhz*]
lead [metal] *n.,* plomb (m) [*plõ*]
lead *v.,* conduire (irreg) [*kõ-dweer*]

leader, chef (m) [*shef*]
leaf, feuille (f) [*fuhy*]
leak *n.*, fuite (f) [*fweet*]
lean *v.*, pencher [*pã-sheh*]
  lean on, s'appuyer sur [*sah-pwee-yeh sür*]
learn *v.*, apprendre [*ah-prãdr*]
lease *n.*, bail (m) [*bahy*]
least, moindre, moins [*mwẽdr, mwẽ*]
  at least, au moins [*oh mwẽ*]
leather, cuir (m) [*kweer*]
leave [allow] *v.*, laisser [*le-seh*]
leave [depart] *v.*, sortir de (irreg; *Aux:* ÊTRE), quitter [*sorteer duh, kee-teh*]
lecture *n.*, conférence (f) [*kõ-feh-rãs*]
lecturer, conférencier (m) [*kõ-feh-rã-syeh*]
left [direction], gauche [*gohsh*]
  to the left, à gauche [*ah gohsh*]
leg, jambe (f) [*zhãb*]
legal, légal, -aux (m, pl) [*leh-gahl, leh-goh*]
legible, lisible [*lee-zeebl*]
legitimate, légitime [*leh-zhee-teem*]
leisure, loisir (m) [*lawh-zeer*]
lemon, citron (m) [*see-trõ*]
lemonade, citron pressé (m) [*see-trõ pre-seh*]
lend, prêter [*pre-teh*]
length, longueur (f) [*lõ-guhr*]
lens [of camera], objectif (m) [*ob-zhek-teef*]
lens [of glasses], verre (m) [*ver*]
less, moins [*mwẽ*]
  more or less, plus ou moins [*plü-zoo mwẽ*]
lesson, leçon (f) [*l(uh)-sõ*]
let [permit] *v.*, permettre (irreg), laisser [*per-metr, le-seh*]
letter, lettre (f) [*letr*]
lettuce, laitue (f) [*le-tü*]
level *n.*, niveau (m), -eaux (pl) [*nee-voh*]
level *adj.*, égal, -aux (m, pl) [*eh-gahl, eh-goh*]
liability, responsabilité (f) [*res-põ-sah-bee-lee-teh*]
liar, menteur (m), menteuse (f) [*mã-tuhr, mã-tuhz*]

liberal, libéral, -aux (m, pl) [*lee-beh-rahl, lee-beh-roh*]
liberty, liberté (f) [*lee-ber-teh*]
library, bibliothèque (f) [*bee-blee-yo-tek*]
license *n.,* permis (m) [*per-mee*]
license plate, plaque d'immatriculation [*plahk dee-mah-tree-kü-lah-syō*]
lid, couvercle (m) [*koo-verkl*]
lie [untruth] *n.,* mensonge (m) [*mã-sōzh*]
lie [tell an untruth] *v.,* mentir (irreg) [*mã-teer*]
lie [rest] *v.,* s'allonger, être couché [*sah-lõ-zheh, etr koo-sheh*]
  lie down, se coucher [*skoo-sheh*]
lieutenant, lieutenant (m) [*lyuht-nã*]
life, vie (f) [*vee*]
lifeboat, canot (m) de sauvetage [*kah-noh tsohv-tahzh*]
life insurance, assurance-vie (f) [*ah-sü-rãs-vee*]
life jacket, gilet de sauvetage (m) [*zhee-leh tsohv-tahzh*]
lift *v.,* soulever [*sool-veh*]
light *n.,* lumière (f) [*lü-myer*]
light *v.,* allumer [*ah-lü-meh*]
light [color] *adj.,* clair [*kler*]
light [weight] *adj.,* léger, -ère [*leh-zheh, leh-zher*]
lighter [cigaret] *n.,* briquet (m) [*bree-keh*]
lighthouse, phare (m) [*fahr*]
lightning, éclairs (m, pl), foudre (f) [*eh-kler, foodr*]
lights [car], phares (m, pl) [*fahr*]
likeable, sympathique [*sẽ-pah-teek*]
like *prep. & adv.,* comme [*kom*]
like *v.,* aimer [*e-meh*]
  Would you like . . . Voudriez-vous . . . [*voo-dree-yeh-voo*]
  I'd like to, Je voudrais bien [*zhvoo-dre byẽ*]
likely, probable [*pro-bahbl*]
likewise, également [*eh-gahl-mã*]
limb [anat.], membre (m) [*mãbr*]
limb [tree], grosse branche [*grohs brãsh*]
limit *n.,* limite (f) [*lee-meet*]
limit *v.,* limiter [*lee-mee-teh*]
line, ligne (f) [*leeñ*]

Hold the line, Ne quittez pas [*nuh kee-teh pah*]
  stand in line *v.*, faire la queue [*fer lah kuh*]
linen [clothing], linge (m) [*lēzh*]
linen [fabric], toile (f) [*twahl*]
lingerie, lingerie (f) pour femmes [*lēzh-ree poor fahm*]
lining, doublure (f) [*doo-blür*]
lip, lèvre (f) [*levr*]
lipstick, rouge (m) à lèvres [*roo-zhah levr*]
liquid, liquide [*lee-keed*]
liquor, boisson (f) alcoolique [*bwah-sõ ahl-ko-leek*]
list *n.*, liste (f) [*leest*]
listen (to) *v.*, écouter [*eh-koo-teh*]
literally, littéralement, [*lee-teh-rahl-mã*]
literature, littérature (f) [*lee-teh-rah-tür*]
little *adj.*, petit [*ptee(t)*]
little *adv.*, peu [*puh*]
  a little (bit), un peu [*ẽ puh*]
  little by little, petit à petit [*ptee-tah ptee*]
  very little, très peu [*tre puh*]
live [be alive] *v.*, vivre (irreg) [*veevr*]
live [reside] *v.*, habiter [*ah-bee-teh*]
lively, vivant [*vee-vã(t)*]
liver, foie (m) [*fwah*]
living room, salon (m) [*sah-lõ*]
load (with) *v.*, charger (de) [*shahr-zheh (duh)*]
loaf [of bread], pain (m) [*pẽ*]
loan [to lender] *n.*, prêt (m) [*pre*]
loan [to borrow] *n.*, emprunt (m) [*ã-prẽ*]
lobby [hotel], foyer (m) [*fwah-yeh*]
lobster, *homard (m) [*o-mahr*]
local, local, -aux (m, pl) [*lo-kahl, lo-koh*]
local train, omnibus (m) [*om-nee-büs*]
locate *v.*, trouver [*troo-veh*]
  be located *v.*, se trouver [*stroo-veh*]
location, emplacement (m) [*ã-plas-mã*]
lock *n.*, serrure (f) [*se-rür*]
lock *v.*, fermer à clef [*fer-meh ah kleh*]
locomotive, locomotive (f) [*loh-koh-mo-teev*]

lodging, logement (m) [*lozh-mã*]
logical, logique [*lo-zheek*]
long [distance], long, longue [*lõ, lõg*]
long [time], longtemps [*lõ-tã*]
  How long? Combien de temps? [*kõ-byẽ duh tã*]
  long ago, il y a longtemps [*eel yah lõ-tã*]
long distance [telephone], interurbain [*ẽ-ter-ür-bẽ*]
longer, plus long, plus longtemps [*plü lõ, plü lõ-tã*]
  no longer, ne . . . plus [*nuh . . . plü*]
look at v., regarder [*r(uh)-gahr-deh*]
look for v., chercher [*sher-sheh*]
  Look out! Attention! [*a-tã-syõ*]
look like v., ressembler à [*r(uh)-sã-bleh ah*]
loosen v., desserrer [*deh-seh-reh*]
lord, seigneur (m) [*seh-nyuhr*]
lose v., perdre [*perdr*]
loss, perte (f) [*pert*]
lost, perdu [*per-dü*]
lost and found, bureau des objets trouvés (m) [*bü-roh deh-zob-zheh troo-veh*]
lot [real estate], terrain (m) [*teh-rẽ*]
lot [quantity], lot (m) [*loh*]
  a lot (of), beaucoup (de) [*boh-koo (duh)*]
loud, fort [*for(t)*]
loudspeaker, *haut-parleur (m) [*oh-pahr-luhr*]
love n., amour (m) [*ah-moor*]
love v., aimer [*e-meh*]
  be in love (with) v., être amoureux, -euse (de) [*et-rah-moo-ruh, ah-moo-ruhz (duh)*]
lovely, beau (bel), belle; beaux, belles [*boh, bel*]
lover [sweetheart], amoureux, -euse [*ah-moo-ruh, ah-moo-ruhz*]
lover [paramour], amant, -te [*ah-mã, ah-mãt*]
low adj., bas, basse [*bah, bahs*]
loyal, loyal, -aux (m, pl) [*lwah-yahl, lwah-yoh*]
lubrication [auto], graissage (m) [*gre-sahzh*]
luck, chance (f) [*shãs*]
  good luck, bonne chance [*bon shãs*]

lucky: to be lucky, avoir de la chance [*ah-vwahr duh lah shãs*]

luggage, bagages (m, pl) [*bah-gahzh*]

lunch *n.*, déjeuner (m) [*deh-zhuh-neh*]
  have lunch *v.*, déjeuner [*deh-zhuh-neh*]

lung, poumon (m) [*poo-mõ*]

luxurious, luxueux, -euse [*lük-swuh, lük-swuhz*]

luxury, luxe (m) [*lüks*]

M

machine, machine (f) [*mah-sheen*]

mad [angry], furieux, -euse [*für-yuh, für-yuhz*]

madam, madame (f) [*mah-dahm*]

made, fait [*fe(t)*]

magazine, revue (f) [*r(uh)-vü*]

magic *adj.*, magique [*mah-zheek*]

magnificent, magnifique [*mah-nyee-feek*]

mahogany, acajou (m) [*ah-kah-zhoo*]

maid, bonne (f) [*bon*]

mail *n.*, courrier (m) [*koor-yeh*]

mail *v.*, poster [*po-steh*]

mailbox, boîte (f) aux lettres [*bwaht oh letr*]

mailman, facteur (m) [*fahk-tuhr*]

main, principal, -aux (m, pl) [*prẽ-see-pahl, prẽ-see-poh*]

mainly, surtout [*sür-too*]

maintain *v.*, maintenir (irreg) [*mẽt-neer*]

majority, majorité (f), la plupart (de) [*mah-zho-ree-teh, lah plü-pahr (duh)*]

make *v.*, faire (irreg) [*fer*]

male, mâle (m) [*mahl*]

man, homme (m) [*om*]
  young man, jeune homme (m), jeunes gens (pl) [*zhuh-nom, zhuhn-zhã*]

manage *v.*, diriger, arranger [*dee-ree-zheh, ah-rã-zheh*]

manager, directeur (m), gérant (m) [*dee-rek-tuhr, zheh-rã*]
manicure, manucure (f) [*mah-nü-kür*]
manner, manière (f) [*mah-nyer*]
manufacture v., fabriquer [*fah-bree-keh*]
manufacturer, fabriquant (m) [*fah-bree-kã*]
many, beaucoup (de) [*boh-koo (duh)*]
   How many? Combien (de)? [*kõ-byē (duh)*]
   too many, trop (de) [*troh (duh)*]
map [of city], plan (m) [*plã*]
map [large scale], carte (f) [*kahrt*]
   road map, carte routière [*kahrt roo-tyer*]
marble, marbre (m) [*mahrbr*]
March, mars (m) [*mahrs*]
march n., marche (f) [*mahrsh*]
mark v., marquer [*mahr-keh*]
market, marché (m) [*mahr-sheh*]
marriage, mariage (m) [*mahr-yahzh*]
married, marié [*mah-ryeh*]
marry [someone] v., épouser [*eh-poo-zeh*]
   get married, se marier [*smahr-yeh*]
marvelous, merveilleux, -euse [*mer-ve-yuh, mer-ve-yuhz*]
mass [quantity], masse (f) [*mahs*]
Mass [eccles.], messe (f) [*mes*]
massage n., massage (m) [*mah-sahzh*]
mass production, fabrication (f) en série [*fah-bree-kah-syõ ã seh-ree*]
master n., maître (m) [*metr*]
masterpiece, chef-d'oeuvre (m) [*sheh-duhvr*]
match [for igniting], allumette (f) [*ah-lü-met*]
material, matériel (m) [*mah-ter-yel*]
mathematics, mathématiques (f, pl) [*mah-teh-mah-teek*]
matter v., importer [*ē-por-teh*]
   What's the matter? Qu'est-ce qu'il y a? [*kes keel-yah*]
   It doesn't matter, Ça ne fait rien [*sahn fe ryē*]
mattress, matelas (m) [*maht-lah*]
mature, mûr [*mür*]
May, mai (m) [*meh*]
may v., pouvoir (irreg) [*poo-vwahr*]

It may be, Il se peut . . . [*eel suh puh*]

May I go? Puis-je partir? [*pweezh pahr-teer*]

maybe, peut-être [*puh-tetr*]

mayor, maire (m) [*mer*]

me, me, moi [*muh, mwah*]

meal, repas (m) [*r(uh)-pah*]

mean v., vouloir (irreg) dire [*vool-wahr deer*]

    What do you mean? Qu'est-ce que vous voulez dire?
    [*kes kuh voo voo-leh deer*]

    What does that mean? Qu'est-ce que cela veut dire?
    [*kes kuh slah vuh deer*]

means, moyen(s) (m, pl) [*mwah-yẽ*]

    by means of, au moyen de [*oh mwah-yẽ d(uh)*]

    by all means, certainement [*ser-ten-mã*]

    by no means, en aucune façon [*ã-noh-kün fah-sõ*]

meanwhile, entretemps, [*ã-truh-tã*]

measles, rougeole (f) [*roo-zhol*]

    German measles, rubéole (f) [*rü-beh-ol*]

measure v., mesurer [*muh-zü-reh*]

meat, viande (f) [*vyãd*]

mechanic, mécanicien (m) [*meh-kah-nee-syẽ*]

mechanical, mécanique [*meh-kah-neek*]

medal, médaille (f) [*meh-dahy*]

medical, médical, -aux (m, pl) [*meh-dee-kahl, meh-dee-koh*]

medicine, médecine (f) [*med-seen*]

Mediterranean, Méditerranée (f) [*meh-dee-te-rah-neh*]

medium adj., moyen, -enne [*mwah-yẽ, mwah-yen*]

meet [for first time] v., faire la connaissance de [*fer lah ko-ne-sãs d(uh)*]

    Glad to meet you, Enchanté [*ã-shã-teh*]

meet [encounter] v., rencontrer [*rã-kõ-treh*]

meeting [group] n., réunion (f) [*re-ü-nyõ*]

meeting [encounter] n., rencontre (f) [*rã-kõtr*]

melon, melon (m) [*m(uh)-lõ*]

melt v., fondre, faire fondre [*fõdr, fer fõdr*]

member, membre (m) [*mãbr*]

memory, mémoire (f) [*meh-mwahr*]

mend v., raccomoder [*rah-ko-mo-deh*]

mental, mental, -aux (m, pl) [*mã-tahl, mã-toh*]
mention v., mentionner [*mã-syo-neh*]
merchandise, marchandise (f) [*mahr-shã-deez*]
merchant, commerçant (m) [*ko-mer-sã*]
merely, simplement [*sẽ-pluh-mã*]
merit n., mérite (m) [*meh-reet*]
merit v., mériter [*meh-ree-teh*]
merry, joyeux, -euse [*zhwah-yuh, zhwah-yuhz*]
message, message (m) [*meh-sahzh*]
messenger, messager (m) [*meh-sah-zheh*]
metal, métal (m), -aux (pl) [*meh-tahl, meh-toh*]
meter [measure] n., mètre (m) [*metr*]
meter [counter] n., compteur (m) [*kõ-tuhr*]
method, méthode (f) [*meh-tod*]
metric system, système métrique (m) [*sees-tem meh-treek*]
middle, milieu (m), -eux (pl) [*meel-yuh*]
midnight, minuit (m) [*mee-nwee*]
midway, à mi-chemin [*ah mee-shmẽ*]
mild, doux, douce [*doo, doos*]
mile, mille [*meel*]
military, militaire [*mee-lee-ter*]
milk, lait (m) [*le*]
milliner, modiste (f) [*mo-deest*]
million, million (m) [*mee-lyõ*]
mind n., esprit (m) [*es-pree*]
mind [attend to] v., faire attention à, s'occuper de [*fer ah-tã-syõ ah, so-kü-peh duh*]
   Mind your own business! Occupez-vous de ce qui vous regarde! [*o-kü-peh-voo duh skee voor-gahrd*]
   I don't mind, Cela m'est égal [*sah me-teh-gahl*]
mine pron., le mien, la mienne; les miens, les miennes [*luh myẽ, lah myen; leh myẽ, leh myen*]
mine n., mine (f) [*meen*]
miner, mineur (m) [*mee-nuhr*]
mineral, minéral, -aux (m, pl) [*mee-neh-rahl, mee-neh-roh*]
minister [government] n., ministre (m) [*mee-neestr*]
minister [religious] n., pasteur (m) [*pahs-tuhr*]
minor [age], mineur, -eure [*mee-nuhr*]

minority, minorité (f) [*mee-no-ree-teh*]
minus, moins [*mwē*]
minute *n.*, minute (f) [*mee-nüt*]
mirror *n.*, miroir (m) [*meer-wahr*]
miserable, misérable [*mee-zeh-rahbl*]
misfortune, malheur (m) [*mah-luhr*]
Miss, Mademoiselle [*mahd-mwah-zel*]
miss *v.*, manquer [*mã-keh*]
  I miss them, Ils me manquent [*eel muh māk*]
  I missed the train, J'ai manqué le train [*zheh mã-kehl trē*]
mistake *n.*, erreur (f), faute (f) [*e-ruhr, foht*]
  make a mistake *v.*, se tromper [*strō-peh*]
mistaken: to be mistaken, se tromper [*strō-peh*]
mistrust *v.*, se méfier (de) [*smeh-fyeh (duh)*]
misunderstanding, malentendu (m) [*mah-lã-tã-dü*]
mix *v.*, mélanger [*meh-lã-zheh*]
mixture, mélange (m) [*meh-lãzh*]
model *n.*, modèle (m) [*mo-del*]
modern, moderne [*mo-dern*]
modest, modeste [*mo-dest*]
moisture, humidité (f) [*ü-mee-dee-teh*]
moment, moment (m) [*mo-mã*]
monarchy, monarchie (f) [*mo-nahr-shee*]
monastery, monastère (m) [*mo-nahs-ter*]
Monday, lundi (m) [*lē-dee*]
money, argent (m) [*ahr-zhã*]
monotonous, monotone [*mo-no-ton*]
month, mois (m) [*mwah*]
monthly, mensuel, -elle [*mã-swel*]
monument, monument (m) [*mo-nü-mã*]
mood, humeur (f) [*ü-muhr*]
  in a bad mood, de mauvaise humeur [*duh mo-ve-zü-muhr*]
  in a good mood, de bonne humeur [*duh bo-nü-muhr*]
moon, lune (f) [*lün*]
moonlight, clair (m) de lune [*kler duh lün*]
mop, balai (m) à laver par terre [*bah-le ah lah-veh pahr ter*]
moral *adj.*, moral, -aux (m, pl) [*mo-rahl, mo-roh*]
moral *n.*, morale (f) [*mo-rahl*]

morale *n.*, moral (m) [*mo-rahl*]
more, plus [*plü(s)*]
  more and more, de plus en plus [*duh plü-zã plü*]
  more or less, plus ou moins [*plü-zoo mwẽ*]
  no more, ne . . . plus [*nuh . . . plü*]
  once more, encore une fois [*ã-ko-rün fwah*]
  the more . . . the more, plus . . . plus [*plü(z) . . plu(z)*]
moreover, de plus [*duh plü(s)*]
morning, matin (m) [*mah-tē*]
  good morning, bonjour [*bõ-zhoor*]
mortgage, hypothèque (f) [*ee-po-tek*]
mosquito, moustique (m) [*moos-teek*]
most, le (la, les) plus [*luh (lah, leh) plü(z)*]
  at the most, au plus [*oh plü(s)*]
  most of, la plupart des [*lah plü-pahr deh*]
  most of the time, la plupart du temps [*lah plü-pahr dü tã*]
mother, mère (f) [*mer*]
mother-in-law, belle-mère (f) [*bel-mer*]
motion, mouvement (m) [*moov-mã*]
motive, motif (m) [*mo-teef*]
motor, moteur (m) [*moh-tuhr*]
motorcycle, motocyclette (f) [*moh-toh-see-klet*]
mountain, montagne (f) [*mõ-tañ*]
mourning *n.*, deuil (m) [*duhy*]
mouth, bouche (f) [*boosh*]
move [change position of] *v.*, bouger [*boo-zheh*]
move [change residence] *v.*, déménager [*deh-meh-nah-zheh*]
movie, film (m) [*feelm*]
  go to the movies *v.*, aller (irreg) au cinéma [*ah-leh oh see-neh-mah*]
movie theater, salle (f) de cinéma (m) [*sahl duh see-neh-mah*]
moving [emotional], émouvant [*eh-moo-vã(t)*]
Mr., Monsieur [*muh-syuh*]
Mrs., Madame [*mah-dahm*]
much, beaucoup (de) [*boh-koo (duh)*]
  as much as, autant que [*oh-tã k(uh)*]
  How much? Combien (de)? [*kõ-byē (duh)*]
  too much, trop (de) [*troh (duh)*]

mud, boue (f) [*boo*]

muffler [scarf], cache-col (m) [*kash-kol*]

muffler [auto], pot (m) d'échappement [*poh deh-shahp-mā*]

murder *n.*, meurtre (m) [*muhrtr*]

murderer, meurtrier (m) [*muhr-tree-yeh*]

muscle, muscle (m) [*müskl*]

museum, musée (m) [*mü-zeh*]

mushroom, champignon (m) [*shā-pee-nyō*]

music, musique (f) [*mü-zeek*]

musical, musical, -aux (m, pl) [*mü-zee-kahl, mü-zee-koh*]

musician, musicien, -enne [*mü-zee-syē, mü-see-syen*]

must *v.*, devoir (irreg) [*duh-vwahr*]

   I must go, Je dois partir [*zhdwah pahr-teer*]

   I must have lost my book, J'ai dû perdre mon livre
    [*zheh dü perdr mō leevr*]

mustache, moustache (f) [*moos-tash*]

mustard, moutarde (f) [*moo-tahrd*]

mutual, mutuel, -elle [*mü-twel*]

   It's mutual, C'est réciproque [*se reh-see-prok*]

my, mon, ma, mes [*mō, mah, meh*]

myself, moi-même [*mwah-mem*]

mysterious, mystérieux, -euse [*mees-ter-yuh, mees-ter-yuhz*]

mystery, mystère (m) [*mee-ster*]

N

nail [fingernail] *n.*, ongle (m) [*ōgl*]

nail [carpentry] *n.*, clou (m) [*kloo*]

nail *v.*, clouer [*kloo-eh*]

naïve, naïf, naïve [*nah-eef, nah-eev*]

naked, nu [*nü*]

name *n.*, nom (m) [*nō*]

   first name, prénom (m) [*preh-nō*]

   last name, nom de famille [*nōd fah-meey*]

name *v.*, nommer [*no-meh*]

namely, à savoir [*ah sah-vwahr*]
nap, sieste (f) [*syest*]
napkin, serviette (f) [*ser-vyet*]
  sanitary napkin, serviette hygiénique [*ser-vyet ee-zhyeh-neek*]
narrate *v.*, raconter [*rah-kõ-teh*]
narrow *adj.*, étroit [*eh-trwah(t)*]
nasty, méchant, vilain [*meh-shã(t); vee-lẽ, vee-len*]
nation, nation (f) [*nah-syõ*]
national, national, -aux (m, pl) [*nah-syo-nahl, nah-syo-noh*]
native *n.*, indigène (m, f) [*ẽ-dee-zhen*]
natural, naturel, -elle [*nah-tü-rel*]
naturally, naturellement [*nah-tü-rel-mã*]
nature, nature (f) [*nah-tür*]
naughty, vilain, méchant [*vee-lẽ, vee-len; meh-shã(t)*]
naval, naval, navals (m, pl) [*nah-vahl*]
navy, marine (f) [*mah-reen*]
near, près (de) [*pre (duh)*]
nearly, presque [*presk*]
neat, bien rangé, soigné, ordonné [*byẽ rã-zheh, swah-nyeh, or-do-neh*]
necessary, nécessaire [*neh-seh-ser*]
neck, cou (m) [*koo*]
necklace, collier (m) [*kol-yeh*]
necktie, cravate (f) [*krah-vaht*]
need *n.*, besoin (m) [*buh-zwẽ*]
need *v.*, avoir besoin de [*ah-vwahr buh-zwẽ d(uh)*]
needle, aiguille (f) [*e-gweey*]
negative *adj.*, négatif, -ive [*neh-gah-teef, neh-gah-teev*]
negative *n.*, négatif (m) [*neh-gah-teef*]
neglect *v.*, négliger [*neh-glee-zheh*]
Negro, noir, noire [*nwahr*]
neighbor, voisin, -ine [*vwah-zẽ, vwah-zeen*]
neighborhood, quartier (m) [*kahr-tyeh*]
neither *conj.*, non plus [*nõ plü*]
neither one *pron.*, aucun . . . ne [*oh-kẽ, oh-kün . . . nuh*]
neither . . . nor, ni . . . ni [*nee . . . nee*]
nephew, neveu (m) [*nuh-vuh*]

nerve *n.*, nerf (m) [*ner*]

nervous, nerveux, -euse [*ner-vuh, ner-vuhz*]

net, filet (m) [*fee-leh*]

network, réseau (m), -eaux (pl) [*reh-zoh*]

network [radio, TV] *n.*, chaîne (f) [*shen*]

neutral, neutre [*nuhtr*]

  in neutral [gear], au point mort [*oh pwē mor*]

never, jamais [*zhah-me*]

  Never mind, Ça ne fait rien [*sahn fe ryē*]

nevertheless, néanmoins [*neh-ã-mwē*]

new [not used] *adj.*, neuf, neuve [*nuhf, nuhv*]

new [newly learned] *adj.*, nouveau, -vel (m, sing), -velle
    (f, sing); nouveaux (m, pl) [*noo-voh, noo-vel*]

news, nouvelles (f, pl) [*noo-vel*]

newspaper, journal (m), -aux (pl) [*zhoor-nahl, zhoor-noh*]

newsstand, kiosque (m) [*kyosk*]

next [in order] *adj.*, suivant [*swee-vã(t)*]

next [position or time] *adj.*, prochain [*pro-shē, pro-shen*]

  next month, le mois prochain [*luh mwah pro-shē*]

  next time, la prochaine fois [*lah pro-shen fwah*]

  next to, à côté de [*ah koh-teh d(uh)*]

nice, gentil, -ille [*zhã-tee, zhã-teey*]

nickname, surnom (m) [*sür-nõ*]

niece, nièce (f) [*nyes*]

night, nuit (f) [*nwee*]

  good night, bonne nuit [*bon nwee*]

nightclub, boîte (f) de nuit [*bwaht duh nwee*]

nightgown, chemise (f) de nuit [*shmeez duh nwee*]

nightmare, cauchemar (m) [*kohsh-mahr*]

nine, neuf [*nuhf, nuhv*]

nineteen, dix-neuf [*deez-nuhf*]

ninety, quatre-vingt-dix [*kah-truh-vē-dees*]

ninth, neuvième [*nuh-vyem*]

nipple, tétine (f) [*teh-teen*]

no *adv.*, non [*nõ*]

no *adj.*, aucun, aucune [*oh-kē, oh-kün*]

no longer [no more], ne ... plus [*nuh ... plü*]

noble, noble [*nobl*]

nobody, personne [*per-son*]
noise, bruit (m) [*brwee*]
noisy, bruyant [*brwee-yã(t)*]
none, aucun, aucune [*ok-kẽ, oh-kün*]
noodles, nouilles (f, pl) [*nooy*]
noon, midi (m) [*mee-dee*]
nor, ni, non plus [*nee, nõ plu*]
normal, normal, -aux (m, pl) [*nor-mahl, nor-moh*]
north, nord (m) [*nor*]
northeast, nord-est (m) [*nor-est*]
northern, du nord [*dü nor*]
northwest, nord-ouest (m) [*nor-west*]
Norway, Norvège (f) [*nor-vezh*]
Norwegian, norvégien, -ienne [*nor-veh-zhyẽ, nor-veh-zhyen*]
nose, nez (m) [*neh*]
not, ne . . . pas [*nuh . . . pah*]
  not at all, pas du tout [*pah dü too*]
  not even, pas même [*pah mem*]
note *n.,* note (f) [*not*]
note *v.,* noter [*no-teh*]
notebook, carnet (m), cahier (m) [*kahr-ne, kah-yeh*]
nothing, rien [*ryẽ*]
  nothing new, rien de nouveau [*ryẽd noo-voh*]
notice *n.,* avis (m) [*ah-vee*]
notice *v.,* remarquer [*ruh-mahr-keh*]
notify *v.,* avertir [*ah-ver-teer*]
notion, notion (f) [*noh-syõ*]
noun, nom (m) [*nõ*]
novel, roman (m) [*roh-mã*]
novelist, romancier (m) [*ro-mã-syeh*]
novelty, nouveauté (f) [*noo-voh-teh*]
November, novembre (m) [*no-vãbr*]
now, maintenant [*mẽt-nã*]
  from now on, à partir de maintenant [*ah pahr-teer duh mẽt-nã*]
  now and then, de temps en temps [*duh tã-zã tã*]
  until now, jusqu'à maintenant [*zhüs-kah mẽt-nã*]
  by now, à l'heure qu'il est [*ah luhr kee-le*]

three days from now, d'ici trois jours [*dee-see trwah zhoor*]
nowhere, nulle part [*nül pahr*]
number, nombre [*nõbr*]
number [of house], numéro (m) [*nü-meh-roh*]
numerous, nombreux, -euse [*nõ-bruh, nõ-bruhz*]
nun, religieuse (f) [*ruh-lee-zhyuhz*]
nurse *n.*, infirmière (f) [*ẽ-feer-myer*]
nursery, chambre (f) des enfants [*shãbr deh-zã-fã*]
nursery school, école maternelle (f) [*eh-kol mah-ter-nel*]
nut [food], noix (f) [*nwah*]
nut [for a bolt], écrou (m) [*eh-kroo*]
nutmeg, noix (f) de muscade [*nwahd müs-kahd*]
nylon, nylon (m) [*nee-lõ*]

O

---

oak, chêne (m) [*shen*]
oar, rame (f) [*rahm*]
oath, serment (m) [*ser-mã*]
take an oath *v.*, prêter serment [*pre-teh ser-mã*]
obedient, obéissant [*o-beh-ee-sã(t)*]
obey *v.*, obéir à [*o-beh-eer ah*]
object *n.*, objet (m) [*ob-zhe*]
object to *v.*, faire objection à [*fer ob-zhek-syõ ah*]
objection, objection (f) [*ob-zhek-syõ*]
obligation, obligation (f) [*ob-lee-gah-syõ*]
oblige [compel] *v.*, obliger [*ob-lee-zheh*]
obliged, obligé [*ob-lee-zheh*]
Much obliged, Merci beaucoup [*mer-see boh-koo*]
obscene, obscène [*op-sen*]
observation, observation (f) [*op-ser-va-syõ*]
observe *v.*, observer [*op-ser-veh*]
obstacle, obstacle (m) [*op-stahkl*]
obtain *v.*, obtenir (irreg) [*op-tuh-neer*]
obvious, évident [*eh-vee-dã(t)*]

occasion, occasion (f) [*o-kah-zyō*]
occasionally, de temps en temps [*duh tã-zã tã*]
occupied, occupé [*o-kü-peh*]
occupy v., occuper [*o-kü-peh*]
occur v., avoir lieu [*ah-vwahr lyuh*]
occurrence, événement (m) [*eh-ven-mã*]
ocean, océan (m) [*oh-seh-ã*]
o'clock, heure(s) (f) [*uhr*]
   at three o'clock, à trois heures [*ah trwah-zuhr*]
   It's three o'clock, Il est trois heures [*ee-le trwah-zuhr*]
October, octobre (m) [*ok-tobr*]
odd [unusual], bizarre [*bee-zahr*]
odd [not even], impair [*ē-per*]
odor, odeur (f) [*oh-duhr*]
of, de, d' [*d(uh)*]
   of course, bien entendu [*byē-nã-tã-dü*]
off, enlevé, écarté [*ãl-veh, eh-kahr-teh*]
   take off [clothing] v., enlever [*ãl-veh*]
   take off [plane] v., décoller [*deh-ko-leh*]
   turn off [light] v., éteindre (irreg) [*eh-tēdr*]
   turn off [water] v., fermer [*fer-meh*]
offend v., offenser [*o-fã-seh*]
offer n., offre (f) [*ofr*]
offer v., offrir (irreg) [*o-freer*]
office, bureau (m), -eaux (pl) [*bü-roh*]
officer [army], officier (m) [*o-fee-syeh*]
officer [organization], responsable (m, f) [*res-põ-sahbl*]
official, officiel, -elle [*o-fee-syel*]
often, souvent [*soo-vã*]
oil [edible] n., huile (f) [*weel*]
oil [petroleum] n., pétrole (m) [*peh-trol*]
oil v., huiler, graisser [*wee-leh, gre-seh*]
oil change, vidange (m) [*vee-dãzh*]
oilcloth, toile (f) cirée [*twahl see-reh*]
oil painting, peinture (f) à l'huile [*pē-tür ah lweel*]
old, vieux (vieil), vieille [*vyuh, vyey*]
   How old are you? Quel âge avez-vous? [*kel ahzh ah-veh-voo*]

older, plus âgé, aîné [*plü-zah-zheh, e-neh*]
old-fashioned, démodé [*deh-mo-deh*]
olive, olive (f) [*o-leev*]
olive oil, huile d'olive [*weel do-leev*]
omelet, omelette (f) [*om-let*]
omission, omission (f) [*o-mee-syõ*]
omit v., omettre (irreg) [*o-metr*]
on, sur, à, en [*sür, ah, ã*]
    turn on [lights] v., allumer [*ah-lü-meh*]
    turn on [water] v., ouvrir (irreg) [*oov-reer*]
    on the contrary, au contraire [*oh kõ-trer*]
    on duty, de service [*d(uh) ser-vees*]
    on foot, à pied [*ah pyeh*]
    on purpose, exprès [*ehk-spre*]
    on the right (left), à droite (gauche) [*ah drwaht (gohsh)*]
    on sale, en vente [*ã vãt*]
    on time, à l'heure [*ah luhr*]
once, une fois (f) [*ün fwah*]
    at once, tout de suite [*toot sweet*]
    once more, encore une fois [*ã-kor ün fwah*]
one, un, une [*ẽ, ün*]
one-way street, rue (f) à sens unique [*rü ah sãs ü-neek*]
one-way ticket, billet aller (m) [*bee-ye ah-leh*]
onion, oignon (m) [*o-nyõ*]
onlooker, spectateur, -trice [*spek-tah-tuhr, spek-tah-trees*]
only adv., seulement [*suhl-mã*]
only adj., seul [*suhl*]
open adj., ouvert [*oo-ver(t)*]
open v., ouvrir (irreg) [*oo-vreer*]
opening, ouverture (f) [*oo-ver-tür*]
opera, opéra (m) [*o-peh-rah*]
operate v., opérer [*o-peh-reh*]
operation, opération (f) [*o-peh-rah-syõ*]
opinion, opinion (f) [*o-pee-nyõ*]
opportunity, occasion (f) [*o-kah-zyõ*]
oppose [be opposed to] v., s'opposer à [*soh-poh-zeh ah*]
opposite adj., opposé, en face [*oh-poh-zeh, ã fahs*]
optional, facultatif, -tive [*fa-kül-tah-teef, fa-kül-tah-teev*]

or, ou [*oo*]
oral, oral, -aux (m, pl) [*o-rahl, o-roh*]
orange, orange (f) [*o-rãzh*]
orange juice, jus (m) d'orange [*zhü do-rãzh*]
orchard, verger (m) [*ver-zheh*]
orchestra, orchestre (m) [*or-kestr*]
orchid, orchidée (f) [*or-kee-deh*]
order *n.,* ordre (m) [*ordr*]
order *v.,* commander [*ko-mã-deh*]
orderly *adj.,* ordonné [*or-do-neh*]
ordinarily, d'habitude [*dah-bee-tüd*]
ordinary, ordinaire [*or-dee-ner*]
organ [music], orgue (m, sing), orgues (f, pl) [*org*]
organization, organisation (f) [*or-gah-nee-zah-syõ*]
oriental, oriental, -aux (m, pl) [*or-yã-tahl, or-yã-toh*]
original [first], originel, -elle [*o-ree-zhee-nel*]
original [unique], original, -aux (m, pl)[*o-ree-zhee-nahl, o-ree-zhee-noh*]
originally, à l'origine [*ah lo-ree-zheen*]
ornament *n.,* ornement (m) [*or-nuh-mã*]
orphan, orphelin, orpheline [*or-fuh-lẽ, or-fuh-leen*]
other, autre [*ohtr*]
  on the other hand, d'autre part [*doh-truh pahr*]
otherwise, autrement [*oh-truh-mã*]
ought *v.,* devoir (irreg) [*duh-vwahr*]
  You ought to come, Vous devriez venir [*voo duh-vree-yeh vneer*]
our, notre, nos [*notr, noh*]
ours, le nôtre, la nôtre; les nôtres [*luh nohtr, lah nohtr; leh nohtr*]
out, dehors [*duh-or*]
  go out *v.,* sortir (irreg; *Aux:* ÊTRE) [*sor-teer*]
  out of, *hors de [*ord(uh)*]
  The telephone is out of order, Le téléphone est en dérangement [*luh teh-leh-fon e-tã deh-rãzh-mã*]
outdoors, dehors [*duh-or*]
outlet [electrical], prise (f) [*preez*]
outside, dehors [*duh-or*]

outstanding, remarquable [*ruh-mahr-kahbl*]
oven, four (m) [*foor*]
  in the oven, au four [*oh foor*]
over *prep.*, sur, au-dessus, par-dessus [*sür, oht-sü, pahr-duh-sü*]
over [finished], fini [*fee-nee*]
overboard, par-dessus bord [*pahr-duh-sü bor*]
overcoat, pardessus (m) [*pahr-duh-sü*]
overcome *v.*, surmonter [*sür-mõ-teh*]
overdo *v.*, faire trop, forcer [*fer troh, for-seh*]
overflow *v.*, déborder [*deh-bor-deh*]
overhead *n.*, frais généraux (m, pl) [*fre zheh-neh-roh*]
overnight, du soir jusqu'au lendemain [*dü swahr zhüs-koh lãd-mẽ*]
  stay overnight with *v.*, passer la nuit chez [*pah-seh lah nwee sheh*]
overseas, outre-mer [*oot-ruh-mer*]
overtime, heures (f, pl) supplémentaires [*uhr sü-pleh-mã-ter*]
overturn *v.*, renverser [*rã-ver-seh*]
owe *v.*, devoir (irreg) [*duh-vwahr*]
owing to, à cause de [*ah kohz d(uh)*]
own *adj.*, propre [*propr*]
own *v.*, posséder [*po-seh-deh*]
owner, propriétaire (m) [*pro-pree-yeh-ter*]
ox, boeuf (m), boeufs (pl) [*buhf, buh*]
oxygen, oxygène (m) [*ok-see-zhen*]
oyster, huître (f) [*weetr*]

P

pack *n.*, paquet (m) [*pah-keh*]
pack *v.*, emballer [*ã-bah-leh*]
pack of cards, jeu de cartes (m) [*zhuht kahrt*]
package, paquet (m) [*pah-keh*]
page *n.*, page (f) [*pahzh*]

page *v.*, appeler [*ah-pleh*]
paid, payé [*peh-yeh*]
pail, seau (m), seaux (pl) [*soh*]
pain, douleur (f) [*doo-luhr*]
painful, douloureux, -euse [*doo-loo-ruh, doo-loo-ruhz*]
paint *n.*, peinture (f) [*pĕ-tür*]
paint *v.*, peindre (irreg) [*pĕdr*]
painter, peintre (m) [*pĕtr*]
painting, peinture (f) [*pĕ-tür*]
pair *n.*, paire (f) [*per*]
pajamas, pyjama (m) [*pee-zhah-mah*]
palace, palais (m) [*pah-le*]
pale *adj.*, pâle [*pahl*]
palm tree, palmier (m) [*pahl-myeh*]
pan, casserole (f) [*kahs-rol*]
pancake, crêpe (f) [*krep*]
panic *n.*, panique (f) [*pah-neek*]
pants [trousers] *n.*, pantalon (m) [*pã-tah-lõ*]
pants [underpants] *n.*, caleçon (m), culotte (f) [*kahl-sõ, kü-lot*]
paper, papier (m) [*pah-pyeh*]
   toilet paper, papier hygiénique [*pah-pyeh ee-zhyeh-neek*]
   writing paper, papier à lettres [*pah-pyeh ah letr*]
parade *n.*, défilé (m) [*deh-fee-leh*]
paradise, paradis (m) [*pah-rah-dee*]
paragraph, paragraphe (m) [*pah-rah-grahf*]
parallel, parallèle [*pah-rah-lel*]
paralyze *v.*, paralyser [*pah-rah-lee-zeh*]
parcel, colis (m) [*ko-lee*]
pardon *n.*, pardon (m) [*pahr-dõ*]
pardon *v.*, pardonner [*pahr-do-neh*]
   Pardon me! Pardon! [*pahr-dõ*]
parent, parent (m) [*pa-rã*]
parish, paroisse (f) [*pahr-wahs*]
park *n.*, parc (m) [*pahrk*]
park *v.*, garer [*gah-reh*]
parking, stationnement (m) [*sta-syon-mã*]
   no parking, stationnement inderdit [*sta-syon-mã ĕ-ter-dee*]
parliament, parlement (m) [*pahr-luh-mã*]

parsley, persil (m) [*per-see*]

part [portion] *n.,* partie (f) [*pahr-tee*]

part [role] *n.,* rôle (m) [*rohl*]

part [in hair] *n.,* raie (f) [*re*]

partial [in part], partiel, -elle [*pahr-syel*]

partial [favoring], partial, -aux (m, pl) [*pahr-syahl, pahr-syoh*]

participate *v.,* participer [*pahr-tee-see-peh*]

particular, particulier, -ière [*pahr-tee-kü-lyeh, pahr-tee-kü-lyer*]

particularly, particulièrement [*pahr-tee-kü-lyer-mã*]

partly, en partie [*ã pahr-tee*]

partner [business], associé, -ée [*ah-so-syeh*]

partner [game], partenaire (m, f) [*pahr-tuh-ner*]

party, fête (f), réception (f), soirée (f) [*fet, reh-sep-syõ, swah-reh*]

pass [mountain] *n.,* col (m) [*kol*]

pass *v.,* passer (*Aux:* ÊTRE if intrans) [*pah-seh*]

   pass an examination, réussir à un examen [*reh-ü-seer ah ẽ-neg-zah-mẽ*]

passenger, passager, -ère [*pah-sah-zheh, pah-sah-zher*]

passenger train, train (m) de voyageurs [*trẽ duh vwah-yah-zhuhr*]

passing *adj.,* passager, -ère [*pah-sah-zheh, pah-sah-zher*]

passion, passion (f) [*pah-syõ*]

passionate, passionné [*pah-syo-neh*]

passive, passif, -ive [*pah-seef, pah-seev*]

passport, passeport (m) [*pahs-por*]

past, passé (m) [*pah-seh*]

pastry, pastry shop, pâtisserie (f) [*pah-tees-ree*]

patch [mending] *n.,* pièce (f) [*pyes*]

path, sentier (m) [*sã-tyeh*]

patience, patience (f) [*pah-syãs*]

patient *adj.,* patient [*pah-syã(t)*]

patient [medical] *n.,* client, -te; malade (m, f) [*klee-yã, klee-yãt; mah-lahd*]

pattern *n.,* modèle (m) [*mo-del*]

pattern [for clothes] *n.,* patron (m) [*pah-trõ*]

pause *n.,* pause (f) [*pohz*]

pause *v.*, faire une pause [*fer ün pohz*]
pavement [sidewalk], trottoir (m) [*tro-twahr*]
pavement [street], chaussée (f) [*shoh-seh*]
paw *n.*, patte (f) [*paht*]
pay *v.*, payer [*peh-yeh*]
   pay a compliment, faire un compliment [*fer ē kõ-plee-mã*]
   pay attention, faire attention [*fer ah-tã-syõ*]
   pay a visit, rendre une visite à [*rē-drün vee-zeet ah*]
   pay cash, payer comptant [*peh-yeh kõ-tã*]
payment, paiement (m) [*pe-mã*]
pea, petit pois (m) [*ptee pwah*]
peace, paix (f) [*pe*]
peaceful, paisible [*pe-zeebl*]
peach, pêche (f) [*pesh*]
peak, sommet (m), pic (m) [*so-meh, peek*]
peanut, cacahuète (f) [*kah-kah-wet*]
pear, poire (f) [*pwahr*]
pearl, perle (f) [*perl*]
pebble, caillou (m), -oux (pl) [*ka-yoo*]
pebble [at beach], galet (m) [*gah-leh*]
peculiar, étrange [*eh-trãzh*]
pedal *n.*, pédale (f) [*peh-dahl*]
peddler, colporteur (m) [*kol-por-tuhr*]
pedestrian, piéton [*pyeh-tõ*]
pen, stylo (m) [*stee-loh*]
penalty, peine (f) [*pen*]
pencil, crayon (m) [*kre-yõ*]
peninsula, presqu'île (f) [*pres-keel*]
people, gens (m, pl) [*zhã*]
pepper, poivre (m) [*pwahvr*]
peppermint, menthe (f) [*mãt*]
percent, pour cent [*poor sã*]
percentage, pourcentage (m) [*poor-sã-tazh*]
perfect *adj.*, parfait [*pahr-fe(t)*]
perfection, perfection (f) [*per-fek-syõ*]
performance [theater], représentation (f) [*ruh-pre-zã-ta-syõ*]
performance [sports], performance (f) [*per-for-mãs*]
perfume, parfum (m) [*pahr-fẽ*]

perhaps, peut-être [*puh-tetr*]
period [punctuation], point final (m) [*pwē fee-nal*]
period [time], périod (f) [*per-yod*]
  menstrual period, règles (f, pl) [*regl*]
permanent *adj.*, permanent [*per-mah-nã(t)*]
permanent wave, permanente (f) [*per-mah-nãt*]
permission, permission (f) [*per-mee-syõ*]
permit *n.*, permis (m) [*per-mee*]
permit *v.*, permettre (irreg) [*per-metr*]
persist *v.*, persister [*per-sees-teh*]
person, personne (f) [*per-son*]
personal, personnel, -elle [*per-so-nel*]
personality, personalité (f) [*per-so-nah-lee-teh*]
personally, personnellement [*per-so-nel-mã*]
personnel, personnel (m) [*per-so-nel*]
perspiration, transpiration (f) [*trãs-pee-rah-syõ*]
perspire *v.*, transpirer [*trãs-pee-reh*]
persuade *v.*, persuader [*per-swah-deh*]
persuasive, persuasif, -ive [*per-swah-zeef, per-swah-zeev*]
pertaining to, relatif à [*ruh-lah-teef ah*]
petition *n.*, pétition (f) [*peh-tee-syõ*]
petroleum, pétrole (m) [*peh-trol*]
pewter, étain (m) [*eh-tē*]
pharmacy, pharmacie (f) [*fahr-mah-see*]
philosopher, philosophe (m) [*fee-lo-zof*]
philosophy, philosophie (f) [*fee-lo-zo-fee*]
phonograph, tourne-disques (m) [*toor-nuh-deesk*]
photograph *n.*, photo (f) [*foh-toh*]
photograph *v.*, photographier [*foh-toh-grah-fyeh*]
photographer, photographe (m) [*foh-toh-grahf*]
physical, physique [*fee-zeek*]
physician, médecin (m) [*med-sē*]
pianist, pianiste (m, f) [*pyah-neest*]
piano, piano (m) [*pyah-noh*]
pick *v.*, cueillir (irreg) [*kuh-yeer*]
pick up *v.*, ramasser [*rah-mah-seh*]
pickpocket, pickpocket [*peek-po-ket*]
picture, tableau (m), -eaux (pl) [*tah-bloh*]

picturesque, pittoresque [*pee-to-resk*]
pie, tarte (f) [*tahrt*]
piece, morceau (m), -eaux (pl) [*mor-soh*]
pier, quai (m), jetée (f) [*ke, zh(uh)-teh*]
pig, cochon (m) [*ko-shõ*]
pigeon, pigeon (m) [*pee-zhõ*]
pile *n.*, tas (m) [*tah*]
pill, pillule (f) [*pee-lül*]
pillow, oreiller (m) [*or-eh-yeh*]
pilot *n.*, pilote (m) [*pee-lot*]
pin *n.*, épingle (f) [*eh-pĕgl*]
pin *v.*, épingler [*eh-pĕ-gleh*]
pinch *v.*, pincer [*pĕ-seh*]
pine, pin (m) [*pĕ*]
pineapple, ananas (m) [*ah-nah-nah*]
pink, rose [*rohz*]
pint, demi-litre (m) [*d(uh)mee-leetr*]
pious, pieux, pieuse [*pyuh, pyuhz*]
pipe [plumbing] *n.*, tuyau (m), -aux (pl) [*twee-yoh*]
pipe [smoking] *n.*, pipe [*peep*]
pistol, pistolet (m) [*pees-to-leh*]
pitcher, pichet (m) [*pee-sheh*]
pity *n.*, pitié (f) [*pee-tyeh*]
   What a pity! Quel dommage! [*kel do-mahzh*]
pity *v.*, avoir pitié de [*ah-vwar pee-tyeh d(uh)*]
place *n.*, lieu (m), endroit (m) [*lyuh, ã-drwah*]
   in place of, au lieu de [*oh lyuh d(uh)*]
   take place *v.*, avoir lieu [*ah-vwahr lyuh*]
place *v.*, placer [*plah-seh*]
plain, simple [*sĕpl*]
plan *n.*, plan (m) [*plã*]
plan *v.*, faire un projet [*fer ĕ pro-zheh*]
planet, planète (f) [*plah-net*]
plant *n.*, plante (f) [*plãt*]
plant *v.*, planter [*plã-teh*]
plaster *n.*, plâtre (m) [*plahtr*]
plastic, plastique [*plahs-teek*]
plate, assiette (f) [*ah-syet*]

platform [train], quai (m) [*ke*]

play [drama] *n.*, pièce (f) [*pyes*]

play [a game] *v.*, jouer à [*zhweh ah*]

play [an instrument] *v.*, jouer de [*zhweh d(uh)*]

playground, terrain (m) de jeu [*te-rēd zhuh*]

playmate, camarade (m, f) de jeu [*kah-mah-rahd duh zhuh*]

pleasant, agréable [*ah-greh-ahbl*]

please *v.*, plaire (à) (irreg) [*pler (ah)*]

   please, s'il vous plaît [*seel voo ple*]

   Pleased to meet you, Enchanté de faire votre connaissance [*ã-shã-teh d(uh) fer vot-ruh ko-ne-sãs*]

pleasure, plaisir (m) [*ple-zeer*]

   with pleasure, avec plaisir [*ah-vek ple-zeer*]

pleasure trip, voyage (m) d'agrément [*vwah-yahzh dah-greh-mã*]

plenty (of), beaucoup (de) [*boh-kood(uh)*]

plot *n.*, complot (m) [*kõ-ploh*]

plow *n.*, charrue (f) [*shah-rü*]

plow *v.*, labourer [*lah-boo-reh*]

plug [electric], prise (f) [*preez*]

plum, prune (f) [*prün*]

plumber, plombier (m) [*plõ-byeh*]

plural, pluriel (m) [*plür-yel*]

plus, plus [*plüs*]

pneumonia, pneumonie (f) [*pnuh-mo-nee*]

pocket, poche (f) [*posh*]

pocketbook, sac à main (m) [*sah-kah mẽ*]

poem, poème (m) [*poh-em*]

poet, poète (m) [*poh-et*]

point [in time or space] *n.*, point (m) [*pwẽ*]

   point of view, point de vue [*pwẽd vü*]

point [tip] *n.*, pointe (f) [*pwẽt*]

point out *v.*, indiquer [*ẽ-dee-keh*]

poison, poison (m) [*pwah-zõ*]

poisonous, vénéneux, -euse [*veh-neh-nuh, veh-neh-nuhz*]

Poland, Pologne (f) [*po-loñ*]

pole [stick], perche (f) [*persh*]

pole [geographical], pôle (m) [*pohl*]

police, police (f) [*po-lees*]
policeman, agent (m) de police [*ah-zhãt po-lees*]
police station, commissariat (m) (de police) [*ko-mee-sahr-yah (duh po-lees)*]
policy, politique (f) [*po-lee-teek*]
Polish, polonais [*po-lo-ne(z)*]
polish *v.,* polir [*po-leer*]
polite, poli [*po-lee*]
political, politique [*po-lee-teek*]
politics, politique (f) [*po-lee-teek*]
pool *n.,* bassin (m) [*bah-sẽ*]
pool [swimming] *n.,* piscine (f) [*pee-seen*]
poor, pauvre [*pohvr*]
Pope, pape (m) [*pahp*]
poppy, coquelicot (m) [*kok-lee-koh*]
popular, à la mode [*ah lah mod*]
population, population (f) [*po-pü-lah-syõ*]
porch, porche (m) [*porsh*]
pork, porc (m) [*por*]
port [harbor] *n.,* port (m) [*por*]
port [wine] *n.,* porto (m) [*por-toh*]
port [right side] *adj.,* bâbord (m) [*bah-bor*]
portable *adj.,* portatif, -tive [*por-tah-teef, por-tah-teev*]
porter, porteur (m) [*por-tuhr*]
porthole, hublot (m) [*ü-bloh*]
portrait, portrait (m) [*por-tre*]
Portugal, Portugal (m) [*por-tü-gahl*]
Portuguese, portugais [*por-tü-ghe(z)*]
pose *v.,* poser [*poh-zeh*]
position, position (f) [*poh-zee-syõ*]
positive, positif, -tive [*poh-zee-teef, poh-zee-teev*]
possess *v.,* posséder [*po-seh-deh*]
possession, possession (f) [*po-se-syõ*]
possibility, possibilité (f) [*po-see-bee-lee-teh*]
possibly, peut-être [*puh-tetr*]
possible, possible [*po-seebl*]
   as soon as possible, aussitôt que possible [*oh-see-tohk po-seebl*]

post, poteau (m), -eaux (pl) [*poh-toh*]
postage, affranchissement (m) [*ah-frã-shees-mã*]
postage stamp, timbre (m) [*tẽbr*]
post card, carte (f) postale [*kahrt pos-tahl*]
post office, bureau (m) de poste, poste (f) [*bü-rohd post, post*]
postpone v., renvoyer à plus tard [*rã-vwah-yeh ah plü tahr*]
pot, pot (m) [*poh*]
potato, pomme de terre (f) [*pom duh ter*]
   mashed potatoes, purée (f) de pommes de terre [*pü-reht pom duh ter*]
pottery, poterie (f) [*pot-ree*]
pound n., livre (f) [*leevr*]
pour v., verser [*ver-seh*]
poverty, pauvreté (f) [*poh-vruh-teh*]
powder, poudre (f) [*poodr*]
power, pouvoir (m) [*poo-vwahr*]
powerful, puissant [*pwee-sã(t)*]
practical, pratique [*prah-teek*]
practice v., s'exercer [*sehg-zer-seh*]
praise v., louer [*loo-eh*]
pray v., prier [*pree-yeh*]
prayer, prière (f) [*pree-yer*]
precaution, précaution (f) [*pre-koh-syõ*]
precede v., précéder [*pre-seh-deh*]
precious, précieux, -euse [*pre-syuh, pre-syuhz*]
precise, précis [*pre-see(z)*]
precisely, précisément [*pre-see-zeh-mã*]
prefer v., préférer [*pre-feh-reh*]
preferable, préférable [*pre-feh-rahbl*]
preference, préférence (f) [*pre-feh-rãs*]
pregnancy, grossesse (f) [*groh-ses*]
pregnant, enceinte [*ã-sẽt*]
prejudice, préjugé (m) [*pre-zhü-zheh*]
preliminary, préliminaire [*preh-lee-mee-ner*]
preparation, préparation (f) [*pre-pah-rah-syõ*]
prepare v., préparer [*preh-pah-reh*]
prescription, ordonnance (f) [*or-do-nãs*]

presence, présence (f) [*pre-zãs*]
present *adj.*, présent [*pre-zã(t)*]
present [gift] *n.*, cadeau (m), -eaux (pl) [*kah-doh*]
present [time] *n.*, présent (m) [*pre-zã*]
present *v.*, présenter [*pre-zã-teh*]
presentable, présentable [*pre-zã-tahbl*]
preserve *v.*, préserver [*pre-ser-veh*]
president, président (m) [*preh-zee-dã*]
press, presse (f) [*pres*]
press [push, squeeze, urge] *v.*, presser [*pre-seh*]
press [clothes] *v.*, repasser [*r(uh)-pah-seh*]
pressure, pression (f) [*pre-syõ*]
prestige, prestige (m) [*pres-teezh*]
presume *v.*, présumer [*pre-zü-meh*]
pretend [claim] *v.*, prétendre [*pre-tãdr*]
pretend [dissemble] *v.*, faire semblant [*fer sã-blã*]
pretentious, prétentieux, -euse [*pre-tã-syuh, pre-tã-syuhz*]
pretty, joli [*zho-lee*]
prevent *v.*, empêcher [*ã-pe-sheh*]
previous, précédent [*pre-seh-dã(t)*]
previously, auparavant [*oh-pah-rah-vã*]
price *n.*, prix (m) [*pree*]
pride, orgueil (m) [*or-guhy*]
priest, prêtre (m) [*pretr*]
primitive, primitif, -tive [*pree-mee-teef, pree-mee-teev*]
prince, prince (m) [*prẽs*]
princess, princesse (f) [*prẽ-ses*]
principal, principal, -aux (m, pl) [*prẽ-see-pahl, prẽ-see-poh*]
principally, principalement [*prẽ-see-pahl-mã*]
principle, principe (m) [*prẽ-seep*]
print [photo] *n.*, épreuve (f) [*eh-pruhv*]
print *v.*, imprimer [*ẽ-pree-meh*]
printed matter, imprimé (m) [*ẽ-pree-meh*]
printer, imprimeur (m) [*ẽ-pree-muhr*]
prior, antérieur [*ã-tehr-yuhr*]
prison, prison (f) [*pree-zõ*]
prisoner, prisonnier, -ière [*pree-zon-yeh, pree-zon-yer*]
private, privé [*pree-veh*]

privilege, privilège (m) [*pree-vee-lezh*]
prize *n.*, prix (m) [*pree*]
probable, probable [*pro-bahbl*]
probably, probablement [*pro-bahb-luh-mā*]
problem, problème (m) [*pro-blem*]
procedure, procédure (f) [*pro-seh-dūr*]
proceed *v.*, procéder [*pro-seh-deh*]
process [method] *n.*, procédé (m) [*pro-seh-deh*]
produce *v.*, produire (irreg) [*pro-dweer*]
product, produit (m) [*pro-dwee*]
production, production (f) [*pro-dük-syō*]
profession, profession (f) [*pro-fe-syō*]
professor, professeur (m) [*pro-fe-suhr*]
profit *n.*, profit (m) [*pro-fee*]
profit *v.*, profiter [*pro-fee-teh*]
program *n.*, programme (m) [*pro-grahm*]
progress *n.*, progrès (m) [*pro-gre*]
progressive, progressif, -ive [*pro-gre-seef, pro-gre-seev*]
prohibit *v.*, défendre [*deh-fādr*]
prohibited, interdit, défendu [*ē-ter-dee(t), deh-fā-dü*]
project *n.*, projet (m) [*pro-zheh*]
prominent, éminent [*eh-mee-nã(t)*]
promise *n.*, promesse (f) [*pro-mes*]
promise *v.*, promettre (irreg) [*pro-metr*]
promotion, promotion (f) [*proh-moh-syō*]
prompt, prompt [*prŏ(t)*]
pronoun *n.*, pronom (m) [*pro-nō*]
pronounce *v.*, prononcer [*pro-nŏ-seh*]
pronunciation, prononciation (f) [*pro-nŏ-syah-syō*]
proof, preuve (f) [*pruhv*]
propaganda, propagande (f) [*pro-pah-gãd*]
propeller, hélice (f) [*eh-lees*]
proper, convenable [*kŏv-nahbl*]
property, propriété (f) [*pro-pree-yeh-teh*]
proportion, proportion (f) [*pro-por-syō*]
proposal, proposition (f) [*proh-poh-zee-syō*]
proposal [marriage], demande (f) en mariage [*duh-mā-dã mahr-yahzh*]

propose v., proposer [*proh-poh-zeh*]
propose [marriage] v., demander en mariage [*dmã-deh ã mahr-yazh*]
proprietor, propriétaire (m) [*pro-pree-yeh-ter*]
prosperity, prospérité (f) [*pros-peh-ree-teh*]
prosperous, prospère [*pros-per*]
protect v., protéger [*pro-teh-zheh*]
protection, protection (f) [*pro-tek-syõ*]
protest v., protester [*pro-tes-teh*]
Protestant, protestant [*pro-tes-tã(t)*]
proud, fier, fière [*fyer*]
prove v., prouver [*proo-veh*]
proverb, proverbe (m) [*pro-verb*]
provide v., fournir [*foor-neer*]
provided that, pourvu que [*poor-vü k(uh)*]
province, province (f) [*pro-vẽs*]
provincial, provincial, -aux (m, pl) [*pro-vẽ-syahl, pro-vẽ-syoh*]
provision [clause], clause (f) [*klohz*]
provisions [supplies], provisions (f, pl) [*pro-vee-zyõ*]
prune, pruneau (m), -eaux (pl) [*prü-noh*]
psychiatrist, psychiatre (m) [*psee-kyahtr*]
psychoanalysis, psychanalyse (f) [*psee-kah-nah-leez*]
psychological, psychologique [*psee-ko-lo-zheek*]
public adj., public, publique [*pü-bleek*]
public n., public (m) [*pü-bleek*]
publication, publication (f) [*pü-blee-kah-syõ*]
publicity, publicité (f) [*pü-blee-see-teh*]
publish v., publier [*pü-blee-yeh*]
pull v., tirer [*tee-reh*]
pulse n., pouls (m) [*poo*]
pump n., pompe (f) [*põp*]
pumpkin, potiron (m), citrouille (f) [*po-tee-rõ, see-trooy*]
punctual, ponctuel, -elle [*põk-twel*]
puncture n., crevaison (f) [*kruh-ve-sõ*]
punish v., punir [*pü-neer*]
punishment, punition (f) [*pü-nee-syõ*]
pupil, élève (m, f) [*eh-lev*]

puppet, marionnette (f) [*mahr-yo-net*]
purchase *n.*, achat (m) [*ah-shah*]
purchase *v.*, acheter [*ahsh-teh*]
pure, pur [*pür*]
purple, violet, -ette [*vyo-leh, vyo-let*]
purpose, but (m) [*bü(t)*]
  on purpose, exprès [*ehk-spre*]
purse, sac (m) [*sahk*]
pursue *v.*, poursuivre (irreg) [*poor-sweevr*]
push *v.*, pousser [*poo-seh*]
put *v.*, mettre (irreg) [*metr*]
  put on [light], allumer [*ah-lü-meh*]
  put on [clothes], mettre (irreg) [*metr*]
  put out [light], éteindre (irreg) [*eh-tĕdr*]
pyramid, pyramide (f) [*pee-rah-meed*]

Q

qualification [limitation], réserve (f) [*reh-zerv*]
qualification [ability], titre (m) [*teetr*]
quality, qualité (f) [*kah-lee-teh*]
quantity, quantité (f) [*kã-tee-teh*]
quarrel *n.*, querelle (f) [*kuh-rel*]
quart, environ un litre (m) [*ã-vee-rõ ĕ leetr*]
quarter, quart (m) [*kahr*]
  quarter hour, quart d'heure [*kahr duhr*]
queen, reine (f) [*ren*]
queer [odd], bizarre [*bee-zahr*]
question *n.*, question (f) [*kes-tyõ*]
question *v.*, questionner [*kes-tyo-neh*]
questionable, contestable [*kõ-tes-tahbl*]
question mark, point (m) d'interrogation [*pwĕ dĕ-teh-ro-gah-syõ*]
questionnaire, questionnaire (m) [*kes-tyo-ner*]
quick, rapide [*rah-peed*]

quickly, vite [*veet*]
quiet, tranquille [*trã-keel*]
  Be quiet, Restez tranquille [*res-teh trã-keel*]
quit [stop] *v.,* arrêter [*ah-re-teh*]
quit [doing something] *v.,* cesser (de) [*seh-seh (duh)*]
quite, tout à fait [*too-tah fe*]
quotation [of words], citation (f) [*see-tah-syõ*]
quotation [of price, terms], devis (m) [*duh-vee*]
quotation marks, guillemets (m, pl) [*gheey-meh*]
quote *v.,* citer [*see-teh*]

R

rabbi, rabbin (m) [*rah-bẽ*]
rabbit, lapin (m) [*lah-pẽ*]
rabies, rage (f) [*rahzh*]
race [ethnic group] *n.,* race (f) [*rahs*]
race [contest] *n.,* course (f) [*koors*]
racetrack, champ (m) de courses [*shã koors*]
racket [in sports], raquette (f) [*rah-ket*]
radiator, radiateur (m) [*rah-dyah-tuhr*]
radical, radical, -aux (m, pl) [*rah-dee-kahl, rah-dee-koh*]
radio, radio (f) [*rah-dyoh*]
radish, radis (m) [*rah-dee*]
rag, chiffon (m) [*shee-fõ*]
railroad, chemin (m) de fer [*shmẽd fer*]
railroad car, wagon (m) [*vah-gõ*]
railroad crossing, passage à niveau [*pah-sah-zhah nee-voh*]
railroad station, gare (f) [*gahr*]
rain *n.,* pluie (f) [*plwee*]
rain *v.,* pleuvoir (irreg) [*pluh-vwahr*]
  It's raining, Il pleut [*eel pluh*]
rainbow, arc (m) en ciel [*ar-kã syel*]
raincoat, imperméable (m) [*ẽ-per-meh-ahbl*]
raise [rear] *v.,* élever [*ehl-veh*]

raise [lift] *v.*, soulever [*sool-veh*]

raisin, raisin sec (m) [*re-zē sek*]

random, at random, au *hasard [*oh ah-zahr*]

rape *n.*, viol (m) [*vyol*]

rape *v.*, violer [*vyo-leh*]

rapid, rapide [*rah-peed*]

rapidly, rapidement [*rah-peed-mã*]

rare [unusual], rare [*rahr*]

rare [undercooked], saignant [*se-nyã(t)*]

rarely, rarement [*rahr-mã*]

rash *n.*, éruption (f) [*eh-rüp-syõ*]

rash *adj.*, téméraire [*teh-meh-rɛr*]

rat, rat (m) [*rah*]

rate [price] *n.*, tarif (m) [*tah-reef*]

rate [speed] *n.*, taux (m) [*toh*]

rather (than), plutôt (que) [*plü-toh (kuh)*]

   I would rather . . . , J'aimerais mieux . . . [*zhem-re myuh*]

raw, cru [*krü*]

raw material, matière (f) première [*mah-tyer pruh-myer*]

ray, rayon (m) [*re-yõ*]

razor, rasoir (m) [*rah-zwahr*]

razor blade, lame (f) de rasoir [*lahm duh rah-zwahr*]

reach *v.*, atteindre (irreg) [*ah-tēdr*]

reaction, réaction (f) [*reh-ahk-syõ*]

read *v.*, lire (irreg) [*leer*]

reading, lecture (f) [*lek-tür*]

ready, prêt [*pre(t)*]

   ready to wear, prêt à porter [*pre-tah por-teh*]

real, réel, réelle [*reh-el*]

real estate, biens immobiliers (m, pl) [*byē-zee-mo-beel-yeh*]

realize *v.*, se rendre compte (de) [*srãdr kõt (duh)*]

really, réellement [*reh-el-mã*]

reason *n.*, raison (f) [*re-zõ*]

reasonable, raisonnable [*re-zo-nahbl*]

reassure *v.*, rassurer [*rah-sü-reh*]

rebel *n.*, rebelle (m, f) [*ruh-bel*]

rebel (against) *v.*, se soulever (contre) [*suh sool-veh (kõtr)*]

recall *v.*, rappeler [*rah-pleh*]

receipt, reçu (m) [*ruh-sü*]
receive *v.*, recevoir (irreg) [*ruh-suh-vwahr*]
recent, récent [*reh-sã(t)*]
recently, récemment [*reh-sah-mã*]
reception, réception (f) [*reh-sep-syõ*]
recession, récession (f) [*reh-se-syõ*]
recipe, recette (f) [*ruh-set*]
recite *v.*, réciter [*reh-see-teh*]
reckless, téméraire [*teh-meh-rer*]
recognize *v.*, reconnaître (irreg) [*ruh-ko-netr*]
recommend *v.*, recommander [*r(uh)-ko-mã-deh*]
recommendation, recommendation (f) [*ruh-ko-mã-dah-syõ*]
record [for phonograph] *n.*, disque (m) [*deesk*]
record [in sports] *n.*, record (m) [*ruh-kor*]
   police record, casier (m) judiciaire [*kah-zyeh zhü-dee-syer*]
   school record, livret (m) scolaire [*lee-vre sko-ler*]
recover [something] *v.*, retrouver [*r(uh)-troo-veh*]
recover [from illness] *v.*, se remettre (irreg) [*sruh-metr*]
recovery, guérison (f) [*gheh-ree-zõ*]
recreation, récréation (f) [*reh-kreh-ah-syõ*]
rectangle, rectangle (m) [*rek-tãgl*]
red, rouge [*roozh*]
Red Cross, Croix Rouge (m) [*krwah roozh*]
redeem *v.*, racheter [*rahsh-teh*]
reduce *v.*, réduire (irreg) [*reh-dweer*]
reduction, réduction (f) [*reh-dük-syõ*]
referee, arbitre (m) [*ahr-beetr*]
reference, référence (f) [*reh-feh-rãs*]
refill *v.*, remplir [*rã-pleer*]
refined, raffiné [*rah-fee-neh*]
reflect [light] *v.*, refléter [*r(uh)-fle-teh*]
reflect [think] *v.*, réfléchir [*reh-fleh-sheer*]
reflection, réflexion (f) [*reh-flek-syõ*]
reflex, réflexe (m) [*reh-fleks*]
reform *n.*, réforme (f) [*reh-form*]
reform *v.*, réformer [*reh-for-meh*]
refrain (from) *v.*, s'abstenir (de) (irreg) [*sahp-stuh-neer (duh)*]

refresh v., rafraîchir [*rah-fre-sheer*]
refreshing, rafraîchissant [*rah-fre-shee-sã(t)*]
refreshment (m) rafraîchissement [*rah-fre-shees-mã*]
refrigerator, frigidaire (m) [*free-zhee-der*]
refuge, refuge (m) [*r(uh)-füzh*]
refugee, réfugié, -ée [*reh-fü-zhyeh*]
refund n., remboursement (m) [*rã-boor-suh-mã*]
refusal, refus (m) [*r(uh)-fü*]
refuse v., refuser [*r(uh)-fü-zeh*]
regain v., regagner [*ruh-gah-nyeh*]
regard: with regard to, quant à [*kã-tah*]
regiment, régiment (m) [*reh-zhee-mã*]
region, région (f) [*reh-zhyõ*]
register n., registre (m) [*ruh-zheestr*]
register [at school] v., s'inscrire (irreg) [*sẽ-skreer*]
register [baggage] v., enregistrer [*ãr-zhees-treh*]
registered letter, lettre (f) recommandée [*letr ruh-ko-mã-deh*]
regret n., regret (m) [*r(uh)-gre*]
regret v., regretter [*r(uh)-gre-teh*]
regular adj., régulier, -ière [*reh-gü-lyeh, re-gü-lyer*]
regular gas, normal [*nor-mahl*]
regulate v., régler [*reh-gleh*]
regulation, règlement (m) [*re-gluh-mã*]
rehearsal, répétition (f) [*reh-peh-tee-syõ*]
reign n., règne (m) [*reñ*]
reject v., rejeter [*ruhsh-teh*]
rejoin v., rejoindre (irreg) [*r(uh)-zhwẽdr*]
relation [connection] n., rapport (m) [*ra-por*]
relationship [by family] n., parenté (f) [*pah-rã-teh*]
relative n., parent, -te [*pah-rã(t)*]
relatively, relativement [*ruh-lah-teev-mã*]
relax v., détendre (irreg), se détendre (irreg) [*deh-tãdr, sdeh-tãdr*]
relaxation, détente (f) [*deh-tãt*]
relevant, pertinent [*per-tee-nã(t)*]
reliable, sur [*sür*]
relieve v., soulager [*soo-lah-zheh*]
religion, religion (f) [*r(uh)-lee-zhyõ*]

religious, religieux, -euse [*ruh-lee-zhyuh, ruh-lee-zhyuhz*]
reluctant, peu disposé [*puh dees-poh-zeh*]
rely (on) *v.,* compter sur [*kõ-teh sür*]
remain *v.,* rester (*Aux:* ÊTRE) [*res-teh*]
remainder, reste (m) [*rest*]
remark *n.,* remarque (f) [*r(uh)-mahrk*]
remark *v.,* remarquer [*r(uh)-mahr-keh*]
remarkable, remarquable [*r(uh)-mahr-kahbl*]
remedy *n.,* remède (m) [*r(uh)-med*]
remember *v.,* se rappeler, se souvenir (de) [*srah-pleh, suh soov-neer (duh)*]
remind *v.,* rappeler (à) [*rah-pleh (ah)*]
remittance, paiement (m) [*pe-mã*]
remorse, remords (m) [*r(uh)-mor*]
remove *v.,* enlever [*ãl-veh*]
renew *v.,* renouveler [*ruh-noo-vleh*]
rent *n.,* loyer (m) [*lwah-yeh*]
rent *v.,* louer [*loo-eh*]
repair *v.,* réparer [*reh-pah-reh*]
repay *v.,* rembourser [*rã-boor-seh*]
repeat *v.,* répéter [*reh-peh-teh*]
replace *v.,* remplacer [*rã-plah-seh*]
reply *n.,* réponse (f) [*reh-põs*]
reply *v.,* répondre [*reh-põdr*]
report *v.,* rendre compte (de) [*rãdr kõt (duh)*]
report *n.,* rapport (m) [*rah-por*]
reporter, journaliste (m, f) [*zhoor-nah-leest*]
represent *v.,* représenter [*r(uh)-preh-zã-teh*]
representative, représentant (m) [*r(uh)-preh-zã-tã*]
reproduction, reproduction (f) [*r(uh)-pro-dük-syõ*]
republic, république (f) [*reh-pü-bleek*]
reputation, réputation (f) [*reh-pü-tah-syõ*]
request *n.,* demande (f) [*d(uh)-mãd*]
request *v.,* demander [*d(uh)-mã-deh*]
require *v.,* exiger [*eg-zee-zheh*]
requirement, exigence (f) [*eg-zee-zhãs*]
rescue *v.,* sauver [*soh-veh*]
research *n.,* recherche (f) [*r(uh)-shersh*]

resemblance, ressemblance (f) [*ruh-sã-blãs*]

resemble *v.*, ressembler (à) [*ruh-sã-bleh (ah)*]

resentment, ressentiment (m) [*ruh-sã-tee-mã*]

reservation, réserve (f) [*reh-serv*]

    We have reservations at . . . Hotel, Nous avons retenu des chambres à l'Hotel . . . [*noo-zah-võ ruht-nü deh shã-brah loh-tel*]

reserve [a room] *v.*, retenir (irreg) [*ruht-neer*]

reserve [a seat] *v.*, louer [*loo-weh*]

residence, résidence (f) [*reh-zee-dãs*]

resident, résident -te [*re-zee-dã(t)*]

resign *v.*, démissionner [*deh-mee-syo-neh*]

resignation, démission (f) [*deh-mee-syõ*]

resist *v.*, résister [*reh-zees-teh*]

resolution, résolution (f) [*reh-zo-lü-syõ*]

respect *n.*, respect (m) [*re-spe*]

respect *v.*, respecter [*re-spek-teh*]

respectable, respectable [*re-spek-tahbl*]

response, réponse (f) [*reh-põs*]

responsibility, responsabilité (f) [*res-põ-sah-bee-lee-teh*]

responsible, responsable [*res-põ-sahbl*]

rest *v.*, se reposer [*sruh-poh-zeh*]

restaurant, restaurant (m) [*res-to-rã*]

restore *v.*, restaurer [*res-to-reh*]

result *n.*, résultat (m) [*reh-zül-tah*]

resume *v.*, reprendre (irreg) [*ruh-prãdr*]

retail, au détail [*oh deh-tahy*]

retire [be pensioned off] *v.*, prendre (irreg) sa retraite [*prãdr sah-tret*]

retire [withdraw] *v.*, se retirer [*sruh-tee-reh*]

return *n.*, retour (m) [*r(uh)-toor*]

reveal *v.*, révéler [*reh-vɛh-leh*]

revelation, révélation (f) [*reh-vɛh-lah-syõ*]

revenge, vengeance (f), revanche (f) [*vã-zhãs, r(uh)-vãsh*]

reverse *n.*, inverse (m) [*ẽ-vers*]

revise *v.*, réviser [*reh-vee-zeh*]

revolution, révolution (f) [*reh-vo-lü-syõ*]

revolver, révolver (m) [*reh-vol-ver*]

reward n., récompense (f) [reh-kŏ-pãs]
reward v., récompenser [reh-kŏ-pā-seh]
rheumatism, rhumatisme (m) [rü-mah-teesm]
rhyme n., rime (f) [reem]
rhythm, rythme (m) [reetm]
rib, côte (f) [koht]
ribbon, ruban (m) [rü-bã]
rice, riz (m) [ree]
rich, riche [reesh]
rid: to get rid of v., se débarasser (de) [sdeh-bah-rah-seh (duh)]
ride n., promenade (f) [prom-nahd]
ridiculous, ridicule [ree-dee-kül]
right [direction], droit [drwah(t)]
  on the right, à droite [ah drwaht]
right [correct], juste, exact [zhüst, eg-zah(kt)]
  all right, très bien [tre byē]
  be right v., avoir raison [ah-vwahr re-zŏ]
  right away, tout de suite [toot sweet]
right n., droit (m) [drwah]
ring [circular band] n., bague (f) [bahg]
ring v., sonner [so-neh]
ringing, sonnerie (f) [son-ree]
rinse n., rinçage (m) [rē-sahzh]
rinse v., rincer [rē-seh]
riot n., émeute (f) [eh-muht]
rip v., déchirer [deh-shee-reh]
ripe, mûr [mür]
ripen v., mûrir [mü-reer]
rise v., se lever [s(uh) luh-veh]
risk n., risque (m) [reesk]
ritual n., rites (m, pl) [reet]
rival adj. & n., rival, -le (sing); -aux, -ales (pl) [ree-vahl, ree-voh]
river, fleuve (m), rivière (f) [fluhv, reev-yer]
road, route (f), chemin (m) [root, shmē]
roar v., rugir [rü-zheer]
roast n., rôti (m) [ro-tee]
roast v., faire rôtir [fer ro-teer]

roasted, rôti [*ro-tee*]
rob *v.*, voler [*vo-leh*]
robber, voleur, -euse [*vo-luhr, vo-luhz*]
robbery, vol (m) [*vol*]
rock *n.*, rocher (m) [*ro-sheh*]
rock *v.*, balancer [*bah-lã-seh*]
rocking chair, chaise (f) à bascule [*shez ah bahs-kül*]
roll [bread] *n.*, petit pain (m) [*ptee pẽ*]
roll *v.*, rouler [*roo-leh*]
Roman, romain [*ro-mẽ, ro-men*]
Romanesque, roman [*ro-mã, ro-mahn*]
romantic, romantique [*ro-mã-teek*]
roof, toit (m) [*twah*]
room [apartment] *n.*, pièce (f) [*pyes*]
   double room, chambre à deux lits [*shãbr ah duh lee*]
   single room, chambre à un lit [*shãbr ah ẽ lee*]
room [space] *n.*, place (f) [*plahs*]
root, racine (f) [*rah-seen*]
rope, corde (f) [*kord*]
rose *n.*, rose (f) [*rohz*]
rotten, pourri [*poo-ree*]
rouge, rouge (m) [*roozh*]
rough, rude [*rüd*]
round [circular], rond [*rõ(d)*]
round trip, aller retour [*ah-leh r(uh)-toor*]
routine, routine (f) [*roo-teen*]
row [line] *n.*, rang (m) [*rã*]
royal, royal, -aux (m, pl) [*rwah-yahl, rwah-yoh*]
rub *v.*, frotter [*fro-teh*]
rubber, caoutchouc (m) [*ka-oot-shoo*]
ruby, rubis (m) [*rü-bee*]
rude, grossier, -ière [*groh-syeh, groh-syer*]
rug, tapis (m) [*tah-pee*]
ruin *n.*, ruine (f) [*rween*]
rule *n.*, règle (f) [*regl*]
rule *v.*, gouverner [*goo-ver-neh*]
ruler [measure], règle (f) [*regl*]
ruler [governor], gouvernant (m) [*goo-ver-nã*]

rum, rhum (m) [*rom*]
rumor, rumeur (f) [*rü-muhr*]
run *v.*, courir (irreg) [*koo-reer*]
   run across, traverser [*trah-ver-seh*]
   run away, partir (irreg; *Aux:* ÊTRE) en courant [*pahr-teer ã koo-rã*]
   run over, écraser [*eh-krah-zeh*]
running, courant [*koo-rã(t)*]
runway, piste (f) d'atterrissage [*peest dah-teh-ree-sahzh*]
rural, rural, -aux (m, pl) [*rü-rahl, rü-roh*]
rush hours, heures d'affluence [*uhr dah-flü-ãs*]
Russian, russe [*rüs*]
rust *n.*, rouille (f) [*rooy*]
rust *v.*, rouiller [*roo-yeh*]
rut *n.*, ornière (f) [*orn-yer*]
rye, seigle (m) [*segl*]

S

sack, sac (m) [*sahk*]
sacred, sacré [*sah-kreh*]
sacrifice *n.*, sacrifice (m) [*sah-kree-fees*]
sad, triste [*treest*]
saddle, selle (f) [*sel*]
sadness, tristesse (f) [*trees-tes*]
safe *adj.*, sûr [*sür*]
   safe and sound, sain et sauf [*sẽ eh sohf*]
safety, sûreté (f) [*sür-teh*]
safety pin, épingle anglaise (f) [*eh-pẽgl ã-glez*]
sail *n.*, voile (f) [*vwahl*]
sail *v.*, aller (irreg; *Aux:* ÊTRE) en bateau [*ah-leh ã bah-toh*]
sailboat, bateau (m) à voile [*bah-toh ah vwahl*]
sailor, matelot (m) [*maht-loh*]
saint *adj. & n.*, saint, -te [*sẽ(t)*]
sake: for the sake of, pour [*poor*]

salad, salade (f) [*sah-lahd*]
salary, traitement (m) [*tret-mã*]
sale, vente (f) [*vãt*]
   for sale, à vendre [*ah vãdr*]
salesclerk, vendeur, -euse [*vã-duhr, vã-duhz*]
salmon, saumon (m) [*soh-mõ*]
salt, sel (m) [*sel*]
salty, salé [*sah-leh*]
same, le même, la même, les mêmes [*luh mem, lah mem, leh mem*]
   all the same, tout de même [*tood mem*]
sample *n.*, échantillon (m) [*eh-shã-tee-yõ*]
sand, sable (m) [*sahbl*]
sandal, sandale (f) [*sã-dahl*]
sandwich, sandwich (m) [*sã-dweetsh*]
sandy, sablonneux, -euse [*sah-blo-nuh, sah-blo-nuhz*]
sane, sain d'esprit [*sẽ des-pree*]
sanitary, sanitaire [*sah-nee-ter*]
sanitary napkins, serviettes (f) hygiéniques [*ser-vyet ee-zhyeh-neek*]
sapphire, saphir (m) [*sah-feer*]
satin, satin (m) [*sah-tẽ*]
satire, satire (f) [*sah-teer*]
satirical, satirique [*sah-tee-reek*]
satisfaction, satisfaction (f) [*sah-tees-fahk-syõ*]
satisfactory, satisfaisant [*sah-tees-fuh-zã(t)*]
satisfied, satisfait [*sah-tees-fe(t)*]
satisfy *v.*, satisfaire (irreg) [*sah-tees-fer*]
Saturday, samedi (m) [*sahm-dee*]
sauce, sauce (f) [*sohs*]
saucer, soucoupe (f) [*soo-koop*]
sausage, saucisse (f) [*soh-sees*]
save [preserve] *v.*, sauver [*soh-veh*]
save [put aside] *v.*, économiser [*eh-ko-no-mee-zeh*]
savings, épargne (f) [*eh-pahrñ*]
savings account, compte (m) à la caisse d'épargne [*kõt ah lah kes deh-pahrñ*]
saw *n.*, scie (f) [*see*]

say *v.*, dire (irreg) [*deer*]

scale [for weighing] *n.*, balance (f) [*bah-lãs*]

scale [proportion] *n.*, échelle (f) [*eh-shel*]

scalp, cuir chevelu (m) [*kweer shuh-vlü*]

scandal, scandale (m) [*skã-dahl*]

scar *n.*, cicatrice (f) [*see-kah-trees*]

scarce, rare [*rahr*]

scarcely, à peine [*ah pen*]

scare *v.*, effrayer [*eh-fre-yeh*]

scarf, écharpe (f), foulard (m) [*eh-shahrp, foo-lahr*]

scarlet, écarlate (f) [*eh-kahr-laht*]

scarlet fever, scarlatine (f) [*skahr-lah-teen*]

scatter *v.*, éparpiller [*eh-pahr-pee-yeh*]

scene, scène (f) [*sen*]

scenery, décor (m) [*deh-kor*]

scent *n.*, parfum (m) [*pahr-fẽ*]

schedule *n.*, horaire (m) [*o-rer*]

scholar, savant (m) [*sah-vã*]

school, école (f) [*eh-kol*]

schoolmate, camarade d'école (m, f) [*kah-mah-rahd deh-kol*]

science, science (f) [*syãs*]

scientist, scientifique (m, f) [*syã-tee-feek*]

scissors, ciseaux (m, pl) [*see-zoh*]

scold *v.*, gronder [*grõ-deh*]

scorch *v.*, roussir [*roo-seer*]

score *n.*, nombre (m) de points [*nõbr duh pwẽ*]

scorn *n.*, mépris (m) [*meh-pree*]

scorn *v.*, mépriser [*meh-pree-zeh*]

Scottish, écossais [*eh-ko-se(z)*]

Scotland, Ecosse (f) [*eh-kos*]

scrape *v.*, érafler [*eh-rah-fleh*]

scratch *n.*, égratignure (f) [*eh-grah-tee-nyür*]

scratch *v.*, gratter [*grah-teh*]

scream *n.*, cri (m) [*kree*]

scream *v.*, pousser des cris [*poo-seh deh kree*]

screen [metal] *n.*, grille (f) [*greey*]

screen [motion picture] *n.*, écran (m) [*eh-krã*]

screw *n.*, vis (f) [*vees*]

screwdriver, tournevis (m) [*toor-nuh-vees*]
scrub *v.,* frotter [*fro-teh*]
sculpture, sculpture (f) [*skül-tür*]
sea, mer (f) [*mer*]
seal [animal] *n.,* phoque (m) [*fok*]
seal [stamp] *n.,* sceau (m), sceaux (pl) [*soh*]
seal *v.,* cacheter [*kahsh-teh*]
seam, couture (f) [*koo-tür*]
search for *v.,* chercher [*sher-sheh*]
seaside, bord (m) de la mer [*bor duh lah mer*]
season *n.,* saison (f) [*seh-zõ*]
season *v.,* assaisonner [*ah-seh-zo-neh*]
seat *n.,* siège (m) [*syezh*]
seatbelt, ceinture (f) de sécurité [*sē-tür duh seh-kü-ree-teh*]
seated, assis [*ah-see(z)*]
second *adj.,* second, deuxième [*suh-gõ(d), duh-zyɛm*]
second *n.,* seconde (f) [*suh-gõd*]
secondary, secondaire [*suh-gõ-der*]
secret *n.,* secret (m) [*suh-kreh*]
secretary, secrétaire (m, f) [*suh-kreh-ter*]
section, section (f) [*sek-syõ*]
securities [financial], valeurs (f, pl) [*vah-luhr*]
security, sécurité (f) [*seh-kü-ree-teh*]
seduce *v.,* séduire (irreg) [*seh-dweer*]
see *v.,* voir (irreg) [*vwahr*]
   Let me see, Faites voir [*fet vwahr*]
   Let's see, Voyons [*vwah-yõ*]
seed, graine (f) [*gren*]
seek *v.,* chercher [*sher-sheh*]
seem *v.,* sembler [*sã-bleh*]
seize *v.,* saisir [*se-zeer*]
seldom, rarement [*rahr-mã*]
select *v.,* choisir [*shwah-zeer*]
self, moi, moi-même [*mwah, mwah-mem*]
self-conscious, gêné [*zhe-neh*]
selfish, égoïste [*ɛh-go-eest*]
sell *v.,* vendre [*vãdr*]
senate, sénat (m) [*seh-nah*]

senator, sénateur (m) [*seh-nah-tuhr*]
send *v.*, envoyer [*ã-vwah-yeh*]
   send for, envoyer chercher, faire venir [*ã-vwah-yeh sher-sheh, fer vuh-neer*]
sender, expéditeur (m) [*ehk-speh-dee-tuhr*]
sense *n.*, sens (m) [*sãs*]
   common sense, bon sens [*bõ sãs*]
sensible, raisonnable [*re-zo-nahbl*]
sensitive, sensible [*sã-seebl*]
sentence, phrase (f) [*frahz*]
sentimental, sentimental, -aux (m, pl) [*sã-tee-mã-tahl, sã-tee-mã-toh*]
separate *adj.*, séparé [*seh-pah-reh*]
separate *v.*, séparer [*seh-pah-reh*]
separately, séparément [*seh-pah-reh-mã*]
separation, séparation (f) [*seh-pah-rah-syõ*]
September, septembre (m) [*sep-tãbr*]
sergeant, sergent (m) [*ser-zhã*]
series, série (f) [*seh-ree*]
serious, sérieux, -euse [*ser-yuh, ser-yuhz*]
seriously, sérieusement [*ser-yuhz-mã*]
sermon, sermon (m) [*ser-mõ*]
servant, domestique (m, f) [*do-mes-teek*]
serve *v.*, servir (irreg) [*ser-veer*]
service, service (m) [*ser-vees*]
service [church], office (m) [*o-fees*]
set *n.*, ensemble (m) [*ã-sãbl*]
set *v.*, mettre (irreg) [*metr*]
set [clock] *v.*, régler [*reh-gleh*]
settle *v.*, arranger [*ah-rã-zheh*]
seven, sept [*set*]
seventeen, dix-sept [*dee-set*]
seventh, septième [*set-yem*]
seventy, soixante-dix [*swah-sãt-dees*]
sever *v.*, rompre [*rõpr*]
several, plusieurs [*plü-zyuhr*]
severe, sévère [*seh-ver*]
sew *v.*, coudre (irreg) [*koodr*]

sewing machine, machine (f) à coudre [*mah-sheen ah koodr*]

sex, sexe (m) [*seks*]

shade, shadow *n.,* ombre (f) [*ŏbr*]

shady, ombragé [*ŏ-brah-zheh*]

shake *v.,* secouer [*suh-kweh*]

   shake hands, serrer la main [*seh-reh lah mē*]

shallow, peu profond [*puh pro-fŏ(d)*]

shame, *honte (f) [*ŏt*]

shameful, *honteux, -euse [*ŏ-tuh, ŏ-tuhz*]

shampoo *n.,* shampooing (m) [*shā-pwē*]

shape *n.,* forme (f) [*form*]

share [portion] *n.,* part (f) [*pahr*]

share [stock] *n.,* action (f) [*ahk-syŏ*]

share *v.,* partager [*pahr-tah-zheh*]

sharp, aiguisé, pointu [*eh-ghee-zeh, pwē-tü*]

sharpen *v.,* aiguiser [*eh-ghee-zeh*]

shave *v.,* se raser [*srah-zeh*]

shaving brush, blaireau (m), -eaux (pl) [*ble-roh*]

shaving soap, savon à barbe [*sah-vŏ ah bahrb*]

shawl, châle (m) [*shahl*]

she, elle [*el*]

sheet [bedding], drap (m) [*drah*]

sheet [leaf], feuille (f) [*fuhy*]

shelf, étagère (f), rayon (m) [*eh-tah-zher, re-yŏ*]

shell [seashell], coquillage (m) [*ko-kee-yazh*]

shell [eggshell], coquille (f) [*ko-keey*]

shelter *n.,* abri (m) [*ah-bree*]

shift *v.,* changer [*shā-zheh*]

   shift gears, changer de vitesse [*shā-zhehd vee-tes*]

shine *v.,* briller [*bree-yeh*]

shine [shoes] *v.,* cirer [*see-reh*]

ship *n.,* navire (m) [*nah-veer*]

ship *v.,* expédier [*ehks-peh-dyeh*]

shipment, envoi (m) [*ā-vwah*]

shipwreck, naufrage (m) [*noh-frazh*]

shirt, chemise (f) [*shmeez*]

shiver *v.,* trembler de froid [*trā-bleh duh frwah*]

shock *n.,* choc (m) [*shok*]

shock *v.*, choquer [*sho-keh*]
shoe, chaussure (f) [*shoh-sür*]
shoemaker, cordonnier (m) [*kor-do-nyeh*]
shoeshine boy, cireur (m) [*see-ruhr*]
shoot *v.*, tirer [*tee-reh*]
shop *n.*, magasin (m), boutique (f) [*mah-gah-zē, boo-teek*]
shop *v.*, faire des achats [*fer deh-zah-shah*]
shop window, vitrine (f) [*vee-treen*]
shore, rivage (m) [*ree-vahzh*]
short, court [*koor(t)*]
  in a short time, dans un petit moment [*dã-zē ptee mo-mã*]
shorts, short (m) [*short*]
shortsighted, myope [*myop*]
should:
    We should leave, Nous devrions partir [*noo duh-vree-yō pahr-teer*]
    We should have left, Nous aurions dû partir [*noo-zor-yō dü pahr-teer*]
shoulder, épaule (f) [*eh-pohl*]
shout *v.*, crier [*kree-yeh*]
shovel, pelle (f) [*pel*]
show *n.*, spectacle (m) [*spek-tahkl*]
show *v.*, montrer [*mõ-treh*]
shower [bath] *n.*, douche (f) [*doosh*]
shower [rain] *n.*, averse [*ah-vers*]
shrimp, crevette (f) [*kruh-vet*]
shrink *v.*, rétrécir [*reh-treh-seer*]
shudder *v.*, frémir [*freh-meer*]
shut *v.*, fermer [*fer-meh*]
  shut in, enfermer [*ã-fer-meh*]
shutter, volet (m) [*vo-leh*]
shy, timide [*tee-meed*]
sick, malade [*mah-lahd*]
sickness, maladie (f) [*mah-lah-dee*]
side, côté (m) [*koh-teh*]
sideboard, buffet (m) [*bü-feh*]
sidewalk, trottoir (m) [*tro-twahr*]
sidewalk café, terrasse (f) du café [*te-ras dü kah-feh*]

sideways, de côté [*duh koh-teh*]

sigh *n.,* soupir (m) [*soo-peer*]

sight, vue (f) [*vü*]

sightseeing, visite (f) des curiosités [*vee-zeet deh kür-yoh-zee-teh*]

sign [mark] *n.,* signe (m) [*seeñ*]

sign [display] *n.,* enseigne (f) [*ã-señ*]

sign *v.,* signer [*see-nyeh*]

signal *n.,* signal (m), -aux (pl) [*see-nyahl, see-nyoh*]

signal *v.,* signaler [*see-nyah-leh*]

signature, signature (f) [*see-nyah-tür*]

signpost, poteau indicateur (m) [*poh-toh ẽ-dee-kah-tuhr*]

silence *n.,* silence (m) [*see-lãs*]

silent, silencieux, -euse [*see-lã-syuh, see-lã-syuhz*]

silently, silencieusement [*see-lã-syuhz-mã*]

silk, soie (f) [*swah*]

silly, sot, sotte [*soh, sot*]

silver, argent (m) [*ahr-zhã*]

   sterling silver, argent massif [*ahr-zhã mah-seef*]

silverware, silver plate, argenterie (f) [*ahr-zhã-tree*]

similar, semblable [*sã-blabl*]

simple, simple [*sẽpl*]

simply, simplement [*sẽ-pluh-mã*]

sin *n.,* péché (m) [*peh-sheh*]

since *conj.,* puisque [*pweesk*]

since *adv. & prep.,* depuis [*duh-pwee*]

   Since when [have you been here], Depuis quand (êtes-vous ici) [*duh-pwee kã (et-voo-zee-see)*]

   I have been here since Friday, Je suis ici depuis vendredi [*zhuh swee-zee-see-seed pwee vã-druh-dee*]

sincere, sincère [*sẽ-ser*]

sincerely yours [close of personal letter], bien amicalement [*byẽ-nah-mee-kahl-mã*]

sincerely yours [close of business letter], Veuillez agréer, Monsieur (Madame), l'expression de mes sentiments distingués [*not spoken*]

sing *v.,* chanter [*shã-teh*]

singer, chanteur, chanteuse [*shã-tuhr, shã-tuhz*]

single [sole], seul [*suhl*]
single [unmarried], célibataire [*seh-lee-bah-ter*]
sink *n.*, évier (m) [*eh-vyeh*]
sir, Monsieur [*muh-syuh*]
  Dear Sir, Monsieur [*muh-syuh*]
sister, soeur (f) [*suhr*]
sister-in-law, belle-soeur (f) [*bel-suhr*]
sit [be seated] *v.*, être assis [*etr ah-see*]
  sit down *v.*, s'asseoir (irreg) [*sahs-wahr*]
  Sit down, Asseyez-vous [*ah-seh-yeh-voo*]
situation, situation (f) [*see-twah-syõ*]
six, six [*sees*]
sixteen, seize [*sez*]
sixth, sixième [*see-zyem*]
sixty, soixante [*swah-sãt*]
size, dimension (f) [*dee-mã-syõ*]
size [of clothing], taille (f) [*tahy*]
skate *v.*, patiner [*pah-tee-neh*]
  ice skates, patins à glace [*pah-tẽ ah glahs*]
  roller skates, patins à roulettes [*pah-tẽ ah roo-let*]
skating rink, patinoire (f) [*pah-tee-nwahr*]
skeleton, squelette (f) [*skuh-let*]
sketch *n.*, croquis (m) [*kro-kee*]
sketch *v.*, esquisser [*es-kee-seh*]
ski *v.*, faire du ski [*fer dü skee*]
skid *v.*, déraper [*deh-rah-peh*]
skill, habileté (f) [*ah-beel-teh*]
skillful, habile [*ah-beel*]
skin, peau (f), peaux (pl) [*poh*]
skinny, maigre [*megr*]
skirt, jupe (f) [*zhüp*]
skull, crâne (m) [*krahn*]
sky, ciel (m), cieux (pl) [*syel, syuh*]
skyscraper, gratte-ciel (m) [*graht-syel*]
slang, argot (m) [*ahr-goh*]
slap *n.*, gifle (f) [*zheefl*]
slap *v.*, giffler [*zhee-fleh*]
slave, esclave (m, f) [*es-klahv*]

slavery, exclavage (m) [*es-klah-vazh*]
sleep *v.,* dormir (irreg) [*dor-meer*]
sleep *n.,* sommeil (m) [*so-mey*]
sleeping car, wagon-lit (m) [*vah-gō-lee*]
sleepy: to be sleepy, avoir sommeil [*ah-vwahr so-mey*]
sleeve, manche (f) [*mãsh*]
slender, mince [*mēs*]
slice *n.,* tranche (f) [*trãsh*]
slice *v.,* couper en tranches [*koo-peh ã trãsh*]
slide *v.,* glisser [*glee-seh*]
slip *v.,* glisser [*glee-seh*]
slip [woman's undergarment] *n.,* combinaison (f) [*kō-bee-ne-zō*]
slipper, pantoufle (f) [*pã-toofl*]
slippery, glissant [*glee-sã(t)*]
slow, lent [*lã(t)*]
slowly, lentement [*lãt-mã*]
small, petit [*ptee(t)*]
smaller, plus petit [*plü ptee(t)*]
smallpox, variole (f) [*vahr-yol*]
smell *n.,* odeur (f) [*oh-duhr*]
smell *v.,* sentir (irreg) [*sã-teer*]
smile *n.,* sourire (m) [*soo-reer*]
smile *v.,* sourire (irreg) [*soo-reer*]
smoke *n.,* fumée (f) [*fü-meh*]
smoke *v.,* fumer [*fü-meh*]
smoking car, fumeur (m) [*fü-muhr*]
smooth, lisse [*lees*]
snack, goûter (m) [*goo-teh*]
snail, escargot (m) [*es-kahr-goh*]
snake, serpent (m) [*ser-pã*]
sneeze *v.,* éternuer [*eh-ter-nweh*]
snore *v.,* ronfler [*rō-fleh*]
snow *n.,* neige (f) [*nezh*]
snow *v.,* neiger [*neh-zheh*]
  It's snowing, Il neige [*eel nezh*]
snowflake, flocon (m) de neige [*flo-kōd nezh*]
snowstorm, tempête (f) de neige [*tã-ped duh nezh*]

so [thus], ainsi [*ē-see*]
  and so forth, et ainsi de suite [*eh ē-seet sweet*]
  I don't think so, Je ne le crois pas [*zhuhn luh krwah pah*]
  I think so, Je crois que oui [*shkrwahk wee*]
  so that, afin que (plus subj. clause); afin de (plus infin.)
    [*ah-fē kuh, ah-fē duh*]
so [much], si, tellement [*see, tel-mã*]
  She was so nice, Elle était si gentille [*e-leh-te see zhã-teey*]
  so far, jusqu'ici; jusqu'à un certain point [*zhüs-kee-see; zhüs-kah ē ser-tē pwē*]
  so much, so many, tant de [*tã duh*]
  so-so, comme ci comme ça [*kom see kom sah*]
soap, savon (m) [*sah-võ*]
sober [temperate], sobre [*sobr*]
sober [not drunk], pas ivre [*pah-zeevr*]
social, social, -aux (m, pl) [*so-syahl, so-syoh*]
socialist *n. & adj.,* socialiste (m, f) [*so-syah-leest*]
society, société (f) [*so-syeh-teh*]
sock [apparel], chaussette (f) [*shoh-set*]
soda [bicarbonate], bicarbonate (m) (de soude) [*bee-kahr-bo-naht (duh sood)*]
soda water, soda (m) [*so-dah*]
sofa, sofa (m) [*soh-fah*]
soft, mou, molle [*moo, mol*]
soiled, sali [*sah-lee*]
soldier, soldat (m) [*sol-dah*]
sole *adj.,* seul, unique [*suhl, ü-neek*]
sole [fish] *n.,* sole (f) [*sol*]
sole [of shoe] *n.,* semelle (f) [*smel*]
solid, solide [*so-leed*]
solitary, solitaire [*so-lee-ter*]
solution, solution (f) [*sol-lü-syõ*]
solve *v.,* résoudre (irreg) [*reh-zoodr*]
some [partitive], de, du, de la, des [*duh, dü, duh lah, deh*]
some [certain], quelque(s) [*kelk*]
someone, quelqu'un [*kel-kē*]
something, quelque chose [*kel-kuh shohz*]
sometimes, quelquefois [*kel-kuh-fwah*]

somewhat, quelque peu [*kel-kuh puh*]
somewhere, quelque part [*kel-kuh pahr*]
somewhere else, quelque part ailleurs [*kel-kuh pahr ah-yuhr*]
son, fils (m) [*fees*]
son-in-law, gendre (m) [*zhãdr*]
song, chanson (f) [*shã-sõ*]
soon, bientôt [*byĕ-toh*]
   as soon as, aussitôt que [*oh-see-toh kuh*]
sooner, plus tôt [*plü toh*]
   sooner or later, tôt ou tard [*toh oo tahr*]
sore *adj.,* douloureux, -euse [*doo-loo-ruh, doo-loo-ruhz*]
sore throat, mal de gorge (m) [*mahl duh gorzh*]
sorrow, chagrin (m) [*shah-grĕ*]
sorrowful, triste [*treest*]
sorry, désolé [*deh-zo-leh*]
   I'm very sorry, Je suis désolé [*zhuh swee deh-zo-leh*]
   be sorry for *v.,* plaindre (irreg) [*plĕdr*]
sort *n.,* sorte (f) [*sort*]
soul, âme (f) [*ahm*]
sound *n.,* son (m) [*sõ*]
sound *v.,* sonner [*so-neh*]
soundproof, insonorisé [*ĕ-so-no-ree-zeh*]
soup, soupe (f) [*soop*]
sour, aigre [*egr*]
south, sud (m) [*süd*]
South America, Amérique du Sud (f) [*ah-me-reek dü süd*]
souvenir, souvenir (m) [*soov-neer*]
space, espace (m) [*es-pahs*]
spacious, spacieux, -euse [*spah-syuh, spah-syuhz*]
Spain, Espagne (f) [*es-pahñ*]
Spaniard, Espagnol, -ole [*es-pah-nyol*]
Spanish, espagnol [*es-pah-nyol*]
spare, de rechange [*duhr-shãzh*]
   spare parts, pièces de rechange [*pyes duhr-shãzh*]
   spare tire, roue (f) de secours [*roo d(uh) suh-koor*]
spark, étincelle (f) [*eh-tĕ-sεl*]
sparkplug, bougie (f) [*boo-zhee*]
speak *v.,* parler [*pahr-leh*]

Do you speak English? Parlez-vous anglais? [*par-leh-voo ã-gle*]

special, spécial, -aux (m, pl) [*speh-syahl, speh-syoh*]

special delivery, express [*ek-spres*]

specialist, spécialiste (m, f) [*speh-syah-leest*]

specialty, spécialité (f) [*speh-syah-lee-teh*]

spectacle, spectacle (m) [*spek-tahkl*]

spectacles [glasses], lunettes (f, pl) [*lii-net*]

spectator, spectateur, -trice [*spek-tah-tuhr, spek-tah-trees*]

speech, discours (m) [*dees-koor*]

speed, vitesse (f) [*vee-tes*]

   at full speed, à toute vitesse [*ah toot vee-tes*]

speed limit, limitation de vitesse (f) [*lee-mee-ta-syõd vee-tes*]

speedy, rapide [*rah-peed*]

spell *v.,* épeler [*eh-pleh*]

spelling, orthographe (f) [*or-toh-grahf*]

spend [money] *v.,* dépenser [*deh-pã-seh*]

spend [time] *v.,* passer [*pah-seh*]

spice, épice (f) [*eh-pees*]

spider, araignée (f) [*ah-re-nyeh*]

spill *v.,* renverser [*rã-ver-seh*]

spinach, épinards (m, pl) [*eh-pee-nahr*]

spine, colonne vertébrale (f) [*ko-lon ver-teh-brahl*]

spirit, esprit (m) [*es-pree*]

spiritual, spirituel, -elle [*spee-ree-twel*]

spit *v.,* cracher [*krah-sheh*]

spite: in spite of, malgré [*mahl-greh*]

splendid, splendide [*splã-deed*]

spoil *v.,* gâter [*gah-teh*]

sponge, éponge (f) [*eh-põzh*]

spoon, cuillère (f) [*kwee-yer*]

spoonful, cuillerée (f) [*kweey-reh*]

sport, sport (m) [*spor*]

spot [stain] *n.,* tâche (f) [*tahsh*]

spouse, époux, -ouse [*eh-poo, eh-pooz*]

sprain *n.,* entorse (f) [*ã-tors*]

sprain *v.,* fouler [*foo-leh*]

spray *v.,* asperger [*ahs-per-zheh*]

spread *v.*, étendre [*eh-tãdr*]

spring [season] *n.*, printemps (m) [*prē-tã*]

spring [water] *n.*, source (f) [*soors*]

spring [of watch] *n.*, ressort (m) [*ruh-sor*]

spy *n.*, espion (m) [*ehs-pyõ*]

square [public], place (f) [*plahs*]

square [plane figure], carré (m) [*kah-reh*]

squeak *v.*, grincer [*grē-seh*]

squeeze *v.*, serrer [*seh-reh*]

stable *n.*, écurie (f) [*eh-kü-ree*]

stadium, stade (m) [*stahd*]

stage [theatre] *n.*, scène (f) [*sen*]

stage [degree] *n.*, stade (m) [*stahd*]

stain *n.*, tâche (f) [*tahsh*]

stain *v.*, tâcher [*tah-sheh*]

stained glass window, vitrail (m), -aux (m, pl) [*vee-trahy, vee-troh*]

stairs, escalier (m) [*es-kah-lyeh*]

stall [auto] *v.*, caler, se caler [*kah-leh, skah-leh*]

stamp *n.*, timbre (m) [*tēbr*]

stand *v.*, être (se tenir, rester) debout [*etr (stuh-neer, res-teh) duh-boo*]

  stand up, se lever [*sluh-veh*]

standing *adj.*, debout [*duh-boo*]

standing *n.*, position sociale (f) [*poh-zee-syõ so-syahl*]

standpoint, point (m) de vue [*pwē d(uh) vü*]

star, étoile (f) [*eh-twahl*]

starboard, tribord (m) [*tree-bor*]

starch, amidon (m) [*ah-mee-dõ*]

start *n.*, départ (m) [*deh-pahr*]

start *v.*, commencer [*ko-mã-seh*]

start [an auto] *v.*, démarrer [*deh-mah-reh*]

starter [auto], démarreur (m) [*deh-mah-ruhr*]

starve *v.*, mourir (irreg) de faim [*moo-reer duh fē*]

state *n.*, état (m) [*eh-tah*]

state *v.*, déclarer [*deh-klah-reh*]

statement, déclaration (f) [*deh-klah-rah-syõ*]

stateroom, cabine (f) [*kah-been*]

statesman, homme (m) d'état [*om deh-tah*]
station, gare (f) [*gahr*]
stationary, stationnaire [*stah-syo-ner*]
stationery, papier (m) à lettres [*pah-pyeh ah letr*]
statue, statue (f) [*stah-tü*]
stay *v.,* rester (*Aux:* ÊTRE) [*res-teh*]
  stay at a hotel, descendre (*Aux:* ÊTRE) dans un hôtel
    [*deh-sãdr dã-zē-noh-tel*]
steady, ferme [*ferm*]
steak, biftek (m) [*beef-tek*]
steal *v.,* voler [*vo-leh*]
steam, vapeur (f) [*vah-puhr*]
steamship line, compagnie de navigation (f) [*kõ-pa-need(uh)*
    nah-vee-gah-syõ]
steel, acier (m) [*ah-syeh*]
steep, raide [*red*]
steering wheel, volant (m) [*vo-lã*]
stenographer, sténo (m, f) [*steh-noh*]
step *n.,* pas (m) [*pah*]
step *v.,* faire un (des) pas [*fer ē (deh) pah*]
stepfather, beau-père (m) [*boh-per*]
stepmother, belle-mère (f) [*bel-mer*]
sterilized *v.,* stérilisé [*steh-ree-lee-zeh*]
steward, garçon (m) de cabine [*gar-sõt kah-been*]
stewardess, hôtesse (f) de l'air [*oh-tes duh ler*]
stick *n.,* bâton (m) [*bah-tõ*]
stick [prick] *v.,* piquer [*pee-keh*]
stick [adhere] *v.,* coller [*ko-leh*]
still [yet], encore [*ã-kor*]
stimulant, stimulant (m) [*stee-mü-lã*]
sting *n.,* piqûre (f) [*pee-kür*]
sting *v.,* piquer [*pee-keh*]
stitch *n.,* point (m) [*pwē*]
stitch *v.,* piquer [*pee-keh*]
stock [supply] *n.,* provision (f) [*pro-vee zyõ*]
  in stock, en magasin [*ã mah-gah-zē*]
stock [financial] *n.,* actions (f, pl) [*ahk-syõ*]
stockbroker, agent (m) de change [*ah-zhãd(uh) shãzh*]

stock exchange, bourse (f) [*boors*]

stocking, bas (m) [*bah*]

   I have a run in my stocking, J'ai filé un bas [*zheh fee-leh
   ē bah*]

stomach, estomac (m) [*es-to-mah*]

stomachache, mal (m) à l'estomac [*mahl ah les-to-mah*]

stone, pierre (f) [*pyer*]

stop *n.,* arrêt (m) [*ah-re*]

stop *v.,* arrêter, s'arrêter [*ah-re-teh, sah-re-teh*]

   stop (from) *v.,* empêcher (de) [*ã-peh-sheh (duh)*]

   Stop! Arrêtez! [*ah-re-teh*]

   Stop that! Arrêtez de faire cela! [*ah-re-teh duh fer sah*]

store *n.,* magasin (m) [*mah-gah-zē*]

   department store, grand magasin (m) [*grã mah-gah-zē*]

store *v.,* mettre en garde-meuble [*met-rã gahr-duh-muhbl*]

storm, orage (m) [*o-rahzh*]

story [tale], histoire (f) [*ees-twahr*]

story [floor], étage (m) [*eh-tahzh*]

stove, cuisinière (f) [*kwee-zee-nyer*]

straight, droit [*drwah(t)*]

   straight ahead, tout droit [*too drwah*]

strain *n.,* tension (f) [*tã-syõ*]

strange, étrange [*eh-trãzh*]

stranger, étranger, -ère [*eh-trã-zheh, eh-trã-zher*]

strap, courroie (f) [*koor-wah*]

straw, paille (f) [*pahy*]

strawberry, fraise (f) [*frez*]

stream, ruisseau (m), -eaux (pl) [*rwee-soh*]

street, rue (f) [*rü*]

streetcar, tramway (m) [*trahm-weh*]

strength, force (f) [*fors*]

strengthen *v.,* renforcer [*rã-for-seh*]

stress *v.,* insister (sur) [*ē-sees-teh (sür)*]

strike [hit] *v.,* frapper [*frah-peh*]

strike [cease working] *v.,* faire grève [*fer grev*]

strike [by labor] *n.,* grève (f) [*grev*]

string, ficelle (f) [*fee-sel*]

strong, fort [*for*]
structure, structure (f) [*strük-tür*]
struggle *n.*, lutte (f) [*lüt*]
struggle *v.*, lutter [*lü-teh*]
stubborn, têtu [*teh-tü*]
student *n. & adj.*, étudiant, -te [*eh-tü-dyã(t)*]
study *n.*, étude (f) [*eh-tüd*]
study *v.*, étudier [*eh-tü-dyeh*]
stumble *v.*, trébucher [*tre-bü-sheh*]
stupid, stupide [*stü-peed*]
style, style (m) [*steel*]
subject *n.*, sujet (m) [*sü-zheh*]
submarine, sous-marin (m) [*soo-mah-rē*]
submit *v.*, soumettre (irreg) [*soo-metr*]
subscribe [to magazine] *v.*, s'abonner [*sah-bo-neh*]
subsidize *v.*, subventionner [*süb-vã-syo-neh*]
subsidy, subvention (f) [*süb-vã-syõ*]
substantial, -elle [*süb-stã-syel*]
substitute *v.*, substituer [*süb-stee-tweh*]
subtraction, soustraction (f) [*soos-trak-syõ*]
suburb, banlieue (f) [*bã-lyuh*]
subway, métro (m) [*meh-troh*]
succeed *v.*, réussir [*reh-ü-seer*]
success, succès (m) [*sük-se*]
such, tel, telle [*tel*]
  such as, tel (telle) que [*tel kuh*]
sudden, soudain [*soo-dē, soo-den*]
suddenly, tout à coup [*too-tah koo*]
suffer *v.*, souffrir (irreg) [*soo-freer*]
sugar, sucre (m) [*sükr*]
sugar bowl, sucrier (m) [*sü-kree-yeh*]
suggest *v.*, suggérer [*süg-zheh-reh*]
suggestion, suggestion (f) [*süg-zhes-tyõ*]
suicide, suicide (m) [*swee-seed*]
  commit suicide *v.*, se suicider [*suh swee-see-deh*]
suit [of clothing] *n.*, costume (m), tailleur (m) [*kos-tüm, tah-yuhr*]

suit *v.*, convenir *(irreg)* [*kŏv-neer*]
suitable, convenable [*kŏv-nahbl*]
suitcase, valise (f) [*vah-leez*]
sum *n.*, somme (f) [*som*]
sum up *v.*, résumer [*reh-zü-meh*]
summary, résumé (m) [*reh-zü-meh*]
summer, été (m) [*eh-teh*]
sun, soleil (m) [*so-ley*]
sunburn, coup (m) de soleil [*koo d(uh) so-ley*]
Sunday, dimanche (m) [*dee-māsh*]
sunglasses, lunettes (f, pl) de soleil [*lü-ned duh so-ley*]
sunrise, lever (m) du soleil [*luh-veh dü so-ley*]
sunset, coucher (m) du soleil [*koo-sheh dü so-ley*]
sunshine, lumière (f) du soleil [*lü-myer dü so-ley*]
   in the sunshine, au soleil [*oh so-ley*]
suntanned, bronzé [*brŏ-zeh*]
superb, superbe [*sü-perb*]
superficial, superficiel, -elle [*sü-per-fee-syel*]
superior, supérieur [*sü-per-yuhr*]
superstitious, superstitieux, -euse [*sü-per-stee-syuh, sü-per-stee-syuhz*]
supper, souper (m) [*soo-peh*]
supply *n.*, provision (f) [*pro-vee-zyŏ*]
supply *v.*, fournir [*foor-neer*]
support *n.*, soutien (m) [*soo-tyĕ*]
support *v.*, soutenir (irreg) [*soot-neer*]
suppose *v.*, supposer [*sü-poh-zeh*]
supreme, suprême [*sü-prem*]
sure, sûr [*sür*]
surely, sûrement [*sür-mā*]
surface *n.*, surface (f) [*sür-fahs*]
surgeon, chirurgien, -ienne [*shee-rür-zhyĕ, shee-rür-zhyen, soop-so-nuhz*]
surgery, chirurgie (f) [*shee-rür-zhee*]
surprise *n.*, surprise (f) [*sür-preez*]
surprise *v.*, surprendre (irreg) [*sür-prādr*]
surprising, surprenant [*sür-pruh-nā(t)*]

surrender v., se rendre [*suh rãdr*]
surround v., entourer [*ã-too-reh*]
surroundings, environs (m, pl) [*ã-vee-rõ*]
survive v., survivre (irreg) [*sür-veevr*]
survivor, survivant, -te [*sür-vee-vã(t)*]
suspect n., suspect, -te [*süs-pe(kt)*]
suspect v., soupçonner [*soop-so-neh*]
suspenders, bretelles (f, pl) [*bruh-tel*]
suspicion, soupçon (m) [*soop-sõ*]
suspicious [distrustful], soupçonneux, -euse [*soop-so-nuh, soop-so-nuhz*]
suspicious [suspected], suspect [*süs-pe(kt)*]
swallow v., avaler [*ah-vah-leh*]
swear v., jurer [*zhü-reh*]
sweater, chandail (m) [*shã-dahy*]
Sweden, Suède (f) [*swed*]
Swedish, suèdois [*sweh-dwah(z)*]
sweep v., balayer [*bah-le-yeh*]
sweet adj., doux, douce; sucré [*doo, doos; sü-kreh*]
sweetheart, chéri, -ie [*sheh-ree*]
swim v., nager [*nah-zheh*]
swimming, nage (f) [*nahzh*]
swimming pool, piscine (f) [*pee-seen*]
swimsuit, maillot (m) de bain [*mah-yoh duh bẽ*]
Swiss, suisse [*swees*]
switch [elec.] n., interrupteur (m) [*ẽ-te-rüp-tuhr*]
Switzerland, Suisse (f) [*swees*]
swollen, enflé [ã-fleh]
sword, épée (f) [*eh-peh*]
syllable, syllabe (f) [*see-lahb*]
sympathy, compassion (f) [*kõ-pah-syõ*]
  My deepest sympathy, Mes condoléances sincères [*meh kõ-do-leh-ãs sẽ-ser*]
symphony, symphonie (f) [*sẽ-fo-nee*]
symptom, symptôme (m) [*sẽp-tohm*]
synthetic, synthétique [*sẽ-teh-teek*]
system, système (m) [*sees-tem*]
systematic, systématique [*sees-teh-mah-teek*]

T

table, table (f) [*tahbl*]
   set the table *v.*, mettre (irreg) le couvert [*metr luh koo-ver*]
tablecloth, nappe (f) [*nahp*]
tablespoon, cuillère (f) à soupe [*kwee-yer ah soop*]
tablet [pill], comprimé (m) [*kõ-pree-meh*]
tack [thumb tack] *n.*, punaise (f) [*pü-nez*]
tack [small nail] *n.*, petit clou (m) [*ptee kloo*]
tact, tact (m) [*tahkt*]
tail, queue (f) [*kuh*]
tailor, tailleur (m) [*tah-yuhr*]
take *v.*, prendre (irreg) [*prãdr*]
   take advantage of, profiter de [*pro-fee-teh duh*]
   take after, ressembler à [*ruh-sã-bleh ah*]
   take a walk, se promener [*sprom-neh*]
   take away, emporter [*ã-por-teh*]
   take back, reprendre (irreg) [*ruh-prãdr*]
   take care of, s'occuper de [*so-kü-peh duh*]
   take off, s'envoler [*sã-vo-leh*]
   take place, avoir lieu [*ah-vwahr lyuh*]
   take a seat, s'asseoir (irreg) [*sah-swahr*]
tale, conte (m) [*kõt*]
talent, talent (m) [*tah-lã*]
   be talented *v.*, avoir du talent [*ah-vwahr dü tah-lã*]
talk [conversation] *n.*, conversation (f) [*kõ-ver-sah-syõ*]
talk [speech] *n.*, discours (m) [*dees-koor*]
talk *v.*, parler [*pahr-leh*]
tall, grand [*grã(d)*]
tame *adj.*, domestiqué, dressé [*do-mes-tee-keh, dre-seh*]
tape, ruban (m), bande (f) [*rü-bã, bãd*]
tapestry, tapisserie (f) [*tah-pees-ree*]
tariff, droit (m) de douane [*drwah duh dwahn*]
task, tâche (f) [*tahsh*]

132

taste n., goût (m) [goo]
taste [something] v., goûter [goo-teh]
   This tastes like . . . Ceci a le goût de . . . [suh-see ahl goo duh]
tax v., imposer [ē-poh-zeh]
tax n., impôt (m) [ē-poh]
tax-free, exempt d'impôts [ehg-zã dē-poh]
taxi, taxi (m) [tahk-see]
tea, thé (m) [teh]
   iced tea, thé glacé [teh glah-seh]
teach v., enseigner [ã-se-nyeh]
teacher, enseignant, -te [ã-se-nyã, ã-se-nyãt]
teaching, enseignement (m) [ã-se-nyuh-mã]
teacup, tasse (f) à thé [tahs ah teh]
team, équipe (f) [eh-keep]
teapot, théière (f) [teh-yer]
tear v., déchirer [deh-shee-reh]
teardrop n., larme (f) [lahrm]
teaspoon, petite cuillère (f) [pteet kwee-yer]
technical, technique [tek-neek]
teeth pl., dents (f, pl) [dã]
telegram n., télégramme (m) [teh-leh-grahm]
telephone n., téléphone (m) [teh-leh-fon]
telephone v., téléphoner [teh-leh-fo-neh]
telephone book, annuaire (m) du téléphone [ah-nwer dü teh-leh-fon]
telephone booth, cabine (f) téléphonique [kah-been teh-leh-fo-neek]
telephone call, coup (m) de téléphone [koot teh-leh-fon]
telephone number, numéro (m) de téléphone [nü-meh-roh duh teh-leh-fon]
telephone operator, téléphoniste [teh-leh-fo-neest]
telescope, téléscope (m) [teh-leh-skop]
television, télévision (f), télé [teh-leh-vee-zyõ, teh-leh]
television set, poste (m) de télévision [pos-tuh duh teh-leh-vee-zyõ]
tell v., dire (irreg) [deer]
teller, caissier -ière [ke-syeh, ke-syer]

temperature, température (f) [*tã-peh-rah-tür*]
temple [church], temple (m) [*tãpl*]
temporary, temporaire [*tã-po-rer*]
temptation, tentation (f) [*tã-tah-syõ*]
ten, dix [*dees*]
tenant, locataire (m, f) [*lo-kah-ter*]
tendancy, tendance (f) [*tã-dãs*]
tender, tendre [*tãdr*]
tenth, dixième [*dee-zyem*]
term, terme (m) [*term*]
terrace, terrasse (f) [*te-rahs*]
terrible, terrible [*teh-reebl*]
territory, territoire (m) [*teh-ree-twahr*]
terror, terreur (f) [*teh-ruhr*]
test *n.*, examen (m) [*eg-zah-mē*]
test *v.*, essayer [*e-se-yeh*]
testify *v.*, témoigner [*teh-mwah-nyeh*]
text, texte (m) [*tekst*]
textile *adj.*, textile [*teks-teel*]
than, que, qu' [*kuh*]
thank *v.*, remercier [*r(uh)-mer-syeh*]
  Thank you, Merci [*mer-see*]
thankful, reconnaissant [*r(uh)-ko-ne-sã(t)*]
that *demons. adj.*, ce (m), cet (m), cette (f) [*suh, set*]
that *demons. pron.*, cela, ça [*suh-lah, sah*]
  Give me that, Donnez-moi cela (ça) [*do-neh-mwah slah
    (sah)*]
that *rel. pron.*, qui, que [*kee, kuh*]
that *conj.*, que [*kuh*]
  I hope (that) you will come, J'espère que vous viendrez
    [*zhes-per kuh voo vyē-dreh*]
the, le (m, sing), la (f, sing), les (m & f, pl) [*luh, lah, leh*]
theater, théâtre (m) [*teh-ahtr*]
theft, vol (m) [*vol*]
their, leur, leurs [*luhr*]
theirs, le leur, la leur; les leurs [*luh luhr, lah luhr; leh luhr*]
them, les; leur; eux (m), elles (f) [*leh; luhr; uh, el*]
themselves, eux-mêmes (m), elles-mêmes (f) [*uh-mem, el-*

mem]

then [at that time], alors [*ah-lor*]
then [afterwards], ensuite [*ã-sweet*]
  now and then, de temps en temps [*duh tã-zã tã*]
theory, théorie (f) [*teh-o-ree*]
there, là [*lah*]
  there is, there are, il y a [*eel yah*]
therefore, donc [*dõk*]
thermometer, thermomètre (m) [*ter-mo-metr*]
these *adj.*, ces [*seh*]
these *pron.*, ceux-ci, celles-ci [*suh-see, sel-see*]
they, ils, eux (m); elles (f); on (impersonal) [*eel, uh; el; õ*]
thick, épais, épaisse [*eh-pe, eh-pes*]
thief, voleur, -euse [*vo-luhr, vo-luhz*]
thin, mince [*mēs*]
thing, chose (f) [*shohz*]
think *v.*, penser [*pã-seh*]
  think of [bring to mind], penser à [*pã-seh ah*]
  think of [have an opinion], penser de [*pã-seh duh*]
third [ordinal] *adj.*, troisième [*trwah-zyem*]
third *n.*, tiers [*tyer*]
thirst, soif (f) [*swahf*]
  be thirsty *v.*, avoir soif [*ah-vwahr swahf*]
thirteen, treize [*trez*]
thirty, trente [*trãt*]
this *pron.*, ceci, ce, c' [*suh-see, suh, s'*]
this *adj.*, ce (m), cet (m), cette (f) [*suh, set, set*]
thorn, épine (f) [*eh-peen*]
thoroughly, à fond [*ah fõ*]
those *adj.*, ces [*seh*]
those *pron.*, ceux-ci, celles-ci [*suh-see, sel-see*]
though, bien que [*byẽ kuh*]
thought *n.*, pensée (f) [*pã-seh*]
thoughtful, attentif, -tive [*ah-tã-teef, ah-tã-teev*]
thousand, mille (m, invar) [*meel*]
thread, fil (m) [*feel*]
threat, menace (f) [*muh-nahs*]
threaten *v.*, menacer [*muh-nah-seh*]

three, trois [*trwah*]
thrifty, économe [*eh-ko-nom*]
throat, gorge (f) [*gorzh*]
throne, trône (m) [*trohn*]
through *prep.,* à travers [*ah trah-ver*]
through [finished] *adj.,* fini [*fee-nee*]
  I'm through, J'ai fini [*zheh fee-nee*]
throw *v.,* jeter [*zh(uh)-teh*]
thumb, pouce (m) [*poos*]
thunder, tonnerre (m) [*to-ner*]
Thursday, jeudi (m) [*zhuh-dee*]
thus, ainsi [*ē-see*]
ticket, billet (m) [*bee-ye*]
ticket collector, contrôleur (m) [*kō-troh-luhr*]
ticket window, guichet (m) [*ghee-she*]
tide, marée (f) [*mah-reh*]
tie [apparel] *n.,* cravate (f) [*krah-vaht*]
tie *v.,* lier [*lee-yeh*]
tight, serré [*se-reh*]
tighten *v.,* resserrer [*ruh-se-reh*]
till [until], jusqu'à [*zhüs-kah*]
time [duration], temps (m) [*tã*]
  at the same time, en même temps [*ã mem tã*]
  Have a good time, Amusez-vous bien [*ah-müz-eh voo byē*]
  What time is it? Quelle heure est-il? [*ke-luhr e-teel*]
time [instance], fois (f) [*fwah*]
  at times, des fois [*deh fwah*]
timetable, horaire (m) [*o-rer*]
timid, timide [*tee-meed*]
tin, étain (m) [*eh-tē*]
tip [gratuity] *n.,* pourboire (m) [*poor-bwahr*]
tip [point] *n.,* bout (m), pointe (f) [*boo, pwēt*]
tire [of a car] *n.,* pneu (m) [*pnuh*]
  flat tire, pneu crevé (m) [*pnuh kruh-veh*]
tired, fatigué [*fah-tee-gheh*]
tissue paper, papier (m) de soie [*pah-pyeh duh swah*]
title, titre (m) [*teetr*]
to, à, en, vers [*ah, ã, ver*]

toast [bread] *n.*, pain grillé (m) [*pē gree-yeh*]

toaster, grille-pain (m) [*greey-pē*]

tobacco, tabac (m) [*tah-bah*]

tobacco store, bureau (m) de tabac [*bü-rohd tah-bah*]

today, aujourd'hui [*oh-zhoor-dwee*]

toe, orteil (m) [*or-tey*]

together, ensemble [*ã-sãbl*]

toilet [bath room], cabinet (m) [*kah-bee-neh*]

toilet [grooming], toilette (f) [*twah-let*]

tolerate *v.*, tolérer [*to-leh-reh*]

toll [fee] *n.*, péage (m) [*peh-ahzh*]

tomato, tomate (f) [*to-maht*]

tomato juice, jus (m) de tomate [*zhüt to-maht*]

tomb, tombe (f) [*tõb*]

tomorrow, demain [*d(uh)-mē*]

  tomorrow evening, demain soir [*d(uh)-mē swahr*]

  tomorrow morning, demain matin [*d(uh)-mē mah-tē*]

ton, tonne (f) [*ton*]

tone, ton (m) [*tõ*]

tongue, langue (f) [*lãg*]

tonight, ce soir [*suh swahr*]

tonsils, amygdales (f, pl) [*ah-mee-dahl*]

too [also], aussi [*oh-see*]

  too much, too many, trop (de) [*troh (duh)*]

tool, outil (m) [*oo-tee*]

tooth, dent (f) [*dã*]

toothache, mal (m) de dents [*mahl duh dã*]

toothbrush, brosse (f) à dents [*bros ah dã*]

toothpaste, pâte dentifrice (f) [*paht dã-tee-frees*]

toothpick, cure-dents (m, inv) [*kür-dã*]

top [highest point] *n.*, *haut (m), sommet (m) [*oh, so-me*]

top [surface] *n.*, dessus (m) [*duh-sü*]

  on top of, sur [*sür*]

tornado, tornade (f) [*tor-nahd*]

torture *n.*, torture (f) [*tor-tür*]

torture *v.*, torturer [*tor-tü-reh*]

toss *v.*, lancer [*lã-seh*]

total *n.*, total, -aux (m, pl) [*to-tahl, to-toh*]

touch *v.*, toucher [*too-sheh*]
touching, touchant [*too-shã(t)*]
touchy, susceptible [*sü-sep-teebl*]
tough, dur [*dür*]
tour *n.*, tour (m) [*toor*]
tourist, touriste (m, f) [*too-reest*]
tourist office, office (m) du tourisme [*o-fees dü too-reesm*]
tow *v.*, remorquer [*r(uh)-mor-keh*]
tow truck, dépanneuse (f) [*deh-pah-nuhz*]
toward, vers [*ver*]
towel [bath], serviette (f) [*ser-vyet*]
tower, tour (f) [*toor*]
town, ville (f) [*veel*]
townhall, mairie (f) [*me-ree*]
toy, jouet (m) [*zhwe*]
trace *n.*, trace (f) [*trahs*]
track, piste (f) [*peest*]
trade *n.*, commerce (m) [*ko-mers*]
trade [exchange] *v.*, échanger [*eh-shã-zheh*]
trade [do business] *v.*, faire du commerce [*fer dü ko-mers*]
trademark, marque (f) de fabrique [*mahrk duh fah-breek*]
tradition, tradition (f) [*trah-dee-syõ*]
traditional, traditionnel, -elle [*trah-dee-syo-nel*]
traffic, circulation (f) [*seer-kü-lah-syõ*]
tragedy, tragédie (f) [*trah-zheh-dee*]
tragic, tragique [*trah-zheek*]
trail *n.*, piste (f) [*peest*]
train *n.*, train (m) [*trẽ*]
train [educate] *v.*, former [*for-meh*]
train [coach] *v.*, entraîner [*ã-tre-neh*]
training [sports], entraînement (m) [*ã-tren-mã*]
training [school, job], formation (f) [*for-mah-syõ*]
traitor, traître (m) [*tretr*]
transfer [connection] *n.*, correspondance (f) [*ko-res-põ-dãs*]
transform *v.*, transformer [*trãs-for-meh*]
transit, transit (m) [*trã-zeet*]
translate *v.*, traduire (irreg) [*trah-dweer*]
translation, traduction (f) [*trah-dük-syõ*]

translator, traducteur, -trice [*trah-dük-tuhr, trah-dük-trees*]
transmission, transmission (f) [*trãs-mee-syõ*]
transmit *v.,* transmettre (irreg) [*trãs-metr*]
transportation, transport (m) [*trãs-por*]
trap *n.,* piège (m) [*pyezh*]
travel *n.,* voyages (m, pl) [*vwah-yahzh*]
travel *v.,* voyager [*vwah-yah-zheh*]
travel agency, agence (f) de voyages [*ah-zhãs duh vwah-yahzh*]
traveler, voyageur, -euse [*vwah-yah-zhuhr, vwah-yah-zhuhz*]
traveler's check, chèque (m) de voyage [*shek duh vwah-yahzh*]
tray, plateau (m), -eaux (pl) [*plah-toh*]
treason, trahison (f) [*trah-ee-sõ*]
treasure *n.,* trésor (m) [*treh-zor*]
treasurer, trésorier (m) [*tre-zor-yeh*]
treasury, trésorerie (f) [*tre-zor-ree*]
treat *n.,* régal (m), régals (pl) [*reh-gahl*]
  It's my treat, C'est moi qui paie [*se mwah kee pe*]
treat [entertain] *v.,* régaler [*reh-gah-leh*]
treat [deal with] *v.,* traiter [*tre-teh*]
treatment, traitement (m) [*tret-mã*]
treaty, traité (m) [*tre-teh*]
tree, arbre (m) [*ahrbr*]
tremble *v.,* trembler [*trã-bleh*]
trespass [on property] *v.,* entrer (*Aux:* ÊTRE) dans la propriété
  de [*ã-treh dã lah pro-pree-yeh-teh duh*]
  No trespassing, Défense d'entrée [*deh-fãs dã-treh*]
trial [test], essai (m) [*e-se*]
  trial and error, essais (m, pl) et erreurs (f, pl) [*e-se-zeh
    eh-ruhr*]
trial [at law], procès (m) [*pro-se*]
triangle, triangle (m) [*tree-yãgl*]
trick *n.,* tour (m) [*toor*]
  play a trick on *v.,* jouer un tour à [*jweh ẽ toor ah*]
tricycle, tricycle (m) [*tree-seekl*]
trip [journey] *n.,* voyage (m) [*vwah-yahzh*]
trip [stumble] *v.,* trébucher [*treh-bü-sheh*]
triumphant, triomphant [*tree-yõ-fã(t)*]

tropical, tropical, -aux (m, pl) [*tro-pee-kahl, tro-pee-koh*]
trouble *n.*, difficulté (f) [*dee-fee-kül-teh*]
   have car trouble *v.*, être en panne [*e-trã pahn*]
trouble *v.*, déranger [*deh-rã-zheh*]
trousers, pantalon (m) [*pã-tah-lõ*]
truck, camion (m) [*kah-myõ*]
true, vrai [*vre*]
trunk [container], malle (f) [*mahl*]
trunk [of tree], tronc (m) [*trõ*]
trunk [of car], coffre (m) [*kofr*]
trust *n.*, confiance (f) [*kõ-fyãs*]
trust *v.*, faire confiance [*fer kõ-fyãs*]
truth, vérité (f) [*veh-ree-teh*]
try *v.*, essayer [*e-se-yeh*]
   try on, essayer [*e-se-yeh*]
tube, tube (m) [*tüb*]
tuberculosis, tuberculose (f) [*tü-ber-kü-lohz*]
Tuesday, mardi (m) [*mahr-dee*]
tugboat, remorqueur (m) [*ruh-mor-kuhr*]
tune [melody], air (m) [*er*]
tunnel, tunnel (m) [*tü-nel*]
turkey, dinde (f) [*dẽd*]
Turkey, Turquie (f) [*tür-kee*]
Turkish, turc, turque [*türk*]
turn [order] *n.*, tour (m) [*toor*]
turn [curve] *n.*, virage (m) [*vee-rahzh*]
turn *v.*, tourner [*toor-neh*]
   turn around, retourner, se retourner [*r(uh)-toor-neh, sruh-toor-neh*]
   turn away, détourner, se détourner [*deh-toor-neh, sdeh-toor-neh*]
   turn off [light], éteindre (irreg) [*eh-tẽdr*]
   turn off [water], fermer [*fer-meh*]
   turn on [light], allumer [*ah-lümeh*]
   turn on [water], ouvrir [*oov-reer*]
turnip, navet (m) [*nah-ve*]
twelfth, douzième [*doo-zyem*]
twelve, douze [*dooz*]

twenty, vingt [*vẽ*]
twice, deux fois (f) [*duh fwah*]
twin *n.*, jumeau, jumelle [*zhü-moh, zhü-mel*]
twine, ficelle (f) [*fee-sel*]
twist *v.*, tordre [*tordr*]
two, deux [*duh*]
type *n.*, type (m) [*teep*]
typewriter, machine (f) à écrire [*mah-sheen ah eh-kreer*]
typical, typique [*tee-peek*]
typist, dactylographe (m, f), dactylo (m, f) [*dahk-tee-loh-graf, dahk-tee-loh*]
tyranny, tyrannie (f) [*tee-rah-nee*]
tyrant, tyran (m) [*tee-rã*]

U

ugly, laid [*le(d)*]
umbrella, parapluie (m) [*pah-rah-plwee*]
unable, incapable [*ẽ-kah-pahbl*]
unanimous, unanime [*ü-nah-neem*]
uncertain, incertain [*ẽ-ser-tẽ, ẽ-ser-ten*]
uncle, oncle (m) [*õkl*]
uncomfortable [of feelings], mal à l'aise [*mahl ah lez*]
uncomfortable [of things], peu confortable [*puh kõ-for-tahbl*]
unconscious, inconscient [*ẽ-kõ-syã(t)*]
uncover *v.*, découvrir (irreg) [*deh-koo-vreer*]
under, sous [*soo*]
underground, souterrain [*soo-te-rẽ, soo-te-ren*]
understand *v.*, comprendre (irreg) [*kõ-prãdr*]
undertake *v.*, entreprendre (irreg) [*ã-truh-prãdr*]
undertaker, entrepreneur (m) de pompes funèbres [*ã-truh-pruh-nuhr duh põp fü-nebr*]
underwear, sous-vêtements (m, pl) [*soo-vet-mã*]
undo *v.*, défaire (irreg) [*deh-fer*]
undress *v.*, déshabiller, se déshabiller [*deh-zah-bee-yeh,*

sdeh-zah-bee-yeh]
uneasy, mal à l'aise [*mahl ah lez*]
unemployed, en chômage [*ã shoh-mahzh*]
unemployment, chômage (m) [*shoh-mahzh*]
unequal, inégal, -aux (m, pl) [*ee-neh-gahl, ee-neh-goh*]
unexpected, inattendu [*ee-nah-tã-dü*]
unfair, injuste [*ẽ-zhüst*]
unfaithful, infidèle [*ẽ-fee-del*]
unfavorable, défavorable [*deh-fah-vo-rahbl*]
unforgettable, inoubliable [*ee-noo-blee-yahbl*]
unforeseen, imprévu [*ẽ-preh-vü*]
unforgivable, impardonnable [*ẽ-pahr-do-nahbl*]
unfortunate, malheureux, -euse [*mah-luh-ruh, mah-luh-ruhz*]
unfortunately, malheureusement [*mah-luh-ruhz-mã*]
ungrateful, ingrat [*ẽ-grah(t)*]
unhappy, malheureux, -euse [*mah-luh-ruh, mah-luh-ruhz*]
unhealthy, malsain [*mahl-sẽ, mahl-sen*]
uniform *adj.,* uniforme [*ü-nee-form*]
uniform *n.,* uniforme (m) [*ü-nee-form*]
unimaginable, inimaginable [*ee-nee-mah-zhee-nahbl*]
unimportant, peu important [*puh ẽ-por-tã(t)*]
uninteresting, peu intéressant [*puh ẽ-teh-re-sã(t)*]
union [labor union], syndicat (m) [*sẽ-dee-kah*]
unit, unité (f) [*ü-nee-teh*]
unite *v.,* unir [*ü-neer*]
united, uni [*ü-nee*]
United States, Etats-Unis (m, pl) [*eh-tah-zü-nee*]
unity, unité (f) [*ü-nee-teh*]
universal, universel, -elle [*ü-nee-ver-sel*]
universe, univers (m) [*ü-nee-ver*]
university, université (f) [*ü-nee-ver-see-teh*]
unjust, injuste [*ẽ-zhüst*]
unknown, inconnu [*ẽ-ko-nü*]
unlawful, illégal, -aux (m, pl) [*ee-leh-gahl, ee-leh-goh*]
unless, à moins que [*ah mwẽ kuh*]
unload *v.,* décharger [*deh-shahr-zheh*]
unlock *v.,* ouvrir (irreg) [*oo-vreer*]
unlucky, malheureux, -euse [*mah-luh-ruh, mah-luh-ruhz*]

unoccupied, inoccupé [*ee-no-kü-peh*]
unpack v., défaire (irreg) [*deh-fer*]
unpleasant, désagréable [*deh-zah-greh-ahbl*]
unquestionable, indiscutable [*ē-dees-kü-tahbl*]
unsafe, dangereux, -euse [*dā-zhruh, dā-zhruhz*]
until, jusque [*zhüsk*]
untrue, faux, fausse [*foh, fohs*]
untruthful, menteur, -euse [*mā-tuhr, mā-tuhz*]
unusual, peu commun [*puh ko-mē*]
unwelcome, importun [*ē-por-tē, ē-por-tün*]
unwilling, peu disposé [*puh dees-poh-zeh*]
up, en *haut, vers le *haut [*ā oh, ver luh oh*]
  be up [standing] v., être debout [*e-truh duh-boo*]
  get up v., se lever [*sluh-veh*]
  go up v., monter (Aux: ÊTRE) [*mō-teh*]
  up and down, en *haut et en bas [*ā oh eh ā bah*]
  up to now, jusqu'ici [*zhüs-kee-see*]
upbringing, éducation (f) [*eh-dü-kah-syō*]
uphill, montant [*mō-tā(t)*]
upon, sur [*sür*]
upper, supérieur [*sü-pehr-yuhr*]
uproar, vacarme (m) [*vah-kahrm*]
ups and downs, péripéties (f, pl), les *hauts et les bas [*peh-ree-peh-see, leh oh eh leh bah*]
upset adj., bouleversé [*bool-ver-seh*]
upset v., renverser, bouleverser [*rā-ver-seh, bool-ver-seh*]
upside down, à l'envers [*ah lā-ver*]
upstairs, en *haut [*ā oh*]
up-to-date [fashion], à la mode [*ah lah mod*]
up-to-date [report], à jour [*ah zhoor*]
upward, vers le *haut [*ver luh oh*]
urban, urbain [*ür-bē, ür-ben*]
urgent, urgent [*ür-zhā(t)*]
us, nous [*noo*]
  There are three of us Nous sommes trois [*noo som trwah*]
use n., emploi (m), usage (m) [*ā-plwah, ü-zahzh*]
  personal use, usage (m) personnel [*ü-zahzh per-so-nel*]

use *v.*, employer, se servir de (irreg) [*ã-plwah-yeh, suh ser-veer duh*]
  He is using this table, Il se sert de cette table [*eel suh ser duh set tahbl*]
  What is this used for? A quoi cela sert-il? [*ah kwah suh-lah ser-teel*]
  be used to *v.*, être habitué à [*etr ah-bee-tweh ah*]
used, utilisé [*ü-tee-lee-zeh*]
used [car], d'occasion [*do-kah-zyõ*]
useful, utile [*ü-teel*]
useless, inutile [*ee-nü-teel*]
usual, habituel, -elle [*ah-bee-twel*]
usually, d'habitude [*dah-bee-tiid*]

V

vacancy, vide (m) [*veed*]
  no vacancy, complet [*kõ-pleh*]
vacant, libre [*leebr*]
vacation, vacances (f, pl) [*vah-kãs*]
vaccination, vaccination (f) [*vahk-see-nah-syõ*]
vacuum cleaner, aspirateur (m) [*ah-spee-rah-tuhr*]
vague, vague [*vahg*]
vain, vain [*vẽ, ven*]
  in vain, en vain [*ã vẽ*]
valid, valable [*vah-lahbl*]
valley, vallée (f) [*vah-leh*]
valuable, précieux, -euse [*preh-syuh, preh-syuhz*]
value *n.*, valeur (f) [*vah-luhr*]
value *v.*, estimer [*es-tee-meh*]
valve, soupape (f) [*soo-pahp*]
vanilla, vanille (f) [*vah-neey*]
  vanilla flavored, à la vanille [*ah lah vah-neey*]
vanish *v.*, disparaître (irreg) [*dees-pah-retr*]

vanity, vanité (f) [*vah-nee-teh*]
variety, variété (f) [*vah-ryeh-teh*]
various, divers [*dee-ver(s)*]
vary v., varier [*vah-ryeh*]
vast, vaste [*vahst*]
Vatican, Vatican (m) [*vah-tee-kã*]
vault [burial], caveau (m), -eaux (pl) [*ka-voh*]
veal, veau (m), -eaux (pl) [*voh*]
vegetable, légume (m) [*leh-güm*]
vehicle, véhicule (m) [*veh-ee-kül*]
veil n., voile (m) [*vwahl*]
vein, veine (f) [*ven*]
velvet, velours (m) [*vuh-loor*]
verb, verbe (m) [*verb*]
verdict, verdict (m) [*ver-dee(kt)*]
verge, bord (m) [*bor*]
verify v., vérifier [*veh-ree-fyeh*]
verse, vers (m) [*ver*]
vertical, vertical, -aux (m, pl) [*ver-tee-kahl, ver-tee-koh*]
very, très [*tre*]
  very well, très bien [*tre byẽ*]
vest, gilet (m) [*zhee-le*]
veteran, ancien combattant (m) [*ã-syẽ kõ-bah-tã*]
veterinarian, vétérinaire [*veh-teh-ree-ner*]
vex v., vexer [*vek-seh*]
vice, vice (m) [*vees*]
vicinity, environs (m, pl) [*ã-vee-rõ*]
vicious, méchant [*meh-shã(t)*]
victim, victime (f) [*veek-teem*]
victory, victoire (f) [*veek-twahr*]
view n., vue (f) [*vü*]
viewpoint, point (m) de vue [*pwẽ duh vü*]
vigorous, vigoureux, -euse [*vee-goo-ruh, vee-goo-ruhz*]
village, village (m) [*vee-lahzh*]
villain, scélérat (m) [*seh-leh-rah*]
vine, vigne, (f) [*veeñ*]
vinegar, vinaigre (m) [*vee-negr*]

vineyard, vignoble (m) [*vee-nyobl*]
violate v., violer [*vyo-leh*]
violence, violence (f) [*vyo-lās*]
violet, violette (f) [*vyo-let*]
violin, violon (m) [*vyo-lō*]
virgin, vierge (f) [*vyerzh*]
virtue, vertu (f) [*ver-tü*]
virtuous, vertueux, -euse [*ver-twuh, ver-twuhz*]
visa, visa (m) [*vee-zah*]
visible, visible [*vee-zeebl*]
vision, vision (f) [*vee-zyō*]
visit n., visite (f) [*vee-zeet*]
visit [a person] v., rendre visite à [*rādr vee-zeet ah*]
visit [a place] v., visiter [*vee-zee-teh*]
visiting card, carte (f) de visite [*kahrt duh vee-zeet*]
visitor, visiteur, -euse [*vee-zee-tuhr, vee-zee-tuhz*]
  She has visitors, Elle a du monde [*el ah dü mōd*]
vital, vital, -aux (m, pl) [*vee-tahl, vee-toh*]
vitamin, vitamine (f) [*vee-tah-meen*]
vocabulary, vocabulaire (m) [*vo-kah-bü-ler*]
vocal, vocal, -aux (m, pl) [*vo-kahl, vo-koh*]
vocalist, chanteur (m), cantatrice (f) [*shā-tuhr, kā-tah-trees*]
vocation, vocation (f) [*vo-kah-syō*]
vocational, professionnel, -elle [*pro-fe-syo-nel*]
voice n., voix (f) [*vwah*]
volcano, volcan (m) [*vol-kā*]
volume, volume (m) [*vo-lüm*]
voluntary, volontaire [*vo-lō-ter*]
volunteer n., volontaire (m) [*vo-lō-ter*]
vomit v., vomir [*voh-meer*]
vote n., vote (m) [*vot*]
vote v., voter [*vo-teh*]
vow n., voeu (m), -eux (pl) [*vuh*]
vowel, voyelle (f) [*vwah-yel*]
voyage n., voyage (m) [*vwah-yahzh*]
vulgar, vulgaire [*vül-gher*]
vulnerable, vulnérable [*vül-neh-rahbl*]

W

wages *pl.*, salaire (m, sing) [*sah-ler*]
waist, taille (f) [*tahy*]
wait *n.*, attente (f) [*ah-tãt*]
wait for *v.*, attendre [*ah-tãdr*]
waiter, garçon (m) [*gahr-sõ*]
waiting room, salle (f) d'attente [*sahl dah-tãt*]
waitress, serveuse (f) [*ser-vuhz*]
   Waitress! Mademoiselle! [*mahd-mwah-zel*]
wake *v.*, réveiller [*reh-ve-yeh*]
   wake up [self], se réveiller [*sreh-ve-yeh*]
walk *n.*, promenade (f) [*prom-nahd*]
   take a walk *v.*, se promener [*sprom-neh*]
walk *v.*, marcher [*mahr-sheh*]
wall, mur (m) [*mür*]
wallpaper, papier (m) peint [*pah-pyeh pẽ*]
wallet, portefeuille (m) [*por-tuh-fuhy*]
walnut, noix (f) [*nwah*]
waltz *n.*, valse (f) [*vahls*]
wander *v.*, errer [*eh-reh*]
want *v.*, vouloir (irreg) [*vool-wahr*]
war, guerre (f) [*gher*]
wardrobe [clothes closet], armoire (f) [*ahrm-wahr*]
wardrobe [clothing], vêtements (m, pl) [*vet-mã*]
warehouse, entrepôt (m) [*ã-truh-poh*]
warm *adj.*, chaud [*shoh(d)*]
warm *v.*, chauffer [*shoh-feh*]
warmth, chaleur (f) [*shah-luhr*]
warn *v.*, avertir [*ah-ver-teer*]
warning, avertissement (m) [*ah-ver-tees-mã*]
warrant, mandat (m) [*mã-dah*]
wash *v.*, laver, se laver [*lah-veh, slah-veh*]
washbasin, lavabo (m) [*lah-vah-boh*]

147

washing machine, machine (f) à laver [*mah-sheen ah lah-veh*]
wasp, guêpe (f) [*ghep*]
waste *v.*, gaspiller [*gahs-pee-yeh*]
wastebasket, corbeille (f) à papier [*kor-be-yah pah-pyeh*]
watch *n.*, montre (f) [*mõtr*]
  wristwatch, montre-bracelet (f) [*mõtr-brah-sleh*]
watch *v.*, regarder [*r(uh)-gahr-deh*]
  Watch out! Attention! [*ah-tã-syõ*]
watchmaker, horloger [*or-lo-zheh*]
watchman [night], veilleur (m) (de nuit) [*ve-yuhr (duh nwee)*]
water, eau (f), eaux (pl) [*oh*]
  drinking water, eau potable [*oh po-tahbl*]
  fresh water, eau douce [*oh doos*]
  mineral water, eau minérale [*oh mee-neh-rahl*]
  running water, eau courante [*oh koo-rãt*]
  salt water, eau de mer [*ohd mer*]
water closet, cabinet (m) [*kah-bee-ne*]
watercolor, aquarelle (f) [*ah-kwah-rel*]
waterfall, cascade (f) [*kahs-kahd*]
watermelon, pastèque (f) [*pahs-tek*]
waterproof, imperméable [*ẽ-per-meh-ahbl*]
wave *n.*, vague (f) [*vahg*]
wave *v.*, faire signe [*fer seeñ*]
wax *n.*, cire (f) [*seer*]
way [route], chemin (m) [*sh(uh)-mẽ*]
way [manner], façon (f) [*fah-sõ*]
  by the way, à propos [*ah proh-poh*]
  in this way, de cette façon [*duh set fah-sõ*]
we, nous [*noo*]
weak, faible [*febl*]
weakness, faiblesse (f) [*feh-bles*]
wealth, richesse (f) [*ree-shes*]
wealthy, riche [*reesh*]
wean *v.*, sevrer [*suh-vreh*]
weapon, arme (f) [*ahrm*]
wear *v.*, porter [*por-teh*]
  wear out, user [*ü-zeh*]
weather, temps (m) [*tã*]

weave *v.*, tisser [*tee-seh*]

web [spider], toile (f) d'araignée [*twahl dah-re-nyeh*]

wedding, mariage (m) [*mahr-yahzh*]

wedding ring, alliance (f) [*ah-lyãs*]

Wednesday, mercredi (m) [*mer-kruh-dee*]

weed *n.*, mauvaise herbe (f) [*moh-ve-zerb*]

week, semaine (f) [*s(uh)-men*]
  last week, la semaine dernière [*lah smen der-nyer*]
  next week, la semaine prochaine [*lah smen pro-shen*]

weekend, fin de semaine (f) [*fẽ duh suh-men*]

weekly, hebdomadaire [*eb-do-mah-der*]

weep *v.*, pleurer [*pluh-reh*]

weigh *v.*, peser [*puh-zeh*]

weight, poids (m) [*pwah*]

welcome *n.*, bienvenu (m) [*byẽ-vnü*]
  Welcome! Soyez le bienvenu! [*swo-yeh luh byẽ-vnü*]
  You're welcome, Je vous en prie; Il n'y a pas de quoi
    [*zhvoo-zã pree; eel nyah paht kwah*]

welfare, bien-être (m) [*byẽ-netr*]

well [for water] *n.*, puits (m) [*pwee*]

well *adv.*, bien [*byẽ*]
  very well, très bien [*tre byẽ*]
  Well! Tiens! [*tyẽ*]

well-bred, bien élevé [*byẽ-nehl-yeh*]

well-known, célèbre [*seh-lebr*]

well-off, prospère [*pros-per*]

west, ouest (m) [*west*]

western, occidental, -aux (m, pl) [*ok-see-dã-tahl, ok-see-dã-toh*]

wet, mouillé [*moo-yeh*]

whale, baleine (f) [*bah-len*]

what *interr. adj.*, quel, quelle; quels, quelles [*kel*]
  What road will he take? Quel chemin prendra-t-il? [*kel shuh-mẽ prã-drah-teel*]
  What's the weather like? Quel temps fait-il? [*kel tã fe-teel*]
  What is the date of . . . Quelle est la date de . . . [*ke-le lah daht duh . . .*]

what *interr. pron.*, que, qu'est-ce qui, qu'est-ce que, quoi
   [*kuh, kes-kee, kes-kuh, kwah*]

  What are you doing here? Que faites-vous ici?, Qu'est-ce
   que vous faites ici? [*kuh fet voo-zee-see, kes-kuh voo
   fet ee-see*]

  What do you think? Que pensez-vous?, Qu'est-ce que
   vous pensez? [*kuh pã-seh-voo, kes-kuh voo pã-seh*]

  What's happening? Qu'est-ce qui se passe?, Que se passe-
   t-il? [*kes-kee spahs, kuh spahs-teel*]

  What are you thinking about? A quoi pensez vous?
   [*ah kwah pã-seh-voo*]

  What else? Quoi d'autre? [*kwah dohtr*]

  What for? Pourquoi? [*poor-kwah*]

what *rel. pron.*, ce qui (subj), ce que (obj) [*skee, skuh*]

  I see what is coming, Je vois ce qui arrive [*zhvwah skyah-
   reev*]

  I don't like what I see, Je n'aime pas ce que je vois
   [*zhnem pah skuhzh vwah*]

whatever, quoi qui, quoi que [*kwah kee, kwah kuh*]

  whatever happens, quoi qu'il arrive [*kwah kee-lah-reev*]

  whatever it may be, quoi que ce soit [*kwahk suh swah*]

  whatever they say, quoi qu'on dise [*kwah kõ deez*]

wheat, blé (m) [*bleh*]

wheel, roue (f) [*roo*]

  steering wheel, volant (m) [*vo-lã*]

wheelbarrow, brouette (f) [*broo-et*]

when, quand [*kã*]

whenever, chaque fois que [*shak fwah kuh*]

where, où [*oo*]

  Where is she? Où est-elle? [*we-tel*]

  Where do you come from? D'où venez-vous? [*doo vneh-
   voo*]

wherever, partout où [*pahr-too oo*]

whether, si [*see*]

  whether or not, si, oui ou non [*see, wee oo nõ*]

which *interr. adj.*, quel, quelle; quels, quelles [*kel*]

which *interr. pron.*, lequel, laquelle; lesquels, lesquelles
   [*luh-kel, lah-kel; leh-kel*]

Which have you chosen? Lesquels avez-vous choisis?
[*leh-kel ah-veh-voo shwah-zee*]

which *rel.*, qui, que; lequel [*kee, kuh; luh-kel*]

  the car which is leaving, l'auto qui part [*loh-toh kee pahr*]

  the car which I saw, l'auto que j'ai vue [*loh-tohk zheh vü*]

  the car in which she arrived, l'auto dans laquelle elle est arrivée [*loh-toh dã lah-kel e-le-tah-ree-veh*]

  to which, at which, auquel, à laquelle; auxquels, auxquelles [*oh-kel, ah lah-kel; oh-kel*]

  of which, from which, duquel, de laquelle; desquels, desquelles; dont [*dü-kel, duh lah-kel; deh-kel; dõ*]

  the car of which I speak, l'auto dont je parle [*loh-toh dõsh pahrl*]

while, pendant que [*pã-dã kuh*]

whipped cream, crème Chantilly [*krem shã-tee-yee*]

whisper *v.*, chuchoter [*shü-sho-teh*]

whistle *n.*, sifflet (m) [*see-fleh*]

whistle *v.*, siffler [*see-fleh*]

white, blanc, blanche [*blã, blãsh*]

who, qui [*kee*]

whoever, quiconque [*kee-kõk*]

whole, entier, -ière [*ã-tyeh, ã-tyer*]

wholesale, vente (f) en gros [*vã-tã groh*]

whom *interr.*, qui [*kee*]

whom *rel.*, que; qui [*kuh, kee*]

  The man whom I saw, L'homme que j'ai vu [*lom kuh zheh vü*]

  The man to whom I spoke, L'homme à qui j'ai parlé [*lom ah kee zheh pahr-leh*]

whose *poss. pron.*, de qui, à qui [*duh kee, ah kee*]

  Whose book is this? A qui est ce livre? [*ah kee eh suh leevr*]

whose *rel. pron.*, dont [*dõ*]

  The boy whose book I found, Le garçon dont j'ai trouvé le livre [*luh gar-sõ dõ zheh troo-veh luh leevr*]

why, pourquoi [*poor-kwah*]

  why not, pourquoi pas [*poor-kwah pah*]

wicked, méchant [*meh-shã(t)*]

wide, large [*lahrzh*]

widespread, répandu [*reh-pã-dü*]

widow, veuve (f) [*vuhv*]

widower, veuf (m) [*vuhf*]

width, largeur (f) [*lahr-zhuhr*]

wife, femme (f) [*fam*]

wig, perruque (f) [*pe-rük*]

wild, sauvage [*soh-vahzh*]

will [testament] n., testament (m) [*tes-tah-mã*]

willingly, volontiers [*vo-lõ-tyeh*]

willpower, volonté (f) [*vo-lõ-teh*]

win v., gagner [*gah-nyeh*]

wind n., vent (m) [*vã*]

wind v., remonter [*r(uh)-mõ-teh*]

windmill, moulin (m) à vent [*moo-lẽ ah vã*]

window, fenêtre (f) [*f(uh)-netr*]

   store window, vitrine (f) [*vee-treen*]

windshield, pare-brise (m) [*pahr-breez*]

wine, vin (m) [*vẽ*]

wing, aile (f) [*el*]

winner, gagnant, -ante [*gah-nyã(t)*]

winter, hiver (m) [*ee-ver*]

wipe v., essuyer [*e-swee-yeh*]

wire [filament], fil (m) de fer [*feel duh fer*]

wisdom, sagesse (f) [*sah-zhes*]

wise, sage [*sahzh*]

wish n., souhait (m) [*swe*]

wish v., souhaiter [*swe-teh*]

wit, esprit (m) [*es-pree*]

witch, sorcière (f) [*sor-syer*]

with, avec [*ah-vek*]

withdraw v., retirer, se retirer [*ruh-tee-reh, sruh-tee-reh*]

within, à l'intérieur (de), dedans, dans [*ah lẽ-teh-ryuhr (duh), duh-dã, dã*]

without, sans [*sã*]

witness n., témoin (m) [*teh-mwẽ*]

witness v., être témoin [*etr teh-mwẽ*]

witty, spirituel, -elle [*spee-ree-twel*]
woman, femme (f) [*fahm*]
wonder v., se demander [*s(uh) d(uh)-mã-deh*]
wonderful, merveilleux, -euse [*mer-veh-yuh, mer-veh-yuhz*]
wood, bois (m), [*bwah*]
wooden, en bois [*ã bwah*]
woods, bois (m), forêt (f) [*bwah, fo-re*]
wool, laine (f) [*len*]
woolen, en laine [*ã len*]
word, mot (m) [*moh*]
work [result] n., ouvrage (m) , oeuvre (f) [*oo-vrahzh, uhvr*]
  work of art, oeuvre d'art (f) [*uh-vruh dahr*]
work v., travailler [*trah-vah-yeh*]
  This doesn't work, Ca ne marche pas [*sahn mahrsh pah*]
worker, travailleur, -euse [*trah-vah-yuhr, trah-vah-yuhz*]
  factory worker, ouvrier, -ière [*oo-vree-yeh, oo-vree-yer*]
workshop, atelier (m) [*ah-tuh-lyeh*]
world, monde (m) [*mõd*]
world war, guerre mondiale (f) [*gher mõ-dyahl*]
worm, ver (m) [*ver*]
worn out, usé [*ü-zeh*]
worried, inquiet, -ète [*ẽ-kyeh, ẽ-kyet*]
worry n., inquiétude (f) [*ẽ-kyeh-tüd*]
worry v., s'inquiéter [*sẽ-kyeh-teh*]
worse adj., pire, plus mauvais [*peer, plü mo-ve(z)*]
worse adv., pis, plus mal [*pee, plü mahl*]
worship v., adorer [*ah-do-reh*]
worst, le pire, le plus mauvais [*luh peer, luh plü mo-ve*]
worth: to be worth, valoir (irreg) [*vahl-wahr*]
  It's worth ten francs, Cela vaut dix francs [*sah voh dee
  frã*]
worthwhile: to be worthwhile v., valoir (irreg) la peine
  [*vahl-wahr lah pen*]
worthy, digne [*deeñ*]
wound [injury] n., blessure (f) [*ble-sür*]
wounded, blessé [*ble-seh*]
wrap v., envelopper [*ã-vlo-peh*]
wrench [tool] n., clé (f) [*kleh*]

wrestling, catch (m) [*kahtsh*]
wrinkle [face] *n.*, ride (f) [*reed*]
wrinkle [clothes] *n.*, pli (m) [*plee*]
wrinkle *v.*, plisser [*plee-seh*]
wrist, poignet (m) [*pwah-nye*]
wristwatch, montre-bracelet (f) [*mõtr-brah-sleh*]
write *v.*, écrire (irreg) [*eh-kreer*]
writer, écrivain (m), femme écrivain (f) [*eh-kree-vē, fahm eh-kree-vē*]
writing, écriture (f) [*eh-kree-tür*]
writing paper, papier (m) à lettre [*pah-pyeh ah letr*]
wrong *adj.*, mauvais, incorrect [*mo-vε(z), ē-ko-rektı*]
  be wrong *v.*, avoir tort [*ah-vwahr tor*]
wrong *n.*, mal (m), tort (m) [*mahl, tor*]
wrong *v.*, faire tort à [*fer tor ah*]

X, Y, Z

x-ray, radio-(graphie) (f) [*rah-dyoh-(grah-fee)*]
yard [measure], environ un mètre [*ã-vee-rõ ē metr*]
yard [around house], jardin (m) [*zhahr-dē*]
yarn [filament], fil (m) [*feel*]
yawn *v.*, bâiller [*bah-yeh*]
year, an (m), année, (f) [*ã, ah-neh*]
  last year, l'année dernière [*lah-neh der-nyer*]
  next year, l'année prochaine [*lah-neh pro-shen*]
yearly *adv.*, annuellement [*ah-nwel-mã*]
yearly *adj.*, annuel, -elle [*ah-nwel*]
yell *v.*, *hurler [*ür-leh*]
yellow, jaune [*zhohn*]
yes, oui [*wee*]
yesterday, hier [*yer*]
  the day before yesterday, avant-hier [*ah-vã-tyer*]
yet, encore [*ã-kor*]
you, vous (polite); tu, te, toi (familiar) [*voo; tü, tuh, twah*]

young, jeune [*zhuhn*]

younger, cadet, -ette; plus jeune [*kah-deh, kah-det; plü zhuhn*]

your, votre, vos (polite); ton, ta, tes (familiar) [*votr, voh; tõ, tah, teh*]

yours, le vôtre, la vôtre, les vôtres (polite); le tien, la tienne, les tiens, les tiennes (familiar) [*luh vohtr, lah vohtr, leh vohtr; luh tyẽ, lah tyen, leh tyẽ, leh tyen*]

yourself, vous-même (polite); toi-même (familiar) [*voo-mem; twah-mem*]

yours truly, bien amicalement (personal); Veuillez agréer, Monsieur, l'expression de mes sentiments distingués (business) [*not spoken*]

youth, jeunesse (f) [*zhuh-nes*]

zero, zéro (m) [*zeh-roh*]

zipper, fermeture éclair (f) [*fer-muh-tür eh-kler*]

zone, zone (f) [*zohn*]

zoo, zoo (m) [*zoh-oh*]

French/English

A

a 3d pers. sing. present tense of AVOIR [ah] has
à [ah] at, in; to, into
   à l'anglaise [ah lã-glez] in the English way
abaisser v. [ah-beh-seh] lower
abandonner v. [ah-bã-do-neh] abandon
abbé m. [ah-beh] priest
abeille f. [ah-bey] bee
abimer v. [ah-bee-meh] harm
abolir v. [ah-bo-leer] abolish
abondance f. [ah-bõ-dãs] abundance
abondant [ah-bõ-dã(t)] abundant
abonnement m. [ah-bon-mã] subscription
s'abonner v. [sah-bo-neh] subscribe
d'abord [dah-bor] at first, first
aboutir (à) v. [ah-boo-teer(ah)] lead (to); end (in)
aboyer v. [ah-bwah-yeh] bark
abréviation f. [ah-breh-vyah-syõ] abbreviation
abri m. [ah-bree] shelter
abricot m. [ah-bree-koh] apricot
abriter v. [ah-bree-teh] shelter
absence f. [ahp-sãs] absence
absent [ahp-sã(t)] absent
absolument [ahp-so-lü-mã] absolutely
absorber v. [ahp-sor-beh] absorb
abstrait [ahp-stre(t)] abstract
absurde [ahp-sürd] absurd
acajou m. [ah-kah-zhoo] mahogany
accélérateur m. [ahk-seh-leh-rah-tuhr] accelerator
accent m. [ahk-sã] accent
accentuer v. [ahk-sã-tweh] stress, emphasize
accepter v. [ak-sep-teh] accept
accès m. [ahk-se] access

159

accès interdit [*ahk-se ĕ-ter-dee*] no tresspassing
accident *m.* [*ahk-see-dã*] accident
accidentel, -elle [*ahk-see-dã-tel*] accidental
accommoder *v.* [*ah-ko-mo-deh*] accommodate
accompagner *v.* [*ah-kõ-pah-nyeh*] accompany
accomplir *v.* [*ah-kõ-pleer*] accomplish, achieve
accord *m.* [*ah-kor*] agreement
  être d'accord [*e-truh dah-kor*] agree
  ne pas être d'accord [*nuh pah-ze-truh dah-kor*] disagree
  D'accord [*dah-kor*] All right
accorder *v.* [*ah-kor-deh*] grant
  s'accorder [*sah-kor-deh*] agree
accouchement *m.* [*ah-koosh-mã*] childbirth
accrocher *v.* [*ah-kro-sheh*] hang
accueil *m.* [*ah-kuhy*] reception
accueillir *v. irreg.* [*ah-kuh-yeer*] receive, welcome
accusation *f.* [*ah-kü-zah-syõ*] accusation
accuser *v.* [*ah-kü-zeh*] accuse
  accuser réception de [*ah-kü-zeh reh-sep-syõ duh*]
    acknowledge receipt of
achat *m.* [*ah-shah*] purchase
  faire *v.* **des achats** [*fer deh-zah-shah*] shop
acheter *v.* [*ahsh-teh*] buy
acheteur, -teuse [*ahsh-tuhr, ahsh-tuhz*] buyer
acide *f.* [*ah-seed*] acid
acier *m.* [*ah-syeh*] steel
acompte *m.* [*ah-kõt*] deposit
acquérir *v. irreg.* [*ah-keh-reer*] acquire
acquisition *f.* [*ah-kee-zee-syõ*] acquisition
acquitter *v.* [*ah-kee-teh*] acquit
acte *m.* [*ahkt*] act
acteur *m.* [*ahk-tuhr*] actor
actif, active [*ahk-teef, ahk-teev*] active
activité *f.* [*ahk-tee-vee-teh*] activity
actrice *f.* [*ahk-trees*] actress
actualité *f.* [*ahk-twah-lee-teh*] current events
  les actualités [*leh-zahk-twah-lee-teh*] newsreel
actuel, -elle [*ahk-twel*] current, present

actuellement [*ahk-twel-mã*] currently
adapter *v.* [*ah-dahp-teh*] adapt
addition *f.* [*ah-dee-syõ*] sum
  l'addition [*lah-dee-syõ*] the check
additionnel, -elle [*ah-dee-syo-nel*] additional
additionner *v.* [*ah-dee-syo-neh*] add up, sum up
adieu *m.* [*ah-dyuh*] farewell
adhérer (à) *v.* [*ah-deh-reh (ah)*] adhere (to), join
adjacent [*ahd-zhah-sã(t)*] adjacent
adjectif *m.* [*ahd-zhek-teef*] adjective
adjoint *m.* [*ahd-zhwẽ*] deputy, assistant
admettre *v. irreg.* [*ahd-metr*] admit, acknowledge
administration *f.* [*ahd-mee-nees-trah-syõ*] administration
administrer *v.* [*ahd-mee-nees-treh*] administer
admirable [*ahd-mee-rahbl*] admirable
admirateur, -trice [*ahd-mee-rah-tuhr, ahd-mee-rah-trees*]
    admirer
admiration *f.* [*ahd-mee-rah-syõ*] admiration
admirer *v.* [*ahd-mee-reh*] admire
adopter *v.* [*ah-dop-teh*] adopt
adoption *f.* [*ah-dop-syõ*] adoption
adorable [*ah-do-rahbl*] adorable
adorer *v.* [*ah-do-reh*] adore, love
adresse *f.* [*ah-dres*] address
adresser *v.* [*ah-dreh-seh*] address
  s'adresser (à) [*sah-dreh-seh (ah)*] speak, apply (to)
adroit [*ah-drwah(t)*] skillful
adulte [*ah-dült*] adult
adverbe *m.* [*ahd-verb*] adverb
adversaire *m.* [*ahd-ver-ser*] foe
aérer *v.* [*ah-eh-reh*] air
aérien, -enne [*ah-eh-ryẽ, ah-eh-ryen*] air
aéroport *m.* [*ah-eh-ro-por*] airport
affaires *pl.* [*ah-fer*] belongings, business
affecter *v.* [*ah-fek-teh*] affect
affection *f.* [*ah-fek-syõ*] affection
affectueux, -tueuse [*ah-fek-twuh, ah-fek-twuhz*] affectionate
affiche *f.* [*ah-feesh*] poster

affirmer *v.* [*ah-feer-meh*] affirm
affranchissement *m.* [*ah-frã-shees-mã*] postage
afin que *conj.* [*ah-fẽ kuh*] so that, in order that
afin de *prep.* [*ah-fẽ duh*] so as to, in order to
affreux, -euse [*ah-fruh, ah-fruhz*] horrible
africain [*ah-free-kẽ, ah-free-ken*] African
Afrique *f.* [*ah-freek*] Africa
âge *m.* [*ahzh*] age
   Quel âge avez-vous? [*ke-lahzh ah-veh-voo*] How old are you?
   moyen-âge *m.* [*mwah-ye nahzh*] Middle Ages
agé [*ah-zheh*] elderly, old
   agé de trois ans [*ah-zhehd trwah-zã*] three years old
agence *f.* [*ah-zhãs*] agency, branch office
   agence de voyages [*ah-zhãs duh vwah-yahzh*] travel agency
agenda *m.* [*ah-zhẽ-dah*] date book
agent *m.* [*ah-zhã*] agent
   agent de change [*ah-zhãt shãzh*] stockbroker
   agent de police [*ah-zhãt po-lees*] policeman
aggraver *v.* [*ah-grah-veh*] aggravate
agir *v.* [*ah-zheer*] act
   Il s'agit de [*eel sah-zhee duh*] It's a question of
agité [*ah-zhee-teh*] excited
agiter *v.* [*ah-zhee-teh*] agitate, wave
   s'agiter [*sah-zhee-teh*] move around
agneau, -eaux *m.* [*ah-nyoh*] lamb
agrandir *v.* [*ah-grã-deer*] enlarge
agréable [*ah-greh-ahbl*] agreeable, pleasant
agressif, -sive [*ah-gre-seef, ah-gre-seev*] aggressive
agression *f.* [*ah-gre-syõ*] aggression
agricole [*ah-gree-kol*] agricultural
agriculteur *m.* [*ah-gree-kül-tuhr*] farmer
agriculture *f.* [*ah-gree-kül-tür*] agriculture
aide *f.* [*ed*] aid, assistance
aider *v.* [*e-deh*] help
aigre [*egr*] sour
aigu, -uë [*eh-gü*] sharp
aiguille *f.* [*eh-gweey*] needle

aiguiser v. [*eh-ghee-zeh*] sharpen
ail m. [*ahy*] garlic
aile f. [*el*] wing, fender
ailleurs [*ah-yuhr*] elsewhere
  d'ailleurs [*dah-yuhr*] besides, moreover
aimable [*e-mahbl*] kind
aimer v. [*e-meh*] like, love, enjoy
  J'aimerais mieux . . . [*zhem-re myuh*] I'd rather . . . ,
    I'd prefer . . .
aîné [*eh-neh*] older
ainsi [*ē-see*] thus, so
  ainsi de suite [*ē-seet sweet*] so forth
ainsi que [*ē-see k(uh)*] as, well as
air m. [*er*] air, tune
  courant m. **d'air** m. [*koo-rā der*] draft
  avoir v. **l'air (de)** [*ah-vwahr ler (duh)*] look (like)
aise f. [*ez*] ease
aisé [*eh-zeh*] well off
ajouter v. [*ah-zhoo-teh*] add
ajuster v. [*ah-zhüs-teh*] adjust
alarmer v. [*ah-lahr-meh*] alarm
alcool m. [*ahl-kol*] alcohol
alerte adj. [*ah-lert*] alert
alerte f. [*ah-lert*] alert
aliment m. [*ah-lee-mā*] food
alimentaire [*ah-lee-mā-ter*] nourishing
alimentation f. [*ah-lee-mā-tah-syō*] nourishment, feeding;
  grocery store
allée f. [*ah-leh*] path, aisle
allemand [*ahl-mā(d)*] German
Allemagne f. [*ahl-mahñ*] Germany
aller v. irreg. [*ah-leh*] go
  aller à pied [*ah-leh ah pyeh*] walk
  Comment allez-vous? [*ko-mā-tah-leh-voo*] How do you
    do?, How are you?
  Allez-vous en! [*ah-leh-voo-zā*] Go away!
  s'en aller [*sā-nah-leh*] go away
  aller retour [*ah-lehr-toor*] round trip

alliance *f.* [*ahl-yãs*] alliance; wedding ring
allié, -ée [*ahl-yeh*] ally, allied
Allô [*ah-loh*] Hello
allonger *v.* [*ah-lõ-zheh*] lengthen
  s'allonger *v.* [*sah-lõ-zheh*] lie down
allumage *m.* [*ah-lü-mahzh*] ignition
allumer *v.* [*ah-lü-meh*] light, turn on [lights]
allumette *f.* [*ah-lü-met*] match
alors [*ah-lor*] then
Alpes *f. pl.* [*ahlp*] Alps
Alsace *f.* [*ahl-zahs*] Alsace
altitude *f.* [*ahl-tee-tüd*] altitude
amande *f.* [*ah-mãd*] almond
amant, -te [*ah-mã(t)*] lover
ambassade *f.* [*ã-bah-sahd*] embassy
ambassadeur, -drice [*ã-bah-sah-duhr, ã-bah-sah-drees*]
  ambassador
ambiance *f.* [*ã-byãs*] spirit, atmosphere
ambitieux, -euse [*ã-bee-syuh, ã-bee-syuhz*] ambitious
ambition *f.* [*ã-bee-syõ*] ambition
ambulance *f.* [*ã-bü-lãs*] ambulance
âme *f.* [*ahm*] soul
amélioration *f.* [*ah-meh-lyo-rah-syõ*] improvement
améliorer, s'améliorer *v.* [*ah-meh-lyo-reh, sah-meh-lyo-reh*]
  improve
amende *f.* [*ah-mãd*] fine
amener *v.* [*ahm-neh*] bring
amer, amère [*ah-mer*] bitter
américain [*ah-meh-ree-kẽ, ah-meh-ree-ken*] American
Amérique *f.* [*ah-meh-reek*] America
  Amérique du Nord (Sud) [*ah-meh-reek dü nor (süd)*]
  North (South) America
amertume *f.* [*ah-mer-tüm*] bitterness
ameublement *m.* [*ah-muh-bluh-mã*] furnishings
ami, amie [*ah-mee*] friend
amical, -aux [*ah-mee-kahl, ah-mee-koh*] friendly
  Bien amicalement [*byẽ-nah-mee-kahl-mã*] Sincerely yours
amidon *m.* [*ah-mee-dõ*] starch

amiral, -aux *m.* [*ah-mee-rahl, ah-mee-roh*] admiral
amitié *f.* [*ah-mee-tyeh*] friendship
  avec les amitiés sincères de [*ah-vek leh-zah-mee-tyeh sē-ser duh*] with best regards from
amour *m.* [*ah-moor*] love
amoureux, -euse [*ah-moo-ruh, ah-moo-ruhz*] in love; lover
ampoule *f.* [*ã-pool*] light-bulb; blister [of skin]
amusant [*ah-mü-zā(t)*] entertaining, amusing
amusement *m.* [*ah-müz-mã*] amusement, fun
amuser *v.* [*ah-mü-zeh*] amuse
  s'amuser [*sah-mü-zeh*] have a good time
  Amusez-vous bien! [*ah-mü-zeh-voo byē*] Have a good time!
amygdales *f. pl.* [*ah-mee-dahl*] tonsils
an *m.* [*ã*] year
analyse *f.* [*ah-nah-leez*] analysis, analyses
  analyses de laboratoire [*ah-nah-leez duh lah-bo-rah-twahr*] laboratory tests, lab work
ananas *m.* [*ah-nah-nah*] pineapple
anarchie *f.* [*ah-nar-shee*] anarchy
ancêtre *m., f.* [*ã-setr*] ancestor
anchois *m.* [*ã-shwah*] anchovy
ancien, -nne [*ã-syē, ã-syen*] former (before noun), ancient (after noun)
  objet *m.* **ancien** [*ob-zhe ã-syē*] antique
  ancien combattant *m.* [*ã-syē kõ-bah-tã*] veteran
ancre *f.* [*ãkr*] anchor
âne *m.* [*ahn*] donkey
ange *m.* [*ãzh*] angel
anglais [*ã-gle(z)*] English
angle *m.* [*ãgl*] angle
Angleterre *f.* [*ã-gluh-ter*] England
animal, -aux *m.* [*ah-nee-mahl, ah-nee-moh*] animal
année *f.* [*ah-neh*] year
  l'année prochaine [*lah-neh pro-shen*] next year
  l'année dernière [*lah-neh der-nyer*] last year
  Bonne Année [*bo-nah-neh*] Happy New Year
anniversaire *m.* [*ah-nee-ver-ser*] anniversary, birthday
  Bon anniversaire! [*bon-nah-nee-ver-ser*] Happy Birthday!,

Happy Anniversary!

annonce *f.* [*ah-nõs*] announcement, advertisement

annoncer *v.* [*ah-nõ-seh*] announce

annuaire *m.* **(de téléphone)** [*ah-nwer (duh teh-leh-fon)*] telephone book

annuel, -elle [*ah-nwel*] annual, yearly

annuellement [*ah-nwel-mã*] yearly

annuler *v.* [*ah-nü-leh*] cancel

anonyme [*ah-no-neem*] anonymous

antérieur [*ã-tehr-yuhr*] prior

anticiper *v.* [*ã-tee-see-peh*] anticipate

antiquaire *m., f.* [*ã-tee-ker*] antique dealer

août *m.* [*oo*] August

apercevoir *v. irreg.* [*a-per-suh-vwahr*] catch sight of
s'apercevoir (de) [*sah-per-suh-vwahr (duh)*] realize

apéritif *m.* [*ah-peh-ree-teef*] appetizer

apparence *f.* [*ah-pah-rãs*] appearance; looks

appareil *m.* [*ah-pah-rey*] appliance, gadget
appareil ménagers [*ah-pah-rey meh-nah-zheh*] household appliances
appareil photographique *m.* [*ah-pah-rey foh-toh-grah-feek*] camera

apparaître *v. irreg.* [*ah-pah-retr*] appear

appartement *m.* [*ah-pahr-tuh-mã*] apartment

appartenir *v. irreg.* [*ah-pahr-tuh-neer*] belong

appel *m.* [*ah-pel*] call, bid [in bridge]

appeler *v.* [*ah-pleh*] call
s'appeler [*sah-pleh*] be named

appendicite *f.* [*ah-pẽ-dee-seet*] appendicitis

appétit *m.* [*ah-peh-tee*] appetite

applaudir *v.* [*ah-ploh-deer*] applaud, cheer

applaudissements *m. pl.* [*ah-ploh-dees-mã*] applause

appliquer *v.* [*ah-plee-keh*] apply

apporter *v.* [*ah-por-teh*] bring

apprécier *v.* [*ah-preh-syeh*] appreciate

apprendre *v. irreg.* [*ah-prãdr*] learn

apprenti, -ie [*ah-prã-tee*] apprentice

approbation *f.* [*ah-pro-bah-syõ*] approval

approcher, s'approcher v. [*ah-pro-sheh, sah-pro-sheh*] approach

approprié [*ah-pro-pree-yeh*] appropriate

approprier, s'approprier v. [*ah-pro-pree-yeh, sah-pro-pree-yeh*] appropriate

approuver v. [*ah-proo-veh*] approve

appuyer v. [*ah-pwee-yeh*] lean
 s'appuyer (sur) [*sah-pwee-yeh (sür)*] lean (on); stress

après prep. & adv. [*ah-pre*] after, afterwards
 d'après [*dah-pre*] according to
 après-midi m., f. [*ah-pre-mee-dee*] afternoon
 après demain [*ah-pred-mē*] the day after tomorrow
 après que conj. [*ah-pre kuh*] after

aquarelle f. [*ah-kwah-rel*] watercolor

Arabe m., f. [*ah-rahb*] Arab

Arabie f. [*ah-rah-bee*] Arabia

araignée f. [*ah-reh-nyeh*] spider

arbitraire [*ahr-bee-trer*] arbitrary

arbitre m. [*ahr-beetr*] arbitrator, referee

arbre m. [*ahrbr*] tree

arc m. [*ahrk*] bow [for arrows], arch
 arc-boutant m. [*ahrk-boo-tā*] flying buttress
 arc-en-ciel m. [*ahr-kā-syel*] rainbow
 arc en plein cintre [*ahr-kā plē sētr*] semi-circular arch

architecte m. [*ahr-shee-tekt*] architect

architecture f. [*ahr-shee-tek-tür*] architecture

ardoise f. [*ahr-dwahz*] slate

arête f. [*ah-ret*] fishbone

argent m. [*ahr-zhā*] money, silver
 argent massif [*ahr-zhā mah-seef*] sterling silver

argenterie f. [*ahr-zhā-tree*] silverware, silver plate

argot m. [*ahr-goh*] slang

argument m. [*ahr-gü-mā*] argument

aristocrate m., f. [*ah-rees-to-kraht*] aristocrat

aristocratique [*ah-rees-to-krah-teek*] aristocratic

arme f. [*ahrm*] weapon

armée f. [*ahr-meh*] army

armoire f. [*ahr-mwahr*] closet, cupboard

arracher v. [*ah-rah-sheh*] pull out, pull away
arranger v. [*ah-rā-zheh*] arrange, fix
arrêt m. [*ah-re*] stop
arrêter v. [*ah-reh-teh*] stop, arrest
  s'arrêter [*sah-reh-teh*] stop (oneself), halt
  Arrêtez! [*ah-reh-teh*] Stop!
arrhes f. pl. [*ahr*] deposit
arrière m. [*ahr-yer*] back, rear
  en arrière [*ã-nahr-yer*] backwards, behind
  à l'arrière [*ah lahr-yer*] in the back
  arrière-grand-mère f. [*ahr-yer-grā-mer*] great-grandmother
  arrière-pensée f. [*ahr-yer-pã-seh*] ulterior motive
  arrière-plan m. [*ahr-yer-plã*] background
arrivée f. [*ah-ree-veh*] arrival
arriver v. [*ah-ree-veh*] arrive, happen
arrondissement m. [*ah-rõ-dees-mã*] district
arroser v. [*ah-roh-zeh*] water
art m. [*ahr*] art
artère f. [*ahr-ter*] artery
artichaut m. [*ahr-tee-shoh*] artichoke
article m. [*ahr-teekl*] article
artificiel, -elle [*ahr-tee-fee-syel*] artificial
artisan m. [*ahr-tee-zã*] craftsman
artiste m., f. [*ahr-teest*] artist
as m. [*ahs*] ace
ascenseur m. [*ah-sā-suhr*] elevator
Asie f. [*ah-zee*] Asia
asile m. [*ah-zeel*] asylum
asperge f. [*ah-sperzh*] asparagus
aspirateur m. [*ah-spee-rah-tuhr*] vacuum cleaner
aspirine f. [*ah-spee-reen*] aspirin
assaisonnement m. [*ah-se-zon-mã*] seasoning
assaisonner v. [*ah-se-zo-neh*] flavor, season
assemblée f. [*ah-sā-bleh*] assembly, meeting
asseoir v. irreg. [*ah-swahr*] seat
  s'asseoir [*sah-swahr*] sit down
  Asseyez-vous [*ah-seh-yeh voo*] Sit down, Have a seat,
    Be seated

être assis [*e-trah-see(z)*] be seated
assez [*ah-seh*] enough
assiette *f.* [*ah-syet*] plate
assis [*ah-see(z)*] seated
assistant, -te [*ah-sees-tã(t)*] assistant
assister *v.* [*ah-sees-teh*] assist
  assister à [*ah-sees-teh ah*] attend
associé, -ée [*ah-so-syeh*] associate
associer, s'associer *v.* [*ah-so-syeh, sah-so-syeh*] associate
assurance *f.* [*ah-sü-rãs*] insurance [life, fire]; assurance
  compagnie *f.* **d'assurances** [*kõ-pah-nyee dah-sü-rãs*]
    insurance company
  police *f.* **d'assurance** [*po-lees dah-sü-rãs*] insurance policy
assurément [*ah-sü-reh-mã*] certainly
assurer *v.* [*ah-sü-reh*] assure, insure
atelier *m.* [*ah-tuh-lyeh*] workshop
athlétique [*aht-leh-teek*] athletic
Atlantique *m.* [*aht-lã-teek*] Atlantic
atmosphère *f.* [*aht-mos-fer*] atmosphere
atomique [*ah-to-meek*] atomic
attacher *v.* [*ah-tah-sheh*] attach, fasten
attaque *f.* [*ah-tahk*] attack
attaquer *v.* [*ah-tah-keh*] attack
atteindre *v. irreg.* [*ah-tẽdr*] reach
attendre *v.* [*ah-tãdr*] wait (for)
  s'attendre à [*sah-tã-drah*] expect
  en attendant [*ã-nah-tã-dã*] meanwhile
attente *f.* [*ah-tãt*] wait
attentif, -ve [*ah-tã-teef, ah-tã-teev*] attentive
attention *f.* [*ah-tã-syõ*] attention
  Attention! [*uh-tã-syõ*] Look out!
atterrir *v.* [*ah-teh-reer*] land
attérrissage *m.* [*ah-teh-ree-sahzh*] landing
attirer *v.* [*ah-tee-reh*] attract
attitude *f.* [*ah-tee-tüd*] attitude
attraper *v.,* [*ah-trah-peh*] catch
au: à le [*oh*] to the, at the
aube *f.* [*ohb*] dawn

aucun *adj. & pron.* [*oh-kẽ, oh-kün*] no, none
audacieux, -euse [*oh-dah-syuh, oh-dah-syuhz*] bold
au-dessous (de) [*ot-soo (duh)*] below
au-dessus (de) [*oht-sü (duh)*] above
auditeur, -trice [*oh-dee-tuhr, oh-dee-trees*] listener
augmentation *f.* [*og-mã-tah-syõ*] increase
augmenter *v.* [*og-mã-teh*] increase
aujourd'hui [*oh-zhoor-dwee*] today
auparavant [*oh-pah-rah-vã*] previously
auprès (de) [*oh-pre (duh)*] near
auquel [*oh-kel*] to whom, which
au revoir [*ohr-vwahr*] good-bye
aussi [*oh-see*] also, too
  aussi . . . que [*oh-see . . . k(uh)*] as . . . as
aussitôt [*oh-see-toh*] immediately
  aussitôt que [*oh-see-toh k(uh)*] as soon as
Australie *f.* [*os-trah-lee*] Australia
australien, -enne [*os-trah-lyẽ, os-trah-lyen*] Australian
autant de, autant que [*oh-tã d(uh), oh-tã k(uh)*] as much
  (as), so much (as)
autel *m* [*o-tel*] altar
auteur *m.* [*oh-tuhr*] author
auto *f.* [*oh-toh*] car
autobus *m.* [*oh-toh-büs*] bus
autocar *m.* [*oh-toh-kahr*] bus
automatique [*oh-toh-mah-teek*] automatic
automne *m.* [*o-ton*] autumn
automobile *f.* [*o-to-mo-beel*] automobile
autoriser *v.* [*o-to-ree-zeh*] authorize
autorité *f.* [*o-to-ree-teh*] authority, control
auto-stop *m.* [*o-to-stop*] hitch-hiking
autour *adv.* [*oh-toor*] around
autour de *prep.* [*oh-toor duh*] around, about
autre [*ohtr(uh)*] other
  un (une) autre [*ẽ-nohtr, ü-nohtr*] another
  l'un l'autre, les uns les autres [*lẽ lohtr, leh-zẽ leh-zohtr*]
    each other
  d'autre [*dohtr*] else

quoi d'autre? [*kwah dohtr*] what else?
autrefois [*oh-truh-fwah*] formerly
autrement [*oh-truh-mã*] otherwise
Autriche *f.* [*oh-treesh*] Austria
autrichien, -enne [*oh-tree-shẽ, oh-tree-shyen*] Austrian
aux: à les [*oh*] to the, at the
auxquels, auxquelles [*oh-kel*] to which, to whom
avalanche *f.* [*ah-vah-lãsh*] avalanche
avaler *v.* [*ah-vah-leh*] swallow
avance *f.* [*ah-vãs*] advance
  à l'avance [*ah lah-vãs*] beforehand, ahead of time
  en avance [*ã-nah-vãs*] in advance, early
avancer, s'avancer *v.* [*ah-vã-seh, sah-vã-seh*] advance
avant *prep. & adv.* [*ah-vã*] before
  en avant (de) [*ã-nah-vã (duh)*] ahead (of)
  avant de faire [*ah-vãd fer*] before doing
avant-hier [*ah-vã-tyer*] the day before yesterday
avant que *conj.* [*ah-vã kuh*] before
avantage *m.* [*uh-vã-tahzh*] advantage
avare *m., f.* [*ah-vahr*] miser
avec [*ah-vek*] with
avenir *m.* [*ahv-neer*] future
  à l'avenir [*ah lahv-neer*] in the future
aventure *f.* [*ah-vã-tür*] adventure
avenue *f.* [*ahv-nii*] avenue
averse *f.* [*ah-vers*] shower
avertir *v.* [*ah-ver-teer*] warn, notify
avertissement *m.* [*ah-ver-tees-mã*] warning
aveugle [*ah-vuhgl*] blind
avez *2d pers. pl. pres. tense of* AVOIR [*ah-veh*] you have
avion *m.* [*ah-vyõ*] airplane
  avion à réaction [*ah-vyõ ah reh-ahk-syõ*] jet
  par avion [*pah-rah-vyõ*] airmail
avis *m.* [*ah-vee*] notice, opinion
avocat *m.* [*ah-vo-kah*] attorney, lawyer
avoir *v. irreg.* [*ah-vwahr*] have
  avoir besoin [*ah-vwahr buhz-wẽ*] need
  avoir chaud [*ah-vwahr shoh*] be hot

avoir faim [*ah-vwahr fẽ*] be hungry
avoir froid [*ah-vwahr frwah*] be cold
avoir l'air (de) [*ah-vwahr ler (duh)*] look (like)
avoir peur [*ah-vwahr puhr*] be afraid
avoir raison [*ah-vwahr re-zõ*] be right
avoir soif [*ah-vwahr swahf*] be thirsty
avoir tort [*ah-vwahr tor*] be wrong
avons *1st pers. pl. present tense of* AVOIR [*ah-võ*] we have
avouer *v.* [*ah-vweh*] confess, admit
avril *m.* [*ah-vreel*] April
ayant [*pres. part. of* AVOIR] [*e-yã*] having

B

bâbord *m.* [*bah-bor*] port
baccalauréat (bac, bachot) *m.* [*bah-kah-lo-reh-ah (bahk, bah-shoh)*] baccalaureate examination
bagages *m. pl.* [*bah-gahzh*] baggage, luggage
bague *f.* [*bahg*] ring
baigner *v.* [*beh-nyeh*] bathe, wash
  se baigner [*s(uh) beh-nyeh*] take a bath, go swimming
baignoire *f.* [*behñ-wahr*] bathtub
bail *m.* [*bahy*] lease
bâiller *v.* [*bah-yeh*] yawn
bain *m.* [*bẽ*] bath
  salle *f.* **de bains** [*sahl duh bẽ*] bathroom
  prendre un bain [*prã-drẽ bẽ*] take a bath
baiser *m.* [*beh-zeh*] kiss
baisse *f.* [*bes*] drop
  en baisse [*ã bes*] falling
baisser *v.* [*beh-seh*] lower
bal *m.* [*bahl*] dance, ball
balai *m.* [*bah-le*] broom
balance *f.* [*bah-lãs*] scale
balancer *v.* [*bah-lã-seh*] rock

balayer *v.* [*bah-leh-yeh*] sweep
balcon *m.* [*bahl-kō*] balcony
balle *f.* [*bahl*] ball
ballet *m.* [*bah-le*] ballet
ballon *m.* [*bah-lō*] ball
banane *f.* [*bah-nahn*] banana
banc *m.* [*bã*] bench
banlieue *f.* [*bã-lyuh*] suburbs
banque *f.* [*bãk*] bank
banquier *m.* [*bã-kyeh*] banker
baptême *m.* [*bah-tem*] baptism
bar *m.* [*bahr*] bar
barbe *f.* [*bahrb*] beard
barrage *m.* [*bah-rahzh*] dam
barrer *v.* [*bah-reh*] bar
barrière *f.* [*bahr-yer*] barrier, fence
bas, basse [*bah(s)*] low
  À bas . . . ! [*ah bah*] Down with . . . !
  en bas [*ã bah*] down, downstairs
bas *m.* [*bah*] stocking
  J'ai filé un bas [*zheh fee-leh ē bah*] I have a run in my
    stocking
base *f.* [*bahz*] base
basse-cour *f.* [*bahs-koor*] farmyard
bataille *f.* [*bah-tahy*] battle
bateau, -eaux *m.* [*bah-toh*] boat
  bateau à voile [*bah-toh ah vwahl*] sailboat
bâtiment *m.* [*bah-tee-mã*] building
bâton *m.* [*bah-tō*] stick
battement *m.* [*baht-mã*] beat
batterie *f.* [*bah-tree*] battery
battre *v. irreg.* [*bahtr*] beat, defeat
  se battre [*s(uh) bahtr*] fight
beau (bel), belle; beaux, belles [*boh, bel*] beautiful,
  handsome
beaucoup (de) [*boh-koo (duh)*] much, many; a great deal
  (of), a lot (of)
beau-frère, beaux-frères *m.* [*boh-frer*] brother-in-law,

brothers-in-law

beau-père *m.* [*boh-per*] father-in-law, stepfather

beauté *f.* [*boh-teh*] beauty

   produits *m. pl.* **de beauté** [*pro-dwee d(uh) boh-teh*] cosmetics

bébé *m.* [*beh-beh*] baby, infant

belge [*belzh*] Belgian

Belgique [*bel-zheek*] Belgium

belle-fille *f.* [*bel-feey*] daughter-in-law

belle-mère *f.* [*bel-mer*] mother-in-law, stepmother

belle-soeur *f.* [*bel-suhr*] sister-in-law

bénédicité *m.* [*beh-neh-dee-see-teh*] grace, blessing

bénédiction *f.* [*beh-neh-deek-syō*] blessing

bénéfice *m.* [*beh-neh-fees*] benefit, profit

bénir *v.* [*beh-neer*] bless

berceau, -eaux *m.* [*ber-soh*] cradle

besoin *m.* [*buh-zwē*] need

   avoir besoin de [*ah-vwahr buh-zwē d(uh)*] need

bétail *m.* [*beh-tahy*] cattle, livestock

bête *f.* [*bet*] beast

bête *fam.* [*bet*] stupid

beurre *m.* [*buhr*] butter

biberon *m.* [*bee-brō*] baby bottle

bible *f.* [*beebl*] bible

bibliothèque *f.* [*bee-blee-yo-tek*] library, bookcase

bicarbonate *m.* **de soude** [*bee-kahr-bo-naht duh sood*] sodium bicarbonate

bicyclette *f.* [*bee-see-klet*] bicycle

bien *m.* [*byē*] good

bien *adv.* [*byē*] well, quite

   très bien [*tre byē*] very well

   bien entendu [*byē-nã-tã-dü*] of course

bien-être *m.* [*byē-netr*] welfare, well-being

bien que *conj.* [*byē (k(uh)*] although

bientôt [*byē-toh*] soon

bienvenu *m.* [*byē-vnü*] welcome

   Soyez le bienvenu! [*swah-yehl byē-vnü*] Welcome!

bière *f.* [*byer*] beer

biftek *m.* [*beef-tek*] steak

bijou, -oux *m.* [*bee-zhoo*] jewel
bijouterie *f.* [*bee-zhoo-tree*] jewelry
billet *m.* [*bee-ye*] ticket
  billet de banque [*bee-yed bāk*] banknote
biscuit *m.* [*bees-kwee*] cracker, cookie
blaireau, -eaux *m.* [*ble-roh*] shaving brush; badger
blâme *m.* [*blahm*] blame
blâmer *v.* [*blah-meh*] blame
blanc, blanche [*blã(sh)*] white
blanchir *v.* [*blã-sheer*] bleach, blanch
blanchisserie *f.* [*blã-shees-ree*] laundry
blé *m.* [*bleh*] wheat
blesser *v.* [*ble-seh*] injure, wound
blessure *f.* [*ble-sür*] injury
bleu [*bluh*] blue
bloc *m.* [*blok*] block
blond, blonde [*blõ(d)*] blond
blouse *f.* [*blooz*] smock, lab coat
bocal, -aux *m.* [*bo-kal, bo-koh*] jar
boeuf, -s *m.* [*buhf, buh*] ox, steer; beef
bois *m.* [*bwah*] wood, woods
  en bois [*ã bwah*] wooden
boire *v. irreg.* [*bwahr*] drink
boisson *f.* [*bwah-sõ*] drink
boîte *f.* [*bwaht*] box
  boîte de conserve [*bwaht duh kõ-serv*] can
  boîte aux lettres [*bwah-toh letr*] mail box
bombardements *m. pl.* [*bõ-bahr-duh-mã*] bombing
bombe *f.* [*bõb*] bomb
bon, bonne [*bõ, bon*] good
  bon marché [*bõ mahr-sheh*] cheap
bonbon *m.* [*bõ-bõ*] a piece of candy
  des bonbons [*deh bõ-bõ*] candy
bonheur *m.* [*bo-nuhr*] happiness
bonne *f.* [*bon*] maid
Bonjour! [*bõ-zhoor*] Good morning!, Good afternoon!
Bonsoir! [*bõ-swahr*] Good evening!
bonté *f.* [*bõ-teh*] goodness, kindness

bord *m.* [*bor*] edge
  à bord (de) [*ah bor (duh)*] aboard
  le bord de la mer [*luh bor d(uh) lah mer*] sea-shore
botte *f.* [*bot*] boot
bouche *f.* [*boosh*] mouth
boucher *m.* [*boo-sheh*] butcher
boucherie *f.* [*boosh-ree*] butcher shop
bouchon *m.* [*boo-shõ*] stopper, cork
  tire-bouchon *m.* [*teer boo-shõ*] corkscrew
boucle *f.* [*bookl*] curl [of hair], buckle [of belt]
boucle d'oreille [*bookl do-rey*] earring
boue *f.* [*boo*] mud
bougeoir *m.* [*boozh-wahr*] candlestick
bouger *v.* [*boo-zheh*] move
bougie *f.* [*boo-zhee*] candle, sparkplug
bouillant [*boo-yã(t)*] boiling
bouillie *f.* [*boo-yee*] baby cereal, porridge
bouillir *v. irreg.* [*boo-yeer*] boil
bouilloire *f.* [*booy-wahr*] kettle
bouillon *m.* [*boo-yõ*] broth
boulangerie *f.* [*boo-lãzh-ree*] bakery
boule *f.* [*bool*] ball
bouleverser *v.* [*bool-ver-seh*] upset
boulon *m.* [*boo-lõ*] bolt
Bourgogne *f.* [*boor-goñ*] Burgundy
Bourse *f.* [*boors*] stock exchange
bout *m.* [*boo*] end
bouteille *f.* [*boo-tey*] bottle
boutique *f.* [*boo-teek*] shop
bouton *m.* [*boo-tõ*] button, pimple
boxe *f.* [*boks*] boxing
bracelet *m.* [*brahs-le*] bracelet
branche *f.* [*brãsh*] branch
bras *m.* [*brah*] arm
brasserie *f.* [*brahs-ree*] brewery; saloon, café
bref, brève [*bref, brev*] brief
Bretagne *f.* [*bruh-tahñ*] Brittany
bretelle *f.* [*bruh-tel*] suspender; by-pass

breton, -onne [*bruh-tõ, bruh-ton*] Breton
brillant [*bree-yã(t)*] bright, brilliant
briller v. [*bree-yeh*] shine
brique f. [*breek*] brick
briquet m. [*bree-ke*] lighter
brise f. [*breez*] breeze
briser v. [*bree-zeh*] break
britannique [*bree-tah-neek*] British
broderie f. [*brod-ree*] embroidery
bronze [*brõz*] bronze
brosse f. [*bros*] brush
   brosse à dents [*bro-sah dã*] toothbrush
brosser v. [*bro-seh*] brush
brouette f. [*broo-et*] wheelbarrow
brouillard m. [*broo-yahr*] fog
   Il fait du brouillard [*eel fe dü broo-yahr*] It's foggy
bruit m. [*brwee*] noise
brûler v. [*brü-leh*] burn
brûlure f. [*brü-lür*] burn
brun [*brẽ, brün*] brown, brunette
bruyant [*brwee-ã(t)*] noisy
budget m. [*büd-zhe*] budget
buffet m. [*bü-fe*] buffet, sideboard
buisson m. [*bwee-sõ*] bush
bulgare [*bül-gahr*] Bulgarian
Bulgarie f. [*bül-gah-ree*] Bulgaria
bulletin m. [*bül-tẽ*] bulletin, baggage check, ballot
bureau, -eaux m. [*bü-roh*] desk, office
   bureau de poste [*bü-rohd post*] post office
   bureau de location [*bü-rohd lo-kah-syõ*] box office
   bureau de tabac [*bü-rohd tah-bah*] tobacco store
but m. [*bü*] aim, goal, purpose
buvard m. [*bü-vahr*] blotter

C

ça (cela) [*sah*] that
cabane *f.* [*kah-bahn*] cabin
cabine *f.* [*kah-been*] cabin, stateroom
  cabine téléphonique [*kah-been teh-leh-fo-neek*]
    télephone booth
cabinet *m.* [*kah-bee-ne*] cabinet; toilet
cable *m.* [*kahbl*] cable
cacahuète *f.* [*kah-kah-wet*] peanut
cacao *m.* [*kah-kah-oh*] cocoa
cacher *v.* [*kah-sheh*] hide, conceal
  se cacher [*skah-sheh*] hide oneself
cachot *m.* [*kah-shoh*] dungeon
cadeau, -eaux *m.* [*kah-doh*] gift
cadet, -ette [*cah-de(t)*] younger, youngest
cadran *m.* [*kah-drã*] dial
cadre *m.* [*kahdr*] frame [for picture]; framework [theoretical]
café *m.* [*kah-feh*] café, coffee
cafetière *f.* [*kahf-tyer*] coffee pot
cage *f.* [*kahzh*] cage
cahier *m.* [*kah-yeh*] notebook
caillou, -oux *m.* [*kah-yoo*] pebble
caisse *f.* [*kes*] case, crate; cashier
  Payez à la caisse [*peh-yeh ah lah kes*] Pay the cashier
caissier, -ière [*kes-yeh, kes-yer*] cashier, bank teller
calculer *v.* [*kahl-kü-leh*] calculate
caleçon *m.* [*kahl-sõ*] underpants
calendrier *m.* [*kah-lã-dree-yeh*] calender
calme [*kahlm*] calm
caler, se caler *v.* [*kah-leh, s(uh) kah-leh*] stall
camarade *m., f.* [*kah-mah-rahd*] comrade
  camarade de classe [*kah-mah-rahd duh klahs*] classmate
  camarade de jeu [*kah-mah-rahd duh zhuh*] playmate

Why We Make This Generous Offer

There are three important reasons why the Cortina Institute of Languages is pleased to make this special Free Cassette and Sample Lesson offer:

First, never before have there been so many fascinating opportunities open to those who speak foreign languages fluently. Besides the cultural and travel benefits, there are many practical dollars-and-cents advantages—and an ever-increasing number of interesting, well-paying jobs.

The Natural Method

Second, our long experience in the language field has convinced us that the "learn-by-listening" method is the fastest, most convenient and most effective one. It enables you to learn *naturally*—the way you learned English as a child. You acquire a perfect accent and perfect grammar—because that's all you hear.

Just Listen—and Learn

Finally, our professional standing in the field of languages has enabled us to make these generous arrangements with one of the foremost language schools—the inventors of the "learn-by-listening" method. And we are pleased to provide this service for those of our students who want to speak and understand a foreign language "like a native."

There is no obligation and *no salesman will call.* Just mail the card TODAY for your FREE Cassette and Sample Lesson.

What Others Say:

Bob Hope says... "I am studying the course in French ... I think it's a great way to study a language."

Enjoyed by Children "It is surprising how much our two children have absorbed by listening."
—Mrs. C.M.J.

"A Good Investment" "Just returned from Mexico ... Course good investment!"
—Phillips B. Iden

CORTINA INSTITUTE OF LANGUAGES
19 Newtown Turnpike, Westport, CT 06880

cambrioleur *m.* [*kã-bree-o-luhr*] burglar
caméra *m.* [*kah-meh-rah*] movie camera
camion *m.* [*kah-myõ*] truck
camp *m.* [*kã*] camp
campagne *f.* [*kã-pahñ*] country
  à la campagne [*ah lah kã-pahñ*] in the country
camper *v.* [*kã-peh*] camp
Canada *m.* [*kah-nah-dah*] Canada
canadien, -enne [*kah-nah-dyẽ, kah-nah-dyen*] Canadian
canal, -aux *m.* [*kah-nal, kah-noh*] canal
canapé *m.* [*kah-nah-peh*] sofa, couch
canard *m.* [*kah-nahr*] duck
candidat [*kã-dee-dah(t)*] candidate
caniche *f.* [*kah-neesh*] poodle
canne *f.* [*kahn*] cane
canon *m.* [*kah-nõ*] cannon
canot *m.* [*kah-noh*] small boat
  canot de sauvetage [*kah-nohd sohv-tahzh*] life-boat
caoutchouc *m.* [*kah-oot-shoo*] rubber
capable [*kah-pahbl*] able, capable
capacité *f.* [*kah-pah-see-teh*] capacity, ability
capitaine *m.* [*kah-pee-ten*] captain
capital, -aux *adj.* [*kah-pee-tahl, kah-pee-toh*] capital
capital, -aux *m.* [*kah-pee-tahl, kah-pee-toh*] capital
car [*kahr*] for
caractère *m.* [*kah-rahk-ter*] character, disposition
  de bon (mauvais) caractère [*duh bõ (mo-ve) kah-rahk-ter*] good- (bad-) tempered
carafe *f.* [*kah-rahf*] decanter [for wine], pitcher
carburant *m.* [*kahr-bü-rã*] fuel
cardinal, -aux *m.* [*kahr-dee-nahl, kahr-dee-noh*] cardinal
caresser *v.* [*kah-reh-seh*] caress
cargaison *f.* [*kahr-ghe-zõ*] cargo
carie *f.* [*kah-ree*] cavity [of a tooth]
carnaval, -als *m.* [*kahr-nah-vahl*] carnival
carnet *m.* [*kahr-ne*] notebook
  carnet de chèques [*kahr-ned shek*] checkbook
carotte *f.* [*kah-rot*] carrot

carré m. [*kah-reh*] square
carrefour m. [*kahr-foor*] crossroads, intersection
carrelage m. [*kahr-lahzh*] tile floor
carrément [*kah-reh-mã*] squarely, frankly
carrière f. [*kahr-yer*] career
carte f. [*kahrt*] card; map, chart
  cartes à jouer [*kahr-tah zhweh*] playing cards
  carte postale [*kahrt pos-tahl*] postcard
  carte de séjour [*kahrt duh seh-zhoor*] resident's card
  carte de visite [*kahrt duh vee-zeet*] calling card
carton m. [*kahr-tō*] carton, cardboard
cas m. [*kah*] case, situation
  au cas où [*oh kah oo*] in the event of
  en cas de [*ã kah d(uh)*] in case of
  dans ce cas [*dãs kah*] in that case
  en tout cas [*ã too kah*] anyhow, in any case
  selon le cas [*suh-lõl kah*] as the case may be
caserne f. [*kah-zern*] barracks
casier judiciaire m. [*kah-zyeh zhü-dee-syer*] police record
casquette f. [*kahs-ket*] cap
casser v. [*kah-seh*] break
casserole f. [*kahs-rol*] pan
catch m. [*kahtsh*] wrestling
catégorie f. [*kah-teh-go-ree*] category
cathédrale f. [*kah-teh-drahl*] cathedral
catholique [*kah-to-leek*] Catholic
cauchemar m. [*kosh-mahr*] nightmare
cause f. [*kohz*] cause, reason
  à cause de [*ah kohz d(uh)*] because of, on account of
cave f. [*kahv*] cellar
caveau, -eaux m. [*kah-voh*] tomb, vault
ce dem. adj. m. [*s(uh)*] this, that
ce, c' demons. pron. [*s(uh)*] it, this, he, she
ceci [*suh-see*] this
céder v. irreg. [*seh-deh*] cede, give in
ceinture f. [*sē-tür*] belt
  ceinture de sécurité [*sē-tür d(uh) seh-kü-ree-teh*] safety belt
cela (ça) pron. [*s(uh)-lah (sah)*] that

C'est cela [*se slah*] That's it
célèbre [*seh-lebr*] famous
céleri *m.* [*sel-rée*] celery
célibataire *adj.* [*seh-lee-bah-ter*] single
célibataire *m., f.* [*seh-lee-bah-ter*] bachelor, single woman
celle-ci, celle-là; celles-ci, celles-là [*sel-see, sel-lah*]
    this one, that one; these, those
celui-ci, celui-là [*suh-lwee-see, suh-lwee-lah*] this one, that
    one
cendre *f.* [*sãdr*] ash, cinder
cendrier *m.* [*sã-dree-yeh*] ashtray
censé [*sã-seh*] supposed to
cent [*sã*] hundred
centime *m.* [*sã-teem*] centime
centimètre *m.* [*sã-tee-metr*] centimeter [.39 inch]
ce qui, ce que [*skee, skuh*] what, that which
central, -aux [*sã-trahl, sã-troh*] central
centre *m.* [*sãtr*] center
  centre-ville *m.* [*sã-truh-veel*] downtown
cependant [*s(uh)-pã-dã*] however
cercle *m.* [*serkl*] circle
cercueil *m.* [*ser-kuhy*] coffin
céréale *f.* [*seh-reh-ahl*] cereal
cérémonie *f.* [*seh-reh-mo-nee*] ceremony
cerf-volant *m.* [*ser-vo-lã*] kite
cerise *f.* [*s(uh)-reez*] cherry
certain [*ser-tẽ, ser-ten*] certain
certainement [*ser-ten-mã*] certainly
certificat *m.* [*ser-tee-fee-kah*] certificate
cerveau, -eaux *m.* [*ser-voh*] brain [anat.]
cervelle *f.* [*ser-vel*] brains [food]
ces [*seh*] these, those
cesser (de faire) *v.* [*seh-seh (duh fer)*] cease (doing),
    discontinue
c'est-à-dire [*se-tah deer*] that's to say
cet, cette *dem. adj.* [*set*] this, that
ceux [*suh*] the ones, they
ceux-ci, ceux-là [*suh-see, suh-lah*] these, those

chacun, -une [*shah-kē, shah-kün*] each, every one
chagrin *m.* [*shah-grē*] sorrow
chaîne *f.* [*shen*] chain; network [radio, T.V.]
chair *f.* [*sher*] flesh
chaise *f.* [*shez*] chair
châle *m.* [*shahl*] shawl
chaleur *f.* [*shah-luhr*] heat, warmth
chambre *f.* [*shãbr*] room
   chambre à coucher [*shã-brah koo-sheh*] bedroom
   chambre d'hôtel [*shã-bruh doh-tel*] hotel room
   chambre à un lit [*shã-brah ē lee*] single room
   chambre à deux lits [*shã-brah duh lee*] double room
   chambre meublée [*shã-bruh muh-bleh*] furnished room
   chambre forte [*shã-bruh fort*] vault
champ *m.* [*shã*] field
   champ de courses [*shãd koors*] racetrack
champagne *m.* [*shã-pahñ*] champagne
champignon *m.* [*shã-pee-nyõ*] mushroom
champion, -onne [*shã-pyõ, shã-pyon*] champion
chance *f.* [*shãs*] chance, luck
   avoir *v.* **de la chance** [*ah-vwahr dlah shãs*] have good luck,
     be lucky
   Bonne chance! [*bon shãs*] Good luck!
chandail *m.* [*shã-dahy*] sweater
chandelier *m.* [*shã-duh-lyeh*] candlestick
chandelle *f.* [*shã-del*] candle
change *m.* [*shãzh*] foreign exchange
   taux *m.* **de change** [*tohd shãzh*] rate of exchange
changement *m.* [*shãzh-mã*] change
changer *v.* [*shã-zheh*] change
   se changer [*s(uh) shã-zheh*] change clothes
chanson *f.* [*shã-sõ*] song
chanter *v.* [*shã-teh*] sing
chanteur, chanteuse [*shã-tuhr, shã-tuhz*] singer
chantier *m.* [*shã-tyeh*] construction site
chapeau, -eaux *m.* [*shah-poh*] hat
chapelle *f.* [*shah-pel*] chapel
chapiteau, -eaux *m.* [*shah-pee-toh*] capital

chapitre m. [*shah-peetr*] chapter
chaque [*shahk*] each, every
charbon m. [*shahr-bō*] coal
charcuterie f. [*shahr-kü-tree*] pork butcher's, delicatessen
charger v. [*shahr-zheh*] load, burden entrust
  charger une batterie [*shahr-zheh ün bah-tree*] charge a
    battery
  personne f. **à charge** [*per-son ah shahrzh*] dependent
charité f. [*shah-ree-teh*] charity
charmant [*shar-mā(t)*] charming
charme m. [*shahrm*] charm
charnière f. [*shahr-nyer*] hinge
charrue f. [*shah-rü*] plow
chasse f. [*shahs*] hunting
chasser v. [*shah-seh*] chase, hunt
chasseur m. [*shah-suhr*] hunter; bellboy
chat m. [*shah*] cat
château, -eaux m. [*shah-toh*] castle
chaud [*shoh*] hot
  Il fait chaud [*eel fe shoh*] It's hot
  avoir v. **chaud** [*ah-vwahr shoh*] be hot
chauffage m. [*shoh-fahzh*] heating
chauffer v. [*shoh-feh*] heat
chauffeur m. [*shoh-fuhr*] driver, chauffeur
chaussée f. [*shoh-seh*] street, roadway
chaussette f. [*shoh-set*] sock
chaussure f. [*shoh-sür*] shoe
chauve [*shohv*] bald
chef m. [*shef*] chief, leader
chef-d'oeuvre m. [*she-duhvr*] masterpiece
chemin m. [*sh(uh)-mĕ*] road, path, way
  chemin de fer [*sh(uh)-mĕd fer*] railroad
  à mi-chemin [*ah meesh-mĕ*] midway
cheminée f. [*sh(uh)-mee-neh*] chimney, fireplace, mantel
chemise f. [*sh(uh)-meez*] shirt
  chemise de nuit [*sh(uh)-meez duh nweet*] nightgown
chemisier m. [*sh(uh)-mee-zyeh*] blouse
chêne m. [*shen*] oak

chèque *m.* [*shek*] check
  chèque de voyage [*shek duh vwah-yahzh*] traveler's check
cher, chère [*sher*] dear, expensive
chercher *v.* [*sher-sheh*] look for, search for
chéri, -ie [*sheh-ree*] sweetheart, darling
cheval, -aux *m.* [*sh(uh)-vahl, sh(uh)-voh*] horse
  monter *v.* **à cheval** [*mõ-teh ahsh-vahl*] ride
chevalier *m.* [*sh(uh)-vah-lyeh*] knight
cheveux *m. pl.* [*sh(uh)-vuh*] hair
  se faire *v.* **couper les cheveux** [*sfer koo-peh leh-shvuh*] have
    a haircut
cheville *f.* [*sh(uh)-veey*] ankle
chèvre *f.* [*shevr*] goat
chevreau, -eaux *m.* [*shuh-vroh*] kid
chez [*sheh*] at the home of, at the place of business of
  chez-soi *m. inv.* [*sheh-swah*] home
  Faites comme chez vous [*fet kom sheh voo*] Make yourself
    at home
chic [*sheek*] smart
chien *m.* [*shyē*] dog
chiffon *m.* [*shee-fõ*] rag
chiffre *m.* [*sheefr*] figure
chimique *adj.* [*shee-meek*] chemical
Chine *f.* [*sheen*] China
chinois [*shee-nwah(z)*] Chinese
chirurgie *f.* [*shee-rür-zhee*] surgery
chirurgien, -ienne [*shee-rür-zhyē, shee-rür-zhyen*] surgeon
choc *m.* [*shok*] shock
chocolat *m.* [*sho-ko-lah*] chocolate
choisir *v.* [*shwah-zeer*] choose
choix *m.* [*shwah*] choice
chômage *m.* [*shoh-mahzh*] unemployment
  en chômage [*ã shoh-mahzh*] unemployed
choquant [*sho-kã(t)*] offensive, shocking
choquer *v.* [*sho-keh*] shock
chose *f.* [*shohz*] thing
chou, choux *m.* [*shoo*] cabbage
chou-fleur, choux-fleurs *m.* [*shoo-fluhr*] cauliflower

chrétien, -enne [*kreh-tyē, kreh-tyen*] Christian
chuchoter *v.* [*shü-sho-teh*] whisper
chute *f.* [*shüt*] fall
cicatrice *f.* [*see-kah-trees*] scar
cidre *m.* [*seedr*] cider
ciel, cieux *m.* [*syel, syuh*] sky, heaven
cierge *f.* [*syerzh*] candle
cigare *f.* [*see-gahr*] cigar
cigarette *f.* [*see-gah-ret*] cigarette
cil *m.* [*seel*] eyelash
ciment *m.* [*see-mã*] cement
cimetière *m.* [*seem-tyer*] cemetery
cinéma *m.* [*see-neh-mah*] movies, movie theater
cinq [*sē(k)*] five
cinquante [*sē-kãt*] fifty
cinquième [*sē-kyem*] fifth
circonscription *f.* [*seer-kõ-skreep-syõ*] electoral district
circonstance *f.* [*seer-kõ-stãs*] circumstance
circulation *f.* [*seer-kü-lah-syõ*] circulation [of blood], traffic
cire *f.* [*seer*] wax
cirer *v.* [*see-reh*] shine, wax
cireur *m.* [*see-ruhr*] shoeshine boy
cirque *m.* [*seerk*] circus
ciseau *m.* [*see-zoh*] chisel
  ciseaux *pl.* [*see-zoh*] scissors
citation *f.* [*see-tah-syõ*] quotation
citer *v.* [*see-teh*] quote
citoyen, -enne [*see-twah-yē, see-twah-yen*] citizen
citron *m.* [*see-trõ*] lemon
citrouille *f.* [*see-trooy*] pumpkin
civil, -le [*see-veel*] civilian
civilisation *f.* [*see-vee-lee-zah-syõ*] civilization
civisme *m.* [*see-veezm*] good citizenship
clair [*kler*] light, bright, clear
clair *m.* **de lune** [*kler duh lün*] moonlight
classe *f.* [*klahs*] class
classer *v.* [*klah-seh*] classify
classique [*klah-seek*] classic

clef *f.* [*kleh*] key; wrench
clergé *m.* [*kler-zheh*] clergy
client, -te [*klee-ã(t)*] customer, client
clientèle *f.* [*klee-ã-tel*] clientele
climat *m.* [*klee-mah*] climate
clinique *f.* [*klee-neek*] private hospital
cloche *f.* [*klosh*] bell
clocher *m.* [*klo-sheh*] steeple
cloître *m.* [*klwahtr*] cloister
clou *m.* [*kloo*] nail
clouer *v.* [*kloo-eh*] nail
cochon *m.* [*ko-shõ*] pig
cocktail *m.* [*kok-tel*] cocktail
coeur *m.* [*kuhr*] heart
  par coeur [*pahr kuhr*] by heart
coffre *m.* [*kofr*] chest; auto trunk
cognac *m.* [*ko-nyahk*] brandy
coiffer, se coiffer *v.* [*kwah-feh, s(uh) kwah-feh*] comb [one's] hair
coiffeur *m.* [*kwah-fuhr*] barber, beauty operator
coin *m.* [*kwẽ*] corner
coincidence *f.* [*ko-ẽ-see-dãs*] coincidence
col *m.* [*kol*] collar; mountain pass
colère *f.* [*ko-ler*] anger
  en colère [*ã ko-ler*] angry
colis *m.* [*ko-lee*] parcel
colle *f.* [*kol*] glue
collection *f.* [*ko-lek-syõ*] collection
collectionner *v.* [*ko-lek-syo-neh*] collect
collègue *m., f.* [*ko-leg*] colleague
coller *v.* [*ko-leh*] stick, glue
collier *m.* [*kol-yeh*] necklace, beads
colline *f.* [*ko-leen*] hill
collision *f.* [*ko-lee-zyõ*] collision, crash
colonel *m.* [*ko-lo-nel*] colonel
colonie *f.* [*ko-lo-nee*] colony
coloniser *v.* [*ko-lo-nee-zeh*] colonize, settle
colonne *f.* [*ko-lon*] column

colonne vertébrale f. [*ko-lon ver-teh-brahl*] spine
colorer v. [*ko-lo-reh*] color
combat m. [*kõ-bah*] fight
Combien (de)? [*kõ-byē (duh)*] How much? How many?
  Combien de temps? [*kõ-byēd tã*] How long?
combinaison f. [*kõ-bee-ne-zõ*] combination, slip
  [undergarment]
combiner v. [*kõ-bee-neh*] combine
combler v. [*kõ-bleh*] fill
comédie f. [*ko-meh-dee*] comedy
comédien, -enne [*ko-meh-dyē, ko-meh-dyen*] comedian
comité m. [*ko-mee-teh*] committee
commander v. [*ko-mã-deh*] command, order
comme [*kom*] like, as
  comme ci comme ça [*kom see kom sah*] so-so
commencement m. [*ko-mãs-mã*] beginning
commencer (à faire) v. [*ko-mã-seh (ah fer)*] begin (to do)
comment [*ko-mã*] how
commerçant, -te [*ko-mer-sã(t)*] merchant, storekeeper
commerce m. [*ko-mers*] trade
commercial, -aux [*ko-mer-syahl, ko-mer-syoh*] commercial
commettre v. irreg. [*ko-metr*] commit
commissaire m. **de police** [*ko-mee-ser duh po-lees*] police
  superintendent
commissariat m. **de police** [*ko-mee-sahr-yah duh po-lees*]
  police station
commission f. [*ko-mee-syõ*] commission
commode [*ko-mod*] convenient
commode f. [*ko-mod*] dresser, chest of drawers
commun [*ko-mē, ko-mün*] common
communauté f. [*ko-mü-noh-teh*] community
commune f. [*ko-mün*] municipality
communication f. [*ko-mü-nee-kah-syõ*] communication,
  telephone call
communiquer v. [*ko-mü-nee-keh*] communicate
communisme m. [*ko-mü-neezm*] communism
communiste n. & adj. [*ko-mü-neest*] communist
compagnie f. [*kõ-pah-nyee*] company

compagnie aérienne [kõ-pah-nyee ah-eh-ryen] airline
compagnie de navigation [kõ-pah-nyeed nah-vee-gah-syõ] steamship line
compagnon m. [kõ-pah-nyõ] companion
comparaison f. [kõ-pah-re-zõ] comparison
comparer v. [kõ-pah-reh] compare
compartiment m. [kõ-pahr-tee-mã] compartment
compatriote m., f. [kõ-pah-tree-ot] compatriot
compensation f. [kõ-pã-sah-syõ] compensation
compétent [kõ-peh-tã(t)] competent
compétition f. [kõ-peh-tee-syõ] competition
complément m. [kõ-pleh-mã] complement
complet, -ète [kõ-ple(t)] complete
  Complet [kõ-ple] Full, No vacancy
complet m. [kõ-ple] suit
complètement [kõ-plet-mã] completely
completer v. [kõ-pleh-teh] complete
compliment m. [kõ-plee-mã] compliment
compliqué [kõ-plee-keh] complicated
compliquer v. [kõ-plee-keh] complicate
complot m. [kõ-ploh] plot
comportement m. [kõ-por-tuh-mã] behavior
comporter v. [kõ-por-teh] comprise
  se comporter [s(uh) kõ-por-teh] behave
composé [kõ-poh-zeh] compound
composer v. [kõ-poh-zeh] compose, dial [a telephone]
compositeur m. [kõ-poh-zee-tuhr] composer
comprendre v. irreg. [kõ-prãdr] understand
comprimé m. [kõ-pree-meh] tablet
comprimer v. [kõ-pree-meh] compress
compromis m. [kõ-pro-mee] compromise
comptable m. [kõ-tahbl] accountant, bookkeeper
comptabilité f. [kõ-tah-bee-lee-teh] bookkeeping, accounts
comptant [kõ-tã] cash
compte m. [kõt] account
  compte courant [kõt koo-rã] checking account
  compte-cheques [kõt-shek] checking account
  compte-rendu [kõt-rã-dü] report, book review

rendre v. **compte de** [*rãdr kõt d(uh)*] account for
se rendre v. **compte de** [*s(uh) rãdr kõt d(uh)*] realize
compter (sur) v. [*kõ-teh (sür)*] count; rely (on)
comptoir m. [*kõ-twahr*] counter
concentrer, se concentrer v. [*kõ-sã-treh, skõ-sã-treh*] concentrate
concept m. [*kõ-sept*] concept
concernant [*kõ-ser-nã*] concerning
concert m. [*kõ-ser*] concert
concevoir v. irreg. [*kõ-s(uh)-vwahr*] conceive
concièrge m., f. [*kõ-syerzh*] housekeeper, doorkeeper
conclure v. irreg. [*kõ-klür*] conclude
conclusion f. [*kõ-klü-zyõ*] conclusion
concombre m. [*kõ-kõbr*] cucumber
concours m. [*kõ-koor*] contest, competitive examination
concurrence f. [*kõ-kü-rãs*] competition
condamnation f. [*kõ-dah-nah-syõ*] condemnation
condamner v. [*kõ-dah-neh*] condemn
condenser v. [*kõ-dã-seh*] condense
condition f. [*kõ-dee-syõ*] condition
conditionnel, -elle [*kõ-dee-syo-nel*] conditional
conduire v. irreg. [*kõ-dweer*] drive, lead
se conduire [*s(uh) kõ-dweer*] behave
conduite f. [*kõ-dweet*] conduct
confection f. [*kõ-fek-syõ*] ready-to-wear
conférence f. [*kõ-feh-rãs*] lecture
conférencier m. [*kõ-feh-rã-syeh*] lecturer
confesser v. [*kõ-feh-seh*] confess
se confesser [*s(uh) kõ-feh-seh*] go to confession
confession f. [*kõ-fe-syõ*] confession
confiance f. [*kõ-fyãs*] confidence, trust
faire v. **confiance** [*fer kõ-fyãs*] trust
confiant [*kõ-fyã(t)*] trusting, confident
confidentiel, -elle [*kõ-fee-dã-syel*] confidential
confier v. [*kõ-fyeh*] entrust
confirmer v. [*kõ-feer-meh*] confirm
confiture f. [*kõ-fee-tür*] jam
conflit m. [*kõ-flee*] conflict

confondre v. [kõ-fõdr] confuse

confort m. [kõ-for] comfort

confortable [kõ-for-tahbl] comfortable

  peu (pas) confortable [puh (pah) kõ-for-tahbl] uncomfortable

confusion f. [kõ-fü-zyõ] confusion

congé m. [kõ-zheh] holiday

congrès m. [kõ-gre] congress, conference

connaissance f. [ko-ne-sãs] acquaintance, knowledge

  faire v. **la connaissance de** [fer lah ko-ne-sãs duh] meet, make the acquaintance of

connaissement m. [ko-nes-mã] bill of lading

connaître v. irreg. [ko-netr] know

conquérir v. irreg. [kõ-keh-reer] conquer

consacrer v. [kõ-sah-kreh] devote

conscience f. [kõ-syãs] consciousness, conscience

consciencieux, -euse [kõ-syã-syuh, kõ-syã-syuhz] conscientious

conscient [kõ-syã(t)] aware, conscious

conseil m. [kõ-sey] advice, council

  conseil m. **de ministres** [kõ-seyd mee-neestr] cabinet

conseiller v. [kõ-se-yeh] advise, recommend

consentir v. irreg. [kõ-sã-teer] consent

conséquence f. [kõ-seh-kãs] consequence

  en conséquence [ã kõ-seh-kãs] therefore, accordingly

conséquent [kõ-seh-kã(t)] consistent

  par conséquent [pahr kõ-seh-kã] consequently

conservateur, -trice [kõ-ser-vah-tuhr, kõ-ser-vah-trees] conservative

conservatoire m. [kõ-ser-vah-twahr] music school

conserver v. [kõ-ser-veh] preserve

considérable [kõ-see-deh-rahbl] considerable

considérer v. [kõ-see-deh-reh] consider

consigne f. [kõ-seeñ] baggage check

  mettre v. irreg. **à la consigne** [me-trah lah kõ-seeñ] check

consister à v. [kõ-sees-teh (ah)] consist in

  consister en [kõ-sees-teh ã] consist of

consoler f. [kõ-so-leh] console, comfort

consommateur m. [kõ-so-mah-tuhr] consumer

consommation f. [kõ-so-mah-syõ] consumption; beverage, drink

consommer v. [kõ-so-meh] consume, consummate

constamment [kõ-stah-mã] constantly

constant [kõ-stã(t)] constant

constater v. [kõ-stah-teh] note

constituer v. [kõ-stee-tweh] constitute

constitution f. [kõ-stee-tü-syõ] constitution

construction f. [kõ-strük-syõ] construction

construire v. irreg. [kõ-strweer] build

consul m. [kõ-sül] consul

consulat m. [kõ-sü-lah] consulate

consultation f. [kõ-sül-tah-syõ] office call, conference

consulter v. [kõ-sül-teh] consult

contact m. [kõ-tahkt] contact

contagieux, -euse [kõ-tah-zhyuh, kõ-tah-zhyuhz] contagious

conte m. [kõt] tale

contemporain [kõ-tã-po-rẽ, kõ-tã-po-ren] contemporary

contenir v. irreg. [kõt-neer] contain

content [kõ-tã(t)] happy, glad

contenu m. [kõt-nü] contents

contestable [kõ-tes-tahbl] questionable

continent m. [kõ-tee-nã] continent

continuer (à, de) v. [kõ-tee-nweh (ah, duh)] continue (to)

contraire [kõ-trer] contrary

   au contraire [oh kõ-trer] on the contrary

contraste m. [kõ-trahst] contrast

contrat m. [kõ-trah] contract

contre [kõtr] against

contribuer v. [kõ-tree-bweh] contribute

contrôle m. [kõ-trohl] check

contrôler v. [kõ-troh-leh] check, verify

contrôleur m. [kõ-troh-luhr] inspector; ticket-taker, train conductor

controverse f. [kõ-tro-vers] controversy

convaincre v. irreg. [kõ-vẽkr] convince, convict

convenable [kõ-vnahbl] suitable, proper

convenir v. irreg. [kŏ-vneer] suit
conversation f. [kŏ-ver-sah-syŏ] conversation
convertir v. [kŏ-ver-teer] convert
coopération f. [ko-o-peh-rah-syŏ] cooperation
copie f. [ko-pee] copy
copier v. [ko-pyeh] copy
coquelicot m. [kok-lee-koh] poppy
coquillage m. [ko-kee-yahzh] seashell
coquille f. [ko-keey] shell
corbeau, -eaux m. [kor-boh] crow
corbeille f. [kor-bey] basket
  corbeille à papier [kor-bey ah pah-pyeh] wastebasket
corde f. [kord] cord, rope
cordial, -iaux [kor-dyahl, kor-dyoh] cordial
cordonnier m. [kor-do-nyeh] shoemaker
corne f. [korn] horn
corps m. [kor] body
correct adj. [ko-rekt] correct
correction f. [ko-rek-syŏ] correction
correspondance f. [ko-res-pŏ-dãs] correspondence; train
    connection
correspondre v. [ko-res-pŏdr] correspond
corriger v. [ko-ree-zheh] correct
corrompre v. [ko-rŏpr] corrupt, bribe
corrompu [ko-rŏ-pü] corrupt
corruption f. [ko-rüp-syŏ] corruption
corsage m. [kor-sahzh] blouse, dress bodice
costume m. [kos-tüm] suit
côte f. [koht] coast; rib
côté m. [koh-teh] side
  à côté de [ah koh-teh d(uh)] beside, near, next to
  de côté [d(uh) koh-teh] aside, sideways
côtelette f. [koht-let] chop, cutlet
coton m. [ko-tŏ] cotton
cou m. [koo] neck
couche f. [koosh] diaper
coucher m. **de soleil** [koo-shehd so-ley] sunset
coucher v. [koo-sheh] lay, put to bed

se coucher [*s*(*uh*) *koo-sheh*] lie down, go to bed
couchette *f.* [*koo-shet*] berth
coude *m.* [*kood*] elbow
coudre *v. irreg.* [*koodr*] sew
   machine *f.* **à coudre** *f.* [*mah-shee-nah koodr*] sewing machine
couler *v.* [*koo-leh*] flow
couleur *f.* [*koo-luhr*] color
couloir *m.* [*kool-wahr*] hall, corridor
coup *m.* [*koo*] blow
   coup de feu [*kood fuh*] shot
   coup d'oeil [*koo duhy*] glance
   coup de pied [*kood pyeh*] kick
   coup de soleil [*kood so-ley*] sunburn
   tout à coup [*too-tah koo*] suddenly
coupable [*koo-pahbl*] guilty
coupe *f.* [*koop*] cut
couper *v.* [*koo-peh*] cut
couple *m.* [*koopl*] couple
coupure *f.* [*koo-pür*] cut
cour *f.* [*koor*] court, courtyard
   faire *v.* **la cour à** [*fer lah koor ah*] court
courage *m.* [*koo-rahzh*] courage
courageux, -euse [*koo-rah-zhuh, koo-rah-zhuhz*] brave
couramment [*koo-rah-mã*] fluently
courant *adj.* [*koo-rã(t)*] running, current
courant *m.* [*koo-rã*] current
   courant d'air [*koo-rã der*] draft
courbe *f.* [*koorb*] curve
courir *v. irreg.* [*koo-reer*] run
couronne *f.* [*koo-ron*] crown
courrier *m.* [*koor-yeh*] mail
cours *m.* [*koor*] course
   cours du change [*koor dü shãzh*] rate of exchange
   Quel est le cours du dollar? [*kel el koor dü do-lahr*]
      What is the rate of exchange for dollars?
course *f.* [*koors*] race, errand
court [*koor(t)*] short
courtois [*koor-twah(z)*] courteous

cousin, -ine [*koo-zē, koo-zeen*] cousin
  cousin (-ine) germain (-aine) [*koo-zē zher-mē, koo-zeen zher-men*] first cousin
coussin *m.* [*koo-sē*] cushion
coût *m.* [*koo*] cost
  coût de la vie [*kood lah vee*] cost of living
couteau, -eaux *m.* [*koo-toh*] knife
coûter *v.* [*koo-teh*] cost
couteux, -euse [*koo-tuh, koo-tuhz*] costly
coutume *f.* [*koo-tüm*] custom
couture *f.* [*koo-tür*] sewing, seam
couturière *f.* [*koo-tür-yer*] dressmaker
couvent *m.* [*koo-vā*] convent, monastery
couvercle *m.* [*koo-verkl*] lid
couvert *adj.* [*koo-ver(t)*] covered
  vente *f.* **à couvert** [*vā-tah koo-ver*] sale for delivery
couvert *m.* [*koo-ver*] fork and spoon, place at table, restaurant cover charge
  mettre *v. irreg.* **le couvert** [*metr luh koo-ver*] set the table
couverture *f.* [*koo-ver-tür*] blanket, cover
couvrir *v. irreg.* [*koov-reer*] cover
crabe *m.* [*krahb*] crab
cracher *v.* [*krah-sheh*] spit
craie *f.* [*kre*] chalk
craindre *v. irreg.* [*krēdr*] fear
crainte *f.* [*krēt*] fear
crâne *m.* [*krahn*] skull
cravate *f.* [*krah-vaht*] necktie
crayon *m.* [*kre-yō*] pencil
créancier *m.* [*kreh-ā-syeh*] creditor
création *f.* [*kreh-ah-syō*] creation
créature *f.* [*kreh-ah-tür*] creature
crédit *m.* [*kreh-dee*] credit
créer *v.* [*kreh-eh*] create
crème *f.* [*krem*] cream
  crème Chantilly [*krem shā-tee-yee*] sugared whipped cream
crêpe *f.* [*krep*] crepe, pancake

crépuscule *m.* [*kreh-püs-kül*] dusk
creuser *v.* [*kruh-zeh*] dig
creux, -euse [*kruh, kruhz*] hollow
crevaison *f.* [*kruh-ve-zõ*] blow-out
crever *v.* [*kruh-veh*] burst
   J'ai crevé [*zheh kruh-veh*] I have (had) a flat tire
crevette *f.* [*kruh-vet*] shrimp
cri *m.* [*kree*] cry, scream
   pousser *v.* **des cris** [*poo-seh deh kree*] scream
cric *m.* [*kreek*] jack
crier *v.* [*kree-eh*] call, shout
crime *m.* [*kreem*] crime
criminel, -elle *adj. & n.* [*kree-mee-nel*] criminal
crise *f.* [*kreez*] crisis, heart attack
cristal, -aux *m.* [*krees-tahl, krees-toh*] crystal
critique *adj.* [*kree-teek*] critical
critique *f.* [*kree-teek*] review, criticism
critique *m.* [*kree-teek*] critic
critiquer *v.* [*kree-tee-keh*] criticize
crochet *m.* [*kro-she*] hook, crochet work
croire *v. irreg.* [*krwahr*] believe
   Je crois que oui [*zhuh krwahk wee*] I think so
   Je ne le crois pas [*zhuhn luh krwah pah*] I don't think so
croisement *m.* [*krwahz-mã*] crossing
croiser *v.* [*krwah-zeh*] cross
croisière *f.* [*krwah-zyer*] cruise
croître *v. irreg.* [*krwahtr*] grow
croix *f.* [*krwah*] cross
   Croix Rouge *m.* [*krwah roozh*] Red Cross
croquis *m.* [*kro-kee*] sketch
croûte *f.* [*kroot*] crust
croyance *f.* [*krwah-yãs*] belief
cru [*krü*] raw
cru *past part. of* CROIRE [*krü*] believed
cruauté *f.* [*krü-oh-teh*] cruelty
crudités *f. pl.* [*krü-dee-teh*] raw vegetables
cruel, -elle [*krü-el*] cruel
Cuba *m.* [*kü-bah*] Cuba

cubain [*kü-bē, kü-ben*] Cuban
cube *m.* [*küb*] cube, block
cueillir *v. irreg.* [*kuh-yeer*] pick
cuillère *f.* [*kwee-yer*] spoon
  petite cuillère [*p(uh)-teet kwee-yer*] teaspoon
  cuillère à soupe [*kwee-yer ah soop*] tablespoon
cuillerée *f.* [*kweey-reh*] spoonful
cuir *m.* [*kweer*] leather
  cuir chevelu [*kweer chuhv-lü*] scalp
cuire *v. irreg.* [*kweer*] cook
  cuire au four [*kweer oh foor*] bake
cuisine *f.* [*kwee-zeen*] kitchen, cooking
  faire *v.* **la cuisine** [*fer lah kwee-zeen*] cook
cuisinier, -ière, *m., f.* [*kwee-zee-nyeh, kwee-zee-nyer*] cook
cuisinière *f.* [*kwee-zee-nyer*] stove
cuisse *f.* [*kwees*] thigh
cuit [*kwee(t)*] cooked
  bien cuit [*byē kwee(t)*] well done
cuivre *m.* [*kweevr*] copper, brass
culotte *f.* [*kü-lot*] pants
culte *m.* [*kült*] worship
cultivateur *m.* [*kül-tee-vah-tuhr*] farmer
cultiver *v.* [*kül-tee-veh*] cultivate, grow
culture *f.* [*kül-tür*] culture; crop
cure *f.* [*kür*] cure
curé *m.* [*kü-reh*] pastor
cure-dents *m. inv.* [*kür-dā*] toothpick
curieux, -euse [*kür-yuh, kür-yuhz*] curious
curiosité *f.* [*kür-yoh-zee-teh*] curiosity
cuvette *f.* [*kü-vet*] basin
cycliste *m., f.* [*see-kleest*] cyclist

D

d': de [*duh*] of, from
dame *f.* [*dahm*] lady
danger *m.* [*dã-zheh*] danger
dangereux, -euse [*dãzh-ruh, dãzh-ruhz*] dangerous
dans [*dã*] in
dactylographe, dactylo *m., f.* [*dahk-tee-lo-grahf, dahk-tee-loh*] typist
danse *f.* [*dãs*] dance
danser *v.* [*dã-seh*] dance
danseur, -euse [*dã-suhr, dã-suhz*] dancer
date *f.* [*daht*] date
datte *f.* [*daht*] date [fruit]
davantage [*dah-vã-tahzh*] more
de [*d(uh)*] of, from
dé *m.* [*deh*] die [gambling], thimble
déballer *v.* [*deh-bah-leh*] unpack
débarquer *v.* [*deh-bahr-keh*] disembark
débarrasser *v.* [*deh-bah-rah-seh*] rid
  se débarrasser de [*s(uh) deh-bah-rah-seh duh*] get rid of
déborder *v.* [*deh-bor-deh*] overflow
debout *adv.* [*duh-boo*] upright, standing
  être (se tenir, rester) debout [*e-truh (stuh-neer, res-teh) duh-boo*] stand
se débrouiller *v.* [*s(uh) deh-broo-yeh*] get along
début *m.* [*deh-bü*] beginning
décédé [*deh-seh-deh*] deceased
décembre *m.* [*deh-sãbr*] December
décence *f.* [*deh-sãs*] decency
décent [*deh-sã(t)*] decent
décevoir *v. irreg.* [*dehs-vwahr*] disappoint
décharger *v.* [*deh-shahr-zheh*] unload, relieve
déchirer *v.* [*deh-shee-reh*] tear, rip

décider *v.* [*deh-see-deh*] decide
  se décider [*sdeh-see-deh*] make up one's mind
décision *f.* [*deh-see-zyō*] decision
déclaration *f.* [*deh-klah-rah-syō*] declaration, statement
déclarer *v.* [*deh-klah-reh*] declare
décommander *v.* [*deh-ko-mā-deh*] call off
décor *m.* [*deh-kor*] decoration, scenery
décoration *f.* [*deh-ko-rah-syō*] decoration
décorer *v.* [*deh-ko-reh*] decorate
découper *v.* [*deh-koo-peh*] cut up, cut out, carve [meat]
décourager *v.* [*deh-koo-rah-zheh*] discourage
découvert [*deh-koo-ver(t)*] uncovered, exposed
  compte *m.* **découvert** [*kōt deh-koo-ver*] overdrawn account
  crédit *m.* **à découvert** [*kreh-dee ah deh-koo-ver*] unsecured
  credit
  vente *f.* **à découvert** [*vā-tah deh-koo-ver*] sale for futures
découverte *f.* [*deh-koo-vert*] discovery
découvrir *v. irreg.* [*deh-koo-vreer*] discover, uncover
décret *m.* [*deh-kre*] decree
décrire *v. irreg.* [*deh-kreer*] describe
décrocher *v.* [*deh-kro-sheh*] unhook, disconnect
déçu [*deh-sü*] disappointed
dedans [*duh-dā*] inside, indoors
défaire *v. irreg.* [*deh-fer*] undo, unpack
défaite *f.* [*deh-fet*] defeat
défaut *m.* [*deh-foh*] defect
défavorable [*deh-fah-vo-rahbl*] unfavorable
défectueux, -euse [*deh-fek-twuh, deh-fek-twuhz*] defective
défendre *v.* [*deh-fādr*] defend, prohibit
défendu [*deh-fā-dü*] forbidden
Défense d'entrer [*deh-fās dā-treh*] Keep out
défi *m.* [*deh-fee*] challenge, dare
défilé *m.* [*deh-fee-leh*] parade
définir *v.* [*deh-fee-neer*] define
définition *f.* [*deh-fee-nee-syō*] definition
défunt [*deh-fĕ(t)*] deceased
dégouté [*deh-goo-teh*] disgusted
degré *m.* [*duh-greh*] degree

déguisement *m.* [*deh-gheez-mã*] disguise

dehors [*duh-or*] out, outside, outdoors

déjà [*deh-zhah*] already

déjeuner *m.* [*deh-zhuh-neh*] lunch, noon meal
  petit déjeuner [*ptee deh-zhuh-neh*] breakfast

déjeuner *v.* [*deh-zhuh-nèh*] have breakfast, have lunch

delà: au dela de [*ohd lahd(uh)*] beyond

délai *m.* [*deh-le*] delay, time-limit

délibéré [*deh-lee-beh-reh*] deliberate

délicat [*deh-lee-kah(t)*] delicate

délicieux, -euse [*deh-lee-syuh, deh-lee-syuhz*] delicious

délivrer *v.* [*deh-lee-vreh*] deliver

demain [*d(uh)-mē*] tomorrow
  demain matin [*d(uh)-mē mah-tē*] tomorrow morning
  après-demain [*ah-pred-mē*] the day after tomorrow

demande *f.* [*d(uh)-mãd*] request, application
  demande en mariage [*d(uh)-mã-dã mahr-yahzh*] proposal

demander *v.* [*d(uh)-mã-deh*] ask, ask for
  demander à [someone] **de faire** [something] [*d(uh)-mã-deh
    ah . . . dfer . . .*] ask [someone] to do [something]
  demander [something] **à** [someone] [*d(uh)-mã-deh . . .
    ah . . .*] ask [someone] for [something]
  se demander [*suhd-mã-deh*] wonder

démarrer *v.* [*deh-mah-reh*] start [car]

démarreur *m.* [*deh-mah-ruhr*] starter

déménager *v.* [*deh-meh-nah-zheh*] move [change residence]

démenti *m.* [*deh-mã-tee*] denial

démentir *v.* [*deh-mã-teer*] deny, contradict

demi [*d(uh)-mee*] half
  deux heures et demie [*duh-zuhr ed-mee*] half past two

démission *f.* [*deh-mee-syō*] resignation

démissionner *v.* [*deh-mee-syo-neh*] resign

démocratie *f.* [*deh-mo-krah-see*] democracy

démodé [*deh-mo-deh*] old-fashioned

demoiselle *f.* [*d(uh)-mwah-zel*] young lady
  demoiselle d'honneur [*d(uh)-mwah-zel do-nuhr*] bridesmaid,
    flower girl

démolir *v.* [*deh-mo-leer*] demolish

démonstration f. [deh-mõ-strah-syõ] demonstration
démontrer v. [deh-mõ-treh] demonstrate, prove
dense [dãs] dense
densité f. [dã-see-teh] density
dent f. [dã] tooth
   mal m. **de dents** [mahl duh dã] toothache
   brosse f. **à dents** [bro-sah dã] toothbrush
dentelle f. [dã-tel] lace
dentifrice f. [dã-tee-frees] toothpaste
dentiste m. [dã-teest] dentist
dépanneuse f. [deh-pah-nuhz] tow truck
départ m. [deh-pahr] departure, start
département m. [deh-pahr-tuh-mã] department
dépasser v. [deh-pah-seh] exceed, pass
se dépêcher v. [s(uh)-deh-pe-sheh] hurry
   Dépêchez-vous! [deh-pe-sheh-voo] Hurry up!
dépendre (de) v. [deh-pãdr (duh)] depend (on)
   Cela dépend [slah deh-pã] That depends
dépense f. [deh-pãs] expense, cost
dépenser v. [deh-pã-seh] spend
déplacement m. [deh-plahs-mã] traveling
déplacer v. [deh-plah-seh] move
déposer v. [deh-poh-zeh] deposit
depuis [d(uh)-pwee] since, for [time, duration]
   Depuis quand êtes-vous ici? [duh-pwee kã et-voo ee-see]
      Since when have you been here?
   Je suis ici depuis vendredi [shswee-zee-seed-pwee vã-
      druh-dee] I have been here since Friday
   Je suis ici depuis trois jours [shswee-zee-seed-pwee trwah
      zhoor] I have been here for three days
dérangement m. [deh-rãzh-mã] inconvenience
   en dérangement [ã deh-rãzh-mã] out of order
déranger v. [deh-rã-zheh] bother, disturb
déraper v. [deh-rah-peh] skid
dernier, -ière [der-nyeh, der-nyer] last, latest; latter
dernièrement [der-nyer-mã] lately
derrière m. [der-yer] rear, bottom
   de derrière [duh der-yer] back, hind

derrière *prep. & adv.* [*der-yer*] behind, in back (of)
des: de les [*deh*] some, any; of the
dès [*de*] from
désagréable [*deh-zah-greh-ahbl*] disagreeable
désapprouver *v.* [*deh-zah-proo-veh*] disapprove
désastre *m.* [*deh-zahstr*] disaster
désavantage *m.* [*deh-zah-vã-tahzh*] disadvantage
descendre *v.* [*deh-sãdr*] descend, come down, go down,
    take down
descente *f.* [*deh-sãt*] descent
description *f.* [*des-kreep-syõ*] description
désert *m.* [*deh-zer*] desert
déserter *v.* [*deh-zer-ıeh*] desert
désespéré [*deh-zes-peh-reh*] desperate
désespérer *v.* [*deh-zes-peh-reh*] despair
désespoir *m.* [*deh-zes-pwahr*] despair
déshabiller *v.* [*deh-zah-bee-yeh*] undress [someone or
    something]
  se déshabiller [*sdeh-zah-bee-ych*] undress [oneself], get
    undressed
désigner *v.* [*deh-zee-nyeh*] designate
désintéressé [*deh-zẽ-ıeh-re-seh*] disinterested
désir *m.* [*deh-zeer*] desire
désirable [*deh-zee-rahbl*] desirable
désirer *v.* [*deh-zee-reh*] desire
désobéir (à) *v.* [*deh-zo-beh-eer (ah)*] disobey
désolé [*deh-zo-leh*] desolate
  Je suis désolé [*shswee deh-zo-leh*] I'm very sorry
désordre *m.* [*deh-zordr*] disorder
désormais [*deh-zor-me*] from now on
desquels, -quelles [*deh-kel*] of whom, of which, from whom,
    from which
dessein *m.* [*deh-sẽ*] plan
desserrer *v.* [*deh-seh-reh*] loosen
dessert *m.* [*deh-ser*] dessert
desservir *v.* [*deh-ser-veer*] clear the table
dessin *m.* [*deh-sẽ*] drawing
dessiner *v.* [*deh-see-neh*] draw

dessous *m.* [*d(uh)-soo*] lower part, bottom

dessus *m.* [*d(uh)-sü*] top

destin *m.* [*des-tē*] destiny, fate

destinataire *m.* [*des-tee-nah-ter*] addressee

destruction *f.* [*des-trük-syõ*] destruction

détaché [*deh-tah-sheh*] unfastened, loose

détail *m.* [*deh-tahy*] detail
  au détail [*oh deh-tahy*] retail

détective *m.* [*deh-tek-teev*] detective

déteindre *v. irreg.* [*deh-tēdr*] fade

détendre, se détendre *v.* [*deh-tãdr, sdeh-tãdr*] relax

détente *f.* [*deh-tãt*] relaxation

déterminé [*deh-ter-mee-neh*] determined, definite

déterminer *v.* [*deh-ter-mee-neh*] determine

détester *v.* [*deh-tes-teh*] detest

détour *m.* [*deh-toor*] detour

détourner *v.* [*deh-toor-neh*] turn aside, turn away
  se détourner [*sdeh-toor-neh*] turn away

détresse *f.* [*deh-tres*] distress

détruire *v. irreg.* [*deh-trweer*] destroy

dette *f.* [*det*] debt

deuil *m.* [*duhy*] mourning

deux [*duh*] two
  les deux [*leh duh*] both

deuxième [*duh-zyem*] second

devant [*d(uh)-vã*] before, in front of

devant *m.* [*d(uh)-vã*] front

développement *m.* [*dehv-lop-mã*] development

développer *v.* [*dehv-lo-peh*] develop

devenir *v. irreg.* [*duhv-neer*] become

déviation *f.* [*deh-vyah-syõ*] detour

deviner *v.* [*d(uh)-vee-neh*] guess

devis *m.* [*d(uh)-vee*] estimate

devoir *m.* [*d(uh)-vwahr*] duty

devoir *v. irreg.* [*d(uh)-vwahr*] owe
  devoir (plus infin.) [*d(uh)-vwahr*] must, have to

dévotion *f.* [*deh-voh-syõ*] devotion

dévoué [*deh-vweh*] devoted

diable *m.* [*dyahbl*] devil
diagnostic *m.* [*dyahg-nos-teek*] diagnosis
dialecte *m.* [*dyah-lekt*] dialect
dialogue *m.* [*dyah-log*] dialogue
diament *m.* [*dyah-mã*] diamond
diarrhée *f.* [*dyah-reh*] diarrhea
dictée *f.* [*deek-teh*] dictation
dicter *v.* [*deek-teh*] dictate
dictionnaire *m.* [*deek-syo-ner*] dictionary
dieu *m.* [*dyuh*] god
   Mon Dieu! [*mõ dyuh*] Good heavens!
différence *f.* [*dee-feh-rãs*] difference
différent [*dee-feh-rã(t)*] different
difficile [*dee-fee-seel*] difficult, hard
difficulté *f.* [*dee-fee-kül-teh*] difficulty, trouble
digérer *v.* [*dee-zheh-reh*] digest
digestion *f.* [*dee-zhes-tyõ*] digestion
digne [*deeñ*] worthy
dignité *f.* [*dee-nyee-tch*] dignity
dimanche *m.* [*dee-mãsh*] Sunday
dimension *f.* [*dee-mã-syõ*] dimension, size
diminuer *v.* [*dee-mee-nweh*] decrease
dinde *f.* [*dẽd*] turkey
dîner *m.* [*dee-neh*] dinner
dîner *v.* [*dee-neh*] dine, have dinner
diplomate *adj.* [*dee-plo-maht*] diplomatic
diplomate *m.* [*dee-plo-maht*] diplomat
diplôme *m.* [*dee-plohm*] diploma
dire *v. irreg.* [*deer*] say, tell
direct [*dee-rekt*] direct
directement [*dee-rek-tuh-mã*] directly
directeur *m.* [*dee-rek-tuhr*] director, manager
direction *f.* [*dee-rek-syõ*] direction, management
diriger *v.* [*dee-ree-zheh*] direct, control
discipline *f.* [*dee-see-pleen*] discipline
discontinuer *v.* [*dees-kõ-tee-nweh*] discontinue
discours *m.* [*dees-koor*] speech, talk
discussion *f.* [*dees-kü-syõ*] discussion

discuter *v.* [*dees-kü-teh*] discuss
disgrâce *f.* [*dees-grahs*] disgrace
disparaître *v. irreg.* [*dees-pah-retr*] disappear
disponible [*dees-po-neebl*] available
dispute *f.* [*dees-püt*] dispute
disputer *v.* [*dees-pü-teh*] dispute, contest
  se disputer [*s(uh) dees-pü-teh*] argue
disque *m.* [*deesk*] record
dissoudre *v. irreg.* [*dee-soodr*] dissolve
distance *f.* [*dees-tãs*] distance
  A quelle distance? [*ah kel dees-tãs*] How far?
distant [*dees-tã(t)*] distant, reserved
distinct [*dees-tẽ(kt)*] distinct
distingué [*dees-tẽ-gheh*] distinguished
distinguer *v.* [*dees-tẽ-gheh*] distinguish
distrait [*dees-tre(t)*] absent-minded
distribuer *v.* [*dees-tree-bweh*] distribute, deal [cards]
distribution *f.* [*dees-tree-bü-syõ*] distribution, cast [theatre]
divan *m.* [*dee-vã*] couch
divers [*dee-ver(s)*] various
divertissement *m.* [*dee-ver-tees-mã*] amusement, entertainment
divin [*dee-vẽ, dee-veen*] divine
diviser *v.* [*dee-vee-zeh*] divide
division *f.* [*dee-vee-syõ*] division
divorce *m.* [*dee-vors*] divorce
divorcer *v.* [*dee-vor-seh*] divorce
dix [*dees*] ten
dix-huit [*deez-weet*] eighteen
dixième [*dee-zyem*] tenth
dix-neuf [*deez-nuhf*] nineteen
dix-sept [*dee-set*] seventeen
dizaine *f.* [*dee-zen*] ten
docteur *m.* [*dok-tuhr*] doctor
document *m.* [*do-kü-mã*] document
doigt *m.* [*dwah*] finger
dollar *m.* [*do-lahr*] dollar
domaine *m.* [*do-men*] estate
dôme *m.* [*dohm*] dome

domestique [*do-mes-teek*] domestic

domestique *m.*, *f.* [*do-mes-teek*] servant

dommage *m.* [*do-mahzh*] damage

  Quel dommage! [*kel do-mahzh*] What a pity!

domicile *m.* [*do-mee-seel*] residence

don *m.* [*dõ*] gift

donc [*dõ(k)*] therefore, so

donne *f.* [*don*] deal [of cards]

donner *v.* [*do-neh*] give, deal [cards]

dont [*dõ*] of whom, of which, from whom, from which, whose

  L'homme dont je parle [*lom dõzh parl*] The man of whom
    I am speaking

dormir *v. irreg.* [*dor-meer*] sleep

dortoir *m.* [*dor-twahr*] dormitory

dos *m.* [*doh*] back

dose *f.* [*dohz*] dose

dossier *m.* [*doh-syeh*] file

dot *f.* [*dot*] dowry

douane *f.* [*dwahn*] customs

  droit *m.* **de douane** [*drwahd dwahn*] customs duty

douanier *m.* [*dwah-nyeh*] customs officer

double [*doobl*] double

doublure *f.* [*doo-blür*] lining

doucement [*doos-mã*] gently

douche *f.* [*doosh*] shower

doué [*dweh*] gifted

douleur *f.* [*doo-luhr*] pain, sorrow, grief

douloureux, -euse [*doo-loo-ruh, doo-loo-ruhz*] painful

doute *m.* [*doot*] doubt

  sans doute [*sã doot*] doubtless

douter *v.* [*doo-teh*] doubt

  J'en doute [*zhã doot*] I doubt it

  se douter [*sdoo-teh*] suspect

  Je m'en doutais [*zhmã doo-te*] I thought as much

douteux, -euse [*doo-tuh, doo-tuhz*] doubtful

doux, douce [*doo(s)*] gentle, soft, mild [weather]

douzaine *f.* [*doo-zen*] dozen

douze [*dooz*] twelve

douzième [*doo-zyem*] twelfth
dramatique [*drah-mah-teek*] dramatic
drame *m.* [*drahm*] drama
drap *m.* [*drah*] sheet
drapeau, -eaux *m.* [*drah-poh*] flag
drogue *f.* [*drog*] drug
droit [*drwah(t)*] straight, right
  à droite [*ah drwaht*] on the right
  tout droit [*too drwah*] straight ahead
droit *m.* [*drwah*] law, right
  droits civiques *m. pl.* [*drwah see-veek*] civil rights
drôle [*drohl*] funny
  une drôle d'histoire [*ün drohl dees-twahr*] a strange story
du : de le [*dü*] of the, from the, some, any
duquel [*dü-kel*] of whom, of which
dur [*dür*] hard, tough
durable [*dü-rahbl*] durable
durée *f.* [*dü-reh*] duration
durer *v.* [*dü-reh*] last
dynamite *f.* [*dee-nah-meet*] dynamite

E

eau, eaux *f.* [*oh*] water
  eau courante [*oh koo-rãt*] running water
  eau douce [*oh doos*] fresh water
  eau de Javel [*ohd zhah-vel*] bleach
  eau de mer [*ohd mer*] salt water
  eau minérale [*oh mee-neh-rahl*] mineral water
  eau potable [*oh po-tahbl*] drinking water
écarter *v.* [*eh-kar-teh*] separate
  s'écarter [*seh-kar-teh*] turn away
échange *m.* [*eh-shãzh*] exchange
échanger *v.* [*eh-shã-zheh*] exchange
échantillon *m.* [*eh-shã-tee-yõ*] sample

prendre *v. irreg.* **un échantillon** [*prã-drĕ-neh-shã-tee-yŏ*] sample

échapper, s'échapper *v.* [*eh-shah-peh, seh-shah-peh*] escape

écharpe *f.* [*eh-sharp*] scarf

échec *m.* [*eh-shek*] failure

échecs *m. pl.* [*eh-shek*] chess

échelle *f.* [*eh-shel*] scale, ladder

écho *m.* [*eh-koh*] echo

échouer *v.* [*eh-shweh*] fail

éclair *m.* [*eh-kler*] eclair, flash of lightning

éclaircir *v.* [*eh-kler-seer*] clarify

éclairer *v.* [*eh-kleh-reh*] light

éclater *v.* [*eh-klah-teh*] burst, explode

école *f.* [*eh-kol*] school
  école secondaire [*eh-kol suh-gŏ-der*] high school

écolier, -ière [*eh-kol-yeh, eh-kol-yer*] pupil

économe *adj.* [*eh-ko-nom*] thrifty

économie *f.* [*eh-ko-no-mee*] economy

économique [*eh-ko-no-meek*] economical

économiser *v.* [*eh-ko-no-mee-zeh*] save, economize

écorce *f.* [*eh-kors*] bark

écossais [*eh-ko-se(z)*] Scottish; plaid [fabric]

Ecosse *f.* [*eh-kos*] Scotland

écouter *v.* [*eh-koo-teh*] listen to

écran *m.* [*eh-krã*] screen

écraser *v.* [*eh-krah-zeh*] crush
  s'écraser [*seh-krah-zeh*] crash

écrevisse *f.* [*eh-kruh-vees*] crayfish

s'écrier *v.* [*seh-kree-eh*] cry out

écrire *v. irreg.* [*eh-kreer*] write

écriture *f.* [*eh-kree-tür*] writing

écrivain *m.*, **femme écrivain** *f.* [*eh-kree-vē, fah-meh-kree-vē*] writer

écrou *m.* [*eh-kroo*] nut

écume *f.* [*eh-küm*] foam

écurie *f.* [*eh-kü-ree*] stable

édifice *m.* [*eh-dee-fees*] building

éditeur, -trice [*eh-dee-tuhr, eh-dee-trees*] editor

édition *f.* [*eh-dee-syõ*] edition
éducation *f.* [*eh-dü-kah-syõ*] education, bringing up
effacer *v.* [*eh-fah-seh*] erase
effectivement [*eh-fek-teev-mã*] indeed, really
effet *m.* [*e-fe*] effect; bill [commerce]
  en effet [*ã-ne-fe*] indeed
effets *m. pl.* [*e-fe*] belongings
efficace [*eh-fee-kahs*] efficient, effective
effort *m.* [*e-for*] effort
effrayer *v.* [*eh-freh-yeh*] scare, frighten
égal, -aux [*eh-gahl, eh-goh*] equal, regular
  Ça m'est égal [*sah me-teh-gahl*] I don't care
également [*eh-gahl-mã*] likewise
égalité *f.* [*eh-gah-lee-teh*] equality
égard *m.* [*eh-gahr*] regard
  à cet égard [*ah se-teh-gahr*] in this respect
égarer *v.* [*eh-gah-reh*] mislead
  s'égarer [*seh-gah-reh*] get lost
église *f.* [*eh-gleez*] church
égoiste [*eh-go-eest*] selfish
égout *m.* [*eh-goo*] sewer
égoutter *v.* [*eh-goo-teh*] drain
égratignure *f.* [*eh-grah-tee-nyür*] scratch
Egypte *f.* [*eh-zheept*] Egypt
égyptien, -ienne [*eh-zheep-syẽ, eh-zheep-syen*] Egyptian
élastique [*eh-lahs-teek*] elastic
élection *f.* [*eh-lek-syõ*] election
électricien, -enne [*eh-lek-tree-syẽ, eh-lek-tree-syen*] electrician
électricité *f.* [*eh-lek-tree-see-teh*] electricity
électrique [*eh-lek-treek*] electric
électrophone *m.* [*eh-lek-tro-fon*] record player
élégance *f.* [*eh-leh-gãs*] elegance
élégant [*eh-leh-gã(t)*] elegant
élément *m.* [*eh-leh-mã*] element
élémentaire [*eh-leh-mã-ter*] elementary
éléphant *m.* [*eh-leh-fã*] elephant
élève *m., f.* [*eh-lev*] pupil
élever *v.* [*el-veh*] raise, lift up; rear, bring up [children]

bien élevé [*byē-nel-veh*] well bred
s'élever [*sel-veh*] rise, stand, amount
éliminer *v.* [*eh-lee-mee-neh*] eliminate
élire *v. irreg.* [*eh-leer*] elect
elle [*el*] she, her, it
  elle-même [*el mem*] herself, itself
elles *f.* [*el*] they, them
  elles-mêmes [*el mem*] themselves
éloigner *v.* [*eh-lwah-nyeh*] take away
embargo *m.* [*ã-bahr-goh*] embargo
emballage *m.* [*ã-bah-lahzh*] packing
emballer *v.* [*ã-bah-leh*] pack, wrap
embarrasser *v.* [*ã-bah-rah-seh*] embarrass
s'embarquer *v.* [*sã-bahr-keh*] embark
embrasser *v.* [*ã-brah-seh*] kiss
embrayage *m.* [*ã-bre-yahzh*] clutch
embrayer *v.* [*ã-bre-yeh*] put in gear
émeraude *f.* [*em-rohd*] emerald
émettre *v. irreg.* [*eh-metr*] emit
émeute *f.* [*eh-muht*] riot
émigrant, -te [*eh-mee-grã(t)*] emigrant
émigration *f.* [*eh-mee-grah-syõ*] emigration
éminent [*eh-mee-nã(t)*] prominent
émission *f.* [*eh-mee-syõ*] program, broadcast
emmagasiner *v.* [*ã-mah-gah-zee-neh*] store, accumulate
emmener *v.* [*ãm-neh*] take away
émotion *f.* [*eh-moh-syõ*] emotion
émouvant [*eh-moo-vã(t)*] moving
empêcher (de) *v.* [*ã-pe-sheh (duh)*] stop (from), keep (from)
  s'empêcher (de) [*sã-pe-sheh (duh)*] refrain (from), keep (from)
empereur *m.* [*ã-pruhr*] emperor
emplacement *m.* [*ã-plahs-mã*] location
emploi *m.* [*ã-plwah*] employment, use
  emploi du temps [*ã-plwah dü tã*] schedule
employé, -ée [*a-plwah-yeh*] employee, clerk
employer *v.* [*ã-plwah-yeh*] employ
employeur *m.* [*ã-plwah-yuhr*] employer

emporter *v.* [*ã-por-teh*] carry away
  s'emporter [*sã-por-teh*] become angry
  l'emporter sur [*lã-por-teh sür*] prevail over
emprunt *m.* [*ã-prẽ*] loan
emprunter *v.* [*ã-prẽ-teh*] borrow
en [*ã*] in, into, to; as
en *pron.* [*ã*] some, any
  Il en a [*ee-lã nah*] He has some [of them]
  Je n'en ai pas [*zhnã-neh pah*] I don't have any [of them]
enceinte [*ã-sẽt*] pregnant
enchanter *v.* [*ã-shã-teh*] delight
  Enchanté! [*ã-shã-teh*] Glad to meet you!
encombré [*ã-kõ-breh*] burdened, crowded
encore [*ã-kor*] again, still, more
  encore une fois [*ã-kor ün fwah*] once more
  pas encore [*pah ã-kor*] not yet
encouragement *m.* [*ã-koo-rahzh-mã*] encouragement
encre *f.* [*ãkr*] ink
encourager *v.* [*ã-koo-rah-zheh*] encourage, cheer
en-dessous (de) [*ãd-soo*] below, beneath
endommagé [*ã-do-mah-zheh*] damaged
endommager *v.* [*ã-do-mah-zheh*] damage
s'endormir *v. irreg.* [*sã-dor-meer*] fall asleep
endosser *v.* [*ã-do-seh*] endorse, assume
endroit *m.* [*ã-drwah*] place
énergie *f.* [*eh-ner-zhee*] energy
énergique [*eh-ner-zheek*] energetic
enfance *f.* [*ã-fãs*] childhood
enfant *m.* [*ã-fã*] child
enfer *m.* [*ã-fer*] hell
enfermer *v.* [*ã-fer-meh*] shut in
enfin [*ã-fẽ*] at last
enflé [*ã-fleh*] swollen
enfler *v.* [*ã-fleh*] swell
engagement *m.* [*ã-gahzh-mã*] engagement
engager *v.* [*ã-gah-zheh*] engage, hire
enlever *v.* [*ãl-veh*] take off, remove
ennemi *m.* [*en-mee*] enemy

ennui *m.* [ã-nwee] boredom
ennuyer *v.* [ã-nwee-yeh] bore, bother
ennuyeux, -euse [ã-nwee-yuh, ã-nwee-yuhz] annoying, boring
enorme [eh-norm] enormous, huge
enquête *f.* [ã-ket] inquiry
enregistrer *v.* [ãr-zhees-treh] record, check [luggage]
s'enrhumer *v.* [sã-rü-meh] catch a cold
enseignant, -te [ã-se-nyã(t)] teacher
enseigne *f.* [ã-señ] sign
enseignement *m.* [ã-señ-mã] teaching, education
enseigner *v.* [ã-se-nyeh] teach
ensemble *adv.* [ã-sãbl] together
ensemble *m.* [ã-sãbl] set, whole
ensuite [ã-sweet] afterwards, then
entendre *v.* [ã-tãdr] hear
   entendre dire (que) [ã-tãdr deer (kuh)] hear (that)
   entendre parler de [ã-tãdr pahr-leh d(uh)] hear of (about)
entendu [ã-tã-dü] agreed, understood
   bien entendu [byẽ-nã-tã-dü] of course
enterrement *m.* [ã-ter-mã] burial, funeral
enterrer *v.* [ã-teh-reh] bury
enthousiasme *m.* [ã-too-zyahsm] enthusiasm
entier, -tière [ã-tyeh, ã-tyer] entire, whole
entièrement [ã-tyer-mã] entirely
entorse *f.* [ã-tors] sprain
entourer *v.* [ã-too-reh] surround
entr'acte *m.* [ã-trahkt] intermission
entraîner *v.* [ã-tre-neh] bring about, train [sports]
entre [ãtr] between, among
entrée *f.* [ã-treh] entrance, admission
entrepôt *m.* [ã-truh-poh] warehouse
entreprendre *v. irreg.* [ã-truh-prãdr] undertake
entrepreneur *m.* [ã-truh-pruh-nuhr] contractor, businessman
entreprise *f.* [ã-truh-preez] enterprise, firm
entrer (dans) *v.* [ã-treh (dã)] enter, go in, come in
entretemps [ã-truh-tã] meanwhile
entretien *m.* [ã-truh-tyẽ] upkeep
entrevue *f.* [ã-truh-vü] interview

enveloppe *f.* [*ãv-lop*] envelope
envelopper *v.* [*ãv-lo-peh*] wrap
envers *m.* [*ã-ver*] wrong side
  à l'envers [*ah lã-ver*] upside down, inside out
envie *f.* [*ã-vee*] wish, desire
  avoir *v.* **envie de** [*ah-vwahr ã-veed*] want, feel like
envier *v.* [*ã-vyeh*] envy
environ *adv.* [*ã-vee-rõ*] about, approximately
environnement *m.* [*ã-vee-ron-mã*] surroundings, environment
environs *m. pl.* [*ã-vee-rõ*] surroundings, vicinity
envisager *v.* [*ã-vee-zah-zheh*] consider
envoi *m.* [*ã-vwah*] shipment, sending
s'envoler *v.* [*sã-vo-leh*] take off [plane], fly away
envoyer *v.* [*ã-vwah-yeh*] send
  envoyer chercher [*ã-vwah-yeh sher-sheh*] send for
épais, épaisse [*eh-pe, eh-pes*] thick
épargne *f.* [*eh-pahrñ*] savings
  caisse *f.* **d'épargne** [*kes deh-pahrñ*] savings bank
épargner *v.* [*eh-pahr-nyeh*] save
épaule *f.* [*eh-pohl*] shoulder
épée *f.* [*eh-peh*] sword
épeler *v.* [*eh-pleh*] spell
épice *f.* [*eh-pees*] spice
épicerie *f.* [*eh-pees-ree*] grocery store
épinards *m. pl.* [*eh-pee-nar*] spinach
épine *f.* [*eh-peen*] thorn
épingle *f.* [*eh-pẽgl*] pin
  épingle anglaise [*eh-pẽ-glã-glez*] safety pin
épingler *v.* [*eh-pẽ-gleh*] pin
éponge *f.* [*eh-põzh*] sponge
époque *f.* [*eh-pok*] period
épouser *v.* [*eh-poo-zeh*] marry
époux, -ouse [*eh-poo, eh-pooz*] spouse; husband, wife
épreuve *f.* [*eh-pruhv*] trial; photo, print
éprouver *v.* [*eh-proo-veh*] test
épuisé [*eh-pwee-zeh*] exhausted
épuiser *v.* [*eh-pwee-zeh*] exhaust
équilibre *m.* [*eh-kee-leebr*] equilibrium, balance

équilibrer *v.* [*eh-kee-lee-breh*] balance
équipage *m.* [*eh-kee-pahzh*] crew
équipe *f.* [*eh-keep*] team
équipement *m.* [*eh-keep-mā*] equipment
équivalent *m.* [*eh-kee-vah-lā*] equivalent
érafler *v.* [*eh-rah-fleh*] scrape
errer *v.* [*e-reh*] wander
erreur *f.* [*e-ruhr*] error
éruption *f.* [*eh-rüp-syō*] rash
escalier *m.* [*es-kah-lyeh*] staircase, stairs
escargot *m.* [*es-kahr-goh*] snail
esclavage *m.* [*es-klah-vahzh*] slavery
esclave *m.*, *f.* [*es-klahv*] slave
escompte *m.* [*es-kõt*] discount
escrime *f.* [*es-kreem*] fencing
espace *m.* [*es-pahs*] space
Espagne *f.* [*es-pahñ*] Spain
espagnol *n.* & *adj.* [*es-pah-nyol*] Spaniard, Spanish
espèce *f.* [*es-pes*] kind
espérance *f.* [*es-peh-rãs*] hope
espérer *v.* [*es-peh-reh*] hope
espion *m.* [*es-pyō*] spy
espoir *m.* [*es-pwahr*] hope
   plein d'espoir [*plē des-pwahr*] hopeful
   sans espoir [*sā-zes-pwahr*] hopeless
esprit *m.* [*es-pree*] mind, spirit, wit
esquisser *v.* [*es-kee-seh*] sketch
essai *m.* [*eh-se*] trial
   essais *m. pl.* **et erreurs** *f. pl.* [*eh-se-zeh e-ruhr*] trial
   and error
essayage *m.* [*eh-se-yahzh*] fitting
essayer *v.* [*eh-seh-yeh*] try, try on [clothing]
essence *f.* [*eh-sãs*] gasoline
essential, -elle [*eh-sã-syel*] essential
essieu *m.* [*eh-syuh*] axle
essuyer *v.* [*eh-swee-yeh*] wipe
est *m.* [*est*] east
est *3d pers. sing. pres. tense of* ÊTRE [*e*] is

Est-ce que . . . [*es k(uh)*] Is it that . . .
estimer *v.* [*es-tee-meh*] estimate, esteem
estomac *m.* [*es-to-mahk*] stomach
et [*eh*] and
établir *v.* [*eh-tah-bleer*] establish
établissement *m.* [*eh-tah-blees-mã*] institution, establishment
étage *m.* [*eh-tahzh*] floor, story
étagère *f.* [*eh-tah-zher*] shelf
étain *m.* [*eh-tē*] tin, pewter
étalage *m.* [*eh-tah-lahzh*] display
étaler *v.* [*eh-tah-leh*] display
étang *m.* [*eh-tã*] pool
état *m.* [*eh-tah*] state, condition
état-civil *m.* [*eh-tah-see-veel*] civil status
Etats-Unis *m. pl.* [*eh-tah-zü-nee*] United States
été *m.* [*eh-teh*] summer
éteindre *v. irreg.* [*eh-tēdr*] turn off, turn out [a light]; extinguish [a fire]
étendre *v.* [*eh-tãdr*] hang out, lay out, spread
étendue *f.* [*eh-tã-dü*] extent, range
éternel, -elle [*eh-ter-nel*] eternal
éternuer *v.* [*eh-ter-nweh*] sneeze
êtes *2d pers. pl. pres. tense of* ÊTRE [*et*] you are
étincelle *f.* [*eh-tē-sel*] spark
étiquette *f.* [*eh-tee-ket*] label, tag
étoile *f.* [*eh-twahl*] star
étonnant [*eh-to-nã(t)*] astonishing, surprising
étonner *v.* [*eh-to-neh*] surprise
étouffer *v.* [*eh-too-feh*] smother
étrange [*eh-trãzh*] strange
étranger, -ère *n.* [*eh-trã-zheh, eh-trã-zher*] foreigner
    à l'étranger [*ah leh-trã-zheh*] abroad
étranger, -ère *adj.* [*eh-trã-zheh, eh-trã-zher*] foreign
être *m.* [*etr*] being
être *v. irreg.* [*etr*] be
étroit [*eh-trwah(t)*] narrow
étude *f.* [*eh-tüd*] study

étudiant, -te *n. & adj.* [*eh-tü-dyã(t)*] student
étudier *v.* [*eh-tü-dyeh*] study
étui *m.* [*eh-twee*] case
Europe *f.* [*uh-rop*] Europe
européen, -enne [*uh-ro-peh-ē, uh-ro-peh-en*] European
eux *m.* [*uh*] them
eux-mêmes [*uh-mem*] themselves
s'évanouir *v.* [*seh-vahn-weer*] faint
événement *m.* [*eh-ven-mã*] event
évêque *m.* [*eh-vek*] bishop
éventail *m.* [*eh-vã-tahy*] fan
évidemment [*eh-vee-dah-mã*] evidently
évident [*eh-vee-dã(t)*] evident
évier *m.* [*eh-vyeh*] sink
éviter *v.* [*eh-vee-teh*] avoid
évolution *f.* [*eh-vo-lü-syõ*] evolution, change
exact [*eg-zah(kt)*] exact
exactement [*eg-zahk-tuh-mã*] exactly
exagérer *v.* [*eg-zah-zheh-reh*] exaggerate
examen *m.* [*eg-zah-mē*] examination
   réussir *v.* **à un examen** [*reh-ü-see-rah ē-neg-zah-mē*] pass
   an examination
examiner *v.* [*eg-zah-mee-neh*] examine
excellent [*ek-se-lã(t)*] excellent
excepté [*ek-sep-teh*] except
exception *f.* [*ek-sep-syõ*] exception
excès *m.* [*ek-se*] excess
exclusif, -ive [*eks-klü-zeef, eks-klü-zeev*] exclusive
excursion *f.* [*eks-kür-syõ*] excursion, trip
excuse *f.* [*eks-küz*] excuse
excuser *v.* [*eks-kü-zeh*] excuse, pardon
   s'excuser [*seks-kü-zeh*] apologize
exemplaire *m.* [*eg-zã-pler*] copy
exemple *m.* [*eg-zãpl*] example
   par exemple [*pah-reg-zãpl*] for instance, for example
s'exercer *v.* [*seg-zer-seh*] practice
exercise *m.* [*eg-zer-sees*] exercise
exigence *f.* [*eg-zee-zhãs*] requirement

exigeant [*eg-zee-zhã(t)*] demanding
exiger *v.* [*eg-zee-zheh*] demand, require
exil *m.* [*eg-zeel*] exile
existence *f.* [*eg-zees-tãs*] existence
exister *v.* [*eg-zees-teh*] exist
expédier *v.* [*eks-peh-dyeh*] send, ship
expéditeur *m.* [*eks-peh-dee-tuhr*] sender
expédition *f.* [*eks-peh-dee-syõ*] expedition
expérience *f.* [*eks-peh-ryãs*] experience, experiment
expert [*eks-per(t)*] expert
explication *f.* [*eks-plee-kah-syõ*] explanation
expliquer *v.* [*eks-plee-keh*] explain
exploiter *v.* [*eks-plwah-teh*] exploit
explorer *v.* [*eks-plo-reh*] explore
explosion *f.* [*eks-ploh-zyõ*] explosion
exporter *v.* [*eks-por-teh*] export
exposer *v.* [*eks-poh-zeh*] exhibit
exposition *f.* [*eks-poh-zee-syõ*] exhibition
exprès [*eks-pre*] on purpose
express *m.* [*eks-pres*] special delivery, express train
expression *f.* [*eks-pre-syõ*] expression
exprimer *v.* [*eks-pree-meh*] express
extérieur [*eks-teh-ryuhr*] exterior, external
extraction *f.* [*eks-trahk-syõ*] extraction
extraire *v. irreg.* [*eks-trer*] extract
extraordinaire [*eks-trah-or-dee-ner*] extraordinary
extrême [*eks-trem*] extreme
extrêmement [*eks-trem-mã*] extremely

F

fabrication *f.* **en série** [*fah-bree-kah-syõ ã seh-ree*]
  mass production
fabriquant *m.* [*fah-bree-kã*] manufacturer
fabriquer *v.* [*fah-bree-keh*] make, manufacture

face *f.* [*fahs*] side
  en face (de) [*ã fahs (duh)*] across the street, on the other side
fâché [*fah-sheh*] angry
fâcher *v.* [*fah-sheh*] make angry
  se fâcher [*sfah-sheh*] get angry
facile [*fah-seel*] easy
facilement [*fah-seel-mã*] easily
facilité *f.* [*fah-see-lee-teh*] ease
façon *f.* [*fah-sõ*] way, manner
  de toute façon [*duh toot fah-sõ*] anyhow, anyway
  en aucune façon [*ã-noh-kün fah-sõ*] by no means
facteur *m.* [*fahk-tuhr*] mailman
facture *f.* [*fahk-tür*] bill, invoice
facultatif, -tive [*fah-kül-tah-teef, fah-kül-tah-teev*] optional
faculté *f.* [*fah-kül-teh*] faculty
faible [*febl*] weak
faiblesse *f.* [*fe-bles*] weakness
faillite *f.* [*fah-yeet*] bankruptcy
faim *f.* [*fẽ*] hunger
  avoir *v.* **faim** [*ah-vwahr fẽ*] be hungry
faire *v. irreg.* [*fer*] make, do
  faire attention [*fe-rah-tã-syõ*] pay attention
  faire beau (chaud, froid) [*fer boh (shoh, frwah)*] be nice
    (hot, cold) [weather]
  Il fait beau aujourd'hui [*eel fe boh oh-zhoor-dwee*] It's a
    nice day today
  faire du soleil (du vent) [*fer dü so-ley (dü vã)*] be sunny
    (windy)
  faire face à [*fer fahs ah*] face
  faire mal à [*fer mahl ah*] hurt
  faire construire une maison [*fer kõ-strwee-rün me-zõ*]
    have a house built
  faire parler [*fer pahr-leh*] make [someone] talk
  faire peur à [*fer puh-rah*] frighten
  faire plaisir à [*fer pleh-zeer ah*] please
  faire une promenade [*fer ün prom-nahd*] take a walk
  se faire [*s(uh) fer*] become, be done
  s'y faire [*see fer*] get used to

s'en faire [*sã fer*] worry
Ne vous en faites pas! [*nuh voo-zã fet pah*] Don't get
  upset!
faire-part *m.* [*fer-pahr*] announcement
fait *m.* [*fe*] fact
  en fait [*ã fe*] in fact
falloir *v. irreg.* [*fahl-wahr*] be necessary
fameux, -euse [*fah-muh(z)*] famous, good
familial, -aux *adj.* [*fah-meel-yahl, fah-meel-yoh*] family
familier, -ière [*fah-meel-yeh, fah-meel-yer*] familiar
famille *f.* [*fah-meey*] family
fantôme *m.* [*fã-tohm*] ghost
farce *f.* [*fahrs*] practical joke
fardeau, -eaux *m.* [*fahr-doh*] burden
farine *f.* [*fah-reen*] flour
fascinant [*fah-see-nã(t)*] fascinating
fatigant [*fah-tee-gã(t)*] tiring
fatigue *f.* [*fah-teeg*] fatigue
fatigué [*fah-tee-gheh*] tired
fatiguer *v.* [*fah-tee-gheh*] tire
faut: il faut [*eel foh*] it is necessary
faute *f.* [*foht*] fault, mistake
fauteuil *m.* [*foh-tuhy*] armchair
faux, fausse [*foh(s)*] false
faveur *f.* [*fah-vuhr*] favor
favoriser *v.* [*fah-vo-ree-zeh*] favor
fédéral, -aux [*feh-deh-rahl, feh-deh-roh*] federal
félicitations *f. pl.* [*feh-lee-see-tah-syõ*] congratulations
féliciter *v.* [*feh-lee-see-teh*] congratulate
féminin [*feh-mee-nē, feh-mee-neen*] feminine
femme *f.* [*fahm*] woman, wife
  femme de chambre [*fahm duh shãbr*] chambermaid
  femme de ménage [*fahm duh meh-nahzh*] cleaning woman
fendre *v.* [*fãdr*] split
fenêtre *f.* [*f(uh)-netr*] window
fer *m.* [*fer*] iron
ferme *adj.* [*ferm*] firm
ferme *f.* [*ferm*] farm

fermé [*fer-meh*] closed
fermer v. [*fer-meh*] close; turn off
  fermer à clef [*fer-meh ah kleh*] lock
fermeture f. [*fer-muh-tür*] closing
  fermeture annuelle [*fer-muh-tü-rahn-wel*] closed for vacation
  fermeture éclair [*fer-muh-tü-reh-kler*] zipper
fermier m. [*fer-myeh*] farmer
festival, -aux m. [*fes-tee-vahl, fes-tee-voh*] festival
fête f. [*fet*] feast, celebration, holiday, party
fêter v. [*feh-teh*] celebrate
feu m. [*fuh*] fire
  Au feu! [*oh fuh*] Fire!
feuille f. [*fuhy*] leaf; sheet of paper
février m. [*feh-vree-yeh*] February
fiançailles f. pl. [*fyã-sahy*] engagement
fiancé [*fyã-seh*] engaged
fiancé, -ée [*fyã-seh*] fiancé, fiancée
  se fiancer v. [*s(uh) fyã-seh*] become engaged
ficelle f. [*fee-sel*] string
fidèle [*fee-del*] faithful
fier, fière [*fyer*] proud
fièvre f. [*fyevr*] fever
figue f. [*feeg*] fig
fil m. [*feel*] thread, yarn
  fil de fer [*feel duh fer*] wire
filet m. [*fee-le*] net
fille f. [*feey*] daughter, girl
filleul, -cule [*fee-yuhl*] godson, goddaughter
film m. [*feelm*] movie, movie film
fils m. [*fees*] son
filtre m. [*feeltr*] filter
fin [*fẽ, feen*] fine, thin, small
fin f. [*fẽ*] end, ending
  sans fin [*sã fẽ*] endless, interminable
  fin de semaine [*fẽd suh-men*] week-end
final, -aux [*fee-nahl, fee-noh*] final
finalement [*fee-nahl-mã*] eventually, finally
financier, -ière [*fee-nã-syeh, fee-nã-syer*] financial

finir *v.* [*fee-neer*] finish, end
firme *f.* [*feerm*] firm
fissure *f.* [*fee-sür*] crack
flamme *f.* [*flahm*] flame
flan *m.* [*flã*] custard
flatter *v.* [*flah-teh*] flatter
flatteur, -euse [*flah-tuhr, flah-tuhz*] flatterer
flèche *f.* [*flesh*] arrow, church spire
fleur *f.* [*fluhr*] flower, blossom
fleurir *v.* [*fluh-reer*] blossom
fleuriste *m.* [*fluh-reest*] florist
fleuve *m.* [*fluhv*] river
flirter *v.* [*fluhr-teh*] flirt
flotte *f.* [*flot*] fleet
flotter *v.* [*flo-teh*] float
flute *f.* [*flüt*] flute
foi *f.* [*fwah*] faith
foie *m.* [*fwah*] liver
foin *m.* [*fwē*] hay
foire *f.* [*fwahr*] fair
fois *f.* [*fwah*] time
  une fois [*ün fwah*] once
  deux fois [*duh fwah*] twice
  encore une fois [*ã-ko-rün fwah*] once more
  des fois [*deh fwah*] at times
  chaque fois que [*shahk fwah k(uh)*] whenever
  Il était une fois [*ee-leh-te-tün fwah*] Once upon a time
    there was (were)
foncé [*fõ-seh*] dark [color]
fonction *f.* [*fõk-syõ*] function
fonctionnaire *m., f.* [*fõk-syo-ner*] civil servant
fonctionnement *m.* [*fõk-syon-mã*] working
fonctionner *v.* [*fõk-syo-neh*] function, work
fond *m.* [*fõ*] bottom
  à fond [*ah fõ*] thoroughly
  au fond [*oh fõ*] after all
fondamental, -aux [*fõ-dah-mã-tahl, fõ-dah-mã-toh*] basic,
  fundamental

fondation *f.* [*fõ-dah-syõ*] foundation
fondre *v.* [*fõdr*] melt
fonds *m. pl.* [*fõ*] funds
fontaine *f.* [*fõ-ten*] fountain
football *m.* [*foot-bohl*] soccer
forçat *m.* [*for-sah*] convict
force *f.* [*fors*] force
forcer *v.* [*for-seh*] compel, force
forêt *f.* [*fo-re*] forest
forgeron *m.* [*for-zhuh-rõ*] blacksmith
formalité *f.* [*for-mah-lee-teh*] formality
formation *f.* [*for-mah-syõ*] formation, training
forme *f.* [*form*] form, shape
formel, -elle [*for-mel*] formal
former *v.* [*for-meh*] form, train
formidable [*for-mee-dahbl*] wonderful
formule *f.* [*for-mül*] formula
fort [*for(t)*] strong, loud
fort *m.* [*for*] fort
forteresse *f.* [*for-tuh-res*] fort
fortune *f.* [*for-tün*] fortune
fossé *m.* [*fo-seh*] ditch
fou, folle [*foo, fol*] crazy, foolish, insane
foudre *f.* [*foodr*] lightning, thunderbolt
fouet *m.* [*fweh*] whip
fouiller *v.* [*foo-yeh*] search
foulard *m.* [*foo-lahr*] scarf
foule *f.* [*fool*] crowd
fouler *v.* [*foo-leh*] sprain
four *m.* [*foor*] oven
  au four [*oh foor*] in the oven
fourchette *f.* [*foor-shet*] fork
fourmi *f.* [*foor-mee*] ant
fournir *v.* [*foor-neer*] furnish, provide
fourrure *f.* [*foo-rür*] fur
foyer *m.* [*fwah-yeh*] hearth; lobby
fracture *f.* [*frahk-tür*] fracture
fragile [*frah-zheel*] fragile

frais, fraîche [*fre(sh)*] chilly, cool; fresh
frais *m. pl.* [*fre*] expenses
  frais généraux [*fre zheh-neh-roh*] overhead
fraise *f.* [*frez*] strawberry
franc, franche [*frã(sh)*] frank
franc *m.* [*frã*] franc
français [*frã-se(z)*] French
France *f.* [*frãs*] France
franchement [*frãsh-mã*] frankly, really
frapper *v.* [*frah-peh*] hit, strike, knock
fraternel, -elle [*frah-ter-nel*] brotherly
fraude *f.* [*frohd*] fraud
frein *m.* [*frẽ*] brake
freiner *v.* [*freh-neh*] brake
frémir *v.* [*freh-meer*] shudder
fréquent [*freh-kã(t)*] frequent
frère *m.* [*frer*] brother
frêt *m.* [*fre*] freight
frigidaire *m.* [*free-zhee-der*] refrigerator
frire *v. irreg.* [*freer*] fry
frit [*free(t)*] fried
froid [*frwah(d)*] cold
  Il fait froid [*eel fe frwah*] It's cold
  avoir *v.* **froid** [*ah-vwahr frwah*] be cold
fromage *m.* [*fro-mahzh*] cheese
froncer *v.* **les sourcils** [*frõ-seh leh soor-see*] frown
front *m.* [*frõ*] forehead
frontière *f.* [*frõ-tyer*] border
frotter *v.* [*fro-teh*] rub, scrub
fruit *m.* [*frwee*] fruit
fuir *v. irreg.* [*fweer*] flee
fuite *f.* [*fweet*] flight, escape; leak
fumée *f.* [*fü-meh*] smoke
fumer *v.* [*fü-meh*] smoke
fumeur *m.* [*fü-muhr*] smoker, smoking car
furieux, -euse [*für-yuh, für-yuhz*] furious
fusil *m.* [*fü-zee*] gun, rifle
futur *m.* [*fü-tür*] future

G

gâcher *v.* [*gah-sheh*] spoil
gagnant, -ante [*gah-nyã(t)*] winner
gagner *v.* [*gah-nyeh*] earn, gain, win
gai [*ghe*] gay
gain *m.* [*ghē*] gain
gaine *f.* [*ghen*] girdle
galet *m.* [*gah-le*] pebble
galon *m.* [*gah-lõ*] braid
gant *m.* [*gã*] glove
garage *m.* [*gah-rahzh*] garage
garagiste *m.* [*gah-rah-zheest*] garage man
garantie *f.* [*gah-rã-tee*] guarantee
garantir *v.* [*gah-rã-teer*] guarantee
garçon *m.* [*gahr-sõ*] boy, waiter
  garçon de cabine [*gahr-sõd kah-been*] steward
garde *m., f.* [*gahrd*] guard
garde-meuble *m.* [*gahr-duh-muhbl*] furniture storage
garder *v.* [*gahr-deh*] keep
gardien *m.* [*gahr-dyē*] guardian, guard
gare *f.* [*gahr*] station
garer *v.* [*gah-reh*] park
garnir *v.* [*gahr-neer*] decorate
gaspiller *v.* [*gahs-pee-yeh*] waste
gâteau, -eaux *m.* [*gah-toh*] cake
gâter *v.* [*gah-teh*] spoil
gauche, à gauche [*gohsh, ah gohsh*] left
gaz *m.* [*gahz*] gas
gazon *m.* [*gah-zõ*] grass
gelée *f.* [*zh(uh)-leh*] frost; jelly
geler *v.* [*zh(uh)-leh*] freeze
gémir *v.* [*zheh-meer*] groan
gémissement *m.* [*zheh-mees-mã*] groan

gencive *f.* [*zhã-seev*] gum

gendarme *m.* [*zhã-dahrm*] policeman

gendre *m.* [*zhãdr*] son-in-law

gêné [*zheh-neh*] inconvenienced, embarrassed, self-conscious

gêner *v.* [*zheh-neh*] inconvenience, bother

général, -aux *n. & adj.* [*zheh-neh-rahl, zheh-neh-roh*] general

   en général [*ã zheh-neh-rahl*] in general

génération *f.* [*zheh-neh-rah-syõ*] generation

généreux, -euse [*zheh-neh-ruh, zheh-neh-ruhz*] generous

génie *m.* [*zheh-nee*] genius

genou, -oux *m.* [*zh(uh)-noo*] knee

   se mettre *v. irreg.* **a genoux** [*sme-trahzh-noo*] kneel

genre *m.* [*zhãr*] gender, kind

gens *m. pl.* [*zhã*] people

gentil, gentille [*zhã-tee(y)*] nice

géographie *f.* [*zheh-o-grah-fee*] geography

géométrie *f.* [*zheh-o-meh-tree*] geometry

gérant *m.* [*zheh-rã*] manager

gibier *m.* [*zhee-byeh*] game [animals]

gifle *f.* [*zheefl*] slap

gifler *v.* [*zhee-fleh*] slap

gilet *m.* [*zhee-le*] vest

   gilet de sauvetage [*zhee-led sohv-tahzh*] life-jacket

gin *m.* [*dzheen*] gin

gitan [*zhee-tã, zhee-tahn*] gypsy

glace *f.* [*glahs*] ice, ice-cream

glaçon *m.* [*glah-sõ*] ice cube

glissant [*glee-sã(t)*] slippery

glisser *v.* [*glee-seh*] slide; slip

gloire *f.* [*glwahr*] glory

golf *m.* [*golf*] golf

gomme *f.* [*gom*] eraser

gonfler *v.* [*gõ-fleh*] inflate

gorge *f.* [*gorzh*] throat

   avoir *v.* **mal à la gorge** [*ah-vwahr mah-lah lah gorzh*] have a sore throat

gosse *m., f.* [*gos*] kid, youngster

gothique [*go-teek*] gothic
gourmand [*goor-mã(d)*] glutton
goût m. [*goo*] taste
goûter m. [*goo-teh*] snack
goûter v. [*goo-teh*] taste
goutte f. [*goot*] drop
gouttière f. [*goo-tyer*] gutter
gouvernement m. [*goo-ver-nuh-mã*] government
gouverner v. [*goo-ver-neh*] govern, rule
gouverneur m. [*goo-ver-nuhr*] governor
grâce f. [*grahs*] grace
gracieux, -cieuse [*grah-syuh, grah-syuhz*] graceful, gracious
grain m. [*grẽ*] grain, corn; particle, speck
graine f. [*gren*] seed
graissage m. [*gre-sahzh*] lubrication
graisse f. [*gres*] grease, fat
graisser v. [*greh-seh*] grease, oil
gramme m. [*grahm*] gram
grammaire f. [*grah-mer*] grammar
grand [*grã(d)*] big, tall, great, large
Grande Bretagne f. [*grãd bruh-tahñ*] Great Britain
grandeur f. [*grã-duhr*] greatness
grandir v. [*grã-deer*] grow older, taller
grand-mère f. [*grã-mer*] grandmother
grand-père m. [*grã-per*] grandfather
grands-parents m. pl. [*grã-pah-rã*] grandparents
grange f. [*grãzh*] barn
gras, grasse [*grah, grahs*] fat, oily
gratte-ciel m. [*graht-syel*] skyscraper
gratter v. [*grah-teh*] scratch
gratuit [*grah-twee(t)*] free
grave [*grahv*] grave, solemn
gravure f. [*grah-vür*] print, illustration
grec, grecque [*grek*] Greek
Grèce f. [*gres*] Greece
grêle f. [*grel*] hail
grenier m. [*gruh-nyeh*] attic, granary
grenouille f. [*gruh-nooy*] frog

grève *f.* [*grev*] strike
  faire *v.* **grève** [*fer grev*] strike, go on strike
gréviste *m. f.* [*greh-veest*] striker
griffer *v.* [*gree-feh*] scratch
grille *f.* [*greey*] grill, screen
grillé [*gree-yeh*] broiled
grille-pain *m.* [*greey-pē*] toaster
griller *v.* [*gree-yeh*] broil
grimace *f.* [*gree-mahs*] grimace, grin
grimper *v.* [*grē-peh*] climb
grincer *v.* [*grē-seh*] creak
grippe *f.* [*greep*] flu
gris [*gree(z)*] grey
gronder *v.* [*grŏ-deh*] scold
gros, grosse [*groh, grohs*] fat
grossesse *f.* [*groh-ses*] pregnancy
grossier, -ière [*groh-syeh, groh-syer*] coarse, rough, rude
grossièreté *f.* [*groh-syer-teh*] rudeness
grossir *v.* [*groh-seer*] put on weight
grotte *f.* [*grot*] cave
groupe *m.* [*groop*] group
guêpe *f.* [*ghep*] wasp
guère: ne . . . guère [*nuh . . . gher*] hardly, scarcely
guérir *v.* [*gheh-reer*] cure
guérison *f.* [*gheh-ree-zŏ*] recovery, healing
guerre *f.* [*gher*] war
  guerre mondiale [*gher mŏ-dyahl*] world war
guichet *m.* [*ghee-she*] ticket-window, counter
guide *m.* [*gheed*] guide, guide-book
guillemets *m. pl.* [*gheey-me*] quotation marks
guitare *f.* [*ghee-tahr*] guitar
gymnastique *f.* [*zheem-nahs-teek*] gymnastics

H

habile [*ah-beel*] clever
habileté *f.* [*ah-beel-teh*] skill
habiller *v.* [*ah-bee-yeh*] dress
  s'habiller [*sah-bee-yeh*] get dressed
habitant *m.* [*ah-bee-tã*] inhabitant
habiter *v.* [*ah-bee-teh*] live, inhabit
habits *m. pl.* [*ah-bee*] clothes
habitude *f.* [*ah-bee-tüd*] habit
  d'habitude [*dah-bee-tüd*] usually, ordinarily
habituer, s'habituer *v.* [*ah-bee-tweh, sah-bee-tweh*] get used to
habitué, -ée (à) [*ah-bee-tweh (ah)*] accustomed (to), used (to)
habituel, -elle [*ah-bee-twel*] customary, usual
***hache** *f.* [*ahsh*] axe
***haine** *f.* [*en*] hate
***haïr** *v. irreg.* [*ah-eer*] hate
***hâle** *m.* [*ahl*] tan
haleine *f.* [*ah-len*] breath
***hanche** *f.* [*ãsh*] hip
***hardi** [*ahr-dee*] bold
***haricot** *m.* [*ah-ree-koh*] bean
***harpe** *f.* [*ahrp*] harp
***hasard** *m.* [*ah-zahr*] chance, luck
  au hasard [*oh ah-zahr*] at random
  par hasard [*pahr ah-zahr*] by chance
  jeu *m.* **de hasard** [*zhuh duh ah-zahr*] game of chance
***hâte** *f.* [*aht*] haste
***hausse** *f.* [*ohs*] increase
***haut** *m.* [*oh*] top
***haut** [*oh(t)*] high
  en haut [*ã oh*] up, at the top, above, upstairs
  vers le haut [*ver luh oh*] upward
***hauteur** *f.* [*oh-tuhr*] height

*haut-parleur *m.* [*oh-pahr-luhr*] loudspeaker
hebdomadaire [*eb-do-mah-der*] weekly
hectare *m.* [*ek-tahr*] two and one-half acres
*hélas [*eh-lahs*] alas
hélice *f.* [*eh-lees*] propeller
herbe *f.* [*erb*] grass
    mauvaise herbe [*mo-ve-zerb*] weed
héritage *m.* [*eh-ree-tahzh*] inheritance
hériter *v.* [*eh-ree-teh*] inherit
héritier *m.* [*eh-ree-tyeh*] heir
héritière *f.* [*eh-ree-tyer*] heiress
*héros *m.* [*eh-roh*] hero
hésiter *v.* [*eh-zee-teh*] hesitate
heure *f.* [*uhr*] hour
    Quelle heure est-il? [*kel uhr e-teel*] What time is it?
    Il est trois heures [*ee-le trwah-zuhr*] It's three o'clock
    Il est trois heures cinq [*ee-le trwah-zuhr sĕk*] It is five
      past three
    Il est trois heures et demie [*ee-le trwah-zuhr ehd-mee*]
      It is half past three
    Il est trois heures moins le quart [*ee-le trwah-zuhr mwē*
      luh kahr] It is a quarter to three
    à l'heure [*ah luhr*] on time
    de bonne heure [*d(uh) bo-nuhr*] early
    tout à l'heure [*too-tah luhr*] a while ago, in a little while
    C'est l'heure [*se luhr*] It's time
    A tout à l'heure! [*ah too-tah luhr*] So long! See you soon!
    toutes les heures [*toot leh-zuhr*] hourly
    à l'heure actuelle [*ah luhr ahk-twel*] nowadays
    heures supplémentaires [*uhr sü-pleh-mã-ter*] overtime
    heures d'affluence [*uhr dah-flü-ãs*] rush hours
heureusement [*uh-ruhz-mã*] fortunately
heureux, -euse [*uh-ruh, uh-ruhz*] happy, lucky, fortunate
*heurter *v.* [*uhr-teh*] strike
hier [*yer*] yesterday
    avant-hier [*ah-vã-tyer*] the day before yesterday
    hier soir [*yer swahr*] last night
histoire *f.* [*ees-twahr*] history; story

historique [*ees-to-reek*] historical
hiver *m.* [*ee-ver*] winter
*****hollandais** [*o-lã-de(z)*] Dutch
*****Hollande** *f.* [*o-lãd*] Holland
*****homard** *m.* [*o-mahr*] lobster
homme *m.* [*om*] man
   homme d'affaires [*om dah-fer*] businessman
   homme d'état [*om deh-tah*] statesman
   jeune homme [*zhuh-nom*] young man
   jeunes gens [*zhuhn zhã*] young people
*****Hongrie** *f.* [*õ-gree*] Hungary
*****hongrois** [*õ-grwah(z)*] Hungarian
honnête [*o-net*] honest
honneur *m.* [*o-nuhr*] honor
honoraires *m. pl.* [*o-no-rer*] fee
honorer *v.* [*o-no-reh*] honor
*****honte** *f.* [*õt*] shame
   avoir *v.* **honte** [*ah-vwahr õt*] be ashamed
*****honteux, -euse** [*õ-tuh, õ-tuhz*] shameful
hôpital, -aux *m.* [*o-pee-tahl, o-pee-toh*] hospital
horaire *adj.* [*o-rer*] hourly
horaire *m.* [*o-rer*] schedule
horloge *f.* [*or-lozh*] clock
horloger *m.* [*or-lo-zheh*] watchmaker
horrible [*o-reebl*] horrible
*****hors de** [*or d(uh)*] out of
*****hors d'oeuvre** *m. invar.* [*or duhvr*] relishes, hors d'oeuvre,
   appetizer
hospitalité *f.* [*os-pee-tah-lee-teh*] hospitality
hostile [*os-teel*] hostile
hôte *m.* [*oht*] host; guest
hôtel *m.* [*oh-tel*] hotel
   hôtel de ville [*oh-tel duh veel*] city hall, town hall
hôtelier *m.* [*oh-tuh-lyeh*] innkeeper, hotel keeper
**hôtesse, ** *f.* [*oh-tes*] hostess
   hôtesse de l'air [*oh-tes duh ler*] stewardess
huile *f.* [*weel*] oil
huiler *v.* [*wee-leh*] oil

*huit [*wee(t)*] eight
*huitième [*wee-tyem*] eighth
huître *f.* [*weetr*] oyster
humain [*ü-mē, ü-men*] human
humanité *f.* [*ü-mah-nee-teh*] humanity
humble [*ēbl*] humble
humeur *f.* [*ü-muhr*] mood
  de bonne humeur [*duh bo-nü-muhr*] in a good mood
humide [*ü-meed*] damp, humid
humidité *f.* [*ü-mee-dee-teh*] humidity, moisture
humoristique [*ü-mo-rees-teek*] humorous
hypothèque *f.* [*ee-po-tek*] mortgage
hypothèse *f.* [*ee-po-tez*] hypothesis, assumption

I

ici [*ee-see*] here
  par ici [*pahr ee-see*] this way
  d'ici trois jours [*dee-see trwah zhoor*] three days from now
idéal, -aux *adj. & n.* [*ee-deh-ahl, ee-deh-oh*] ideal
idée *f.* [*ee-deh*] idea
identifier *v.* [*ee-dā-tee-fyeh*] identify
identique [*ee-dā-teek*] identical
identité *f.* [*ee-dā-tee-teh*] identity
idiot [*ee-dyoh, ee-dyot*] idiot, idiotic
ignorant [*ee-nyo-rā(t)*] ignorant
ignorer *v.* [*ee-nyo-reh*] not know
il [*eel*] he, it
  Il y a [*eel yah*] There is, There are
  il y a trois ans [*eel yah trwah-zā*] three years ago
île *f.* [*eel*] island
illégal, -aux [*ee-leh-gahl, ee-leh-goh*] illegal
ils [*eel*] they
image *f.* [*ee-mahzh*] image
imagination *f.* [*ee-mah-zhee-nah-syō*] imagination

imaginer v. [*ee-mah-zhee-neh*] imagine
imbécile m. [*ē-beh-seel*] fool
imitation f. [*ee-mee-tah-syō*] imitation
imiter v. [*ee-mee-teh*] imitate
immatriculation f. [*ee-mah-tree-kü-lah-syō*] registration
  plaque f. d'immatriculation [*plahk dee-mah-tree-kü-lah-syō*] license plate
immédiat [*ee-meh-dyah(t)*] immediate
immédiatement [*ee-meh-dyaht-mā*] immediately
immense [*ee-mãs*] immense
immeuble m. [*ee-muhbl*] apartment house
immigration f. [*ee-mee-grah-syō*] immigration
immoral, -aux [*ee-mo-rahl, ee-mo-roh*] immoral
impair [*ē-per*] odd
impardonnable [*ē-pahr-do-nahbl*] unforgivable
imparfait [*ē-pahr-fe(t)*] imperfect
impartial, -aux [*ē-pahr-syahl, ē-pahr-syoh*] impartial
impasse f. [*ē-pahs*] dead-end street
impatient [*ē-pah-syã(t)*] impatient, eager
impérialisme m. [*ē-peh-ryah-leesm*] imperialism
imperméable adj. [*ē-per-meh-ahbl*] waterproof
imperméable m. [*ē-per-meh-ahbl*] raincoat
impoli [*ē-po-lee*] impolite
importance f. [*ē-por-tãs*] importance
important [*ē-por-tã(t)*] important
  peu important [*puh ē-por-ta(t)*] unimportant
importé [*ē-por-teh*] imported
importer v. [*ē-por-teh*] import; be important, matter
  n'importe comment [*nē-port ko-mã*] no matter how
  n'importe lequel [*nē-port luh-kel*] either, anyone
  n'importe où [*nē-por-too*] anywhere
  n'importe quand [*nē-port kã*] at any time
  n'importe quel [*nē-port kel*] any
  n'importe qui [*nē-port kee*] just anyone
  n'importe quoi [*nē-port kwah*] anything
  peu importe [*puh ē-port*] no matter; it makes no difference
imposer v. [*ē-po-zeh*] impose; tax
impossible [*ē-po-seebl*] impossible

impôt *m.* [*ē-poh*] tax
   impôt sur le revenu [*ē-poh sür luh ruhv-nü*] income tax
   exempt d'impôts [*eg-zā(t) dē-poh*] tax free
impression *f.* [*ē-preh-syō*] impression
imprévu [*ē-preh-vü*] unforeseen
imprimé *m.* [*ē-pree-meh*] form, printed matter
imprimer *v.* [*ē-pree-meh*] print
imprimeur *m.* [*ē-pree-muhr*] printer
improbable [*ē-pro-bahbl*] improbable
inattendu [*ee-nah-tā-dü*] unexpected
incapable [*ē-kah-pahbl*] incapable
incapacité *f.* [*ē-kah-pah-see-teh*] inability, incompetence
incendie *m.* [*ē-sā-dee*] fire
incertain [*ē-ser-tē, ē-ser-ten*] uncertain
incident *m.* [*ē-see-dā*] incident
incliner *v.* [*ē-klee-neh*] bend, bow
inclure *v. irreg.* [*ē-klür*] include
inclus [*ē-klü(z)*] included
incomparable [*ē-kō-pah-rahbl*] incomparable
incomplet, -ète [*ē-kō-pleh, ē-kō-plet*] incomplete
inconnu [*ē-ko-nü*] unknown
inconscient [*ē-kō-syā(t)*] unconscious
inconvenient *m.* [*ē-kō-veh-nyā*] disadvantage
incorrect [*ē-ko-rekt*] incorrect
incroyable [*ē-krwah-yahbl*] incredible
Inde *f.* [*ēd*] India
indécent [*ē-deh-sā(t)*] indecent
indécis [*ē-deh-see(z)*] undecided
indéfini [*ē-deh-fee-nee*] indefinite
indépendance *f.* [*ē-deh-pā-dās*] independence
independent [*ē-deh-pā-dā(t)*] independent
indicateur *m.* [*ē-dee-kah-tuhr*] timetable
indifférent [*ē-dee-feh-rā(t)*] indifferent
indigène *m., f.* [*ē-dee-zhen*] native
indigestion *f.* [*ē-dee-zhes-tyō*] indigestion
indigné [*ē-dee-nyeh*] indignant
indien, -enne [*ē-dyē, ē-dyen*] Indian
indiquer *v.* [*ē-dee-keh*] point out

indirect [*ē-dee-rekт*] indirect
indiscret, -ète [*ē-dees-kre(t)*] indiscreet
indiscutable [*ē-dees-kü-tahbl*] unquestionable
indispensable [*ē-dees-pā-sahbl*] indispensable
individu m. [*ē-dee-vee-dü*] individual
individuel, -elle [*ē-dee-vee-dwel*] individual
industrie f. [*ē-düs-tree*] industry
industriel, -elle [*ē-düs-tree-el*] industrial
inefficace [*ee-neh-fee-kahs*] inefficient
inégal, -aux [*ee-neh-gahl, ee-neh-goh*] unequal
inexcusable [*ee-nek-skü-zahbl*] inexcusable
infarctus m. [*ē-fahrk-tüs*] heart attack
infection f. [*ē-fek-syō*] infection
inférieur [*ē-feh-ryuhr*] inferior
infidèle [*ē-fee-del*] unfaithful
infiniment [*ē-fee-nee-mā*] infinitely
infinitif m. [*ē-fee-nee-teef*] infinitive
infirmière f. [*ē-feer-myer*] nurse
infirmité f. [*ē-feer-mee-teh*] disease, disability
influence f. [*ē-flü-ās*] influence
influencer v. [*ē-flü-ā-seh*] influence
information f. [*ē-for-mah-syō*] information
informer v. [*ē-for-meh*] inform
ingénieur m. [*ē-zheh-nyuhr*] engineer
initiative f. [*ee-nee-syah-teev*] initiative
injection f. [*ē-zhek-syō*] injection
injure f. [*ē-zhür*] insult
injuste [*ē-zhüst*] unjust, unfair
injustice f. [*ē-zhüs-tees*] injustice
innocent [*ee-no-sā(t)*] innocent
innombrable [*ee-nō-brahbl*] innumerable
inoccupé [*ee-no-kü-peh*] unoccupied
inondation f. [*ee-nō-dah-syō*] flood
inoubliable [*ee-noo-blee-ahbl*] unforgettable
inouï [*een-wee*] unheard-of
inquiet, -ète [*ē-kyeh, ē-kyet*] anxious, uneasy
inquiéter v. [*ē-kyeh-teh*] bother
  s'inquiéter [*sē-kyeh-teh*] worry

inquiétude *f.* [*ē-kyeh-tüd*] worry
inscription *f.* [*ē-skreep-syō*] registration, enrollment
s'inscrire *v. irreg.* [*sē-skreer*] enroll, register
insecte *m.* [*ē-sekt*] insect; bug
insistance *f.* [*ē-sees-tās*] insistance, emphasis
insister (sur) *v.* [*ē-sees-teh*] insist (on), stress
insonorisé [*ē-so-no-ree-zeh*] soundproof
insouciant [*ē-soo-syā(t)*] heedless
inspecter *v.* [*ē-spek-teh*] inspect
inspecteur, -trice [*ē-spek-tuhr, ē-spek-trees*] inspector
inspection *f.* [*ē-spek-syō*] inspection
inspiration *f.* [*ē-spee-rah-syō*] inspiration
installation *f.* [*ē-stah-lah-syō*] moving in, settling
installer *v.* [*ē-stah-leh*] install
  s'installer [*sē-stah-leh*] move in, get settled
instant *m.* [*ē-stā*] instant
  à l'instant [*ah lē-stā*] right now
instinct *m.* [*ē-stē*] instinct
instituteur, -trice [*ē-stee-tü-tuhr, ē-stee-tü-trees*] teacher
institution *f.* [*ē-stee-tü-syō*] institution
instructeur, -trice [*ē-strük-tuhr, ē-strük-trees*] instructor
instruction *f.* [*ē-strük-syō*] instruction, education
instruire *v. irreg.* [*ē-strweer*] instruct
instrument *m.* [*ē-strü-mā*] instrument
insuffisant [*ē-sü-fee-zā(t)*] insufficient
insulte *f.* [*ē-sült*] insult
insulter *v.* [*ē-sül-teh*] insult
intellectuel, -elle [*ē-teh-lek-twel*] intellectual
intelligent [*ē-teh-lee-zhā(t)*] intelligent
intense [*ē-tās*] intense
intention *f.* [*ē-tā-syō*] intention
  avoir *v.* **l'intention (de)** [*ah-vwahr lē-tā-syō (duh)*] intend
interdire *v. irreg.* [*ē-ter-deer*] forbid
interdit [*ē-ter-dee(t)*] forbidden, prohibited
intéressant [*ē-teh-re-sā(t)*] interesting
intéresser *v.* [*ē-teh-reh-seh*] interest
  s'intéresser (à) *v.* [*sē-teh-reh-seh (ah)*] care for, be interested
    (in)

intérêt *m.* [*ē-teh-re*] interest
intérieur *m.* [*ē-tehr-yuhr*] inside, interior
  à l'intérieur [*ah lē-tehr-yuhr*] within
internat *m.* [*ē-ter-nah*] boarding school
international, -aux [*ē-ter-nah-syo-nahl, ē-ter-nah-syo-noh*]
  international
interne [*ē-tern*] internal
interprète *m.* [*ē-ter-pret*] interpreter
interrompre *v.* [*ē-teh-rōpr*] interrupt
interrupteur *m.* [*ē-teh-rüp-tuhr*] switch
interurbain [*ē-ter-ür-bē, ē-ter-ür-ben*] long-distance
intervalle *m.* [*ē-ter-vahl*] interval
intervenir *v. irreg.* [*ē-ter-vuh-neer*] intervene, interfere
intime [*ē-teem*] intimate
introduction *f.* [*ē-tro-dük-syō*] introduction
introduire *v. irreg.* [*ē-tro-dweer*] introduce
intuition *f.* [*ē-twee-syō*] intuition
inutile [*ee-nü-teel*] useless
invalide [*ē-vah-leed*] invalid, disabled
invasion *f.* [*ē-vah-zyō*] invasion
inventeur *m.* [*ē-vā-tuhr*] inventor
invention *f.* [*ē-vā-syō*] invention
inverse *m.* [*ē-vers*] reverse
investir *v.* [*ē-ves-teer*] invest
invisible [*ē-vee-zeebl*] invisible
invitation *f.* [*ē-vee-tah-syō*] invitation
invité, -ée [*ē-vee-teh*] guest, company
inviter *v.* [*ē-vee-teh*] invite
involontaire [*ē-vo-lō-ter*] involuntary
irlandais *n. & adj.* [*eer-lā-de(z)*] Irish
Irlande *f.* [*eer-lād*] Ireland
irrégulier, -ière [*ee-reh-gü-lyeh, ee-reh-gü-lyer*] irregular
irrésistible [*ee-reh-zees-teebl*] irresistible
irriter *v.* [*ee-ree-teh*] irritate
isolé [*ee-zo-leh*] isolated, lonely
israelien, -enne *n. & adj.* [*eez-rah-eh-lyē, eez-rah-eh-lyen*]
  Israeli
israélite *n. & adj.* [*eez-rah-eh-leet*] Jew, Jewish; Israelite

Italie *f.* [*ee-tah-lee*] Italy
italien, -enne *n. & adj.* [*ee-tahl-yē, ee-tahl-yen*] Italian
itinéraire *m.* [*ee-tee-neh-rer*] itinerary
ivoire *m.* [*ee-vwahr*] ivory

J

jadis [*zhah-dees*] formerly
jalousie *f.* [*zhah-loo-zee*] jealousy
jaloux, -ouse [*zhah-loo, zhah-looz*] jealous
jamais [*zhah-me*] ever, never
jambe *f.* [*zhãb*] leg
jambon *m.* [*zhã-bõ*] ham
janvier *m.* [*zhã-vyeh*] January
Japon *m.* [*zhah-põ*] Japan
japonais *n. & adj.* [*zhah-po-ne(z)*] Japanese
jardin *m.* [*zhahr-dē*] garden
jardinier, -ière [*zhahr-dee-nyeh, zhahr-dee-nyer*] gardener
jarretière *f.* [*zhahr-tyer*] garter
jauge *f.* [*zhohzh*] gauge
jaune [*zhohn*] yellow
jazz *m.* [*dzhahz*] jazz
je [*zhuh*] I
jetée *f.* [*zh(uh)-teh*] pier
jeter *v.* [*zh(uh)-teh*] throw
jeu *m.* [*zhuh*] game
   jeu de cartes [*zhuhd kahrt*] deck of cards
jeudi *m.* [*zhuh-dee*] Thursday
jeune [*zhuhn*] young
jeunesse *f.* [*zhuh-nes*] youth
jockey *m.* [*zho-ke*] jockey
joie *f.* [*zhwah*] joy, delight
joindre *v. irreg.* [*zhwēdr*] join, bring together, meet
   se joindre à [*suh zhwē-drah*] join with [someone]
joli [*zho-lee*] pretty, nice

joue *f.* [*zhoo*] cheek
jouer *v.* [*zhweh*] play; gamble
   jouer à un jeu [*zhweh ah ē zhuh*] play a game
   jouer d'un instrument [*zhweh dē-nē-strü-mã*] play an
     instrument
jouet *m.* [*zhwe*] toy
jouir *v.* [*zhweer*] enjoy
jour *m.* [*zhoor*] day
   tous les jours [*too leh zhoor*] daily, every day
journal, -aux *m.* [*zhoor-nahl, zhoor-noh*] newspaper, journal
journaliste *m., f.* [*zhoor-nah-leest*] journalist, reporter
journée *f.* [*zhoor-neh*] day
   toute la journée [*toot lah zhoor-neh*] all day long
joyeux, -euse [*zhwah-yuh, zhwah-yuhz*] cheerful, joyful
juge *m.* [*zhüzh*] judge
jugement *m.* [*zhüzh-mã*] judgment
juger *v.* [*zhü-zheh*] judge
juif, juive [*zhweef, zhweev*] Jew, Jewish
juillet *m.* [*zhwee-ye*] July
juin *m.* [*zhwē*] June
jumeau, jumelle [*zhü-moh, zhü-mel*] twin brother, twin sister
jumelles *f. pl.* [*zhü-mel*] opera glasses, field glasses
jument *f.* [*zhü-mã*] mare
jungle *f.* [*zhēgl*] jungle
jupe *f.* [*zhüp*] skirt
jupon *m.* [*zhü-pō*] petticoat
jurer *v.* [*zhü-reh*] swear
jury *m.* [*zhü-ree*] jury
jus *m.* [*zhü*] juice
jusque [*zhüsk*] until, up to
   jusqu'Ici [*zhüs-kee-see*] so far
juste *adj. & adv.* [*zhüst*] just, accurate, fair
justement [*zhüs-tuh-mã*] precisely
justice *f.* [*zhüs-tees*] justice
justifier *v.* [*zhüs-tee-fyeh*] justify

K

kilogramme *m.* [*kee-lo-grahm*] kilogram [2.2 pounds]
kilomètre *m.* [*kee-lo-metr*] kilometer [.61 mile]
kiosque *m.* [*kyosk*] newsstand
klaxon *m.* [*klahk-son*] horn

L

l': **le, la** [*l*] the; him, her, it
la *art.* [*lah*] the
la *pron.* [*lah*] her, it
là [*lah*] there
   là-bas [*lah-bah*] over there
   là-haut [*lah-oh*] up there
laboratoire *m.* [*lah-bo-rah-twahr*] laboratory
labourer *v.* [*lah-boo-reh*] plow
lac *m.* [*lahk*] lake
lacet *m.* [*lah-se*] lace
lâche *m. f.*; *n. & adj.* [*lahsh*] coward, cowardly
lâcher *v.* [*lah-sheh*] let go
laid [*le(d)*] ugly
lainage *m.* [*le-nahzh*] wool garment
laine *f.* [*len*] wool
   en laine [*ã len*] woolen
laisser *v.* [*leh-seh*] leave (behind); let, allow
   laisser entrer [*leh-seh ã-treh*] admit
lait *m.* [*le*] milk
laiterie *f.* [*let-ree*] dairy
laitue *f.* [*leh-tü*] lettuce
lame *f.* [*lahm*] blade

lame de rasoir [*lahm duh rahz-wahr*] razor blade
lampe *f.* [*lãp*] lamp
lancer *v.* [*lã-seh*] toss
langage *m.* [*lã-gahzh*] language
langouste *f.* [*lã-goost*] spiny lobster
langue *f.* [*lãg*] tongue, language
lapin *m.* [*lah-pē*] rabbit
laquelle [*lah-kel*] which, who, whom
lard *m.* [*lahr*] bacon
large [*lahrzh*] wide, broad
   large d'esprit [*lahrzh des-pree*] broad-minded
largeur *f.* [*lahr-zhuhr*] width
larme *f.* [*lahrm*] tear
lavabo *m.* [*lah-vah-boh*] washbasin
laver *v.* [*lah-veh*] wash
   se laver [*slah-veh*] wash [oneself]
le *art.* [*luh*] the
le *pron.* [*luh*] him, it
leçon *f.* [*l(uh)-sõ*] lesson
lecteur, -trice [*lek-tuhr, lek-trees*] reader
lecture *f.* [*lek-tür*] reading
légal, -aux [*leh-gahl, leh-goh*] legal, lawful
léger, -ère [*leh-zheh, leh-zher*] light
légitime [*leh-zhee-teem*] legitimate
légume *m.* [*leh-güm*] vegetable
lendemain *m.* [*lãd-mē*] the next day
lent [*lã(t)*] slow
lentement [*lãt-mã*] slowly
lequel, laquelle; lesquels, lesquelles [*luh-kel, lah-kel, leh-kel*]
   whom, which
   La chaise sur laquelle j'étais assise [*lah shez sür lah-kel
   zheh-te ah-seez*] The chair on which I was sitting
lequel, laquelle *interr.* [*luh-kel, lah-kel*] which, which one
   Lequel voulez-vous? [*luh-kel voo-leh-voo*] Which [one] do
   you want?
les *art.* [*leh*] the
les *pron.* [*leh*] them
lesquels, -quelles [*leh-kel*] which, whom

lessive *f.* [*leh-seev*] washing
lettre *f.* [*letr*] letter
   lettre recommandée [*letr ruh-ko-mã-deh*] registered letter
leur, leurs *adj.* [*luhr*] their
leur *pron.* [*luhr*] to them
le leur, la leur *pron.* [*luh luhr, lah luhr*] theirs
lever *m.* **de soleil** [*l(uh)-vehd so-ley*] sunrise
se lever *v. irreg.* [*sluh-veh*] get up, stand up, rise
lèvre *f.* [*levr*] lip
libéral, -aux [*lee-beh-rahl, lee-beh-roh*] liberal
libérer *v.* [*lee-beh-reh*] free
liberté *f.* [*lee-ber-teh*] liberty, freedom
librairie *f.* [*lee-bre-ree*] bookstore
libre [*leebr*] free, vacant
libre-service *m.* [*lee-bruh-ser-vees*] cafeteria
licence *f.* [*lee-sãs*] university diploma, masters
lier *v.* [*lee-eh*] bind, tie up
lieu *m.* [*lyuh*] place
   avoir *v.* **lieu** [*ah-vwahr lyuh*] take place
   au lieu de [*oh lyuh duh*] instead of
lièvre *m.* [*lyevr*] hare
ligne *f.* [*leeñ*] line
lime *f.* [*leem*] file
limitation *f.* [*lee-mee-tah-syõ*] limitation
   limitation de vitesse [*lee-mee-tah-syõd vee-tes*] speed limit
limite *f.* [*lee-meet*] limit
limiter *v.* [*lee-mee-teh*] limit
linge *m.* [*lẽzh*] linen, clothes
liquide [*lee-keed*] liquid
lire *v. irreg.* [*leer*] read
lisible [*lee-zeebl*] legible
lisse [*lees*] smooth
liste *f.* [*leest*] list
lit *m.* [*lee*] bed
   lit d'enfant [*lee dã-fã*] crib
litre *m.* [*leetr*] liter [1.1 quarts]
littéralement [*lee-teh-rahl-mã*] literally
littérature *f.* [*lee-teh-rah-tür*] literature

livre *f.* [*leevr*] pound
livre *m.* [*leevr*] book
livrer *v.* [*lee-vreh*] deliver
livret *m.* [*lee-vre*] booklet
local, -aux [*lo-kahl, lo-koh*] local
locataire *m., f.* [*lo-kah-ter*] tenant
locomotive *f.* [*lo-ko-mo-teev*] engine, locomotive
logement *m.* [*lozh-mã*] housing, accommodations
loger *v.* [*lo-zheh*] house
logique [*lo-zheek*] logical, consistent
loi *f.* [*lwah*] law
loin (de) [*lwẽ (duh)*] far (from)
  au loin [*oh lwẽ*] far away
lointain [*lwẽ-tẽ, lwẽ-ten*] far away
loisir *m.* [*lwah-zeer*] leisure
long, longue [*lõ, lõg*] long
  le long de [*luh lõ d(uh)*] along
  à la longue [*ah lah lõg*] in the end
longtemps [*lõ-tã*] long, a long time
  il y a longtemps [*eel yah lõ-tã*] long ago
longueur *f.* [*lõ-guhr*] length
lorsque [*lorsk*] when
louer *v.* [*lweh*] rent; praise; reserve [a place]
lourd [*loor(d)*] heavy
loyal, -aux [*lwah-yahl, lwah-yoh*] loyal
loyer *m.* [*lwah-yeh*] rent
lui [*lwee*] him, her, it
  lui-même [*lwee-mem*] himself; itself
lumière *f.* [*lü-myer*] light
lundi *m.* [*lẽ-dee*] Monday
lune *f.* [*lün*] moon
  lune de miel [*lün duh myel*] honeymoon
lunettes *f. pl.* [*lü-net*] eyeglasses
  lunettes de soleil [*lü-net duh so-ley*] sunglasses
lutte *f.* [*lüt*] struggle
lutter *v.* [*lü-teh*] struggle
luxe *m.* [*lüks*] luxury

luxueux, -euse [*lük-swuh, lük-swuhz*] luxurious
lycée *m.* [*lee-seh*] high school, junior college

M

m': me [*m*] me
M.: Monsieur [*muh-syuh*] Mr.
ma [*mah*] my
mâcher *v.* [*mah-sheh*] chew
machine *f.* [*mah-sheen*] machine
  machine à écrire [*mah-sheen ah eh-kreer*] typewriter
  machine à laver [*mah-sheen ah lah-veh*] washing machine
mâchoire *f.* [*mah-shwahr*] jaw
Madame, Mesdames *f.* [*mah-dahm, meh-dahm*] madam, Mrs.
Mademoiselle, Mesdemoiselles *f.* [*mahd-mwah-zel, med-mwah-zel*] Miss
  Mademoiselle! [*mahd-mwah-zel*] Waitress!
magasin *m.* [*mah-gah-zē*] store, shop
  grand magasin *m.* [*grã mah-gah-zē*] department store
magique [*mah-zheek*] magic
magistrat *m.* [*mah-zhee-strah*] judge
magnifique [*mah-nyee-feek*] magnificent, gorgeous
mai *m.* [*me*] May
maigre [*megr*] thin
maigrir *v.* [*me-greer*] lose weight
maille *f.* [*mahy*] stitch
maillot *m.* **de bain** [*may-yoh duh bē*] swimsuit, bathing suit
main *f.* [*mē*] hand
  fait main [*fe mē*] handmade
main-d'oeuvre *f.* [*mē-duhvr*] labor
maintenant [*mēt-nã*] now
  à partir de maintenant [*ah pahr-teer duh mēt-nã*] from now on
  jusqu'à maintenant [*zhüs-kah mēt-nã*] until now
maintenir *v. irreg.* [*mēt-neer*] maintain

maire *m.* [*mer*] mayor
mairie *f.* [*meh-ree*] town hall
mais [*me*] but
maïs *m.* [*mah-ees*] corn
maison *f.* [*me-zõ*] house, home
  à la maison [*ah lah me-zõ*] at home
maître *m.* [*metr*] master
maîtresse *f.* [*me-tres*] mistress
  maîtresse de maison [*me-tres duh me-zõ*] housewife
maîtrise *f.* [*meh-treez*] control, mastery
majeur [*mah-zhuhr*] major
majorité *f.* [*mah-zho-ree-teh*] majority
mal, maux *m.* [*mahl, moh*] pain, evil, difficulty
  mal de gorge [*mahl duh gorzh*] sore throat
  mal de mer [*mahl duh mer*] sea-sickness
  mal à l'aise [*mah-lah lez*] uneasy, uncomfortable
  avoir *v.* **mal à** [*ah-vwahr mah-lah*] have a . . . ache
  avoir *v.* **mal à la tête** [*ah-vwahr mah-lah lah tet*] have a
    headache
  faire *v.* **mal** [*fer mahl*] hurt
  J'ai mal! [*zheh mahl*] It hurts!, I have a pain!
mal *adv.* [*mahl*] badly
  pas mal [*pah mahl*] not bad, pretty good
malade *adj.* [*mah-lahd*] sick, ill
malade *n.* [*mah-lahd*] patient
maladie *f.* [*mah-lah-dee*] disease, sickness, illness
maladroit [*mah-lah-drwah(t)*] awkward
malentendu *m.* [*mah-lã-tã-dü*] misunderstanding
malgré [*mahl-greh*] despite, in spite of
malheur *m.* [*mah-luhr*] bad luck, misfortune
malheureusement [*mah-luh-ruhz-mã*] unfortunately
malheureux, -euse [*mah-luh-ruh, mah-luh-ruhz*] unfortunate,
    unhappy
malhonnête [*mah-lo-net*] dishonest
malle *f.* [*mahl*] trunk
malsain [*mahl-sẽ, mahl-sen*] unhealthy
manche *m.* [*mãsh*] handle
manche *f.* [*mãsh*] sleeve; English Channel

manchette f. [mã-shet] cuff
  bouton m. **de manchette** [boo-tõd mã-shet] cuff links
mandat m. [mã-dah] money order; arrest warrant
mangeable [mã-zhahbl] edible
manger v. [mã-zheh] eat
manière f. [mah-nyer] manner
manifestation f. [man-nee-fes-tah-syõ] manifestation, demonstration
manifester v. [mah-nee-fes-teh] show, demonstrate [politically]
manivelle f. [mah-nee-vel] crank
manoeuvre m. [mah-nuhvr] unskilled worker
manoeuvre f. [mah-nuhvr] maneuver
manoeuvrer v. [mah-nuh-vreh] maneuver
manque m. [mãk] lack
manquer v. [mã-keh] be lacking, miss
  manquer (de) [mã-keh (duh)] lack
  J'ai manqué le train [zheh mã-kehl trẽ] I missed the train
  Ils me manquent [eel muh mãk] I miss them
manteau, -eaux m. [mã-toh] coat
manucure f. [mah-nü-kür] manicurist
maquillage m. [mah-kee-yahzh] make-up
marais m. [mah-re] marsh
marbre m. [mahrbr] marble
marchand m. [mahr-shã] merchant, dealer
marchander v. [mahr-shã-deh] bargain
marchandise f. [mahr-shã-deez] goods, merchandise
marche f. [mahrsh] step [of stairs], walk, march
  faire v. **marche arrière** [fer mar-shahr-yer] back up
marché m. [mahr-sheh] market
  bon marché [bõ mahr-sheh] cheap
  marché aux puces [mahr-sheh oh püs] flea-market
marcher v. [mahr-sheh] walk
mardi m. [mahr-dee] Tuesday
marée f. [mah-reh] tide
marguerite f. [mahr-guh-reet] daisy
mari m. [mah-ree] husband
mariage m. [mahr-yahzh] marriage, wedding

marié *m.* [*mahr-yeh*] bridegroom, groom
mariée *f.* [*mahr-yeh*] bride
se marier *v.* [*smahr-yeh*] get married
marin *m.* [*mah-rē*] sailor
marine *f.* [*mah-reen*] navy
marionnette *f.* [*mah-ryo-net*] puppet
marmite *f.* [*mahr-meet*] pot
marque *f.* [*mahrk*] mark, brand
   marque de fabrique [*mahrk duh fah-breek*] trademark
marquer *v.* [*mahr-keh*] mark
marraine *f.* [*mah-ren*] godmother
marron *m.* [*mah-rō*] chestnut; brown [color]
mars *m.* [*mahrs*] March
marteau, -eaux *m.* [*mahr-toh*] hammer
masculin [*mahs-kü-lē, mahs-kü-leen*] masculine
massage *m.* [*muh-sahzh*] massage
masse *f.* [*mahs*] mass
mât *m.* [*mah*] mast
matelas *m.* [*maht-lah*] mattress
matelot *m.* [*maht-loh*] sailor
matériel *m.* [*mah-tehr-yel*] material, equipment
maternel, -elle [*mah-ter-nel*] maternal
   ècole *f.* **maternelle** [*eh-kol mah-ter-nel*] nursery school
mathématiques *f. pl.* [*mah-teh-mah-teek*] mathematics
matière *f.* [*mah-tyer*] matter, material
   matières premières [*mah-tyer pruh-myer*] raw materials
matin *m.* [*mah-tē*] morning
matinée *f.* [*mah-tee-neh*] morning; matinee [theater]
mauvais *adj.* [*mo-ve(z)*] bad
me [*muh*] me
mécanicien *m.* [*meh-kah-nee-syē*] mechanic; engineer
   [of train]
mécanique [*meh-kah-neek*] mechanical
mécanisme *m.* [*meh-kah-neesm*] mecanism
méchant [*meh-shã(t)*] bad, michievous, naughty
mécontent [*meh-kō-tã(t)*] unhappy
médecin *m.* [*med-sē*] doctor
médecine *f.* [*med-seen*] medicine [profession]

médical, -aux [*meh-dee-kahl, meh-dee-koh*] medical
médicament m. [*meh-dee-kah-mã*] medication
Méditerranée f. [*meh-dee-te-rah-neh*] Mediterranean (Sea)
méfiance f. [*meh-fyãs*] distrust
meilleur, le meilleur [*meh-yuhr, luh meh-yuhr*] better, best
mélange m. [*meh-lãzh*] mixture
mélanger v. [*meh-lã-zheh*] mix
melon m. [*m(uh)-lõ*] melon
membre m. [*mãbr*] member; limb [of body]
même adj. [*mem*] same, very, self
même adv. [*mem*] even
  à meme de [*ah mem d(uh)*] able to
  de même [*duh mem*] likewise
  de même que [*duh mem kuh*] just as
  tout de même [*tood mem*] all the same
memoire f. [*mem-wahr*] memory
menace f. [*muh-nahs*] threat
menacer v. [*muh-nah-seh*] threaten
ménage m. [*meh-nahzh*] housework, household
ménagère f. [*meh-nah-zher*] housekeeper, housewife
mendiant, -te [*mã-dyã(t)*] beggar
mendier v. [*mã-dyeh*] beg
mener v. [*muh-neh*] lead, conduct
mensonge m. [*mã-sõzh*] lie
mensuel, -elle [*mã-swel*] monthly
menteur, -euse [*mã-tuhr, mã-tuhz*] liar
menthe f. [*mãt*] mint
mentionner v. [*mã-syo-neh*] mention
mentir v. irreg. [*mã-teer*] lie
menton m. [*mã-tõ*] chin
menu m. [*muh-nii*] menu
menuisier m. [*muh-nwee-zyeh*] carpenter
mépris m. [*meh-pree*] contempt
mépriser v. [*meh-pree-zeh*] scorn
mer f. [*mer*] sea
mercerie f. [*mer-suh-ree*] notions, dry goods
Merci [*mer-see*] Thank you
mercredi m. [*mer-kruh-dee*] Wednesday

mère *f.* [*mer*] mother
mérite *m.* [*meh-reet*] merit
mériter *v.* [*meh-ree-teh*] deserve
merveilleux, -euse [*mer-ve-yuh, mer-ve-yuhz*] wonderful
mes [*meh*] my
mesdames, mesdemoiselles [*meh-dahm, med-mwah-zel*]
　　ladies, young ladies
message *m.* [*meh-sahzh*] message
messager *m.* [*meh-sah-zheh*] messenger
messe *f.* [*mes*] mass [eccl.]
mesure *f.* [*muh-zür*] measure
　fait sur mesure [*fe sür muh-zür*] custom made
mesurer *v.* [*muh-zü-reh*] measure
métal, -aux *m.* [*meh-tahl, meh-toh*] metal
méthode *f.* [*meh-tod*] method
métier *m.* [*meh-tyeh*] trade
mètre *m.* [*metr*] meter [39.4 inches]
métro *m.* [*meh-troh*] subway
metteur en scène *m.* [*me-tuhr ã sen*] director [films]
mettre *v. irreg.* [*metr*] put, set; put on [clothing]
meuble *m.* [*muhbl*] a piece of furniture, furniture
meubler *v.* [*muh-bleh*] furnish
　chambre *f.* **meublée** [*shã-bruh muh-bleh*] furnished room
meurtre *m.* [*muhrtr*] murder
meurtrier *m.* [*muhr-tree-yeh*] murderer
microbe *m.* [*mee-krob*] germ
midi *m.* [*mee-dee*] noon
miel *m.* [*myel*] honey
le mien, la mienne [*luh myẽ, la myen*] mine
miette *f.* [*myet*] crumb
mieux, le mieux [*myuh, luh myuh*] better, best
mignon, -nne [*mee-nyõ, mee-nyon*] cute
milieu, *m.* [*meel-yuh*] middle; social circle, surroundings
militaire [*mee-lee-ter*] military
mille *m. inv.* [*meel*] thousand
milliard *m.* [*meel-yahr*] billion
million *m.* [*meel-yõ*] million
mince [*mẽs*] thin

mine *f.* [*meen*] looks, appearance
  Elle a bonne mine [*el ah bon meen*] She looks well
minéral, -aux [*mee-neh-rahl, mee-neh-roh*] mineral
mineur *m.* [*mee-nuhr*] miner
mineur, -eure [*mee-nuhr*] minor, infant
minimum *m.* [*mee-nee-mom*] minimum
ministère *f.* [*mee-nees-ter*] ministry
ministre *m.* [*mee-neestr*] minister
minorité *f.* [*mee-no-ree-teh*] minority
minuit *m.* [*mee-nwee*] midnight
minuscule [*mee-nüs-kül*] tiny
minute *f.* [*mee-nüt*] minute
miroir *m.* [*meer-wahr*] mirror
misérable [*mee-zeh-rahbl*] miserable
mode *f.* [*mod*] fashion, style
  à la mode [*ah lah mod*] fashionable
modèle *m.* [*mo-del*] model
moderne [*mo-dern*] modern
modeste [*mo-dest*] modest
modifier *v.* [*mo-dee-fyeh*] modify, change
modiste *f.* [*mo-deest*] milliner
moi [*mwah*] me; I
  moi-même [*mwah-mem*] myself
moi *m.* [*mwah*] self, ego
moindre [*mwēdr*] less
  le moindre [*luh mwēdr*] the least
moins [*mwē*] less, fewer, minus
  au moins [*oh mwē*] at least
  à moins de, à moins que [*ah mwē d(uh), ah mwē kuh*]
    unless
  de moins en moins [*duh mwē-zã mwē*] less and less
mois *m.* [*mwah*] month
moisson *f.* [*mwah-sõ*] harvest
moitié *f.* [*mwah-tyeh*] half
moment *m.* [*mo-mã*] moment
mon [*mõ*] my
monarchie *f.* [*mo-nahr-shee*] monarchy
monastère *m.* [*mo-nah-ster*] monastery

monde *m.* [*mõd*] world
mondial, -aux [*mõ-dyahl, mõ-dyoh*] world, world-wide
monétaire [*mo-neh-ter*] monetary
monnaie *f.* [*mo-ne*] money, currency
  de la monnaie [*dlah mo-ne*] change
monotone [*mo-no-ton*] monotonous
monsieur, messieurs [*muh-syuh, meh-syuh*] gentleman, gentlemen
  Monsieur [*muh-syuh*] Mister, Sir
montagne *f.* [*mõ-tahñ*] mountain
montant [*mõ-tã(t)*] uphill
montant *m.* [*mõ-tã*] amount, post
monter *v.* [*mõ-teh*] go up; carry up
montre *f.* [*mõtr*] watch
montrer *v.* [*mõ-treh*] show
monument *m.* [*mo-nü-mã*] monument
moral, -aux [*mo-rahl, mo-roh*] moral
moral *m.* [*mo-rahl*] morale, spirit
morale *f.* [*mo-rahl*] moral
morceau, -eaux *m.* [*mor-soh*] piece
mordre *v.* [*mordr*] bite
mort *f.* [*mor*] death
mort *adj.* [*mor(t)*] dead
mortel, -elle [*mor-tel*] deadly
mot *m.* [*moh*] word
moteur *m.* [*mo-tuhr*] motor, engine
motif *m.* [*mo-teef*] motive
motocyclette *f.* [*mo-to-see-klet*] motorcycle
mou, molle [*moo, mol*] soft
mouche *f.* [*moosh*] fly
se moucher *v.* [*smoo-sheh*] blow one's nose
mouchoir *m.* [*moo-shwahr*] handkerchief
moudre *v. irreg.* [*moodr*] grind
mouillé [*moo-yeh*] wet
moule *f.* [*mool*] mussel
moule *m.* [*mool*] mold
moulin *m.* [*moo-lẽ*] mill
  moulin à vent [*moo-lẽ ah vã*] windmill

moulu [*moo-lü*] ground
mourir *v. irreg.* [*moo-reer*] die
mousse *f.* [*moos*] moss; foam [of a beverage]
moustache *f.* [*moos-tahsh*] mustache
moustique *m.* [*moos-teek*] mosquito
moutarde *f.* [*moo-tahrd*] mustard
mouvement *m.* [*moov-mã*] movement, motion
moyen, -enne [*mwah-ē, mwah-en*] average, medium
   au moyen de [*oh mwah-ēd(uh)*] by means of
moyens *m. pl.* [*mwah-ē*] means
moyenne *f.* [*mwah-yen*] average
muet, muette [*mweh, mwet*] dumb
munitions *f. pl.* [*mü-nee-syõ*] munitions, ammunition
mur *m.* [*mür*] wall
mûr [*mür*] mature, ripe
mûrir *v.* [*mü-reer*] ripen
muscle *m.* [*müskl*] muscle
musée *m.* [*mü-zeh*] museum
musical, -aux [*mü-zee-kahl, mü-zee-koh*] musical
musicien, -enne [*mü-zee-syē, mü-zee-syen*] musician
musique *f.* [*mü-zeek*] music
mutilé [*mü-tee-leh*] mutilated, disabled
mutuel, -elle [*mü-twel*] mutual
myope [*myop*] near-sighted
mystère *m.* [*mees-ter*] mystery
mystérieux, -euse [*mees-teh-ryuh, mees-teh-ryuhz*] mysterious

N

nager *v.* [*nah-zheh*] swim
naïf, naïve [*nah-eef, nah-eev*] naive
naissance *f.* [*ne-sãs*] birth
naître *v. irreg.* [*netr*] be born
   Je suis né en France [*zhuh swee neh ã frãs*] I was born
   in France

nappe *f.* [*nahp*] tablecloth
nation *f.* [*nah-syõ*] nation
national, -aux [*nah-syo-nahl, nah-syo-noh*] national
nationalité *f.* [*nah-syo-nah-lee-teh*] nationality, citizenship
natte *f.* [*naht*] braid
nature *f.* [*nah-tür*] nature
naturel, -elle [*nah-tü-rel*] natural
naturellement [*nah-tü-rel-mã*] naturally
naufrage *m.* [*noh-frahzh*] shipwreck
naval, navals *adj.* [*nah-vahl*] naval
navet *m.* [*nah-ve*] turnip
navire *m.* [*nah-veer*] ship
ne, n' [*nuh*] not
  ne ... pas [*nuh ... pah*] not
  ne ... guère [*nuh ... gher*] hardly
  ne ... plus [*nuh ... plü*] no more, no longer
  ne ... que [*nuh ... kuh*] only
néanmoins [*nch-ã-mwẽ*] nevertheless
nécessaire [*neh-seh-ser*] necessary
nef *f.* [*nef*] nave
négatif, -ive [*neh-gah-teef, neh-gah-teev*] negative
négatif *m.* [*neh-gah-teef*] negative
négliger *v.* [*neh-glee-zheh*] neglect
négociant *m.* [*neh-go-syã*] dealer
neige *f.* [*nezh*] snow
  flocon *m.* **de neige** [*flo-kõd nezh*] snowflake
  tempête *f.* **de neige** [*tã-pet duh nezh*] snow storm, blizzard
neiger *v.* [*ne-zheh*] snow
  Il neige [*eel nezh*] It's snowing
nerf *m.* [*ner*] nerve
nerveux, -euse [*ner-vuh, ner-vuhz*] nervous
n'est-ce pas [*nes pah*] isn't that so
  Il est allé, n'est-ce pas? [*ee-le-tah-leh, nes pah*] He went, didn't he?
net, nette [*net*] neat, clear
nettoyage *m.* [*ne-twah-yahzh*] cleaning
nettoyer *v.* [*ne-twah-yeh*] clean
  nettoyer à sec [*ne-twah-yeh ah sek*] dry-clean

neuf [*nuhf*] nine
neuf, neuve [*nuhf, nuhv*] new
neutre [*nuhtr*] neutral
neveu, -eux *m.* [*nuh-vuh*] nephew
nez *m.* [*neh*] nose
ni . . . ni [*nee . . . nee*] neither . . . nor
nid *m.* [*nee*] nest
nièce *f.* [*nyes*[niece
nier *v.* [*nee-eh*] deny
niveau, -aux *m.* [*nee-voh*] level
noble [*nobl*] noble
Noël *m.* [*no-el*] Christmas
   Joyeux Noël! [*zhwah-yuh no-el*] Merry Christmas!
noeud *m.* [*nuh*] knot, bow
noir *adj.* [*nwahr*] black
noir, noire *n.* [*ňwahr*] Negro
noix *f.* [*nwah*] nut, walnut
   noix de muscade [*nwahd müs-kahd*] nutmeg
nom *m.* [*nõ*] name; noun
   nom de famille [*nõd fah-meey*] last name
nombre *m.* [*nõbr*] number
nombreux, -euse [*nõ-bruh, nõ-bruhz*] numerous
   famille *f.* **nombreuse** [*fah-meey nõ-bruhz*] large family
nommer *v.* [*no-meh*] name, appoint
non [*nõ*] no
nord *m.* [*nor*] north
   nord-est *m.* [*nor-est*] northeast
   nord-ouest *m.* [*nor-west*] northwest
normal, -aux [*nor-mahl, nor-moh*] normal
Norvége *f.* [*nor-vezh*] Norway
norvègien, -ienne [*nor-veh-zhyē, nor-veh-zhyen*] Norwegian
nos *pl.* [*noh*] our
notamment [*no-tah-mã*] notably
note *f.* [*not*] note, memo; grade, mark; bill, invoice
noter *v.* [*no-teh*] note
notion *f.* [*noh-syõ*] notion
notre [*notr*] our
   le nôtre [*luh nohtr*] ours

nouer *v.* [*nweh*] tie
nouilles *f. pl.* [*nooy*] noodles
nourrir *v.* [*noo-reer*] feed
nous [*noo*] we, us
  nous trois [*noo trwah*] the three of us
nouveau, -vel, -velle [*noo-voh, noo-vel*] new
nouveauté *f.* [*noo-voh-teh*] novelty
nouvelle *f.* [*noo-vel*] a piece of news
novembre *m.* [*no-vãbr*] November
noyer, se noyer *v.* [*nwah-yeh, s(uh) nwah-yeh*] drown
nu [*nü*] bare, nude
nuage *m.* [*nwahzh*] cloud
nuageux, -euse [*nwah-zhuh, nwah-zhuhz*] cloudy
nuisible [*nwee-zeebl*] harmful
nuit *f.* [*nwee*] night
  Bonne nuit [*bon nwee*] Good night
nul, nulle [*nül*] null, worthless; no
  nulle part [*nül pahr*] nowhere
numéro *m.* [*nü-meh-roh*] number
  numéro de téléphone [*nü-meh-rohd teh-leh-fon*]
    telephone number
nylon *m.* [*nee-lõ*] nylon

O

obéir (à) *v.* [*o-beh-eer (ah)*] obey
obéissant [*o-beh-ee-sã(t)*] obedient
objectif *m.* [*ob-zhek-teef*] objective; lens
objection *f.* [*ob-zhek-syõ*] objection
  faire *v.* **objection** [*fer ob-zhek-syõ*] object
objet *m.* [*ob-zhe*] object
obligation *f.* [*o-blee-gah-syõ*] obligation, bond
obligatoire [*o-blee-gah-twahr*] obligatory, compulsory
obliger *v.* [*o-blee-zheh*] oblige
obscurité *f.* [*op-skü-ree-teh*] obscurity, darkness

observation *f.* [*op-ser-vah-syõ*] observation
observer *v.* [*op-ser-veh*] observe
obstacle *m.* [*op-stahkl*] obstacle
obtenir *v. irreg.* [*op-tuh-neer*] obtain, get
occasion *f.* [*o-kah-syõ*] occasion, opportunity; bargain
  d'occasion [*do-kah-syõ*] second-hand, used
occidental, -aux [*ok-see-dã-tahl, ok-see-dã-toh*] western
occupé [*o-kü-peh*] busy, occupied
occuper *v.* [*o-kü-peh*] occupy
  s'occuper (de) [*so-kü-peh (duh)*] take care of, handle
océan *m.* [*o-seh-ã*] ocean
octobre *m.* [*ok-tobr*] October
oculiste *m.* [*o-kü-leest*] eye doctor
odeur *f.* [*o-duhr*] odor, smell
ouvre-boîte *m.* [*oo-vruh-bwaht*] can opener
oeil *m.* **yeux** *pl.* [*uhy, yuh*] eye
  coup *m.* **d'oeil** [*koo-duhy*] glance
  jeter *v.* **un coup d'oeil** [*zh(uh)-teh ẽ koo duhy*] glance
oeuf, oeufs *m.* [*uhf, uh*] egg
  oeuf à la coque [*uh-fah lah kok*] soft boiled egg
  oeufs brouillés [*uh broo-yeh*] scrambled eggs
  oeuf dur [*uhf diir*] hard boiled egg
  oeuf au plat [*uh-foh plah*] fried egg
oeuvre *f.* [*uhvr*] work
  oeuvre d'art *f.* [*uh-vruh dahr*] work of art
offenser *v.* [*o-fã-seh*] offend
offensif, -ive [*o-fã-seef, o-fã-seev*] offensive
office *m.* [*o-fees*] service
officiel, -elle [*o-fee-syel*] official
officier *m.* [*o-fee-syeh*] officer
offre *f.* [*ofr*] offer, supply, bid
offrir *v.* [*o-freer*] offer
oignon *m.* [*o-nyõ*] onion
oiseau, -eaux *m.* [*wah-zoh*] bird
olive *f.* [*o-leev*] olive
  huile *f.* **d'olive** [*weel do-leev*] olive oil
ombragé [*õ-brah-zheh*] shady
ombre *f.* [*õbr*] shade, shadow

omelette *f.* [*om-let*] omelet
omettre *v. irreg.* [*o-metr*] omit
omission *f.* [*o-mee-syõ*] omission
omnibus *m.* [*om-nee-büs*] local bus
on *impers. pron.* [*õ*] one, they, people
oncle *m.* [*õkl*] uncle
ondes courtes *f. pl.* [*õd koort*] short wave
ongle *m.* [*õgl*] nail
ont *3d pers. pl. pres. tense of* AVOIR [*õ*] have
onze [*õz*] eleven
opéra *m.* [*o-peh-rah*] opera
opération *f.* [*o-peh-rah-syõ*] operation
opérer *v.* [*o-peh-reh*] operate
opinion *f.* [*o-pee-nyõ*] opinion
opposé [*o-poh-zeh*] opposite
s'opposer à *v.* [*so-poh-zeh ah*] oppose, be opposed to
opposition *f.* [*o-poh-zee-syõ*] opposition
or *conj.* [*or*] now
or *m.* [*or*] gold
 d'or [*dor*] golden
orage *m.* [*o-rahzh*] storm
oral, -aux [*o-rahl, o-roh*] oral
orange *f.* [*o-rãzh*] orange
orchestre *m.* [*or-kestr*] orchestra, band
orchidée *f.* [*or-kee-deh*] orchid
ordinaire [*or-dee-ner*] ordinary, common
ordonnance *f.* [*or-do-nãs*] prescription
ordonné [*or-do-neh*] orderly
ordre *m.* [*ordr*] order, command
ordures *f. pl.* [*or-dür*] garbage
oreille *f.* [*o-rey*] ear
oreiller *m.* [*o-reh-yeh*] pillow
organe *m.* [*or-gahn*] organ
organisation *f.* [*or-gah-nee-zah-syõ*] organization
organiser *v.* [*or-gah-nee-zeh*] organize
orgue *m.*, **orgues** *f. pl.* [*org*] organ [music]
orgueil *m.* [*or-guhy*] pride
orgueilleux, -euse [*or-guh-yuh, or-guh-yuhz*] proud

Orient *m.* [*or-yã*] East
   Extrême Orient [*ek-strem or-yã*] Far East
   Moyen Orient [*mwah-yĕ-nor-yã*] Middle East
   Proche Orient [*pro-shor-yã*] Near East
oriental, -aux [*or-yã-tahl, or-yã-toh*] oriental, eastern
original, -aux [*o-ree-zhee-nahl, o-ree-zhee-noh*] original
origine *f.* [*o-ree-zheen*] origin
   à l'origine [*ah lo-ree-zheen*] originally
originel, -elle [*o-ree-zhee-nel*] original
ornement *m.* [*or-nuh-mã*] ornament
ornière *f.* [*or-nyer*] rut
orphelin *m., f.* [*or-fe-lĕ*] orphan
orteil *m.* [*or-tey*] toe
orthographe *f.* [*or-to-grahf*] spelling
os *m.* [*os*; pl.: *o*] bone
oser *v.* [*oh-zeh*] dare
otage *m.* [*o-tahzh*] hostage
ôter *v.* [*oh-teh*] remove
ou [*oo*] or
   ou . . . ou [*oo . . . oo*] either . . . or
   où [*oo*] where
oublier *v.* [*oo-blee-eh*] forget
ouest *m.* [*west*] west
oui [*wee*] yes
ours *m.* [*oors*] bear
outil *m.* [*oo-tee*] tool, implement
outre-mer [*oo-truh-mer*] overseas
ouvert [*oo-ver(t)*] open
ouverture *f.* [*oo-ver-tiir*] opening
ouvrage *m.* [*oo-vrahzh*] work
ouvreuse *f.* [*oo-vruhz*] usher
ouvrier, -ière [*oo-vree-eh, oo-vree-er*] worker
ouvrir *v. irreg.* [*oo-vreer*] open; turn on [water]
oxygène *m.* [*ok-see-zhen*] oxygen

P

page *f.* [*pahzh*] page
paiement *m.* [*pe-mã*] payment
paille *f.* [*pahy*] straw
pain *m.* [*pẽ*] bread
   pain grillé [*pẽ gree-yeh*] toast
pair *adj.* [*per*] even
paire *f.* [*per*] pair
paisible [*peh-zeebl*] peaceful
paix *f.* [*pe*] peace
palais *m.* [*pah-le*] palace
pâle [*pahl*] pale
pâlir *v.* [*pah-leer*] grow pale
palmier *m.* [*pahl-myeh*] palm
palourde *f.* [*pah-loord*] clam
pamplemousse *f.* [*pã-pluh-moos*] grapefruit
pancarte *f.* [*pã-kahrt*] sign
panier *m.* [*pah-nyeh*] basket
panique *f.* [*pah-neek*] panic
panne *f.* [*pahn*] breakdown
   en panne [*ã pahn*] having [car] trouble
   en panne d'essence [*ã pahn deh-sãs*] out of gas
pansement *m.* [*pãs-mã*] bandage
pantalon *m.* [*pã-tah-lõ*] trousers, pants, slacks
pantoufle *f.* [*pã-toofl*] slipper
pape *m.* [*pahp*] Pope
papeterie *f.* [*pah-peh-tree*] stationer's
papier *m.* [*pah-pyeh*] paper
   papier hygénique [*pah-pyeh-ee-zheh-neek*] toilet paper
   papier peint [*pah-pyeh pẽ*] wallpaper
   papier à lettres [*pah-pyeh ah letr*] writing paper, stationery
papillon *m.* [*pah-peé-yõ*] butterfly
paquebot *m.* [*pahk-boh*] steamship

Pâques *m. pl.* [*pahk*] Easter
paquet *m.* [*pah-ke*] package, pack
par [*pahr*] through, by
  par-ci par-là [*pahr-see pahr-lah*] here and there
  par hasard [*pahr ah-zahr*] by chance
paradis *m.* [*pah-rah-dee*] paradise
paragraphe *m.* [*pah-rah-grahf*] paragraph
paraître *v. irreg.* [*pah-retr*] appear, seem
  il paraît [*eel pah-re*] it seems
parallèle [*pah-rah-lel*] parallel
paralyser *v.* [*pah-rah-lee-zeh*] paralyze
parapluie *m.* [*pah-rah-plwee*] umbrella
parc *m.* [*pahrk*] park
parce que [*pahrs kuh*] because
parcourir *v. irreg.* [*pahr-koo-reer*] travel through; look
    through
parcours *m.* [*pahr-koor*] distance covered; route
pardessus *m.* [*pahr-duh-sü*] overcoat
par-dessus [*pahrd-sü*] over
pardon *m.* [*pahr-dõ*] pardon
pardonner *v.* [*pahr-do-neh*] forgive, pardon
  Pardon! [*pahr-dõ*] Excuse me!
pare-brise *m.* [*pahr-breez*] windshield
pare-choc *m.* [*pahr-shok*] bumper
pareil, -eille [*pah-rey*] alike, like
parent *m.* [*pah-rã*] relative
parenté *f.* [*pah-rã-teh*] relationship, kindred
paresse *f.* [*pah-res*] laziness
paresseux, -euse [*pah-re-suh, pah-re-suhz*] lazy
parfait [*pahr-fe(t)*] perfect
parfois [*pahr-fwah*] sometimes
parfum *m.* [*pahr-fẽ*] perfume; flavor
pari *m.* [*pah-ree*] bet
parier *v.* [*pahr-yeh*] bet
parlement *m.* [*pahr-luh-mã*] parliament
parler *v.* [*pahr-leh*] talk, speak
  Parlez-vous français? [*pahr-leh-voo frã-se*] Do you speak
    French?

parmi [*pahr-mee*] among
paroisse *f.* [*pahr-wahs*] parish
parole *f.* [*pah-rol*] (spoken) word, remark, promise
parrain *m.* [*pah-rē*] godfather
part *f.* [*pahr*] part, share
  à part [*ah pahr*] apart, except for, aside
  nulle part [*nül pahr*] nowhere
  quelque part [*kel-kuh pahr*] somewhere
  d'autre part [*doh-truh pahr*] moreover
  d'une part ... d'autre part [*dün pahr ... doh-truh pahr*]
    on the one hand ... on the other hand
  de la part de [*dlah pahr duh*] on behalf of, from, sent by
  faire *v.* **part** [*fer pahr*] announce
  faire-part *m.* [*fer-pahr*] announcement
partager *v.* [*pahr-tah-zheh*] share, divide
parti *m.* [*pahr-tee*] party
participe *m.* [*pahr-tee-seep*] participle
participer *v.* [*pahr-tee-see-peh*] participate
particulier, -iere [*pahr-tee-kü-lyeh, pahr-tee-kü-lyer*]
  particular, individual
partie *f.* [*pahr-tee*] part
  en partie [*ã pahr-tee*] partly
partir (de) *v. irreg.* [*pahr-teer (duh)*] leave, depart
  à partir de ... [*ah pahr-teer duh*] from ... on
  partir en courant [*pahr-teer ã koo-rã*] run away
  Il est temps de partir [*ee-le tãd pahr-teer*] It's time to
    be going
partout [*pahr-too*] everywhere
  partout où [*pahr-too oo*] wherever
parvenir *v. irreg.* [*pahr-vuh-neer*] reach, succeed
pas [*pah*] not
  pas du tout [*pah dü too*] not at all
pas *m.* [*pah*] step, pace
  faire *v.* **un (des) pas** [*fer ē (deh) pah*] step, take a step
passage *m.* [*pah-sahzh*] passage
  passage à niveau [*pah-sah-zhah nee-voh*] railroad crossing
passager, -ère *adj.* [*pah-sah-zheh, pah-sah-zher*] passing,
  fleeting, momentary

passager, -ère n. [*pah-sah-zheh, pah-sah-zher*] passenger
passant, -te [*pah-sã(t)*] passer-by
passé m. [*pah-seh*] past
passeport m. [*pahs-por*] passport
passer v. [*pah-seh*] pass; spend [time]
  se passer de [*spah-seh duh*] do without
passerelle f. [*pahs-rel*] bridge; gangplank
passif, -ive [*pah-seef, pah-seev*] passive
passion f. [*pah-syõ*] passion
passionné [*pah-syo-neh*] passionate
pastèque f. [*pahs-tek*] watermelon
pasteur m. [*pahs-tuhr*] minister
pâte f. [*paht*] dough, pasta
pâté m. [*pah-teh*] pâté
patience f. [*pah-syãs*] patience
patient [*pah-syã(t)*] patient
patin m. [*pah-tẽ*] skate
  patins à glace [*pah-tẽ ah glahs*] ice skates
  patins à roulettes [*pah-tẽ ah roo-let*] roller skates
patiner v. [*pah-tee-neh*] skate
patinoire f. [*pah-tee-nwahr*] skating rink
patisserie f. [*pah-tees-ree*] pastry, pastry shop
patrie f. [*pah-tree*] native country
patriotique [*pah-tree-o-teek*] patriotic
patron m. [*pah-trõ*] pattern [for sewing]; boss, employer
patte f. [*paht*] paw
paupière f. [*poh-pyer*] eyelid
pause f. [*pohz*] pause
pauvre [*pohvr*] poor
pauvreté f. [*poh-vruh-teh*] poverty
payer v. [*peh-yeh*] pay
  C'est moi qui paie [*se mwah kee peh*] It's my treat
pays m. [*peh-ee*] country, nation
paysage m. [*peh-ee-zahzh*] landscape
péage m. [*peh-ahzh*] toll
peau, peaux f. [*poh*] skin
pêche f. [*pesh*] peach; fishing
péché m. [*peh-sheh*] sin

pêcher *v.* [*peh-sheh*] fish
pécher *v.* [*peh-sheh*] sin
pêcheur *m.* [*peh-shuhr*] fisherman
pédale *f.* [*peh-dahl*] pedal
peigne *m.* [*peñ*] comb
peigner *v.* [*pe-nyeh*] comb
peindre *v. irreg.* [*pēdr*] paint
peine *f.* [*pen*] penalty, suffering
  à peine [*ah pen*] hardly
peintre *m.* [*pĕtr*] painter
peinture *f.* [*pē-tür*] painting, paint
  peinture à l'huile [*pē-tur ah lweel*] oil painting
pelle *f.* [*pel*] shovel
pellicule *f.* [*peh-lee-kül*] film
pelouse *f.* [*p(uh)-looz*] lawn
pelure *f.* [*p(uh)-lür*] peel
pencher *v.* [*pã-sheh*] lean
  se pencher [*spã-sheh*] lean over
pendant [*pã-dã*] during
  pendant que [*pã-dã k(uh)*] while
pendre *v.* [*pãdr*] hang
pendule *f.* [*pã-dül*] clock
pénétration *f.* [*peh-neh-trah-syō*] penetration, insight
pénible [*peh-neebl*] hard
péniche *f.* [*peh-neesh*] barge
pensée *f.* [*pã-seh*] thought
penser *v.* [*pã-seh*] think
  penser à [*pã-seh ah*] think of, about; reflect on; remember
  penser de [*pã-seh duh*] think about, have an opinion on
pension *f.* [*pã-syō*] boarding house
pensionnaire *m., f.* [*pã-syo-ner*] boarder
pensionnat *m.* [*pã-syo-nah*] boarding school
pente *f.* [*pãt*] slope
percer *v.* [*per-seh*] break through
perche *f.* [*persh*] pole
perdre *v.* [*perdr*] lose
perdu [*per-dü*] lost
père *m.* [*per*] father

perfection *f.* [*per-fek-syõ*] perfection
période *f.* [*pehr-yod*] period
périr *v.* [*peh-reer*] perish
perle *f.* [*perl*] pearl
permanent [*per-mah-nã(t)*] permanent
permanente *f.* [*per-mah-nãt*] permanent (wave)
permettre *v. irreg.* [*per-metr*] allow, let, permit
  permettre à ... de faire ... [*per-me-trah ... duh fer ...*]
    allow [someone] to do [something]
permis *m.* [*per-mee*] license, permit
  permis de conduire [*per-meed kõ-dweer*] driver's license
permission *f.* [*per-mee-syõ*] permission; leave
perruque *f.* [*peh-rük*] wig
persil *m.* [*per-see*] parsley
persister *v.* [*per-sees-teh*] persist
personalité *f.* [*per-so-nah-lee-teh*] personality
personnage *m.* [*per-so-nahzh*] person
personne *pron.* [*per-son*] nobody, no one; anybody, anyone
personne *f.* [*per-son*] person
personnel, -elle [*per-so-nel*] personal
personnel *m.* [*per-so-nel*] personnel
personnellement [*per-so-nel-mã*] personally
persuader *v.* [*per-swah-deh*] persuade
perte *f.* [*pert*] loss
pertinent [*per-tee-nã(t)*] relevant
peser *v.* [*puh-zeh*] weigh
pessimiste *adj.* [*peh-see-meest*] pessimistic
pessimiste *m., f.* [*peh-see-meest*] pessimist
petit [*p(uh)-tee(t)*] little, small
  petite fille *f.* [*p(uh)-teet feey*] granddaughter
  petits-enfants *m. pl.* [*p(uh)-tee-zã-fã*] grandchildren
  petit fils *m.* [*p(uh)-tee fees*] grandson
  petit à petit [*ptee-tah ptee*] little by little
pétition *f.* [*peh-tee-syõ*] petition
pétrole *m.* [*peh-trol*] oil, petroleum
peu [*puh*] little, few
  un peu [*ẽ puh*] a little, a few
  peu à peu [*puh ah puh*] little by little

peuple *m.* [*puhpl*] people, nation; lower classes
peur *f.* [*puhr*] fear
   avoir *v.* **peur** [*ah-vwahr puhr*] be afraid
   faire *v.* **peur à** [*fer puhr ah*] frighten
peureux, -euse [*puh-ruh(z)*] fearful
peut-être [*puh-tetr*] maybe, perhaps
phare *m.* [*fahr*] lighthouse; headlight
pharmacie *f.* [*fahr-mah-see*] drugstore, pharmacy
philosophe *m.* [*fee-lo-sof*] philosopher
philosophie *f.* [*fee-lo-so-fee*] philosophy
phoque *m.* [*fok*] seal
photo *f.* [*fo-to*] photo, photograph
photographe *m.* [*fo-to-grahf*] photographer
photographier *v.* [*fo-to-gra-fyeh*] photograph
phrase *f.* [*frahz*] sentence
physique [*fee-zeek*] physical
pianiste *m., f.* [*pyah-neest*] pianist
piano *m.* [*pyah-noh*] piano
pic *m.* [*peek*] peak
pichet *m.* [*pee-she*] pitcher
pièce *f.* [*pyes*] coin; play [theatre]; patch; room
   pièces de rechange [*pyes duhr-shāzh*] spare parts
pied *m.* [*pyeh*] foot
   pieds nus [*pyeh nü*] barefoot
   à pied [*ah pyeh*] on foot
   coup *m.* **de pied** [*kood pyeh*] kick
piège *m.* [*pyezh*] trap
pierre *f.* [*pyer*] stone
piété *f.* [*pyeh-teh*] piety
piéton *m.* [*pyeh-tõ*] pedestrian
pieux, pieuse [*pyuh, pyuhz*] pious
pigeon *m.* [*pee-zhõ*] pigeon
pile *f.* [*peel*] pile, heap; battery
pilier *m.* [*peel-yeh*] pillar
pillule *f.* [*peel-lül*] pill
pilote *m.* [*pee-lot*] pilot
pin *m.* [*pē*] pine
pinceau, -aux *m.* [*pē-soh*] brush

pincer *v.* [*pē-seh*] pinch
pioche *f.* [*pyosh*] pick
pipe *f.* [*peep*] pipe
piquer *v.* [*pee-keh*] sting; stitch
piqûre *f.* [*pee-kür*] insect bite; injection, shot
pire [*peer*] worse
  le pire [*luh peer*] worst
pis [*pee*] worse
piscine *f.* [*pee-seen*] swimming pool
piste *f.* [*peest*] track
  piste d'atterrissage [*pees-tuh dah-teh-ree-sahzh*] runway
pistolet *m.* [*pees-to-le*] pistol
pitié *f.* [*pee-tyeh*] pity
  avoir *v.* **pitié de** [*ah-vwahr pee-tyeh duh*] pity
pittoresque [*pee-to-resk*] picturesque
placard *m.* [*plah-kahr*] cupboard, closet
place *f.* [*plahs*] place; public square
  à la place [*ah lah plahs*] instead
  de la place [*duh lah plahs*] room
placer *v.* [*plah-seh*] place; invest
plafond *m.* [*plah-fõ*] ceiling
plage *f.* [*plahzh*] beach
plaie *f.* [*ple*] wound, sore
plaindre *v. irreg.* [*plēdr*] pity, be sorry for
  se plaindre (de) *v. irreg.* [*s(uh) plēdr (duh)*] complain
    (of, about)
plaine *f.* [*plen*] plain
plaire à *v. irreg.* [*pler ah*] please
  S'il vous plaît [*seel voo ple*] Please
plaisanter *v.* [*ple-zã-teh*] joke
plaisanterie *f.* [*ple-zã-tree*] joke
plaisir *m.* [*ple-zeer*] pleasure
  avec plaisir [*ah-vek ple-zeer*] with pleasure
plan *m.* [*plã*] plan; city map
planche *f.* [*plãsh*] board
plancher *m.* [*plã-sheh*] floor
planète *f.* [*plah-net*] planet
plante *f.* [*plãt*] plant

planter v. [plã-teh] plant
plastique [plahs-teek] plastic
plat [plah] flat
plat m. [plah] dish
plateau, -eaux m. [plah-toh] tray
plâtre m. [plahtr] plaster, plaster cast
plein [plẽ, plen] full
   Le plein normal [luh plẽ nor-mahl] Fill up with regular
pleurer v. [pluh-reh] cry
pleuvoir v. irreg. [pluh-vwahr] rain
   Il pleut [eel pluh] It's raining
pli m. [plee] fold, wrinkle
plier v. [plee-yeh] bend, fold
plomb m. [plõ] lead
plombage m. [plõ-bahzh] filling
plombier m. [plõ-byeh] plumber
plonger v. [plõ-zheh] dive
pluie f. [plwee] rain
plume f. [plüm] feather
plupart [plü-pahr] most, majority
   la plupart du temps [lah plü-pahr dü tã] most of the time
pluriel m. [plür-yel] plural
plus [plü(s)] more, plus
   le plus [luh plü(s)] the most
   au plus [oh plüs] at the most
   de plus [duh plüs] besides, furthermore
   de plus en plus [duh plü-zã plü] more and more
   ne . . . plus [nuh . . . plü] no longer, no more, not again
   plus . . . plus [plü . . . plü] the more . . . the more
plusieurs [plü-zyuhr] several
plutôt (que) [plü-toh (kuh)] rather (than)
pneu m. [pnuh] tire
   pneu crevé [pnuh kruh-veh] flat tire
poche f. [posh] pocket
poêle f. [pwahl] frying pan
poêle m. [pwahl] stove
poème m. [po-em] poem
poète m. [po-et] poet

poids *m.* [*pwah*] weight
poignée *f.* [*pwah-nyeh*] handful; handle
poignet *m.* [*pwah-nye*] wrist
poil *m.* [*pwahl*] hair
poing *m.* [*pwē*] fist
  coup *m.* **de poing** [*kood pwē*] punch, blow
point *m.* [*pwē*] point; stitch
  point final [*pwē fee-nahl*] period
  point d'interrogation [*pwē dē-teh-ro-gah-syō*] question mark
  point de vue [*pwēd vü*] point of view, viewpoint
  point mort [*pwē mor*] neutral [gear]
pointe *f.* [*pwēt*] point
pointu [*pwē-tü*] pointed, sharp
pointure *f.* [*pwē-tür*] size
poire *f.* [*pwahr*] pear
poireau, -eaux *m.* [*pwah-roh*] leek
pois, petits pois *m.* [*pwah, ptee-pwah*] pea, peas
poison *m.* [*pwah-zō*] poison
poisson *m.* [*pwah-sō*] fish
poitrine *f.* [*pwah-treen*] breast, chest
poivre *m.* [*pwahvr*] pepper
pôle *m.* [*pohl*] pole
poli [*po-lee*] polite, courteous
police *f.* [*po-lees*] police
  commissariat *m.* **de police** [*ko-mee-sahr-yahd po-lees*]
    police station
policier *m.* [*po-lee-syeh*] policeman
polir *v.* [*po-leer*] polish
politesse *f.* [*po-lee-tes*] courtesy
politique *adj.* [*po-lee-teek*] political
politique *f.* [*pol-lee-teek*] policy; politics
  politique extérieure [*po-lee-teek ek-stehr-yuhr*] foreign
    policy
Pologne *f.* [*po-loñ*] Poland
polonais [*po-lo-ne(z)*] Polish
pommade *f.* [*po-mahd*] cream
pomme *f.* [*pom*] apple
pomme de terre *f.* [*pom duh ter*] potato

pompe *f.* [*pŏp*] pump
pompier *m.* [*pŏ-pyeh*] fireman
ponctuel, -elle [*pŏk-twel*] punctual
pont *m.* [*pŏ*] bridge; deck [of a ship]
population *f.* [*po-pü-lah-syŏ*] population
porc *m.* [*por*] pork
porcelaine *f.* [*por-suh-len*] porcelain, china
porche *m.* [*porsh*] porch
port *m.* [*por*] port, harbor
portail *m.* [*por-tahy*] gate
portatif, -tive [*por-tah-teef, por-tah-teev*] portable
porte *f.* [*port*] door
portée *f.* [*por-teh*] range
portefeuille *m.* [*por-tuh-fuhy*] wallet
porte-monnaie *m.* [*port-mo-ne*] change-purse
porter *v.* [*por-teh*] carry, bear, wear
porteur *m.* [*por-tuhr*] porter
portier *m.* [*por-tyeh*] doorman
portière *f.* [*por-tyer*] car door
portrait *m.* [*por-tre*] portrait
portugais [*por-tü-ghe(z)*] Portuguese
Portugal *m.* [*por-tü-gahl*] Portugal
pose *f.* [*pohz*] pose
poser *v.* [*poh-zeh*] put, place, lay, pose
  poser une question [*poh-zeh ün kes-tyŏ*] ask a question
position *f.* [*po-zee-syŏ*] position
posséder *v.* [*po-seh-deh*] possess, own
possession *f.* [*po-se-syŏ*] possession
possibilité *f.* [*po-see-bee-lee-teh*] possibility
possible [*po-seebl*] possible
poste *f.* [*post*] post office
  poste restante [*post res-tãt*] general delivery
poste *m.* [*post*] position, post, station; receiver, set
  poste à essence [*post ah eh-sãs*] gas station
poster *v.* [*pos-teh*] mail
pot *m.* [*poh*] pot
potage *m.* [*po-tahzh*] soup
pot d'échappement *m.* [*poh deh-shahp-mã*] muffler

pot-de-vin *m.* [*pohd-vē*] bribe
poteau, -eaux *m.* [*po-toh*] post
poterie *f.* [*pot-ree*] pottery
potiron *m.* [*po-tee-rõ*] pumpkin
poubelle *f.* [*poo-bel*] garbage can
pouce *m.* [*poos*] thumb; inch
poudre *f.* [*poodr*] powder
poule *f.* [*pool*] hen
poulet *m.* [*poo-le*] chicken
pouls *m.* [*poo*] pulse
poumon *m.* [*poo-mõ*] lung
poupée *f.* [*poo-peh*] doll
pour [*poor*] for
pourboire *m.* [*poor-bwahr*] tip
pour cent [*poor sã*] percent
pourcentage *m.* [*poor-sã-tahzh*] percentage
pourquoi [*poor-kwah*] why
　pourquoi pas? [*poor-kwah pah*] why not?
pourri [*poo-ree*] rotten
poursuivre *v. irreg.* [*poor-sweevr*] pursue
pourtant [*poor-tã*] however
pourvu que [*poor-vü k(uh)*] provided that
pousser *v.* [*poo-seh*] push; grow
poussière *f.* [*poo-syer*] dust
poussiéreux, -euse [*poo-syeh-ruh, poo-syeh-ruhz*] dusty
poutre *f.* [*pootr*] beam, girder
pouvoir *m.* [*poo-vwahr*] power
pouvoir *v. irreg.* [*poo-vwahr*] be able, can, may
　Il se peut . . . [*eel suh puh*] It may be . . .
　Puis-je partir? [*pweezh pahr-teer*] May I go?
　Je n'y peux rien [*zhnee puh ryē*] I can't do anything
　　about it
pratique [*prah-teek*] practical
pratiquement [*prah-teek-mã*] practically
pratiquer *v.* [*prah-tee-keh*] practice
pré *m.* [*preh*] meadow
précaution *f.* [*preh-koh-syõ*] precaution, caution
précédemment [*preh-seh-dah-mã*] formerly

précédent [*preh-seh-dã(t)*] previous
précéder *v.* [*preh-seh-deh*] precede
précieux, -euse [*preh-syuh, preh-syuhz*] precious
précis [*preh-see(z)*] precise
précisément [*preh-see-zeh-mã*] precisely
préciser *v.* [*preh-see-zeh*] specify
préférable [*preh-feh-rahbl*] preferable
préféré [*preh-feh-reh*] favorite, preferred
préférence *f.* [*preh-feh-rãs*] preference
préférer *v.* [*preh-feh-reh*] prefer
préfet *m.* [*preh-fe*] perfect
préjugé *m.* [*preh-zhü-zheh*] prejudice
préliminaire [*preh-lee-mee-ner*] preliminary
prématuré [*preh-mah-tü-reh*] premature
premier, -ière [*pruh-myeh, pruh-myer*] first
  premiers secours *m.* [*pruh-myehs-koor*] first aid
prendre *v. irreg.* [*prãdr*] take, pick up
  prendre part à [*prãdr pahr ah*] participate in
prénom *m.* [*preh-nõ*] first name
préparation *f.* [*preh-pah-rah-syõ*] preparation
préparer *v.* [*preh-pah-reh*] prepare
près (de) [*pre d(uh)*] near; close (to)
présence *f.* [*preh-zãs*] presence
présent *adj.* [*preh-zã(t)*] present
présentation *f.* [*preh-zã-tah-syõ*] introduction, presentation
présenter *v.* [*preh-zã-teh*] introduce, present
préserver *v.* [*preh-zer-veh*] preserve
président *m.* [*preh-zee-dã*] president
presque [*presk*] almost, nearly
presqu'île *f.* [*pres-keel*] peninsula
presse *f.* [*pres*] press
pressé [*preh-seh*] in a hurry
presser *v.* [*preh-seh*] press
pressing *m.* [*preh-seeng*] dry-cleaners
pression *f.* [*pre-syõ*] pressure
prestige *m.* [*pres-teezh*] prestige
présumer *v.* [*preh-zü-meh*] presume
prêt *m.* [*pre*] loan

prêt [*pre(t)*] ready
prêt-à-porter *m.* [*pre-tah-por-teh*] ready-to-wear
prétendre *v.* [*preh-tädr*] pretend
prétentieux, -euse [*preh-tä-syuh, preh-tä-syuhz*] pretentious
prêter *v.* [*pre-teh*] lend
prêtre *m.* [*pretr*] priest
preuve *f.* [*pruhv*] proof, evidence
prévenir *v. irreg.* [*prev-neer*] warn, notify [in advance]
prévoir *v. irreg.* [*preh-vwahr*] forsee
prier *v.* [*pree-yeh*] pray
prière *f.* [*pree-yer*] prayer
primitif, -tive [*pree-mee-teef, pree-mee-teev*] primitive
principal, -aux [*prē-see-pahl, prē-see-poh*] principal, main
principalement [*prē-see-pahl-mä*] principally, mainly
principe *m.* [*prē-seep*] principle
printemps *m.* [*prē-tä*] spring
prise *f.* [*preez*] plug; outlet
prison *f.* [*pree-zō*] prison, jail
prisonnier, -ière [*pree-zo-nyeh, pree-zo-nyer*] prisoner
privé [*pree-veh*] private
priver *v.* [*pree-veh*] deprive
privilège *m.* [*pree-vee-lezh*] privilege
prix *m.* [*pree*] price, prize
probable [*pro-bahbl*] probable, likely
probablement [*pro-bah-bluh-mä*] probably
problème *m.* [*pro-blem*] problem
procédé *m.* [*pro-seh-deh*] method
procédure *f.* [*pro-seh-dür*] procedure
procès *m.* [*pro-se*] case, suit
prochain [*pro-shē, pro-shen*] next
proche [*prosh*] close
procuration *f.* [*pro-kü-rah-syō*] proxy
procurer *v.* [*pro-kü-reh*] obtain
production *f.* [*pro-dük-syō*] production
produire *v. irreg.* [*pro-dweer*] produce
produit *m.* [*pro-dwee*] product
professeur *m.*, **femme professeur** *f.* [*pro-fe-suhr, fahm pro-fe-suhr*] professor, teacher

profession *f.* [*pro-fe-syõ*] profession
professionnel, -elle [*pro-fe-syo-nel*] professional, vocational
profit *m.* [*pro-fee*] profit
profiter *v.* [*pro-fee-teh*] profit
  profiter de [*pro-fee-teh duh*] take advantage of
profond [*pro-fõ(d)*] deep
  peu profond [*puh pro-fõ(d)*] shallow
profondeur *f.* [*pro-fõ-duhr*] depth
programme *m.* [*pro-grahm*] program
progrès *m.* [*pro-gre*] progress
progresser *v.* [*pro-gre-seh*] progress
progressif, -ive [*pro-gre-seef, pro-gre-seev*] progressive
projet *m.* [*pro-zhe*] project
prolonger *v.* [*pro-lõ-zheh*] prolong
promenade *f.* [*prom-nahd*] outing
  promenade à pied [*prom-nahd ah pyeh*] walk
  promenade à bicyclette [*prom-nahd ah bee-see-klet*]
    bike ride
  promenade à cheval [*prom-nahd ah shvahl*] horseback ride
  promenade en voiture [*prom-nahd ã vwah-tür*] ride, drive
se promener *v.* [*sprom-neh*] go for a walk, ride
promesse *f.* [*pro-mes*] promise
promettre *v. irreg.* [*pro-metr*] promise
promotion *f.* [*pro-moh-syõ*] promotion
prompt [*prõ(t)*] prompt
pronom *m.* [*pro-nõ*] pronoun
prononcer *v.* [*pro-nõ-seh*] pronounce
prononciation *f.* [*pro-nõ-syah-syõ*] pronunciation
propagande *f.* [*pro-pah-gãd*] propaganda
proportion *f.* [*pro-por-syõ*] proportion
à propos [*ah pro-poh*] by the way
proposer *v.* [*pro-poh-zeh*] propose
proposition *f.* [*pro-poh-zee-syõ*] proposal, proposition
propre [*propr*] clean; one's own
propreté *f.* [*pro-pruh-teh*] cleanliness
propriétaire *m., f.* [*pro-pree-yeh-ter*] landlord, landlady,
    owner
propriété *f.* [*pro-pree-yeh-teh*] property, estate

prospère [*pros-per*] prosperous
prospérité *f.* [*pros-peh-ree-teh*] prosperity
protection *f.* [*pro-tek-syõ*] protection
protéger *v.* [*pro-teh-zheh*] protect, guard
protestant [*pro-tes-tã(t)*] Protestant
protester *v.* [*pro-tes-teh*] protest
prouver *v.* [*proo-veh*] prove
provenir *v. irreg.* [*prov-neer*] come from
proverbe *m.* [*pro-verb*] proverb
province *f.* [*pro-vēs*] province
provincial, -aux [*pro-vē-syahl, pro-vē-syoh*] provincial
provisions *f. pl.* [*pro-vee-zyõ*] provisions
provoquer *v.* [*pro-vo-keh*] provoke
prudence *f.* [*prü-dãs*] prudence
prune *f.* [*prün*] plum
pruneau, -eaux *m.* [*prü-noh*] prune
psychanalyse *f.* [*psee-kah-nah-leez*] psychoanalysis
psychiatre *m.* [*psee-kyahtr*] psychiatrist
psychologique [*psee-ko-lo-zheek*] psychological
public *m.* [*püb-leek*] public, audience
public, -lique [*püb-leek*] public
publication *f.* [*püb-lee-kah-syõ*] publication
publicité *f.* [*püb-lee-see-teh*] publicity, advertising
publier *v.* [*püb-lee-yeh*] publish
puce *f.* [*püs*] flea
puis [*pwee*] then
puisque [*pweesk*] since
puissant [*pwee-sã(t)*] powerful
puits *m.* [*pwee*] well
pull-over *m.* [*pül-o-vuhr*] pullover
punaise *f.* [*pü-nez*] bedbug; thumb tack
punir *v.* [*pü-neer*] punish
punition *f.* [*pü-nee-syõ*] punishment
pur [*pür*] pure
purée *f.* **de pommes de terre** [*pü-rehd pom duh ter*] mashed
    potatoes
pyjama *m.* [*pee-zhah-mah*] pajamas
pyramide *f.* [*pee-rah-meed*] pyramid

Q

qu': que [*k(uh)*] that
quai *m.* [*keh*] dock, pier
qualité *f.* [*kah-lee-teh*] quality
quand [*kã*] when
  quand même [*kã mem*] all the same
quant à [*kã-tah*] as for
quantité *f.* [*kã-tee-teh*] quantity, amount
quarante [*kah-rãt*] forty
quart *m.* [*kahr*] quarter
  quart d'heure [*kahr duhr*] quarter hour
quartier *m.* [*kar-tyeh*] neighborhood
  quartier général [*kar-tyeh zheh-neh-rahl*] headquarters
quatorze [*kah-torz*] fourteen
quatre [*kahtr*] four
quatre-vingt-dix [*kah-ıruh-vẽ-dees*] ninety
quatre-vingts [*kah-truh-vẽ*] eighty
que *conj.* [*k(uh)*] that; than
  J'espère que vous viendrez [*zhes-per kuh voo vyẽ-dreh*]
    I hope (that) you will come
  Il est plus grand que son frère [*ee-le plü grãk sõ frer*]
    He is taller than his brother
que *interr. pron.* [*k(uh)*] what
que *rel. pron.* [*k(uh)*] whom, which, that
  l'arbre que j'ai vu [*lahrbr kuh zheh vü*] the tree (which,
    that) I saw
  l'homme que j'ai vu [*lom kuh zheh vü*] the man (whom,
    that) I saw
quel, quelle *interr. adj.* [*kel*] which, what
  Quelle auto prenez-vous? [*ke-loh-toh pruh-neh voo*]
    Which car are you taking?
  Quelle est la date de . . . [*ke-le lah daht duh*] What is the
    date of . . .

273

Quel âge a-t-il? [*ke-lahzh ah-teel*] How old is he?

quelconque [*kel-kõk*] whatever

quelque, quelques [*kel-k(uh)*] some, any

   quelque peu [*kel-kuh puh*] somewhat

quelque chose [*kel-kuh shohz*] something, anything

quelquefois [*kel-kuh fwah*] sometimes

quelque part [*kel-kuh pahr*] somewhere

   quelque part ailleurs [*kel-kuh pahr ah-yuhr*] somewhere else

quelqu'un [*kel-kẽ*] someone, anyone

querelle *f.* [*kuh-rel*] quarrel

qu'est-ce que *interr. pron.* [*kes-k(uh)*] what [as object of verb]

   Qu'est-ce que c'est? [*kes kuh se*] What is this?, What is it?

   Qu'est-ce que c'est que cela? [*kes kuh sek slah*] What's that?

qu'est-ce qui *interr. pron.* [*kes kee*] what [as subject]

question *f.* [*kes-tyõ*] question

questionnaire *m.* [*kes-tyo-ner*] questionnaire

questionner *v.* [*kes-tyo-neh*] question

quête *f.* [*ket*] search; collection

queue *f.* [*kuh*] tail; line, file, queue

   faire *v.* **la queue** [*fer lah kuh*] stand in line

qui *interr. pron.* [*kee*] who, whom

   qui est-ce qui [*kee es kee*] who

   qui est-ce que [*kee es k(uh)*] whom

qui *rel. pron.* [*kee*] who, that, whom, which

quiconque [*kee-kõk*] whoever

quinine *f.* [*kee-neen*] quinine

quinze [*kẽz*] fifteen

quittance *f.* [*kee-tãs*] receipt

quitter *v.* [*kee-teh*] leave

   Ne quittez pas [*nuh kee-teh pah*] Hold the line

quoi [*kwah*] what

   A quoi pensez-vous? [*ah kwah pã-seh voo*] What are you thinking about?

   Il n'y a pas de quoi [*eel nee yah pahd kwah*] Don't mention it

quoi qui, quoi que [*kwah kee, kwah k(uh)*] whatever

   quoi qu'on dise [*kwah kõ deez*] whatever they say

quoique [*kwahk*] although
quotidien, -enne [*ko-tee-dyē, ko-tee-dyen*] daily

R

rabbin *m.* [*rah-bē*] rabbi
raccomoder *v.* [*rah-ko-mo-deh*] mend, darn
raccourcir *v.* [*rah-koor-seer*] shorten
raccrocher *v.* [*rah-kro-sheh*] hang up
race *f.* [*rahs*] race
racheter *v.* [*rahsh-teh*] redeem
racine *f.* [*rah-seen*] root
raconter *v.* [*rah-kō-teh*] tell
radiateur *m.* [*rah-dyah-tuhr*] radiator
radical, -aux [*rah-dee-kahl, rah-dee-koh*] radical
radio *f.* [*rah-dyoh*] radio
radio(graphie) *f.* [*rah-dyoh-(grah-fee)*] x-ray
radis *m.* [*rah-dee*] radish
rafraîchlr *v.* [*rah-freh-sheer*] cool, refresh
rafraîchissant [*rah-freh-shee-sã(t)*] refreshing
rafraîchissement *m.* [*rah-freh-shees-mã*] refreshment
rage *f.* [*rahzh*] rage; rabies
ragoût *m.* [*rah-goo*] stew
raide [*red*] steep; stiff
raie *f.* [*re*] part
raisin *m.* [*re-zē*] grapes
  raisin sec [*re-zē sek*] raisin
raison *f.* [*re-zō*] reason
  avoir *v.* **raison** [*ah-vwahr re-zō*] be right
raisonnable [*re-zo-nahbl*] reasonable, sensible
ralentir, se ralentir *v.* [*rah-lã-teer, s(uh) rah-lã-teer*] slow
  down
  Ralentissez! [*rah-lã-tee-seh*] Slow down!
ramasser *v.* [*rah-mah-seh*] gather (up, together)
rame *f.* [*rahm*] oar

ramener *v.* [*rahm-neh*] bring back
rancune *f.* [*rã-kün*] grudge, bitterness
rang *m.* [*rã*] row
ranger *v.* [*rã-zheh*] put in order, clean up
rapide [*rah-peed*] fast, rapid, quick
rapide *m.* [*rah-peed*] express (train)
rapidement [*rah-peed-mã*] rapidly
rappeler *v.* [*rah-pleh*] remind, recall
  se rappeler *v.* [*srah-pleh*] remember
rapport *m.* [*rah-por*] profit; relation; report
rapprochement *m.* [*rah-prosh-mã*] bringing together
rapprocher *v.* [*rah-pro-sheh*] bring closer
raquette *f.* [*rah-ket*] racket
rare [*rahr*] rare, scarce
rarement [*rahr-mã*] rarely, seldom
se raser *v.* [*srah-zeh*] shave
rasoir *m.* [*rah-zwahr*] razor
rassembler *v.* [*rah-sã-bleh*] assemble
rassurer *v.* [*rah-sü-reh*] reassure
rat *m.* [*rah*] rat
raté *m.* [*rah-teh*] failure
rateau, -eaux *m.* [*rah-toh*] rake
rater *v.* [*rah-teh*] miss
rattraper *v.* [*rah-trah-peh*] catch up with
ravi [*rah-vee*] overjoyed
rayon *m.* [*re-yõ*] ray; spoke; shelf; department (store)
rayonne *f.* [*re-yon*] rayon
réaction *f.* [*reh-ahk-syõ*] reaction
réaliser *v.* [*reh-ah-lee-zeh*] carry out
réalité *f.* [*reh-ah-lee-teh*] reality
récemment [*reh-sah-mã*] recently
récent [*reh-sã(t)*] recent
réception *f.* [*reh-sep-syõ*] party, reception
récession *f.* [*reh-se-syõ*] recession
recette *f.* [*ruh-set*] recipe
recevoir *v. irreg.* [*ruh-suh-vwahr*] receive, get; entertain
réchaud *m.* [*reh-shoh*] hot plate
recherche *f.* [*r(uh)-shersh*] search, research

rechercher *v.* [*r(uh)-sher-sheh*] look for
récif *m.* [*reh-seef*] reef
récipient *m.* [*reh-see-pyã*] container
réciproque [*reh-see-prok*] mutual
  C'est réciproque [*se reh-see-prok*] It's mutual
récit *m.* [*reh-see*] account
réciter *v.* [*reh-see-teh*] recite
réclamation *f.* [*reh-klah-mah-syõ*] complaint, claim
réclame *f.* [*reh-klahm*] advertisement, special offer
réclamer *v.* [*reh-klah-meh*] complain, protest
récolte *f.* [*reh-kolt*] crop, harvest
recommandation *f.* [*r(uh)-ko-mã-dah-syõ*] recommendation
recommander *v.* [*r(uh)-ko-mã-deh*] recommend
  lettre *f.* **recommandée** [*letr ruh-ko-mã-deh*] registered letter
recommencer *v.* [*r(uh)-ko-mã-seh*] begin again
récompense *f.* [*reh-kõ-pãs*] reward
récompenser *v.* [*reh-kõ-pã-seh*] reward
reconnaissance *f.* [*r(uh)-ko-ne-sãs*] gratitude
reconnaissant [*r(uh)-ko-ne-sã(t)*] grateful, thankful
  Je vous suis très reconnaissant [*zhvoo swee trer-ko-ne-sã*]
    I am much obliged to you
reconnaître *v. irreg.* [*r(uh)-ko-netr*] recognize
record *m.* [*r(uh)-kor*] record
récréation *f.* [*reh-kreh-ah-syõ*] recreation; recess [school]
rectangle *m.* [*rek-tãgl*] rectangle
reçu *m.* [*r(uh)-sü*] receipt
recueillir *v. irreg.* [*r(uh)-kuh-yeer*] gather, take in
reculer *v.* [*r(uh)-kü-leh*] move back
rédacteur *m.* [*reh-dahk-tuhr*] editor
redouter *v.* [*r(uh)-doo-teh*] fear
réduction *f.* [*reh-dük-syõ*] reduction
réduire *v. irreg.* [*reh-dweer*] reduce
réel, réelle [*reh-el*] real, actual
réellement [*reh-el-mã*] really, actually
référence *f.* [*reh-feh-rãs*] reference
réfléchir *v.* [*reh-fleh-sheer*] reflect
refléter *v.* [*r(uh)-fleh-teh*] reflect
réflexe *m.* [*reh-fleks*] reflex

réflexion *f.* [*reh-flek-syõ*] reflection
réforme *f.* [*reh-form*] reform
réformer *v.* [*reh-for-meh*] reform
réfrigérateur *m.* [*reh-free-zheh-rah-tuhr*] refrigerator
refroidir *v.* [*r(uh)-frwah-deer*] cool
refuge *m.* [*r(uh)-füzh*] refuge
réfugié, -ée [*reh-fü-zhyeh*] refugee
refus *m.* [*r(uh)-fü*] refusal
refuser (de) *v.* [*r(uh)-fü-zeh (duh)*] refuse, decline (to)
regagner *v.* [*r(uh)-gah-nyeh*] regain
regard *m.* [*r(uh)-gahr*] look
regarder *v.* [*r(uh)-gahr-deh*] look at, watch
régime *m.* [*reh-zheem*] diet
  suivre *v. irreg.* **un régime** [*sweev-rĕ reh-zheem*] be on a diet
régiment *m.* [*reh-zhee-mã*] regiment
région *f.* [*reh-zhyõ*] region, area, district
registre *m.* [*r(uh)-zheestr*] register
règle *f.* [*regl*] rule; ruler, measure
règlement *m.* [*re-gluh-mã*] regulation
régler *v.* [*reh-gleh*] regulate, settle, set
règles *f. pl.* [*regl*] menstrual period
règne *m.* [*reñ*] reign
régner *v.* [*reh-nyeh*] reign
regret *m.* [*r(uh)-gre*] regret
regretter *v.* [*r(uh)-greh-teh*] regret
régulier, -ière [*reh-gü-lyeh, reh-gü-lyer*] regular
rein *m.* [*rẽ*] kidney [anat.]
  reins *m. pl.* [*rẽ*] lower back
reine *f.* [*ren*] queen
rejeter *v.* [*ruhzh-teh*] reject
rejoindre *v. irreg.* [*r(uh)-zhwẽdr*] rejoin
relatif à [*r(uh)-lah-teef ah*] pertaining to
relation *f.* [*r(uh)-lah-syõ*] relation, connection
relativement [*r(uh)-lah-teev-mã*] relatively
relever *v.* [*ruhl-veh*] pick up; note
religieuse *f.* [*r(uh)-lee-zhyuhz*] nun, sister
religieux, -euse [*r(uh)-lee-zhyuh, r(uh)-lee-zhyuhz*] religious
religion *f.* [*r(uh)-lee-zhyõ*] religion

remarquable [*r(uh)-mahr-kahbl*] remarkable, outstanding

remarque *f.* [*r(uh)-mahrk*] remark

remarquer *v.* [*r(uh)-mahr-keh*] notice, remark

remboursement *m.* [*rã-boors-mã*] refund

rembourser *v.* [*rã-boor-seh*] repay

remède *m.* [*r(uh)-med*] remedy

remerciements *m. pl.* [*r(uh)-mer-see-mã*] thanks

remercier *v.* [*r(uh)-mer-syeh*] thank

remettre *v. irreg.* [*r(uh)-metr*] put on again; remit; postpone
  se remettre [*s(uh) r(uh)-metr*] recover

remise *f.* [*r(uh)-meez*] reduction, discount

remonter *v.* [*r(uh)-mõ-teh*] wind [a watch]; climb back up
  [a hill]

remords *m.* [*r(uh)-mor*] remorse

remorquer *v.* [*r(uh)-mor-keh*] tow

remorqueur *m.* [*r(uh)-mor-kuhr*] tugboat

remplacer *v.* [*rã-plah-seh*] replace

remplir *v.* [*rã-pleer*] fill

rencontre *f.* [*rã-kõtr*] encounter, meeting

rencontrer *v.* [*rã-kõ-treh*] meet, encounter

rendement *m.* [*rãd-mã*] yield

rendez-vous *m.* [*rã-deh-voo*] appointment, date

rendre *v.* [*rãdr*] return, give back
  rendre compte de [*rãdr kõt duh*] report
  se rendre [*s(uh) rãdr*] surrender
  se rendre compte (de) [*s(uh) rãdr kõt (duh)*] realize

renforcer *v.* [*rã-for-seh*] strengthen

renommée *f.* [*r(uh)-no-meh*] fame

renoncer (à) *v.* [*r(uh)-nõ-seh (ah)*] renounce

renouveler *v.* [*r(uh)-noo-vleh*] renew

renseignement *m.* [*rã-se-nyuh-mã*] piece of information

renseigner *v.* [*rã-se-nyeh*] inform

rentrée *f.* [*rã-treh*] reopening; first day of classes

rentrer *v.* [*rã-treh*] return

renverser *v.* [*rã-ver-seh*] spill; turn over

renvoyer *v. irreg.* [*rã-vwah-yeh*] send back; expel, dismiss
  renvoyer à plus tard [*rã-vwah-yeh ah plü tahr*] postpone

répandu [*reh-pã-dü*] widespread

réparation f. [*reh-pah-rah-syõ*] repair
réparer v. [*reh-pah-reh*] repair, fix
répartition f. [*reh-pahr-tee-syõ*] distribution
repas m. [*r(uh)-pah*] meal
repasser v. [*r(uh)-pah-seh*] iron
répéter v. [*reh-peh-teh*] repeat; rehearse
répétition f. [*reh-peh-tee-syõ*] repetition; rehearsal
  répétition générale [*reh-peh-tee-syõ zheh-neh-rahl*]
    dress rehearsal
répondre (à) v. [*reh-põdr (ah)*] reply, answer
réponse f. [*reh-põs*] answer, reply
reporter v. [*r(uh)-por-teh*] take back; carry forward
repos m. [*r(uh)-poh*] rest
se reposer v. [*s(uh) r(uh)-poh-zeh*] rest
reprendre v. irreg. [*r(uh)-prãdr*] resume, take back
représentant m. [*r(uh)-preh-zã-tã*] representative,
    congressman
  représentant de commerce [*r(uh)-preh-zã-tãd ko-mers*]
    traveling salesman
représentation f. [*r(uh)-preh-zã-tah-syõ*] performance
    [theatre]
représenter v. [*r(uh)-preh-zã-teh*] represent
repriser v. [*r(uh)-pree-zeh*] mend
reproche f. [*r(uh)-prosh*] reproach
reprocher v. [*r(uh)-pro-sheh*] reproach
reproduction f. [*r(uh)-pro-dük-syõ*] reproduction
reproduire v. irreg. [*r(uh)-pro-dweer*] reproduce; copy
république f. [*reh-püb-leek*] republic
réputation f. [*reh-pü-tah-syõ*] reputation
réseau, -eaux m. [*reh-zoh*] network
réserve f. [*reh-zerv*] reserve, restriction
réservoir m. **à essence** [*reh-zer-vwah-rah eh-sãs*] gas tank
résidence f. [*reh-zee-dãs*] residence
  résidence universitaire [*reh-zee-dã-sü-nee-ver-see-ter*]
    dormitory
résident, -te [*reh-zee-dã(t)*] resident
résister v. [*reh-zees-teh*] resist
résolution f. [*reh-zo-lü-syõ*] resolution

résoudre v. irreg. [reh-zoodr] solve
respect m. [res-pe] respect
respectable [res-pek-tahbl] respectable
respecter v. [res-pek-teh] respect
respirer v. [res-pee-reh] breathe
responsabilité f. [res-põ-sah-bee-lee-teh] responsibility, liability
responsable adj. [res-põ-sahbl] responsible
responsable m., f. [res-põ-sahbl] officer; person in charge
ressemblance f. [r(uh)-sã-blãs] resemblance
ressembler v. [r(uh)-sã-bleh] resemble
resserrer v. [r(uh)-seh-reh] tighten
ressort m. [r(uh)-sor] spring
ressource f. [r(uh)-soors] resource
restaurant m. [res-to-rã] restaurant
restaurer v. [res-to-reh] restore
reste m. [rest] remainder; leftover (food)
rester v. [res-teh] remain, stay
résultat m. [reh-zül-tah] result
résumé m. [reh-zü-meh] summary
résumer v. [reh-zü-meh] sum up
retard m. [r(uh)-tahr] delay
  en retard [ãr-tahr] late
retenir v. irreg. [r(uh)-t(uh)-neer] keep, detain; reserve
retirer v. [r(uh)-tee-reh] withdraw
  se retirer [sruh-tee-reh] retire, withdraw
retouche f. [r(uh)-toosh] alteration
retour m. [r(uh)-toor] return
retourner v. [r(uh)-toor-neh] return, go back, turn around, turn over
  se retourner [s(uh) r(uh)-toor-neh] turn around, over
retraite f. [r(uh)-tret] retreat; retirement
  prendre v. **sa retraite** [prãdr sahr-tret] retire
rétrécir v. [reh-treh-seer] shrink
retrouver v. [r(uh)-troo-veh] recover
réunion f. [reh-ü-nyõ] meeting
réunir v. [reh-ü-neer] bring together
réussir v. [reh-ü-seer] succeed

revanche *f.* [*r(uh)-vãsh*] revenge
rêve *m.* [*rev*] dream
réveil *m.* [*reh-vey*] awakening
réveil *m.* [*reh-vey*] alarm clock
réveiller *v.* [*reh-veh-yeh*] wake
  se réveiller [*sreh-veh-yeh*] wake up
révéler *v.* [*reh-veh-leh*] disclose, reveal
revendication *f.* [*r(uh)-vã-dee-kah-syõ*] claim, demand
revenir *v. irreg.* [*ruhv-neer*] come back, come again, return
revenu *m.* [*ruhv-nü*] income
rêver *v.* [*reh-veh*] dream
rêverie *f.* [*rev-ree*] daydream
réviser *v.* [*reh-vee-zeh*] revise
revoir *v. irreg.* [*r(uh)-vwahr*] see again
  au revoir [*ohr-vwahr*] good-bye
révolution *f* [*reh-vo-lü-syõ*] revolution
revolver *m.* [*reh-vol-ver*] revolver
revue *f.* [*r(uh)-vü*] magazine, review
rcz-de-chaussée *m.* [*rehd-shoh-seh*] ground floor
rhum *m.* [*rom*] rum
rhumatisme *m.* [*rii-mah-teesm*] rheumatism
rhume *m.* [*rüm*] cold
riche [*reesh*] rich
richesse *f.* [*ree-shes*] wealth
ride *f.* [*reed*] wrinkle
rideau, -eaux *m.* [*ree-doh*] curtain
ridicule [*ree-dee-kül*] ridiculous
ridiculiser *v.* [*ree-dee-kü-lee-zeh*] ridicule
rien [*ryẽ*] nothing, anything
  Ça ne fait rien [*sahn fe ryẽ*] Never mind
rime *f.* [*reem*] rhyme
rinçage *m.* [*rẽ-sahzh*] rinse
rincer *v.* [*rẽ-seh*] rinse
rire *m.* [*reer*] laugh, laughter
rire *v. irreg.* [*reer*] laugh
risque *m.* [*reesk*] risk
rite *m.* [*reet*] rite
rivage *m.* [*ree-vahzh*] shore

rive *f.* [*reev*] bank, shore
rivière *f.* [*ree-vyer*] river
riz *m.* [*ree*] rice
robe *f.* [*rob*] dress
   robe du soir [*rob dü swahr*] evening dress
robinet *m.* [*ro-bee-ne*] faucet
rocher *m.* [*ro-she*] rock
rognon *m.* [*ro-nyŏ*] kidney [food]
roi *m.* [*rwah*] king
rôle *m* [*rohl*] role
romain [*ro-mĕ, ro-men*] Roman
roman [*ro-mã, ro-mahn*] Romanesque
roman *m.* [*ro-mã*] novel
romancier, -ière [*ro-mã-syeh, ro-mã-syer*] novelist
romantique [*ro-mã-teek*] romantic
rompre *v. irreg.* [*rŏpr*] sever, break (off)
rond [*rŏ(d)*] round
ronfler *v.* [*rŏ-fleh*] snore
rose *adj.* [*rohz*] pink
rose *f.* [*rohz*] rose
rosée *f.* [*roh-zeh*] dew
rôti [*roh-tee*] roasted
rôti *m.* [*roh-tee*] roast
rôtir *v.* [*roh-teer*] roast
roue *f.* [*roo*] wheel
   roue de secours [*rood suh-koor*] spare tire
rouge [*roozh*] red
rouge *m.* [*roozh*] rouge
   rouge à levres [*roo-zhah levr*] lipstick
rougeole *f.* [*roo-zhol*] measles
rouille *f.* [*rooy*] rust
rouiller *v.* [*roo-yeh*] rust
rouleau, -eaux *m.* [*roo-loh*] roll, roller
rouler *v.* [*roo-leh*] roll
roulette *f.* [*rou-let*] little wheel, castor
roussir *v.* [*rou-seer*] scorch
route *f.* [*root*] road, highway
routine *f.* [*roo-teen*] routine

roux, rousse [*roo(s)*] red-headed
royal, -aux [*rwah-yahl, rwah-yoh*] royal
royaume *m.* [*rwah-yom*] kingdom
ruban *m.* [*rü-bã*] ribbon
rubéole *f.* [*rü-beh-ol*] rubella, German measles
rubis *m.* [*rü-bee*] ruby
rude [*rüd*] rough
rue *f.* [*rü*] street
ruée *f.* [*rweh*] rush
rugir *v.* [*rü-zheer*] roar
ruine *f.* [*rween*] ruin
ruisseau, -eaux *m.* [*rwee-soh*] stream; gutter
rumeur *f.* [*rü-muhr*] rumor
rural, -aux [*rü-rahl, rü-roh*] rural
russe [*rüs*] Russian
rythme *m.* [*reetm*] rhythm

S

s': **se, si** See SE, SI
sa [*sah*] his, her, its
sable *m.* [*sahbl*] sand
sablonneux, -euse [*sah-blo-nuh, sah-blo-nuhz*] sandy
sabot *m.* [*sah-boh*] wooden shoe
sac *m.* [*sahk*] bag, sack
   sac à main [*sah-kah mẽ*] purse, handbag
sacré [*sah-kreh*] sacred
sacrifice *m.* [*sah-kree-fees*] sacrifice
sage [*sahzh*] wise
sagesse *f.* [*sah-zhes*] wisdom
saignant [*se-nyã(t)*] bloody; rare [meat]
saigner *v.* [*se-nyeh*] bleed
sain [*sẽ, sen*] healthy
   sain et sauf [*sẽ eh sohf*] safe and sound
   sain d'esprit [*sẽ des-pree*] sane

saint [sẽ(t)] holy; Saint
saint, -te [sẽ(t)] saint
saisir v. [seh-zeer] seize
saison f. [se-zõ] season
salade f. [sah-lahd] salad
salaire m. [sah-ler] wages
salarié, -ée [sah-lahr-yeh] wage earner
sale [sahl] dirty
salé [sah-leh] salty
saleté f. [sahl-teh] dirt, dirtiness
sali [sah-lee] soiled
salière f. [sahl-yer] salt shaker
salle f. [sahl] room, hall
    salle d'attente [sahl dah-tãt] waiting room
    salle de bains [sahl duh bẽ] bathroom
    salle de classe [sahl duh klahs] classroom
    salle à manger [sahl ah mã-zheh] dining room
salon m. [sah-lõ] living room
    salon de coiffure [sah-lõd kwah-für] beauty parlor
saluer v. [sah-lweh] greet; bow
salut m. [sah-lü] safety; salute
salutations f. pl. [sah-lü-tah-syõ] greetings
samedi m. [sahm-dee] Saturday
sandale f. [sã-dahl] sandal
sandwich m. [sã-dweetsh] sandwich
sang m. [sã] blood
sang-froid m. [sã-frwah] composure
sanitaire [sah-nee-ter] sanitary
sans [sã] without
    sans que [sã k(uh)] without
    Il est parti sans que je le voie [ee-le pahr-tee sãk zhuhl
      vwah] He left without my seeing him
santé f. [sã-teh] health
    A votre santé! [ah votr sã-teh] Here's to you!, To your
      health!
sapin m. [sah-pẽ] fir tree, Christmas tree
sarcastique [sahr-kahs-teek] sarcastic
satin m. [sah-tẽ] satin

satire *f.* [*sah-teer*] satire
satirique [*sah-tee-reek*] satirical
satisfaction *f.* [*sah-tees-fahk-syõ*] satisfaction
satisfaire *v. irreg.* [*sah-tees-fer*] satisfy
satisfaisant [*sah-tees-fuh-zã(t)*] satisfactory
satisfait [*sah-tees-fe(t)*] satisfied
sauce *f.* [*sohs*] sauce, gravy
saucisse *f.* [*soh-sees*] sausage
sauf *prep.* [*sohf*] except
saumon *m.* [*soh-mõ*] salmon
saut *m.* [*soh*] jump
sauter *v.* [*soh-teh*] jump
sauvage [*soh-vahzh*] wild
sauver *v.* [*soh-veh*] save, rescue
sauvetage *m.* [*sohv-tahzh*] rescue
savant *m.* [*sah-vã*] scholar
saveur *f.* [*sah-vuhr*] flavor, taste
savoir *v. irreg.* [*sah-vwahr*] know [something], know of,
    know how to
  à savoir [*ah sah-vwahr*] namely
savon *m.* [*sah-võ*] soap
scandale *m.* [*skã-dahl*] scandal
scarlatine *f.* [*skahr-lah-teen*] scarlet fever
sceau *f.* [*soh*] seal
scène *f.* [*sen*] scene; stage
schéma *m.* [*sheh-mah*] diagram, outline
scie *f.* [*see*] saw
science *f.* [*syãs*] science
scientifique *adj.* [*syã-tee-feek*] scientific
scientiste *m., f.* [*syã-teest*] scientist
scier *v.* [*see-eh*] saw
scierie *f.* [*see-ree*] sawmill
scolaire [*sko-ler*] school
sculpture *f.* [*skül-tür*] sculpture
se *refl. pron.* [*suh*] him-, her-, itself; themselves, oneself
séance *f.* [*seh-ãs*] session
seau *m.* [*soh*] bucket, pail
sec, sèche [*sek, sesh*] dry

sécher v. [*seh-sheh*] dry
second adj. [*s(uh)-gõ(d)*] second
secondaire [*s(uh)-gõ-der*] secondary
seconde f. [*s(uh)-gõd*] second
secouer v. [*s(uh)-kweh*] shake
secours m. [*s(uh)-koor*] help
  Au secours! [*ohs-koor*] Help!
secret m. [*s(uh)-kre*] secret
secrétaire m., f. [*s(uh)-kreh-ter*] secretary
section f. [*sek-syõ*] section
sécurité f. [*seh-kü-ree-teh*] security
séduire v. irreg. [*seh-dweer*] seduce
seigle m. [*segl*] rye
seigneur m. [*se-nyuhr*] lord
sein m. [*sẽ*] breast
  au sein de [*oh sẽ duh*] in the bosom of, within
seize [*sez*] sixteen
séjour m. [*seh-zhoor*] stay
sel m. [*sel*] salt
selle f. [*sel*] saddle
selon [*s(uh)-lõ*] according to
semaine f. [*s(uh)-men*] week
  la semaine prochaine [*lahs-men pro-shen*] next week
  la semaine dernière [*lahs-men der-nyer*] last week
semblable [*sã-blahbl*] similar
sembler v. [*sã-bleh*] seem
  faire v. **semblant** [*fer sã-blã*] pretend
semelle f. [*s(uh)-mel*] sole [of shoe]
semer v. [*s(uh)-meh*] sow
sénat m. [*seh-nah*] senate
sénateur m. [*seh-nah-tuhr*] senator
sens m. [*sãs*] sense
  bon sens [*bõ sãs*] common sense
  sens unique [*sã-sü-neek*] one way
sensible [*sã-seebl*] sensitive
sentence f. [*sã-tãs*] sentence
sentier m. [*sã-tyeh*] path
sentiment m. [*sã-tee-mã*] feeling

sentimental, -aux [*sã-tee-mã-tahl, sã-tee-mã-toh*]
   sentimental
sentir *v. irreg.* [*sã-teer*] feel; smell
   se sentir [*suh sã-teer*] feel
séparation *f.* [*seh-pah-rah-syõ*] separation
séparé [*seh-pah-reh*] separate
séparément [*seh-pah-reh-mã*] separately
séparer *v.* [*seh-pah-reh*] separate
sept [*set*] seven
septembre *m.* [*sep-tãbr*] September
septième [*set-yem*] seventh
sergent *m.* [*ser-zhã*] sergeant
série *f.* [*seh-ree*] series
sérieusement [*sehr-yuhz-mã*] seriously
sérieux, -euse [*sehr-yuh, sehr-yuhz*] serious
serment *m.* [*ser-mã*] oath
   prêter *v.* **serment** [*pre-teh ser-mã*] take an oath
sermon *m.* [*ser-mõ*] sermon
serpent *m.* [*ser-pã*] snake
serpillière *f.* [*ser-pee-yer*] rag [to wash the floor]
serré [*seh-reh*] tight
serrer *v.* [*seh-reh*] tighten, squeeze
   serrer la main [*seh-reh lah mē*] shake hands
serrure *f.* [*seh-rür*] lock
serrurier *m.* [*seh-rür-yeh*] locksmith
serveuse *f.* [*ser-vuhz*] waitress
service *m.* [*ser-vees*] service
   de service [*duh ser-vees*] on duty
serviette *f.* [*ser-vyet*] napkin; towel; briefcase
   serviettes hygiéniques [*ser-vyet ee-zhyeh-neek*] sanitary
      napkins
servir *v. irreg.* [*ser-veer*] serve
   se servir de [*suh ser-veer duh*] use
ses [*seh*] his, her, its
seuil *m.* [*suhy*] threshold
seul [*suhl*] alone, only
   tout seul, toute seule [*too suhl, toot suhl*] all alone
seulement [*suhl-mã*] only

sévère [*seh-ver*] severe
sevrer *v.* [*suh-vreh*] wean
sexe *m.* [*seks*] sex
shampooing *m.* [*shã-pwē*] shampoo
short *m.* [*short*] shorts
si *conj.* [*see*] if, whether
  même si [*mem see*] even if
  si, oui ou non [*see wee oo nō*] whether or not
si *adv.* [*see*] so, such a, such
siècle *m.* [*syekl*] century
  au quinzième siècle [*oh kēz-yem syekl*] in the fifteenth
    century
siège *m.* [*syezh*] seat; headquarters
sien, sienne *poss. pron.* [*luh syē*] hers, his, its
sieste *f.* [*syest*] nap
siffler *v.* [*see-fleh*] whistle
sifflet *m.* [*see-fle*] whistle
signal, -aux *m.* [*see-nyahl, see-nyoh*] signal
signaler *v.* [*see-nyah-leh*] signal
signature *f.* [*see-nyah-tür*] signature
signe *m.* [*seeñ*] sign
  faire *v.* **signe** [*fer seeñ*] wave
signer *v.* [*see-nyeh*] sign
signifier *v.* [*see-nyee-fyeh*] mean
silence *m.* [*see-lãs*] silence
silencieusement [*see-lã-syuhz-mã*] silently
silencieux, -euse [*see-lã-syuh, see-lã-syuhz*] silent
simple [*sēpl*] simple, mere, casual
simplement [*sē-pluh-mã*] merely
sincère [*sē-ser*] sincere
sinon [*see-nō*] otherwise
situation *f.* [*see-twah-syō*] situation
situé [*see-tweh*] situated
six [*sees*] six
sixième [*see-zyem*] sixth
ski *m.* [*skee*] skiing
  faire *v.* **du ski** [*fer dü skee*] ski
slip *m.* [*sleep*] underpants

smoking *m.* [*smo-keeng*] tuxedo, dinner jacket
sobre [*sobr*] sober
S.N.C.F. *f.* [*es-en-seh-ef*] French National Railways
social, -aux [*so-syahl, so-syoh*] social
socialisme *m.* [*so-syah-leesm*] socialism
socialiste *m., f.* [*so-syah-leest*] socialist
société *f.* [*so-syeh-teh*] society
  société anonyme [*so-syeh-teh ah-no-neem*] corporation
soda *m.* [*so-dah*] soda water
soeur *f.* [*suhr*] sister
sofa *m.* [*so-fah*] sofa
soi [*swah*] oneself, himself, herself; it
  soi-même [*swah-mem*] oneself
  chez soi [*sheh swah*] at one's home, home
soie *f.* [*swah*] silk
soif *f.* [*swahf*] thirst
  avoir *v.* **soif** [*ah-vwahr swahf*] be thirsty
soigner *v.* [*swah-nyeh*] take care of, heal
soigneusement [*swah-nyuhz-mã*] carefully
soigneux, -euse [*swah-nyuh, swah-nyuhz*] careful
soin *m.* [*swē*] care
  premiers soins [*pruh-myeh swē*] first aid
soir *m.* [*swahr*] evening
  le soir [*luh swahr*] in the evening
  ce soir [*suh swahr*] tonight
soirée *f.* [*swah-reh*] evening, evening party
soit *3d pers. pres. subj. of* ÊTRE [*swah*] so be it
  soit . . . soit [*swah . . . swah*] either . . . or
soixante [*swah-sãt*] sixty
soixante-dix [*swah-sãt-dees*] seventy
sol *m.* [*sol*] ground
soldat *m.* [*sol-dah*] soldier
solde *m.* [*sold*] balance; clearance (sale)
sole *f.* [*sol*] sole [fish]
soleil *m.* [*so-ley*] sun
  coup *m.* **de soleil** [*kood so-ley*] sunburn
solide [*so-leed*] solid
solitaire [*so-lee-ter*] solitary

solitude *f.* [*so-lee-tüd*] solitude
solliciter *v.* [*so-lee-see-teh*] solicit, apply for
solution *f.* [*so-lü-syō*] solution
sombre [*sōbr*] dark, dismal
sombrer *v.* [*sō-breh*] sink
somme *f.* [*som*] sum
  en somme [*ã som*] all told
sommeil *m.* [*so-mey*] sleep
  avoir *v.* **sommeil** [*ah-vwahr so-mey*] be sleepy
sommet *m.* [*so-me*] summit, top
somnoler *v.* [*som-no-leh*] doze
son *poss. pron.* [*sō*] his, her, its
son *m.* [*sō*] sound
songer (à) *v.* [*sō-zheh (ah)*] think about
sonner *v.* [*so-neh*] ring, sound
sonnerie *f.* [*son-ree*] ringing
sont *3d pers. pl. pres. tense of* ÊTRE [*sō*] are
sorcière *f.* [*sor-syer*] witch
sort *m.* [*sor*] lot
sorte *f.* [*sort*] sort, kind
sortie *f.* [*sor-tee*] evening out; exit
sortir (de) *v. irreg.* [*sor-teer (duh)*] leave, go out (of); take out
souci *m.* [*soo-see*] worry, care
se soucier (de) *v.* [*suh soo-syeh (duh)*] care (for, about)
soucoupe *f.* [*soo-koop*] saucer
soudain [*soo-dē, soo-den*] sudden
souffle *m.* [*soofl*] breath, wind
souffler *v.* [*soo-fleh*] blow, blow out
souffrir *v. irreg.* [*soo-freer*] suffer
souhait *m.* [*swe*] wish
souhaiter *v.* [*swe-teh*] wish
soulagement *m.* [*soo-lahzh-mã*] relief
soulager *v.* [*soo-lah-zheh*] relieve
soulever *v.* [*sool-veh*] lift, raise
  se soulever [*suh sool-veh*] rise; revolt
soulier *m.* [*sool-yeh*] shoe
souligner *v.* [*soo-lee-nyeh*] underline; stress

soumettre *v. irreg.* [*soo-metr*] submit
soupape *f.* [*soo-pahp*] valve
soupçon *m.* [*soop-sõ*] suspicion
soupçonner *v.* [*soop-so-neh*] suspect
soupe *f.* [*soop*] soup
soupière *f.* [*soo-pyer*] soup tureen
soupir *m.* [*soo-peer*] sigh
souple [*soopl*] flexible
source *f.* [*soors*] source; spring, well
sourcil *m.* [*soor-see*] eyebrow
sourd [*soor(d)*] deaf
sourire *m.* [*soo-reer*] smile
sourire *v. irreg.* [*soo-reer*] smile
souris *f.* [*soo-ree*] mouse
sous [*soo*] under
sous-marin *m.* [*soo-mah-rẽ*] submarine
sous-sol *m.* [*soo-sol*] basement, cellar
soustraction *f.* [*soos-trahk-syõ*] subtraction
sous-vêtement *m.* [*soo-vet-mã*] underwear
soutenir *v. irreg.* [*soot-neer*] support
souterrain [*soo-te-rẽ, soo-te-ren*] underground
soutien *m.* [*soo-tyẽ*] support
soutien-gorge *m.* [*soo-tyẽ-gorzh*] brassiere
souvenir *m.* [*soov-neer*] memory, souvenir
se souvenir (de) *v.* [*suh soov-neer (duh)*] remember
souvent [*soo-vã*] frequently, often
spacieux, -euse [*spah-syuh, spah-syuhz*] spacious
sparadrap *m.* [*spah-rah-drah*] adhesive tape
speaker, speakerine [*spee-kuhr, speek-reen*] announcer
spécial, -aux [*speh-syahl, speh-syoh*] special
spécialement [*speh-syahl-mã*] especially
spécialité *f.* [*speh-syah-lee-teh*] specialty
spectacle *m.* [*spek-tahkl*] show, spectacle
spectateur, -trice [*spek-tah-tuhr, spek-tah-trees*] spectator, bystander
spirituel, -elle [*spee-ree-twel*] spiritual; witty
splendide [*splã-deed*] splendid
sport *m.* [*spor*] sport, athletics

sportif, -ive [*spor-teef, spor-teev*] athletic
squelette *m.* [*skuh-let*] skeleton
stade *m.* [*stahd*] stadium, athletic field; stage
stage *m.* [*stahzh*] training period
starter *m.* [*stahr-ter*] choke
station *f.* [*stah-syõ*] station
   station service [*stah-syõ ser-vees*] service station,
     gas station
stationnaire [*stah-syo-ner*] stationary
stationnement *m.* [*stah-syon-mã*] parking
   stationnement interdit [*stah-syon-mã ẽ-ter-dee*] no parking
statue *f.* [*stah-tü*] statue
sténo *m., f.* [*steh-noh*] stenographer
strict [*streekt*] strict
strictement [*streek-tuh-mã*] strictly
structure *f.* [*strük-tür*] structure
stupide [*stü-peed*] stupid
style *m.* [*steel*] style
stylo *m.* [*stee-loh*] pen
   stylo-bille [*stee-loh-beey*] ballpoint pen
substance *f.* [*süb-stãs*] substance
substituer *v.* [*süb-stee-tweh*] substitute
substitution *f.* [*süb-stee-tü-syõ*] substitution
subtil [*süb-teel*] subtle
subvention *f.* [*süb-vã-syõ*] subsidy
subventionner *v.* [*sub-vã-syo-neh*] subsidize
succès *m.* [*sük-se*] success
succession *f.* [*sük-seh-syõ*] succession; estate [of deceased]
succursale *f.* [*sü-kür-sahl*] branch
sucre *m.* [*sükr*] sugar
sucré [*sü-kreh*] sweet
sucrier *m.* [*sü-kree-yeh*] sugar bowl
sud *m.* [*süd*] south
Suède *f.* [*swed*] Sweden
suédois [*sweh-dwah*(z)] Swede, Swedish
suffire *v. irreg.* [*sü-feer*] suffice, be enough
   Ça suffit! [*sah sü-fee*] That's enough!
suffisant [*sü-fee-zã(t)*] sufficient

suggérer *v.* [*süg-zheh-reh*] suggest
suggestion *f.* [*süg-zhes-tyõ*] suggestion
suicide *m.* [*swee-seed*] suicide
se suicider *v.* [*suh swee-see-deh*] commit suicide
suis *1st pers. sing. pres. tense of* ÊTRE [*swee*] I am
Suisse *f.* [*swees*] Switzerland
suisse *n & adj.* [*swees*] Swiss
suite *f.* [*sweet*] succession, what follows
   de suite [*duh sweet*] in succession, without stopping
   tout de suite [*tood sweet*] at once
   par la suite [*pahr lah sweet*] later on
   à la suite de [*ah lah sweet duh*] following, as a result of
suivant [*swee-vã(t)*] following, next
suivre *v. irreg.* [*sweevr*] follow
   suivre un cours [*swee-vrẽ koor*] take a course
sujet *m.* [*sü-zhe*] subject
   au sujet de [*oh sü-zhe d(uh)*] about, concerning
superbe [*sü-perb*] superb
superficiel, -elle [*sü-per-fee-syel*] superficial
supérieur [*sü-pehr-yuhr*] superior
superstitieux, -euse [*sü-per-stee-syuh, sü-per-stee-syuhz*] superstitious
supplément *m.* [*sü-pleh-mã*] supplement; extra serving; additional charge
supplémentaire [*sü-pleh-mã-ter*] additional, extra
supplier *v.* [*sü-plee-yeh*] implore
supporter *v.* [*sü-por-teh*] endure, bear
supposer *v.* [*sü-po-zeh*] suppose, assume
supposition *f.* [*sü-po-zee-syõ*] assumption
supprimer *v.* [*sü-pree-meh*] suppress, destroy
sur *prep.* [*sür*] on, over, upon
sûr [*sür*] sure, safe
sûrement [*sür-mã*] surely
sûreté *f.* [*sür-teh*] safety
surface *f.* [*sür-fahs*] surface
surmonter *v.* [*sür-mõ-teh*] overcome
surnom *m.* [*sür-nõ*] nickname
surprenant [*sür-pruh-nã(t)*] surprising

surprendre *v. irreg.* [*sür-prãdr*] surprise
  surprendre . . . à faire . . . [*sür-prãdr . . . ah fer . . .*]
    catch [someone] doing [something]
surprise *f.* [*sür-preez*] surprise
surtout [*sür-too*] mainly, especially
surveiller *v.* [*sür-ve-yeh*] supervise, watch
survie *f.* [*sür-vee*] survival
survivant, -te *n. & adj.* [*sür-vee-vã(t)*] survivor, surviving
survivre *v. irreg.* [*sür-veevr*] survive
susceptible [*sü-sep-teebl*] touchy
suspect *adj.* [*süs-pe(kt)*] suspicious
suspendre *v.* [*süs-pãdr*] suspend, hang up
syllabe *f.* [*see-lahb*] syllable
sympathique [*sē-pah-teek*] likeable
symphonie *f.* [*sē-fo-nee*] symphony
symptôme *m.* [*sēp-tohm*] symptom
syndical, -aux [*sē-dee-kahl, sē-dee-koh*] labor
syndicat *m.* [*sē-dee-kah*] labor union
synthétique [*sē-teh-teek*] synthetic
systématique [*sees-teh-mah-teek*] systematic
système *m.* [*sees-tem*] system
  système métrique [*sees-tem meh-treek*] metric system

T

t': te [*tuh*] to you, yourself
ta [*tah*] your
tabac *m.* [*tah-bah*] tobacco
table *f.* [*tahbl*] table
tableau, -eaux *m.* [*tah-bloh*] picture
  tableau d'affichage [*tah-bloh dah-fee-shahzh*] bulletin board
  tableau noir [*tah-bloh nwahr*] blackboard
tablier *m.* [*tah-blee-yeh*] apron
tache *f.* [*tahsh*] spot, stain
tâche *f.* [*tahsh*] task

tacher *v.* [*tah-sheh*] stain
tâcher *v.* [*tah-sheh*] try
tact *m.* [*tahkt*] tact
taille *f.* [*tahy*] height; waist; size [of clothing]
tailleur *m.* [*tah-yuhr*] suit; tailor
se taire *v. irreg.* [*suh ter*] keep silent
   Taisez-vous! [*te-zeh-voo*] Be quiet!
talent *m.* [*tah-lã*] talent
talon *m.* [*tah-lõ*] heel
tambour *m.* [*tã-boor*] drum
tandis que [*tã-dee k(uh)*] while, whereas
tant de [*tã duh*] so much, so many
   tant que [*tã kuh*] as long as
tante *f.* [*tãt*] aunt
tantôt [*tã-toh*] soon
taper *v.* [*tah-peh*] strike, knock; type [write]
tapis *m.* [*tah-pee*] carpet, rug
tapisserie *f.* [*tah-pees-ree*] tapestry
tard *adv.* [*tahr*] late
   Il est tard [*ee-le-tahr*] It's late
tarder à *v.* [*tahr-deh ah*] be slow to
   tarder de [*tahr-deh duh*] long to
tarif *m.* [*tah-reef*] price, price list
tarte *f.* [*tahrt*] pie
tas *m.* [*tah*] pile
tasse *f.* [*tahs*] cup
tâter *v.* [*tah-teh*] feel
taureau, -eaux *m.* [*toh-roh*] bull
taux *m.* [*toh*] rate
taxi *m.* [*tahk-see*] taxi, cab
te [*tuh*] you
technique [*tek-neek*] technical
teindre *v. irreg.* [*tẽdr*] dye
teinture *f.* [*tẽ-tür*] dye
teinturerie *f.* [*tẽ-tur-ree*] cleaner's shop
tel, telle [*tel*] such
   tel que, telle que [*tel kuh*] such as
télégramme *m.* [*teh-leh-grahm*] telegram

télégramme international [*teh-leh-gram ē-ter-nah-syo-nahl*] cable
téléphone *m.* [*teh-leh-fon*] telephone
  coup *m.* **de téléphone** [*kood teh-leh-fon*] telephone call
téléphoner *v.* [*teh-leh-fo-neh*] telephone
téléphoniste *m., f.* [*teh-leh-fo-neest*] telephone operator
télévision *f.* [*teh-leh-vee-zyō*] television
  poste *m.* **de télévision** [*post duh teh-leh-vee-zyō*]
    television set
téméraire [*teh-meh-rer*] daring, rash
témoignage *m.* [*teh-mwah-nyahzh*] testimony
témoigner *v.* [*teh-mwah-nyeh*] testify
témoin *m.* [*teh-mwē*] witness
  être *v.* **témoin** [*e-truh teh-mwē*] witness
température *f.* [*tā-peh-rah-tür*] temperature
tempête *f.* [*tā-pet*] storm
temple *m.* [*tāpl*] temple, church [of Protestants]
temporaire [*tā-po-rer*] temporary
temps *m.* [*tā*] time, weather
  de temps en temps [*duh tā-zā tā*] from time to time
  en même temps [*ā mem tā*] at the same time
  passer *v.* **du temps** [*pah-seh dü tā*] spend time
  Quel temps fait-il? [*kel tā fe-teel*] What's the weather like?
  Combien de temps faut-il pour . . . ? [*kō-byēd tā foh-teel*
    poor] How long does it take to . . . ?
tendance *f.* [*tā-dās*] tendency, inclination
tendre [*tādr*] tender
tendre *v.* [*tādr*] tend
tendresse *f.* [*tā-dres*] affection
tenir *v. irreg.* [*t(uh)-neer*] hold
  se tenir [*stuh-neer*] stand, behave
  tenir compte de [*t(uh)-neer kōt duh*] take into account
  tenir à [*t(uh)-neer ah*] insist on
  Tiens! [*tyē*] Well!
tension *f.* [*tā-syō*] strain, tension
tentation *f.* [*tā-tah-syō*] temptation
tente *f.* [*tāt*] tent
tenter *v.* [*tā-teh*] try

terme *m.* [*term*] term

terminus *m.* [*ter-mee-nüs*] terminus

terrain *m.* [*te-rĕ*] land, lot
  terrain de jeu [*te-rĕd zhuh*] playground

terrasse *f.* [*te-rahs*] terrace
  terrasse du café [*te-rahs dü kah-feh*] sidewalk café

terre *f.* [*ter*] earth, land, ground
  par terre [*pahr ter*] on the ground, on the floor
  à terre [*ah ter*] ashore

terreur *f.* [*te-ruhr*] terror

terrible [*te-reebl*] terrible, awful

territoire *m.* [*te-ree-twahr*] territory

tes [*teh*] your

testament *m.* [*tes-tah-mã*] will

tête *f.* [*tet*] head
  mal *m.* **à la tete** [*mahl ah lah tet*] headache

tétine *f.* [*teh-teen*] nipple

têtu [*teh-tü*] stubborn

texte *m.* [*tekst*] text

thé *m.* [*teh*] tea

théâtre *m.* [*teh-ahtr*] theatre

théière *f.* [*teh-yer*] teapot

théorie *f.* [*teh-o-ree*] theory

thermomètre *m.* [*ter-mo-metr*] thermometer

ticket *m.* [*tee-ke*] ticket

tiède [*tyed*] lukewarm

le tien, la tienne [*luh tyĕ, lah tyen*] yours

tiers *m.* [*tyer*] third

tige *f.* [*teezh*] stem

timbre(-poste) *m.* [*tĕbr (post)*] postage stamp

timide [*tee-meed*] shy, timid

tirer *v.* [*tee-reh*] draw (out), pull; shoot, fire
  tirer la chasse [*tee-reh lah shahs*] flush the toilet

tiroir *m.* [*teer-wahr*] drawer

tissage *m.* [*tee-sahzh*] weaving

tisser *v.* [*tee-seh*] weave

tissu *m.* [*tee-sü*] cloth

titre [*teetr*] title; diploma

toi [*twah*] you
toi-même [*twah-mem*] yourself
toile *f.* [*twahl*] cloth; painting
   toile cirée [*twahl see-reh*] oilcloth
   toile d'araignée [*twahl dah-reh-nyeh*] spiderweb
toilette *f.* [*twah-let*] toilet, grooming
   faire *v.* **sa toilette** [*fer sah twah-let*] get dressed
toit *m.* [*twah*] roof
tomate *f.* [*to-maht*] tomato
tombe *f.* [*tōb*] tomb
tomber *v.* [*tō-beh*] fall
   laisser *v.* **tomber** [*leh-seh tō-beh*] drop
ton [*tō*] your
ton *m.* [*tō*] tone
tonne *f.* [*ton*] ton
tonneau, -eaux *m.* [*to-noh*] barrel
tonnerre *m.* [*to-ner*] thunder
torchon *m.* [*tor-shō*] dishtowel
tordre *v.* [*tordr*] twist
tordu [*tor-dü*] crooked, twisted
tornade *f.* [*tor-nahd*] tornado
torrent *m.* [*to-rā*] mountain stream
tort *m.* [*tor*] wrong
   avoir *v.* **tort** [*ah-vwahr tor*] be wrong
   faire *v.* **tort à** [*fer tor ah*] wrong
   à tort [*ah tor*] wrongly
   à tort et à travers [*ah tor eh ah trah-ver*] in a haphazard
     way
torture *f.* [*tor-tür*] torture
torturer *v.* [*tor-tü-reh*] torture
tôt [*toh*] early
   plus tôt [*plü toh*] sooner
tôt ou tard [*toh oo tahr*] sooner or later
total, -aux [*to-tahl, to-toh*] total
touchant [*too-shā(t)*] touching
toucher *v.* [*too-sheh*] touch; cash [a check]
toujours [*too-zhoor*] always, forever
tour *f.* [*toor*] tower

tour *m.* [*toor*] turn, tour, trick
  chacun à son tour [*shah-kē ah sõ toor*] each one in turn
  À qui le tour? [*ah keel toor*] Whose turn is it?
  jouer *v.* **un tour à** [*zhweh ē toor ah*] play a trick on
    [someone]
touriste *m., f.* [*too-reest*] tourist
tourne-disques *m.* [*toor-nuh-deesk*] phonograph, record-
  player
tourner *v.* [*toor-neh*] turn, revolve; stir [cooking]
tournevis *m.* [*toor-nuh-vees*] screwdriver
tousser *v.* [*too-seh*] cough
tout, toute [*too(t)*] the whole, all
  tout le monde [*tool mõd*] everybody
tout *pron.* [*too*] everything
  C'est tout! [*se too*] That's all!
tout *adv.* [*too*] altogether, quite
  tout en faisant . . . [*too-tã fuh-zã*] while doing . . .
  tout à coup [*too-tah koo*] suddenly
  Pas du tout [*pah dü too*] Not at all
  tout à fait [*too-tah fe*] altogether, quite
  tout à l'heure [*too-tah luhr*] a while ago; in a little while
  tout de même [*toot mem*] all the same
  tout de suite [*toot sweet*] at once
toutefois [*toot-fwah*] however
toux *f.* [*too*] cough
trac *m.* [*trahk*] stage-fright
trace *f.* [*trahs*] trace
tracteur *m.* [*trahk-tuhr*] tractor
tradition *f.* [*trah-dee-syõ*] tradition
traditionnel, -elle [*trah-dee-syo-nel*] traditional
traducteur, -trice [*trah-dük-tuhr, trah-dük-trees*] translator
traduction *f.* [*trah-dük-syõ*] translation
traduire *v. irreg.* [*trah-dweer*] translate
tragédie *f.* [*trah-zheh-dee*] tragedy
tragique [*trah-zheek*] tragic
trahir *v.* [*trah-eer*] betray
trahison *f.* [*trah-ee-zõ*] treason
train *m.* [*trẽ*] train

train transatlantique [*trē trã-zaht-lã-teek*] boat train
en train de [*ã trē d(uh)*] in the act of
  Il est en train de s'habiller [*ee-le-tã trēd sah-bee-yeh*]
    He is getting dressed
traîner *v.* [*treh-neh*] drag, drag out
trait *m.* [*tre*] characteristic; facial feature
traite *f.* [*tret*] bank draft; milking [of a cow]
traité *m.* [*treh-teh*] treaty
traitement *m.* [*tret-mã*] treatment; salary
traiter *v.* [*treh-teh*] treat, deal with
traître *m.* [*tretr*] traitor
tramway *m.* [*trahm-we*] streetcar
tranche *f.* [*trãsh*] slice
tranquille [*trã-keel*] quiet, calm
  Laissez-moi tranquille [*leh-seh-mwah trã-keel*] Don't
    bother me
transat *m.* [*trã-zaht*] deck chair, lawn chair
transformer *v.* [*trãs-for-meh*] transform
transmettre *v. irreg.* [*trãs-metr*] transmit
transmission *f.* [*trãs-mee-syõ*] transmission
transpiration *f.* [*trãs-pee-rah-syõ*] perspiration
transpirer *v.* [*trãs-pee-reh*] perspire
transport *m.* [*trãs-por*] transportation
transporter *v.* [*trãs-por-teh*] transport, carry
travail, -aux *m.* [*trah-vahy, trah-voh*] work, job, labor
travailler *v.* [*trah-vah-yeh*] work
travailleur *m.* [*trah-vah-yuhr*] worker, laborer
travers *m.* [*trah-ver*] defect
  à travers [*ah trah-ver*] across, through
  de travers [*duh trah-ver*] crooked
traversée *f.* [*trah-ver-seh*] crossing
traverser *v.* [*trah-ver-seh*] cross
trébucher *v.* [*treh-bü-sheh*] stumble
treize [*trez*] thirteen
tremblement de terre *m.* [*trã-bluh-mãd ter*] earthquake
trembler *v.* [*trã-bleh*] tremble
  trembler de froid [*trã-blehd frwah*] shiver
trempé [*trã-peh*] soaking wet

tremper *v.* [*trã-peh*] soak

trente [*trãt*] thirty

très [*tre*] very

  très bien [*tre byē*] very well

trésor *m.* [*treh-zor*] treasure

  trésor public [*treh-zor püb-leek*] treasury

trésorerie *f.* [*treh-zor-ree*] treasury

trésorier, -ière [*treh-zor-yeh, treh-zor-yer*] treasurer

triangle *m.* [*tree-yãgl*] triangle

tribord *m.* [*tree-bor*] starboard

tribunal, -aux *m.* [*tree-bü-nal, tree-bü-noh*] court

tricher *v.* [*tree-sheh*] cheat

tricostéril *m.* [*tree-ko-steh-reel*] bandaid

tricot *m.* [*tree-koh*] knitting; knitted garment

tricoter *v.* [*tree-ko-teh*] knit

trier *v.* [*tree-yeh*] sort

trompette *f.* [*trõ-pet*] trumpet

triomphant [*tree-õ-fã(t)*] triumphant

troubler *v.* [*troo-bleh*] disturb

troupeau, -eaux *m.* [*troo-poh*] flock

triste [*treest*] sad, dismal

tristesse *f.* [*trees-tes*] sadness

trois [*trwah*] three

troisième [*trwah-zyem*] third

trolley *m.* [*tro-le*] trolley (car)

tromper *v.* [*trõ-peh*] deceive, mislead

  se tromper [*strõ-peh*] make a mistake

tromperie *f.* [*trõp-ree*] deceit, cheating

tronc *m.* [*trõ*] trunk

trône *m.* [*trohn*] throne

trop [*troh*] too

  trop de [*troh d(uh)*] too much, too many

trottoir *m.* [*tro-twahr*] sidewalk

trou *m.* [*troo*] hole

trouble *m.* [*troobl*] disturbance

troupe *f.* [*troop*] troop

trouver *v.* [*troo-veh*] find

  se trouver [*stroo-veh*] be, happen; be located

bureau *m.* **des objets trouvés** [*bü-roh deh-zob-zhe troo-veh*] lost and found

truc *m.* [*trük*] device, gadget

truite *f.* [*trweet*] trout

T.S.F. *f.* [*teh-es-ef*] radio

tu [*tü*] you

tube *m.* [*tüb*] tube

tuberculose *f.* [*tü-ber-kü-lohz*] tuberculosis

tuer *v.* [*tü-eh*] kill

tuile *f.* [*tweel*] tile; bad break

tunnel *m.* [*tü-nel*] tunnel

turc, turque *n. & adj.* [*türk*] Turk, Turkish

Turquie *f.* [*tür-kee*] Turkey

tuyau, -aux *m.* [*twee-yoh*] pipe

    tuyau de vidange [*twee-yohd vee-dãzh*] drain

type *m.* [*teep*] type

typique [*tee-peek*] typical

tyran *m.* [*tee-rã*] tyrant

tyrannie *f.* [*tee-rah-nee*] tyranny

U

ultérieur [*ül-tehr-yuhr*] further

un, une [*ẽ, ün*] a, an; one

unanime [*ü-nah-neem*] unanimous

uniforme *adj. & n.* [*ü-nee-form*] uniform

union *f.* [*ü-nyõ*] union

unique [*ü-neek*] sole

uniquement [*ü-neek-mã*] only

unir, s'unir *v.* [*ü-neer, sü-neer*] unite

uni [*ü-nee*] united

unité *f.* [*ü-nee-teh*] unity, unit

univers *m.* [*ü-nee-ver*] universe

universel, -elle [*ü-nee-ver-sel*] universal

université *f.* [*ü-nee-ver-see-teh*] university, college

urbain [*ür-bē, ür-ben*] urban
urgent [*ür-zhã(t)*] urgent
  cas *m.* **urgent** [*kah ür-zhã*] emergency
usage *m.* [*ü-zahzh*] use, custom
  usage personnel [*ü-zahzh per-so-nel*] personal use
usé [*ü-zeh*] worn, worn out
user *v.* [*ü-zeh*] wear out
usine *f.* [*ü-zeen*] factory
ustensile *m.* [*üs-tã-seel*] utensil
utile [*ü-teel*] helpful, useful
utilisé [*ü-tee-lee-zeh*] used
utilité *f.* [*ü-tee-lee-teh*] utility

V

va *3d pers. sing. pres. tense of* ALLER [*vah*] goes
vacances *f. pl.* [*vah-kãs*] vacation
vacarme *m.* [*vah-kahrm*] uproar
vaccination *f.* [*vahk-see-nah-syõ*] vaccination
vache *f.* [*vahsh*] cow
vague [*vahg*] vague
vague *f.* [*vahg*] wave
vain [*vē, ven*] vain
vaincre *v. irreg.* [*vēkr*] conquer
vaisselle *f.* [*ve-sel*] dishes
valable [*vah-lahbl*] valid
valeur *f.* [*vah-luhr*] value
valise *f.* [*vah-leez*] suitcase
vallée *f.* [*vah-leh*] valley
valoir *v. irreg.* [*vahl-wahr*] be worth
  Cela vaut dix dollars [*slah voh dee do-lahr*] It's worth
    ten dollars
  valoir la peine [*vahl-wahr lah pen*] be worthwhile
  valoir mieux [*vahl-wahr myuh*] be better
vanille *f.* [*vah-neey*] vanilla

vanité *f.* [*vah-nee-teh*] vanity
vaniteux, -euse [*vah-nee-tuh, vah-nee-tuhz*] vain
se vanter *v.* [*suh vã-teh*] brag
vapeur *f.* [*vah-puhr*] steam
varicelle *f.* [*vah-ree-sel*] chicken pox
varier *v.* [*vahr-yeh*] vary
variété *f.* [*vahr-yeh-teh*] variety
variole *f.* [*vahr-yol*] smallpox
vase *m.* [*vahz*] vase
vaste [*vahst*] vast
Vatican *m.* [*vah-tee-kã*] Vatican
veau, -eaux *m.* [*voh*] calf; veal
véhicule *m.* [*veh-ee-kül*] vehicle
veille *f.* [*vey*] eve
veiller *v.* [*ve-yeh*] stay wake, watch over
veilleur (de nuit) *m.* [*ve-yuhr (duh nwee)*] (night) watchman
veine *f.* [*ven*] vein; luck (*fam.*)
velours *m.* [*v(uh)-loor*] velvet
vendanges *f. pl.* [*vã-dãzh*] grape harvest
vendeur, -euse [*vã-duhr, vã-duhz*] sales clerk, seller
vendre *v.* [*vãdr*] sell
  à vendre [*ah vãdr*] for sale
vendredi *m.* [*vã-druh-dee*] Friday
venez *2d pers. pl. pres. tense of* VENIR [*v(uh)-neh*] come
vengeance *f.* [*vã-zhãs*] vengeance
venir *v. irreg.* [*v(uh)-neer*] come
  venir de faire [*v(uh)-neer duh fer*] have just done
  faire *v.* **venir** [*fer vuh-neer*] send for
vent *m.* [*vã*] wind
vente *f.* [*vãt*] sale
  vente aux enchères [*vã-toh-zã-sher*] auction
ventilateur *m.* [*vã-tee-lah-tuhr*] fan
ventre *m.* [*vãtr*] stomach
ver *m.* [*ver*] worm
verbe *m.* [*verb*] verb
verdict *m.* [*ver-deekt*] verdict
verger *m.* [*ver-zheh*] orchard
vérifier *v.* [*veh-ree-fyeh*] verify

véritable [*veh-ree-tahbl*] genuine
vérité *f.* [*veh-ree-teh*] truth
verre *m.* [*ver*] glass
verrou, -ous *m.* [*ve-roo*] lock, bolt
vers [*ver*] toward
vers *m.* [*ver*] verse
verser *v.* [*ver-seh*] pour
vert [*ver(t)*] green
vertical, -aux [*ver-tee-kahl, ver-tee-koh*] vertical
vertige *m.* [*ver-teezh*] dizziness
  avoir *v.* **le vertige** [*ah-vwahr luh ver-teezh*] feel dizzy
vertu *f.* [*ver-tü*] virtue
vertueux, -euse [*ver-twuh, ver-ıwuhz*] virtuous
veste *f.* [*vest*] jacket, suit-coat
vestiaire *m.* [*ves-tyer*] cloak-room
veston *m.* [*ves-tõ*] coat, sport jacket
vêtement *m.* [*vet-mã*] garment, clothes
vétérinaire *m.* [*veh-teh-ree-ner*] veterinarian
veuf *m.* [*vuhf*] widower
veuillez *impers. form of* VOULOIR [*vuh-yeh*] please
  Veuillez agréer, etc. [*vuh-yeh-zah-greh-eh . . .*] Sincerely
    yours, Yours truly
veuve *f.* [*vuhv*] widow
vexer *v.* [*vek-seh*] vex
viande *f.* [*vyãd*] meat
vice *m.* [*vees*] vice
victime *f.* [*veek-teem*] victim
victoire *f.* [*veek-twahr*] victory
vidange *m.* [*vee-dãzh*] oil change
vide [*veed*] empty
vider *v.* [*vee-deh*] empty
vie *f.* [*vee*] life
vieil *m.* **vieille** *f.* [*vyey*] old
vieillard *m.* [*vye-yahr*] old man
vieillesse *f.* [*vye-yes*] old age
viens *2d pers. sing. pres. tense of* VENIR [*vyẽ*] come
vierge *f.* [*vyerzh*] virgin
vieux, vieil *m.,* **vieille** *f.* [*vyuh, vyey*] old

vif, vive [*veef, veev*] lively
vigilant [*vee-zhee-lã(t)*] watchful
vigne *f.* [*veeñ*] grapevine
vignoble *m.* [*vee-nyobl*] vineyard
vigoureux, -euse [*vee-goo-ruh, vee-goo-ruhz*] vigorous
vilain [*vee-lẽ, vee-len*] nasty, naughty
village *m.* [*vee-lahzh*] village
ville *f.* [*veel*] city, town
vin *m.* [*vẽ*] wine
vinaigre *m.* [*vee-negr*] vinegar
vingt [*vẽ*] twenty
violence *f.* [*vyo-lãs*] violence
violent [*vyo-lã(t)*] violent
violer *v.* [*vyo-leh*] violate; rape
violet, -ette [*vyo-le(t)*] purple
violette *f.* [*vyo-let*] violet [flower]
violon *m.* [*vyo-lõ*] violin
virage *m.* [*vee-rahzh*] curve, turn
virgule *f.* [*veer-gül*] comma
vis *f.* [*vees*] screw
visa *m.* [*vee-zah*] visa
visage *m.* [*vee-zahzh*] face
viser *v.* [*vee-zeh*] aim at
visible [*vee-zeebl*] visible
vision *f.* [*vee-zyõ*] vision
visite *f.* [*vee-zeet*] visit
   rendre *v.* **visite à** [*rãdr vee-zeet ah*] visit, call on
visiter *v.* [*vee-zee-teh*] visit
visiteur, -euse [*vee-zee-tuhr, vee-zee-tuhz*] visitor
vital, -aux [*vee-tahl, vee-toh*] vital
vitamine *f.* [*vee-tah-meen*] vitamin
vite [*veet*] fast, quickly
vitesse *f.* [*vee-tes*] speed; gear [of auto]
   changer *v.* **de vitesse** [*shã-zhehd vee-tes*] change gear
   à toute vitesse [*ah toot vee-tes*] at full speed
   en seconde (vitesse) [*ã suh-gõd (vee-tes)*] in second gear
vitrail, -aux *m.* [*vee-trahy, vee-troh*] stained glass window
vitre *f.* [*veetr*] window pane

vitrine *f.* [*vee-treen*] shop windowpane
vivant [*vee-vã(t)*] alive, lively
vivre *v. irreg.* [*veevr*] live
vocabulaire *m.* [*vo-kah-bü-ler*] vocabulary
vocation *f.* [*vo-kah-syõ*] vocation
voeu, -eux *m.* [*vuh*] vow
voici [*vwah-see*] here is, here are
voilà [*vwah-lah*] there is, there are
  Le voilà, Les voilà [*luh vwah-lah, leh vwah-lah*] There it is,
    There they are
voile *m.* [*vwahl*] veil
voile *f.* [*vwahl*] sail
voir *v. irreg.* [*vwahr*] see
voisin, -ine [*vwah-zẽ, vwah-zeen*] neighbor
voiture *f.* [*vwah-tür*] car
  En voiture [*ã vwah-tür*] All aboard
voix *f.* [*vwah*] voice
  à haute voix [*ah oht vwah*] aloud
vol *m.* [*vol*] flight; theft
volant *m.* [*vo-lã*] steering wheel
volcan *m.* [*vol-kã*] volcano
voler *v.* [*vo-leh*] fly; steal, rob
volet *m.* [*vo-le*] shutter
voleur, -euse [*vo-luhr, vo-luhz*] robber, thief
volontaire *n. & adj.* [*vo-lõ-ter*] volunteer, voluntary
volonté *f.* [*vo-lõ-teh*] will (power)
volontiers [*vo-lõ-tyeh*] willingly
volume *m.* [*vo-lüm*] volume
volumineux, -euse [*vo-lü-mee-nuh, vo-lü-mee-nuhz*] bulky
vomir *v.* [*vo-meer*] vomit
vont *3d pers. pl. pres. tense of* ALLER [*võ*] go
vos [*voh*] your
vote *m.* [*vot*] vote
voter *v.* [*vo-teh*] vote
votre [*votr*] your
le vôtre, la vôtre [*luh vohtr, lah vohtr*] yours
vouloir *v. irreg.* [*vool-wahr*] want
  Voudriez-vous . . . ? [*voo-dree-yeh voo*] Would you like . . . ?

Je voudrais bien [*zhvoo-dre byĕ*] I'd like (to)
en vouloir à [*ã vool-wahr ah*] have a grudge against
vouloir dire [*vool-wahr deer*] mean
Veuillez agréer, etc. [*vuh-yeh-zah-greh-eh . . .*] Sincerely
   yours, Yours truly
vous [*voo*] you
vous même, vous-mêmes [*voo-mem*] yourself, yourselves
voûte *f.* [*voot*] arch
voyage *m.* [*vwah-yahzh*] journey, trip
voyage d'agrément [*vwah-yahzh dah-greh-mã*] pleasure trip
   Bon voyage? [*bõ vwah-yahzh*] Have a good trip!
   agence *f.* **de voyages** [*ah-zhãs duh vwah-yahzh*] travel
      agency
   chèque *m.* **de voyage** [*shek duh vwah-yahzh*] traveler's
      check
voyager *v.* [*vwah-yah-zheh*] travel
voyageur, -euse [*vwah-yah-zhuhr, vwah-yah-zhuhz*] traveler
voyelle *f.* [*vwah-yel*] vowel
voyons *1st pers. pl. pres. tense of* VOIR [*vwah-yõ*] let's see
vrai [*vre*] true
vraiment [*vre-mã*] really
vraisemblable [*vre-sã-blahbl*] likely
vue *f.* [*vü*] sight, view
vulgaire [*vül-gher*] vulgar
vulnerable [*vül-neh-rahbl*] vulnerable

W — Z

wagon *m.* [*vah-gõ*] railroad car
   wagon-lit *m.* [*vah-gõ-lee*] sleeping car
   wagon-restaurant *m.* [*vah-gõ-res-to-rã*] dining car
W.C. *m. pl.* [*veh-seh*] toilets
y *adv. & pron.* [*ee*] there; to it, at it
   il y a [*eel yah*] there is, there are
   y a-t-il . . . ? [*yah-teel*] is there . . . ?, are there . . . ?

J'y suis! [*zhee swee*] I've got it!

Ca y est [*sah ye*] That's it

Je n'y suis pour rien [*zhnee swee poor ryē*] I had nothing to do with it

tout y est [*too-tee e*] it's all there

zéro *m.* [*zeh-roh*] zero

zone *f.* [*zohn*] zone

zoo *m.* [*zoh-oh*] zoo

Phrases for Use Abroad

Helpful Expressions

Good morning/afternoon/evening.
Bonjour/Bonjour/Bonsoir.
Bõ-zhoor/Bõ-swahr.

Hello. How do you do?
Bonjour. Comment allez-vous?
Bõ-zhoor. ko-mã-tah-leh voo?

Goodbye. See you later.
Au revoir. A tout à l'heure.
Ohr-vwahr. Ah too-tah luhr.

Please.	**Excuse me.**
S'il vous plaît.	Pardon.
Seel voo ple.	*Pahr-dõ.*
Thank you.	**You're welcome.**
Merci.	De rien.
Mer-see.	*Duh ryē.*

This is Mr./Mrs./Miss . . . .
Je vous présente Monsieur/Madame/Mademoiselle . . . .
Zhvoo preh-zãt muh-syuh/mah-dahm/mahd-mwah-zel . . . .

My name is . . . .
Je m'appelle . . . .
Zhuh mah-pel . . . .

What is your name?
Comment vous appelez-vous?
Ko-mã voo-zah-pleh-voo?

I am pleased to meet you.
Je suis enchanté de faire votre connaissance.
Zhuh swee-zã-shã-tehd fer votr ko-ne-sãs.

I don't understand.
Je ne comprends pas.
Zhuhn kõ-prã pah.

I don't know.
Je ne sais pas.
Zhuhn seh pah.

Could you speak more slowly, please?
Pourriez-vous parler plus lentement, s'il vous plaît?
Poor-yeh-voo pahr-leh plü lãt-ma, seel voo ple?

Could you repeat, please?
Pourriez-vous répéter, s'il vous plaît?
Poor-yeh-voo reh-peh-teh, seel voo ple?

Do you speak English?
Parlez-vous anglais?
Pahr-leh-voo ã-gle?

Where?	**When?**
Où?	Quand?
Oo?	*Kã?*

Can you help me, please?
Pardon, pourriez-vous m'aider?
Pahr-dõ, poor-yeh-voo meh-deh?

How do you say . . . in French?
Comment dit-on . . . en français?
Ko-mã dee-tõ . . . ã frã-se?

What does . . . mean?
Que veut dire . . .?
Kuh vuh deer . . . ?

Time and Weather

What time is it?
Quelle heure est-il?
Kel uhr e-teel?

(At) what time . . . ?
A quelle heure . . . ?
Ah kel uhr . . . ?

How is the weather today?
Quel temps fait-il aujourd'hui?
Kel tã fe-teel oh-zhoor-dwee?

It's a beautiful day. There will be rain tomorrow.
Il fait beau. Il va pleuvoir demain.
Eel fe boh. Eel vah pluh-vwahr duh-mẽ.

Customs

May I see your passport/visa/papers, please?
Votre passeport/votre visa/vos papiers, s'il vous plaît?
Vo-truh pahs-por/vo-truh vee-zah/voh pah-pyeh, seel voo ple?

Do you have anything to declare?
Avez-vous quelque chose à déclarer?
Ah-veh-voo kel-kuh shohz ah deh-klah-reh?

It's for my personal use.
C'est pour mon usage personnel.
Se poor mõ-nii-zahzh per-so-nel.

How long are you staying?
Combien de temps allez-vous rester?
Kõ-byẽ duh tã ah-leh-voo res-teh?

I will be here for . . . days/weeks/months.
Je compte rester . . . jours/semaines/mois.
Zhuh kõt res-teh . . . zhoor/smen/mwah.

Money

How much?
C'est combien, s'il vous plaît?
Se kõ-byē, seel voo ple?

Where can I cash this traveler's check?
Où est-ce que je peux toucher ce chèque de voyage?
Oo es kuhzh puh too-sheh suh shek duh vwah-yahzh?

When does the bank open/close?
Quand ouvre/ferme la banque?
Kã oovr/ferm lah bāk?

Please give me some small change.
Je voudrais de la petite monnaie, s'il vous plaît.
Zhvoo-dre dlah pteet mo-ne, seel voo ple.

What is the rate of exchange for dollars?
Quel est le cours du dollar?
Kel el koor dü do-lahr?

At the Hotel

I reserved a single/double room by mail/telephone.
J'ai retenu par lettre/téléphone une chambre à un lit/à deux
   lits.
Zhehr-tuh-nü pahr letr/teh-leh-fon ün shã-brah ē lee/ah duh lee.

I want a room with/without bath.
Je voudrais une chambre avec/sans salle de bain.
Zhvoo-dre ün shãbr ah-vek/sã sahl duh bē.

How much is this room?
Quel est le prix de la chambre?
Kel el preed lah shãbr?

Are meals included?
Est-ce que les repas sont compris?
Es kuh lehr-pah sõ kõ-pree?

Is there a special rate by the week?
Est-ce qu'il y a des prix spéciaux pour une semaine?
Es keel yah deh pree speh-syoh poor ün smen?

I would like something cheaper.
Je voudrais quelque chose de moins cher.
Zhvoo-dre kel-kuh shohz duh mwẽ sher.

Where is the manager?
Je voudrais voir le directeur, s'il vous plaît.
Zhvoo-dre vwahr luh dee-rek-tuhr, seel voo ple.

I want to check my valuables in your safe.
Est-ce que vous avez un coffre pour les objets de valeur?
Es kuh voo-zah-veh ẽ kofr poor leh-zob-zhed vah-luhr?

Please give me the key to my room.
S'il vous plaît, je voudrais la clé de ma chambre.
Seel voo ple, zhvoo-dre lah klehd mah shãbr.

Send a boy for my luggage.
Pouvez-vous m'envoyer quelqu'un pour mes bagages?
Poo-veh-voo mã-vwah-yeh kel-kẽ poor meh bah-gahzh?

Communications

Where is the post office/telegraph office?
Où est la poste?
Oo e lah post?

When does it open/close?
Quelle est l'heure d'ouverture/de fermeture?
Kel e luhr doo-ver-tür/duh fer-muh-tür?

Where can I buy some stamps?
Où est-ce que je peux acheter des timbres?
Oo es kuhzh puh ahsh-teh deh tẽbr?

Where is the nearest mail box?
Où est la boîte aux lettres la plus proche?
Oo e lah bwaht oh letr lah plü prosh?

I want to send this letter/package via airmail/special delivery.
Je voudrais envoyer cette lettre/ce paquet par avion/en exprès.
Zhvoo-dre ã-vwah-yeh set letr/suh pah-keh pahr ah-vyõ/ã-nek-spres.

How much postage do I need on this letter/package?
C'est combien pour affranchir cette lettre/ce paquet?
Se kõ-byẽ poor ah-frã-sheer set letr/spah-keh?

I want to insure this package.
Je veux assurer ce paquet.
Zhvuh ah-sü-reh spah-keh.

Please forward my mail to . . . .
Pouvez-vous faire suivre mon courrier à . . . ?
Poo-veh-voo fer sweevr mõ koor-yeh ah . . . ?

Where is the nearest telephone?
Où est le téléphone le plus proche?
Oo el teh-leh-fon luh plü prosh?

Do you have a telephone directory?
Avez-vous un annuaire?
Ah-veh-voo ẽ-nah-nü-er?

I want to make a long-distance call.
Je voudrais l'inter.
Zhvoo-dre lẽ-ter.

I want to call . . . .
S'il vous plaît, donnez-moi . . . .
Seel voo ple, do-neh mwah . . . .

Please call station-to-station/collect/person-to-person.
Je voudrais faire un appel normal/une communication en
    P.C.V./un appel avec préavis.
*Zhvoo-dre fer ĕ-nah-pel nor-mahl/ün ko-mü-nee-kah-syō ã
    peh-seh-veh/ĕ-nah-pel ah-vek preh-ah-vee.*

The line is busy.
La ligne est occupée.
Lah leeñ e-to-kü-peh.

This is . . . . May I speak to . . . .
Ici . . . . Puis-je parler à . . . ?
Ee-see . . . . Pweezh pahr-leh ah . . . ?

Please hold the line.
Ne quittez pas, s'il vous plaît.
Nuh kee-teh pah, seel voo ple.

Hang up please.
Raccrochez, s'il vous plaît.
Rah-kro-sheh, seel voo ple.

Laundry/Dry Cleaning

Where is a laundry/dry cleaner/laundromat?
Où y a-t-il une blanchisserie/une teinturerie/une laverie
    automatique?
*Oo yah-teel ün blã-shee-sree/ün tĕ-tür-ree/ün lah-vree o-toh-
    mah-teek?*

Please wash these clothes.
Voici du linge à laver, s'il vous plaît.
Vwah-see dü lēzh ah lah-veh, seel voo ple.

I don't want any starch, please.
Je ne veux pas d'amidon, s'il vous plaît.
Zhuhn vuh pah dah-mee-dō, seel voo ple.

When will my clothes be ready?
Quand est-ce que mon linge sera prêt?
Kã-tes kuh mõ lēzh srah pre?

I want these clothes dry cleaned.
Je voudrais faire nettoyer ces vêtements.
Zhvoo-dre fer ne-twah-yeh seh vetmã.

Please press these trousers.
Je voudrais faire repasser ces pantalons.
Zhvoo-dre fer ruh-pah-seh seh pã-tah-lõ.

Hairdresser/Barber

I would like a haircut/trim.
Pouvez-vous me couper les cheveux/rafraîchir ma coupe, s'il
vous plaît?
*Poo-veh-voom koo-peh leh shvuh/rah-fre-sheer mah koop, seel
voo ple?*

Make it shorter, please.
Plus court, s'il vous plaît.
Plü koor, seel voo ple.

I would like a shampoo and set.
Je voudrais un shampooing et une mise en plis.
Zhvoo-dre ẽ shã-pwẽ eh iin mee-zã plee.

Getting Around

When is the next flight to . . . ?
Quand part le prochain vol pour . . . ?
Kã pahr luh pro-shẽ vol poor . . . ?

I want a ticket to . . . , please.
Pardon, je voudrais un billet pour . . . .
Pahr-dõ, zhvoo-dre ẽ bee-ye poor . . . .

Is lunch/dinner served on this flight?
Est-ce qu'il y a un déjeuner/dîner à bord?
Es keel yah ē deh-zhuh-neh/dee-neh ah bor?

I want to reconfirm my flight.
Je voudrais reconfirmer mon vol.
Zhvoo-dre ruh-kō-feer-meh mō vol.

Take my bags to my cabin, please.
S'il vous plaît, pouvez-vous apporter mes affaires à ma cabine?
Seel voo ple, poo-veh-voo ah-por-teh me-zah-fer ah mah kah-been?

What time is lunch/dinner/breakfast?
A quelle heure est le déjeuner/dîner/petit déjeuner?
Ah kel uhr el deh-zhuh-neh/dee-neh/ptee deh-zhuh-neh?

At what time does the boat dock?
A quelle heure est-ce que le bateau arrive à quai?
Ah kel uhr es kuhl bah-toh ah-reev ah keh?

Where is the ticket window?
Où est le guichet des billets?
Oo el ghee-sheh deh bee-ye?

May I have a timetable?
Je voudrais un horaire.
Zhvoo-dre ē-no-rer.

How much is a one-way/round trip first-class/second class ticket to . . . ?
Combien coûte un aller simple/un aller-retour en première/en seconde pour . . . ?
Kō-byē koot ē-nah-leh sēpl/ē-nah-lehr-toor ã pruh-myer/ã suh-gōd poor . . . ?

I want to reserve a seat/a berth.
Je voudrais louer une place/une couchette.
Zhvoo-dre lweh iin plahs/iin koo-shet.

From which track does the train for . . . leave?
De quel quai part le train pour . . . ?
Duh kel keh pahr luh trē poor . . . ?

What time does this train leave?
A quelle heure part ce train?
Ah kel uhr pahr strē?

Is this train an express or a local?
Est-ce que c'est un rapide ou un omnibus?
Es kuh se-tē rah-peed oo ē-nom-nee-büs?

Is this seat taken?
Est-ce que cette place est occupée?
Es kuh set plahs e-to-kü-peh?

When is the dining car open?
A quelle heure ouvre le wagon-restaurant?
Ah kel uhr oovr luh vah-gō-res-to-rã?

Which way to the lavatory, please?
Pourriez-vous m'indiquer les toilettes, s'il vous plaît?
Poor-yeh-voo mē-dee-keh leh twah-let, seel voo ple?

I want to check this baggage.
Je voudrais enregistrer ces bagages.
Zhvoo-dre ãr-zhees-treh seh bah-gahzh.

Where is the bus station?
Où est l'arrêt des cars?
Oo e lah-re deh kahr?

When is the next bus to . . . ?
Quand part le prochain car pour . . . ?
Kã pahr luh pro-shē kahr poor . . . ?

How long is the trip?
Combien de temps dure le trajet?
Kō-byēd tã dür luh trah-zhe?

Where do I get off to go to . . . ?
Où dois-je descendre pour aller à . . . ?
Oo dwahzh deh-sãdr poor ah-leh ah . . . ?

Take me to . . . .
Je veux aller à/au/à la . . . .
Zhvuh ah-leh ah/oh/ah lah . . . .

I am in a hurry to catch a bus/train/plane.
C'est pressé. Je dois prendre un car/un train/un avion.
Se pre-seh. Zhdwah prãd-rẽ kahr/trẽ/nah-vyõ.

Where can I rent a car?
Où est-ce que je peux louer une auto?
Oo es kuhzh puh lweh ü-noh-toh?

Do you charge by the day only, or by the mile as well?
Est-ce qu'on paie à la journée seulement ou aussi au
    kilomètre?
Es kõ pe ah lah zhoor-neh suhl-mã oo oh-see oh kee-lo-metr?

Where is the nearest gas station?
Où se trouve le poste d'essence le plus proche?
Oos troov luh post de-sãs luh plü prosh?

Fill it up with regular/premium, please.
Je voudrais le plein normal/super, s'il vous plaît.
Zhvoo-dre luh plẽ nor-mahl/sü-per, seel voo ple.

Please check the oil/tires/water/battery.
Pouvez-vous vérifier l'huile/les pneus/l'eau/les accus?
Poo-veh-voo veh-ree-fyeh lweel/leh pnuh/loh/leh-zah-kü?

My car doesn't work.   **I have a flat tire.**
Je suis en panne.   J'ai un pneu crevé.
Zhuh swee-zã pahn.   *Zheh ẽ pnuh kruh-veh.*

I am having trouble with the . . . .
J'ai des ennuis de . . . .
Zheh deh-zã-nwee duh . . . .

Is there a mechanic here?
Est-ce qu'il y a un mécanicien ici?
Es keel yah ē meh-kah-nee-syē ee-see?

When will my car be ready?
Quand est-ce que l'auto sera prête?
Kã-tes kuh loh-toh srah pret?

Shopping

Where is there a bookstore?
Où y a-t-il une librairie?
Oo yah-teel ün lee-bre-ree?

. . . a department store?
. . . un grand magasin?
. . . ē grã mah-gah-zē?

. . . a pharmacy?
. . . une pharmacie?
. . . ün fahr-mah-see?

. . . a grocery?
. . . une épicerie?
. . . ün eh-pees-ree?

. . . a photo shop?
. . . un magasin de photo?
. . . ē mah-gah-zēd foh-toh?

On what floor are the clothes/leather goods?
A quel étage sont les vêtements/la maroquinerie?
Ah kel eh-tahzh sõ leh vet-mã/lah mah-ro-keen-ree?

How much does this cost?
Combien est-ce que ça coûte?
Kõ-byē es kuh sah koot?

Have you anything better/cheaper?
Avez-vous quelque chose de mieux/de meilleur marché?
Ah-veh-voo kel-kuh shohz duh myuh/duh me-yuhr mahr-sheh?

Is this handmade?
Est-ce que c'est fait-main?
Es kuh se fe-mẽ?

Does this come in any other color?
Avez-vous la même chose en d'autres couleurs?
Ah-vee-voo lah mem shohz ã doh-truh koo-luhr?

This is too large/small.
C'est trop grand/petit.
Se troh grã/ptee.

Please give me a sales slip for this purchase.
Je voudrais un reçu pour cet achat, s'il vous plaît.
Zhvoo-dre ẽr-sü poor se-tah-shah, seel voo ple.

Do you accept checks/traveler's checks?
Est-ce que vous acceptez des chèques/des chèques de voyage?
Es kuh voo-zahk-sep-teh deh shek/deh shek duh vwah-yahzh?

I would like a roll of color/black and white film.
Je voudrais une pellicule photo en couleurs/en noir et blanc.
Zhvoo-dre ün peh-lee-kül foh-toh ã koo-luhr/ã nwahr eh blã.

I would like a Super-8/8 mm. movie film.
Je voudrais un film Super-8/de 8 millimètres.
Zhvoo-dre ẽ feelm sü-per-weet/duh weet mee-lee-metr.

Here are some films to develop.
Voici des pellicules à développer.
Vwah-see deh peh-lee-kül ah deh-vlo-peh.

I'm just looking.
Je veux seulement regarder ce que vous avez.
Zhvuh suhl-mã ruh-gahr-deh skuh voo-zah-veh.

Sightseeing

How long will the tour last? What will I see?
Combien de temps dure la visite? Qu'est-ce qu'on y voit?
Kõ-byēd tã dür lah vee-zeet? Kes kõ-nee vwah?

Where is the museum/cathedral?
Où est le musée/la cathédrale?
Oo el mü-zeh/lah kah-teh-drahl?

What hours are the museums open?
Quelles sont les heures d'ouverture des musées?
Kel sõ leh-zuhr doo-ver-tür deh mü-zeh?

Do we have to pay to go in?
Est-ce qu'il faut payer pour entrer?
Es keel foht peh-yeh poor ã-treh?

What is the name of that building/monument?
Comment s'appelle ce bâtiment/ce monument?
Ko-mã sah-pel sbah-tee-mã/smo-nü-mã?

Entertainment

I would like to see an opera/a game.
Je voudrais assister à un opéra/à un match.
Zhvoo-dre ah-sees-teh ah ē-no-peh-rah/ah ē mahtsh.

Please let me have two orchestra/balcony seats/a box.
Je voudrais deux fauteuils d'orchestre/deux places au balcon/une loge.
Zhvoo-dre duh foh-tuhy dor-kestr/duh plahs oh bahl-kõ/üin lozh.

I want to eat breakfast/lunch/dinner.
Je voudrais un petit déjeuner/un déjeuner/un dîner.
Zhvoo-dre ē ptee deh-zhuh-neh/ē deh-zhuh-neh/ē dee-neh.

We would like a table for two, please.
Nous voudrions une table pour deux, s'il vous plaît.
Noo voo-dree-yō ün tahbl poor duh, seel voo ple.

May we have a menu/wine list, please?
Je voudrais un menu/la carte des vins, s'il vous plaît.
Zhvoo-dre ē muh-nü/lah kahrt deh vē, seel voo ple.

What do you recommend?
Qu'est-ce que vous nous conseillez?
Kes kuh voo noo kō-seh-yeh?

Please bring the check.
S'il vous plaît, l'addition.
Seel voo ple, lah-dee-syō.

Is the tip included?
Est-ce que le service est compris?
Es kuhl ser-vees e kō-pree?

Where do I pay?
Où faut-il payer?
Oo foh-teel peh-yeh?

There is a mistake in the bill.
Il y a une erreur dans l'addition.
Eel yah ün e-ruhr dã lah-dee-syō.

Health

I don't feel well.
Je ne me sens pas bien.
Zhuhn muh sã pah byē.

I need a doctor/dentist.
Je veux voir un docteur/un dentiste.
Zhvuh vwahr ē dok-tuhr/ē dã-teest.

I have a headache/stomach ache/toothache.
J'ai mal à la tête/mal au ventre/mal aux dents.
Zheh mahl ah lah tet/mahl oh vãtr/mahl oh dã.

I have a bad cold/fever.
J'ai un gros rhume/de la fièvre.
Zheh ẽ groh rüm/dlah fyevr.

My . . . is burned/hurt/bleeding.
Mon/ma . . . s'est brûlé/blessé/perd du sang.
Mõ/mah . . . se brü-leh/bleh-seh/per dü sã.

Please make up this prescription.
Pouvez-vous me préparer cette ordonnance, s'il vous plaît.
Poo-veh-voom preh-pah-reh set or-do-nãs, seel voo ple.

Emergencies

Help!   **Police!**
Au secours!   Police!
Ohs-koor!   *Po-lees!*

Please call a policeman/an ambulance.
S'il vous plaît, appelez la police/une ambulance.
Seel voo ple, ah-pleh lah po-lees/ün ã-bü-lãs.

I need a lawyer.
Je veux un avocat.
Zhvuh ẽ-nah-vo-kah.

I want to call the American Embassy.
Je veux téléphoner à l'ambassade américaine.
Zhvuh teh-leh-fo-neh ah lã-bah-sahd ah-meh-ree-ken.

I've been robbed.
On m'a volé.
Õ mah vo-leh.

Is there anyone here who speaks English?
Est-ce que quelqu'un parle anglais?
Es kuh kel-kē pahrl ã-gle?

I am lost.
Je me suis perdu.
Zhuhm swee per-dü.

I don't know where my hotel/car is.
Je ne sais pas où se trouve mon hôtel/mon auto.
Zhuhn seh pah oos troov mõ-noh-tel/mõ-noh-toh.

I have lost a suitcase/an umbrella/my purse.
J'ai perdu une valise/un parapluie/mon sac.
Zheh per-dü ün vah-leez/ẽ pah-rah-plwee/mõ sahk.

I missed the train/bus/plane.
J'ai manqué le train/le car/l'avion.
Zheh mã-keh luh trẽ/luh kahr/lah-vyõ.

Someone is injured.
Il y a un blessé.
Eel yah ẽ bleh-seh.

Menu Reader

Beverages

apéritif [*ah-peh-ree-teef*] wine or other drink before meals
bière [*byer*] beer
  bière à la pression [*byer ah lah pre-syõ*] draught beer
  un demi de bière [*ẽ duh-meed byer*] a glass of draught beer
café [*kah-feh*] coffee
  café au lait [*kah-feh oh le*] coffee with hot milk
  café-crème [*kah-feh krem*] coffee with cream
chocolat chaud [*shoh-koh-lah shoh*] hot chocolate
cidre [*seedr*] cider
citron pressé [*see-trõ pre-seh*] lemonade
eau [*oh*] water
  eau minérale [*oh mee-neh-rahl*] mineral water
glaçon [*glah-sõ*] ice cube
jus de fruit [*zhüd frwee*] fruit juice
lait [*le*] milk
  lait grenadine [*le gruh-nah-deen*] grenadine syrup mixed
    with milk
limonade [*lee-mo-nahd*] soda
martini [*mahr-tee-nee*] sweet vermouth
menthe à l'eau [*mã-tah loh*] mint-flavored syrup with water
pastis [*pahs-tees*] anis-flavored aperitif
porto [*por-toh*] port
soda orange (citron, etc.) [*so-dah o-rãzh (see-trõ)*] orange
  (lemon, etc.) flavored soft drink
thé [*teh*] tea
  thé au citron [*teh oh see-trõ*] tea with lemon
vin [*vẽ*] wine
  vin blanc [*vẽ blã*] white wine
  vin ordinaire [*vẽ or-dee-ner*] ordinary wine
  vin rosé [*vẽ roh-zeh*] rosé wine
  vin rouge [*vẽ roozh*] red wine

The Menu

à la, à l' (with adjective of country, province, etc.) [*ah lah*] prepared in the style of (the country mentioned)
   à la Française [*ah lah frã-sez*] in the French style (often cooked in butter)
   à la Provençale [*ah lah pro-vã-sahl*] Provençal style (often with tomatoes, olives and olive oil)
abricot [*ah-bree-koh*] apricot
agneau [*ah-nyoh*] lamb
ail [*ahy*] garlic
ananas [*ah-nah-nah*] pineapple
anchois [*ã-shwah*] anchovy
artichaut [*ahr-tee-shoh*] artichoke
   fonds d'artichaut [*fõ dahr-tee-shoh*] artichoke hearts
asperges [*ah-sperzh*] asparagus
aubergine [*oh-ber-zheen*] eggplant
avocat [*ah-vo-kah*] avocado

baba au rhum [*bah-bah oh rom*] sponge cake soaked in rum sauce
baguette [*bah-ghet*] long thin loaf of bread
banane [*bah-nahn*] banana
béchamel [*beh-shah-mel*] cream sauce
beignets [*be-nye*] fritters
betterave [*be-trahv*] beet
beurre [*buhr*] butter
bifteck [*beef-tek*] steak (small)
   bien cuit [*byẽ kwee*] well done
   à point [*ah pwẽ*] medium
   saignant [*se-nyã*] rare
biscuits [*bees-kwee*] cookies, crackers
boeuf [*buhf*] beef
   boeuf bourguignon [*buhf boor-ghee-nyõ*] beef stew cooked in wine
bonbons [*bõ-bõ*] candy
bouilli [*boo-yee*] boiled
boudin [*boo-dẽ*] blood sausage

bouillabaisse [*boo-yah-bes*] thick fish soup, specialty of Marseille

brioche [*bree-osh*] light roll, for breakfast or snack

brochet [*bro-she*] pike

brochette [*bro-shet*] skewer, kebabs

cacahuètes [*kah-kah-wet*] peanuts

canard [*kah-nahr*] duck
  canard à l'orange [*kah-nahr ah lo-rãzh*] duck with orange sauce

carottes [*kah-rot*] carrots

carte [*kahrı*] menu

céleri [*sel-ree*] celery

cerises [*sreez*] cherries

cervelle [*ser-vel*] brains

champignons [*shã-pee-nyõ*] mushrooms

charcuterie [*shahr-kü-tree*] pork products, salami, etc.

Châteaubriand [*shah-toh-bree-yã*] thick fillet steak

chou [*shoo*] cabbage

chou à la crème [*shoo ah lah krem*] cream puff

choucroute garnie [*shoo-kroot gahr-nee*] sauerkraut with different kinds of sausages

chou-fleur [*shoo-fluhr*] cauliflower

choux de Bruxelles [*shood brü-sel*] Brussels sprouts

citron [*see-trõ*] lemon

civet de lièvre [*see-ved lyevr*] hare stewed in wine sauce

compote de fruits [*kõ-pot duh frwee*] stewed fruit
  compote de pommes [*kõ-pot duh pom*] applesauce

concombres [*kõ-kõbr*] cucumbers

confiture [*kõ-fee-tür*] jam

coq au vin [*kok oh vẽ*] chicken cooked in wine

coquille Saint Jacques [*ko-keey sẽ zhahk*] scallops served in shell, with cream sauce

cornichons [*kor-nee-shõ*] small pickles

côtelette, côte [*koht-let, koht*] chop

courgettes [*koor-zhet*] zucchini

couscous [*koos-koos*] steamed semolina, with chicken, mutton, etc., vegetables and sauce; specialty of North Africa

couvert [*koo-ver*] place setting, cover charge
crème [*krem*] cream, pudding
  crème anglaise [*krem ã-glez*] boiled custard
  crème Chantilly [*krem shã-tee-yee*] sweetened whipped cream
crêpes [*krep*] thin pancakes, rolled with jelly or other filling
  crêpes Suzette [*krep sü-zet*] crepes with orange sauce, flamed
cresson [*kre-sõ*] watercress
crevettes [*kruh-vet*] shrimp
croissant [*krwah-sã*] crescent-shaped roll
crudités [*krü-dee-teh*] raw vegetables sometimes marinated
cuisses de grenouille [*kwees duh gruh-nooy*] frogs' legs
cuit [*kwee*] cooked

dattes [*daht*] dates
dinde [*dẽd*] turkey

écrevisses [*eh-kruh-vees*] crayfish
endives [*ã-deev*] Belgian endive
entrecôte [*ã-truh-koht*] steak
épinards [*éh-pee-nahr*] spinach
escalope de veau [*es-kah-lop duh voh*] veal steak
escargots [*es-kahr-goh*] snails
faisan [*fuh-zã*] pheasant
fait maison [*fe me-zõ*] homemade
farci [*fahr-see*] stuffed
fèves [*fev*] lima beans (dried)
figues [*feeg*] figs
flan [*flã*] baked custard
foie [*fwah*] liver
au four [*oh foor*] baked
fraises [*frez*] strawberries
framboises [*frã-bwahz*] raspberries
frit [*free*] fried
fromage [*fro-mahzh*] cheese
  fromage de chèvre [*fro-mahzh duh shevr*] goat cheese
fruit [*frwee*] fruit

   fruits confits [*frwee kõ-fee*] candied fruit
   fruits de mer [*frweed mer*] seafood
fumé [*fü-meh*] smoked
gâteau [*gah-toh*] cake
gauffres [*gohfr*] waffles
gigot [*zhee-goh*] leg of lamb
glace [*glahs*] ice cream
gratiné, au gratin [*grah-tee-neh, oh grah-tẽ*] prepared with
      cream sauce, topped with crumbs and/or cheese
grillade [*gree-yahd*] broiled meat
grillé [*gree-yeh*] broiled, grilled

hareng [*ah-rã*] herring
haricots [*ah-ree-koh*] beans
   haricots blancs [*ah-ree-koh blã*] Navy beans
   haricots verts [*ah-ree-koh ver*] green beans
homard [*oh-mahr*] lobster
huile [*weel*] oil
huîtres [*weetr*] oysters

jambon [*zhã-bõ*] ham

laitue [*leh-tü*] lettuce
langouste [*lã-goost*] small lobster
lapin [*lah-pẽ*] rabbit
lièvre [*lyevr*] hare

macédoine [*mah-seh-dwahn*] mixed diced vegetables
maïs [*mah-ees*] corn
maquereau [*mahk-roh*] mackerel
mariné [*mah-ree-neh*] marinated
melon [*muh-lõ*] melon
menu [*muh-nü*] menu
   menu du jour [*muh-nü dü zhoor*] today's menu
miel [*myel*] honey
morue [*mo-rü*] cod
moules [*mool*] mussels
moutarde [*moo-tahrd*] mustard
mouton [*moo-tõ*] mutton

nature [*nah-tür*] plain
navet [*nah-ve*] turnip

oeuf [*uhf*] egg
    oeuf à la coque [*uh-fah lah kok*] soft-boiled egg
    oeuf au plat [*uh-foh plah*] fried egg
    oeufs brouillés [*uh brooh-yeh*] scrambled eggs
    oeuf dur [*uhf dür*] hard-boiled egg
oie [*wah*] goose
oignon [*o-nyõ*] onion
olives [*o-leev*] olives
omelette [*om-let*] omelet

pain [*pẽ*] bread
pamplemousse [*pã-pluh-moos*] grapefruit
pané [*pah-neh*] breaded
pâté de fois gras [*pah-tehd fwah grah*] paste made from
    goose livers
pâtes alimentaires [*paht ah-lee-mã-ter*] pasta: noodles, etc.
pâtisscrie [*pah-tees-ree*] pastry
paupiettes [*poh-pyet*] thin slices of meat, stuffed, braised
pêche [*pesh*] peach
petits pois [*ptee pwah*] green peas
petits fours [*ptee foor*] small frosted cakes
plat de résistance [*plahd reh-zees-tãs*] main course
plat du chef [*plah dü shef*] specialty of the chef
poché [*po-sheh*] poached
poivre [*pwahvr*] pepper
poivron [*pwah-vrõ*] green pepper
pomme [*pom*] apple
pomme de terre [*pom duh ter*] potato
    pommes de terre au gratin [*pom duh ter oh grah-tẽ*] scalloped
    potatoes
    pommes de terre en robe des champs [*pom duh ter ã rob deh
    shã*] baked potatoes
    pommes (de terre) frites [*pom (duh ter) freet*] French fried
    potatoes

purée de pommes de terre [*pü-rehd pom duh ter*] mashed potatoes
porc [*por*] pork
potage [*po-tahzh*] soup
pot-au-feu [*po-toh-fuh*] beef and vegetables in broth
poule [*pool*] hen
poulet [*poo-le*] chicken
pruneaux [*prü-noh*] prunes
prunes [*prün*] plums

quenelle [*kuh-nel*] ground fish or veal, molded and prepared in sauce; specialty of Lyon

ragoût [*rah-goo*] stew
raisin [*re-zē*] grape
  raisins secs [*re-zē sek*] raisins
ratatouille [*rah-tah-tooy*] tomatoes, zucchini, eggplant, peppers, cooked with herbs and olive oil; specialty of Nice
ris de veau [*reed voh*] sweetbreads
rissolé [*ree-so-leh*] browned
riz [*ree*] rice
rognons [*ro-nyō*] kidneys
rosbif [*roz-beef*] roast beef
rôti [*roh-tee*] roast

salade [*sah-lahd*] salad
  salade de fruits [*sah-lahd duh frwee*] fruit cup
  salade de riz [*sah-lahd duh ree*] rice salad (with tomatoes, olives, anchovies, peppers)
  salade Niçoise [*sah-lahd nee-swahz*] tomatoes, hard-boiled eggs, anchovies, olives, etc.
  salade verte [*sah-lahd vert*] tossed salad
saucisse [*soh-sees*] hot, cooked sausage, or sausage to cook
saucisson [*soh-see-sō*] hard sausage: to slice and serve cold
saumon [*soh-mō*] salmon
sauté [*soh-teh*] sauteed

sel [*sel*] salt
sole [*sol*] sole
soupe [*soop*] soup
  soupe à l'ail [*soop ah lahy*] garlic soup
  soupe à l'oignon [*soop ah lo-nyõ*] onion soup
  soupe de légumes [*soop duh leh-güm*] vegetable soup
spécialité de la maison [*speh-syah-lee-tehd lah me-zõ*] specialty
    of the house
sucre [*sükr*] sugar

tarte [*tahrt*] pie
thon [*tõ*] tuna
tomate [*to-maht*] tomato
tournedos [*toor-nuh-doh*] steak from fillet
truite [*trweet*] trout

veau [*voh*] veal
  blanquette de veau [*blã-ket duh voh*] veal stewed in cream
    sauce
viande [*vyãd*] meat
  viande froide [*vyãd frwahd*] cold meat (roast)
  viande hachée [*vyãd ah-sheh*] ground beef
vinaigrette [*vee-ne-gret*] vinegar and oil sauce
volaille [*vo-lahy*] poultry
vol-au-vent [*vol-oh-vã*] patty shell filled with some creamed
    food

yaourt [*yah-oor*] yogurt

A Concise French Grammar

Nouns

French nouns have grammatical gender: every one is masculine or feminine, and every noun in this dictionary is marked *m.* or *f.* Remembering gender is easier if you learn a new noun with its article or an adjective. For various reasons which you will understand later, it is harder to remember the gender of words beginning with vowel sounds. Make a special effort here, since the gender of the nouns determines much of the grammar of the rest of the sentence.

Nouns usually add *-s* to form the plural, unless the noun ends in *-s*, *-x*, or *-z*, in which case there is no change. All other plural forms are marked in the dictionary. The most common irregular plural is *-aux*.

Articles

An article agrees with the noun it precedes, and in context is often the best clue to the gender and number of the noun.

● The definite article, the, is *le*, m., or *la*, f. Both become *l'* before vowel sounds (one reason why the gender of these nouns is harder to distinguish). The plural article for both genders is *les*. In spoken French, adding an *-s* to a noun normally does not change its pronunciation, and the article is often the only sign that a word is plural:

le livre [*luh leevr*] the book
les livres [*leh leevr*] the books

la table [*lah tahbl*] the table
les tables [*leh tahbl*] the tables

l'arbre [*lahrbr*] the tree
les arbres [*leh-zahrbr*] the trees

The masculine and the plural forms of the definite article, *le*, *les*, always contract with the prepositions *à* and *de*:

à le becomes **au** [*oh*] **à les** becomes **aux** [*oh*]
de le becomes **du** [*dii*] **de les** becomes **des** [*deh*]

● The indefinite article, a, an, is *un*, m., or *une*, f. French also has a plural indefinite article, *des*, m. and f.:

un livre a book **des livres** books
une table a table **des tables** tables

French tends to use articles more than English does. One exception is with nouns indicating profession, nationality, or religion, if they are not modified in any way, and not preceded by *c'est*, it is:

Il est professeur. He is a teacher.
Elle est Américaine. She is an American.

BUT **C'est un bon professeur.** He is a good teacher.

● The partitive article is used when speaking of an indefinite quantity. The best English equivalent would be "some" or "any," but often English does not express the idea at all. The partitive article has four forms: *du* (m.), *de la* (f.), *de l'* (m. and f. before vowel sounds), and *des* (all plural nouns). It is used particularly with words like *have*, *want*, *order*, etc. Examples:

Avez-vous des journaux? Do you have (any) newspapers?
Je voudrais du café, de l'eau, et de la salade.
     I would like (some) coffee, water, and salad.

If you can put *some* or *any* in your English sentence, even if you would not ordinarily use either word, you probably need the partitive in your French sentence.

In negative sentences and after expressions of quantity, both the partitive and the indefinite article are replaced by *de*:

J'ai des frères. I have brothers.
Je n'ai pas de frères. I have no brothers.

Il a des livres. He has books.
Il a beaucoup de livres. He has many books.

Il a un livre. He has a book.
Il n'a pas de livres. He has no books.

Qualifying Adjectives

Adjectives agree with the nouns they modify in gender and number. To make the feminine form of the adjective you add -*e* to the masculine singular, unless it ends in -*e*. To make the plural you add -*s* to the correct (masculine or feminine) singular form, unless it ends in -*s* or -*x*. Examples:

m. sing.	m. pl.	f. sing.	f. pl.	
vert	verts	verte	vertes	green
parfait	parfaits	parfaite	parfaites	perfect
jeune	jeunes	jeune	jeunes	young
mauvais	mauvais	mauvaise	mauvaises	bad

Adding -*e* or -*es* often means that you will pronounce a consonant in the feminine form that is silent in the masculine form. In the dictionary the pronunciation of the masculine singular is always given, and the added consonant pronounced in the feminine is included in parentheses.

   green vert [*ver(t)*]
   bad mauvais [*moh-ve(z)*]

Adjectives that do not follow this pattern are considered irregular, and the feminine singular or masculine plural forms are given in the dictionary. Examples:

   marvellous merveilleux, -euse [*mer-ve-yuh, mer-ve-yuhz*]
   rural rural, -aux (m, pl) [*rü-rahl, rü-roh*]

Be sure to use the feminine singular of these irregular adjectives, not the masculine plural, to form the feminine plural.

Most adjectives follow the noun they modify. Some very common ones precede it: *grand*, big, tall; *petit*, small; *bon*, good; *mauvais*, bad; *joli*, pretty; *gros*, fat, big; *long*, long; *court*, short; *jeune*, young; *beau*, beautiful, handsome; *nouveau*, new; and *vieux*, old. The last three, all irregular, have a special form used before masculine singular words beginning with a vowel sound: *bel, nouvel, vieil*. Examples:

   un beau chapeau a beautiful hat
   un bel enfant a beautiful child

   un nouveau livre a new book
   un nouvel habit a new suit of clothes

un vieux monsieur an old man
un vieil hôtel an old hotel

In English we put one noun before another and use the first as an adjective: bed-room, lawn-mower, night-stand. Not so in French. If the word isn't an adjective, it cannot be used as one, and a phrase must be used:

chambre à coucher room for sleeping
tondeuse à gazon cutter for lawn
table de nuit table for night

With one exception, adjectives are compared regularly:

COMPARATIVE:

more than (-er than) **plus . . . que**
> **Louise est plus grande que Françoise.**
> Louise is taller than Frances.

as . . . as **aussi . . . que**
> **Jean est aussi grand que Pierre.**
> John is as tall as Peter.

less . . . than **moins . . . que**
> **Louise est moins grande que Sophie.**
> Louise is less tall than Sophie.

SUPERLATIVE:

the most (the -est) **le (la, les) plus**
> **Louise est la plus grande fille de la classe.**
> Louise is the tallest girl in the class.

> **Anne et Marie sont les plus petites filles de la classe.**
> Anne and Mary are the smallest girls in the class.

the least **le (la, les) moins**
> **Henri est le garçon le moins intelligent de la classe.**
> Henry is the least intelligent boy in the class.

NOTE: French uses *de* after a superlative; English uses *in*.

The position of the adjective remains the same as for the positive form. If the adjective follows the noun, the definite article is used twice:

le garçon le moins intelligent the least intelligent boy

The one adjective that has irregular comparative and superlative forms is *bon*, good. They are: *meilleur(e)*, better, and *le (la, les) meilleur(e)*, best.

Personal Pronouns

French has subject and object pronouns like English I, me; he, him, plus indirect object pronouns, and a special category of pronouns used in a stressed position.

Subject	Direct Object	Indirect Object	Stressed*
je I	**me** me	**me** to me	**moi**
tu you	**te** you	**te** to you	**toi**
il he, it	**le** him, it	**lui** to him	**lui**
elle she, it	**la** her, it	**lui** to her	**elle**
on (indefinite)	**se** himself, herself, itself	**se** to himself, herself, itself	**soi**
nous we	**nous** us	**nous** to us	**nous**
vous you	**vous** you	**vous** to you	**vous**
ils they, *m.*	**les** them, *m.*	**leur** to them, *m.*	**eux**
elles they, *f.*	**les** them, *f.*	**leur** to them, *f.*	**elles**
	se themselves	**se** to themselves	**soi**

*The translation of the stressed pronouns varies with their use.

The second person singular pronouns, *tu*, etc., need some explanation. The same is true of the corresponding verb forms that we will see later. In English we say *you* to everyone. In French there are two possibilities when speaking to one person: the second person singular, *tu*, called the familiar form, or the second person plural, *vous*, used as a polite singular. In the plural, *vous* is used for everyone. As a foreigner you will say *vous* to almost everyone, except to very young children.

● Subject pronouns are used only as the subject of a verb, never alone or after a comparison (taller than *I*, etc.). In these latter cases, use the stressed pronouns:

Qui parle français? Lui.

Who speaks French? He does.

Elle est plus grande que moi.

She is taller than I.

The stressed forms are also used after prepositions:

J'ai parlé avec elle. I spoke with her.

● The third person direct object pronouns, *le*, *la*, *les*, can refer to persons or things. The indirect object pronouns, *lui*, *leur*, refer only to persons. (*Y* is used for things, as we will see later.) All object pronouns normally precede the verb, where they can be used with *en* and *y*, important French pronouns for which there are no direct English equivalents.

En replaces *de* plus a noun or pronoun referring to things or to a situation, not a person. It also is used instead of a partitive expression or with an expression of quantity. In these latter cases it can refer to persons. Examples:

Voulez-vous des poires? Oui, j'en voudrais.
    Do you want some pears? Yes, I would like some.
Combien de frères avez-vous? J'en ai trois.
    How many brothers do you have? I have three.
Je suis content de cela. J'en suis content.
    I am pleased with that. I am pleased with it.

BUT:

Je suis content de Jean. Je suis content de lui.
    I am pleased with John. I am pleased with him.

Y replaces *à* (and, of course, *au* and *aux*) plus a noun or pronoun signifying a thing, or any expression indicating a place. Examples:

Marie est-elle en ville? Oui, elle y est.
    Is Marie in town? Yes, she is.
Je pense à cela. J'y pense.
    I am thinking about that. I am thinking about it.
Je réponds aux lettres. J'y réponds.
    I am answering the letters. I am answering them.

BUT:

Je réponds à mon père. Je lui réponds.
    I am answering my father. I am answering him.

If more than one pronoun precedes the verb (three is the maximum), their order is as follows:

Y and *en* are closest to the verb, and *y* precedes *en*:

Je m'en souviens. I remember.
Il l'y a mis. He put it there.
Il y en a. There is/are some.

When used together, *le*, *la*, or *les* always precedes *lui* or *leur*:

Elle la lui donne.   She gives it to him/her.
Il les leur donne.   He gives them to them.

The other pronouns come first, farthest from the verb:

Il me le donne.   He gives it to me.
Je vous les apporte.   I bring them to you.
Je t'en remercie.   I thank you (for it).
Elle nous y a amenés.   She brought us there.

After an affirmative imperative all pronouns follow the verb. They keep the same order, except for *nous*, *vous*, *me*, and *te*, which follow everything except *y* and *en*. When *me* and *te* are final, they are replaced by their stressed forms, *moi* and *toi*. Examples:

Donnez-les-leur.   Give them to them.
Donnez-le-moi.   Give it to me.
Donnez m'en.   Give some to me.

You will frequently find French verbs that are translated into English by a verb plus a preposition: *attendre* is translated *wait for*, for example. The reverse is also true: *to obey someone* is translated into French by a verb plus a prepositional phrase: *obéir à quelqu'un*. Pay attention to this difference: if the French expression uses a prepositional phrase, you must use an indirect object pronoun if you want to replace it. Examples:

J'attends Jean. Je l'attends.
  I am waiting for John. I am waiting for him.
J'obéis à mon père. Je lui obéis.
  I obey my father. I obey him.

● The reflexive pronoun *se*, direct or indirect object, singular or plural, can show that the subject acts upon itself, or simply may give a different meaning to the verb.

● *On* is an indefinite third person pronoun used only as subject. It is translated in different ways: "people," "they," "one," "you" (in the impersonal sense — "you go three blocks . . ."), or simply by the passive voice.

on pense que   it is thought that
on dit que   they say that
on dirait que   you'd say that
on vous demande au téléphone   you are wanted on the
   telephone

Other Pronouns and Adjectives

An adjective is used with a noun, a pronoun instead of a noun. But since the words are sometimes the same or similar, we will discuss pronouns and adjectives together.

● Demonstrative adjectives and pronouns: this, that, these, those. The demonstrative adjective has four forms:

m. sing.   **ce** (**cet** before vowel sounds)
f. sing.   **cette**
pl.   **ces** (for both genders)

(Note that expressions like *cet ami*, this friend, m., and *cette amie*, this friend, f., sound exactly alike.)

These demonstrative adjectives generally mean *this* or *these*:

ce matin   this morning   **ces livres**   these books

If you want to say *that* or *those*, add *-là* to the noun the demonstrative adjective modifies:

ce matin-là   that morning   **ces livres-là**   those books

To distinguish between *this* or *these* and *that* or *those*, add *-ci* for this, these, and *-là* for that, those:

Ce livre-ci est rouge; ce livre-là est vert.
   This book is red; that book is green.

The demonstrative pronoun has a neuter form *ceci*, this (in general), and *cela*, that (in general), in addition to the masculine and feminine forms *celui*, *ceux*; *celle*, *celles*. These latter forms are never used alone. You can add *-ci* or *-là*:

celui-ci, *m*.	this one	**celle-ci**, *f*.	this one
celui-là, *m*.	that one	**celle-là**, *f*.	that one
ceux-ci, *m*.	these	**celles-ci**, *f*.	these
ceux-là, *m*.	those	**celles-là**, *f*.	those

These forms can also be followed by *de*:

celle de Jean   the one of John's   *or* John's

or by a subordinate clause:

celui que j'ai trouvé   the one I found

● Possessive adjectives and pronouns: In French these forms agree in gender and number *with the object possessed*.

First the adjectives:

English	If the object possessed is		
	m. sing.	*f. sing.*	*m. or f. pl.*
my	**mon**	**ma (mon)**	**mes**
your	**ton**	**ta (ton)**	**tes**
his, her, its	**son**	**sa (son)**	**ses**
our		**notre**	**nos**
your		**votre**	**vos**
their		**leur**	**leurs**

(Before all nouns beginning with a vowel sound, use *mon, ton, son*.)

The French sentence will not tell you the sex of the possessor. *Son livre* can be "his book" or "her book." If you really need to distinguish (you will be surprised at how often it is clear from the context) add *à lui* or *à elle*:

son livre à lui   his book   **son livre à elle**   her book

Be careful not to confuse *ses* and *leurs*. *Ses* refers to several objects belonging to one person, *leurs* to several objects belong to several persons.

The possessive pronouns resemble the adjectives:

English	If the object possessed is:			
	m. sing.	*f. sing.*	*m. pl.*	*f. pl.*
mine	**le mien**	**la mienne**	**les miens**	**les miennes**
yours	**le tien**	**la tienne**	**les tiens**	**les tiennes**
his, hers, its	**le sien**	**la sienne**	**les siens**	**les siennes**
ours	**le nôtre**	**la nôtre**		**les nôtres**
yours	**le vôtre**	**la vôtre**		**les vôtres**
theirs	**le leur**	**la leur**		**les leurs**

● Interrogative adjectives and pronouns: what, which, who, whom, whose. The interrogative adjective, *quel, quels, quelle*, *quelles*, agrees with the noun it modifies.

Quel jour sommes-nous?
  What day is it? *Literally,* What day are we?
Quelle est la date de . . . ?
  What is the date of . . . ?
A quel livre pensez-vous?
  What book are you thinking about?

There are several interrogative pronouns: *Lequel*, m. sing., *laquelle*, f. sing., *lesquels*, m. pl., and *lesquelles*, f. pl., translate "Which one(s)?" Examples:

Voilà deux livres. Lequel voulez-vous?
  Here are two books. Which one do you want?

But you would use the adjective to say:

Quel livre voulez-vous?
  Which book do you want?

(*A* and *de* contract with these pronouns the same way they do with the definite articles: *auquel*, *auxquels*, *auxquelles*; *duquel*, *desquels*, *desquelles*.)

Qui, who, whom, refers to persons and can be used as subject or object. Very often, particularly in spoken French, *qui* is replaced by a longer form, *Qui est-ce qui* for the subject, *qui est-ce que* for the object. Both forms are correct:

Qui vient?/Qui est-ce qui vient?
  Who comes? Who is coming?
Qui voyez-vous?/Qui est-ce que vous voyez?
  Whom do you see?

Note that when you use *qui est-ce que* you keep the normal word order (subject before verb), but when you use *qui* referring to the object of the verb, the subject follows the verb (*voyez-vous*).

Qui can follow a preposition:

  A qui écrivez-vous?   To whom are you writing?

It is used to translate *whose*? (the question, not the relative pronoun):

  A qui est ce livre?   Whose book is this?

Que (*Qu'*) refers to things. In speech *que*, like *qui*, is usually replaced by a longer form: *Qu'est-ce qui* (subject) or *Qu'est-ce que* (object), but both are correct:

Qu'arrive-t-il?/Qu'est-ce qui arrive?
What is happening
Que fait-il?/Qu'est-ce qu'il fait?
What is he doing?

Again you must invert subject and verb if you use the short form. For more detail, see the section on questions.

Quoi, what, is used after prepositions:

A quoi pensez-vous?   What are you thinking about?
De quoi parlez vous?   What are you talking about?

● Relative pronouns vary according to their roles in the subordinate clause:

The subject, who, which, that, is *qui*:

la fille qui est venue   the girl who came
l'auto qui est en bas   the car which is down below

The direct object, whom, which, that, is *que*:

la fille que j'ai vue   the girl (whom) I saw
l'auto que j'ai achetée   the car (which) I bought

(Note that when it is the object, the relative can often be omitted in English, but never in French.)

The preposition *de* and its object, whose, of whom, of which, is *dont*:

la fille dont j'ai le livre   the girl whose book I have

(Note the word order: French says, "of whom I have the book.")

l'homme dont je parle   the man of whom I am speaking

The object of other prepositions: *qui* for persons (*à qui, pour qui*, etc.), *lequel* for things (*auquel, pour laquelle*, etc.).

l'homme à qui j'ai parlé   the man to whom I spoke
la table sur laquelle j'ai mis mon livre
the table on which I put my book

When using relative pronouns, remember that some verbs are followed by a preposition in English and not in French, and vice versa. If your French verb needs a preposition, choose your relative pronoun accordingly:

l'instrument dont il joue   the instrument he plays
   to play = **jouer de**
l'homme qu'il attend   the man he is waiting for
   to wait for = **attendre**
la lettre à laquelle il répond   the letter he is answering
   to answer = **répondre à**

Adverbs

Regular adverbs are formed by adding *-ment* to the adjective. The comparison of adverbs is regular: *plus* (*moins*) for the comparative form, *le plus* (*le moins*) for the superlative. There are a few irregular forms:

bien well	**mieux** better	**le mieux** best
	aussi bien as well	
	moins bien less well	**le moins bien** least well
beaucoup much, very much, many	**plus** more	**le plus** most
peu little	**moins** less	**le moins** least

Note that *beaucoup* and *peu* by themselves are adverbs, linked to the verb. *Beaucoup de* and *peu de* are expressions of quantity, referring to the following noun:

Je l'aime beaucoup (peu).   I like him very much (little).
J'ai beaucoup (peu) de livres.   I have many (few) books.

This difference exists for many expressions. A word without *de* is an adverb; the same word with *de* refers to the following noun, usually as an expression of quantity or a preposition:

Il habite très près.   He lives very near.
Il habite près de l'église.   He lives near the church.

Many adverbs have a negative meaning. We will talk about them in the section on sentence structure.

Prepositions

Prepositions in different languages never correspond exactly. Here we'll mention just a few points:

- In French you cannot end a sentence with a preposition.
- Remember that a preposition may follow a verb in one language but not in the other.
- In English the real action of a verb is often expressed by a preposition which follows it: go in, come in. French will use a verb to translate the preposition rather than the English verb:

go in, come in   **entrer**
go out, come out   **sortir**
run in, run out   **entrer, sortir (en courant)**
go across, walk across   **traverser**
run across   **traverser en courant** (NOT: **courir à travers**)

Many common examples of this are given in the dictionary. If you don't find the one you want, try to translate the idea contained in the preposition.

Verbs

French verbs have different forms for the different persons and numbers, as well as for the different tenses.

French also has a separate category of verbs, reflexive verbs, in which the subject and object of the verb are the same. They are shown in the dictionary with the reflexive pronoun *se* (or *s'*). When these verbs are conjugated, they take the reflexive pronoun (*me, te, se, nous, vous, se*) that agrees in person and number with the subject (see tables).

The infinitive of the verb is given in the dictionary. The conjugation tables at the end of this grammar show how to form four simple and four compound tenses, plus the subjunctive and the imperative. Note that French has no progressive form. Generally you should translate the progressive form of an English tense as you would the simple form — *I am sleeping* like *I sleep*, for example. There is one exception, as we will see.

The *present* tense translates the English present. *Je parle*, I talk.

The *imperfect* corresponds to the past progressive: *Je parlais*, I was talking; or to expressions showing habitual action: I used to talk, I would talk for hours every day. The imperfect does not translate the ordinary English past (I talked), except for verbs which express a state rather than an action:

I knew it. **Je le savais.**

He was sick. **Il était malade.**

The *past indefinite* (*J'ai parlé*, I talked, I have talked) looks like the present perfect in English, but it also translates the ordinary past tense. It is the past tense you will use most often. Often the past indefinite and the imperfect are used together, the past indefinite to note a fact that happened, and the imperfect to describe the surrounding circumstances:

Je lisais quand il a parlé. I was reading when he spoke.

The *past perfect* (*J'avais parlé*, I had talked) is used as it is in English.

The *future* (*Je parlerai*, I will talk) is used as it is in English. It is also used after *when*, where in English we use the present.

The *future perfect* (*J'aurai parlé*, I will have talked) is used as it is in English, and after *when*.

The *conditional* (*Je parlerais*, I would talk) expresses what you would do *if*. It is not used in the if-clause, but in the other part of the sentence:

Si j'étais riche, j'irais en Floride.

If I were rich, I would go to Florida.

The conditional can also be used in indirect statements, in which case it can follow *si*, if.

Je me demandais s'il serait là.

I wondered if he would be there.

The *conditional perfect* (*J'aurais parlé*, I would have talked) expresses what would have happened if something else had or had not happened.

The *subjunctive* (. . . *que je parle*, . . . that I may, should, etc., talk) is used almost exclusively in the subordinate clauses. It is used to indicate doubt, wish, joy, sorrow, etc. Some verbs are always followed by the subjunctive: *désirer*, desire;

préférer, prefer; *souhaiter*, wish; *regretter*, regret; *vouloir*, want; and the impersonal expression *il faut*, it is necessary. Note that these verbs can also take an infinitive. This is possible only if both verbs have the same subject. Say:

Je regrette d'être ici.   I am sorry to be here.
NOT **Je regrette que je sois ici.**

But you must say:

Je regrette qu'il soit ici.
   I am sorry that he is here.

Avoid *il . . . que . . . il, je . . . que . . . je*, and so on.

Some other verbs are followed by the indicative when they are affirmative, but by the subjunctive when negative or interrogative: *penser*, think; *croire*, believe; *espérer*, hope. Certain conjunctions must always be followed by the subjunctive: *avant que*, before; *jusqu'à ce que*, until; *en attendant que*, until; *bien que*, although; *quoique*, although; *à moins que*, unless; *pourvu que*, provided that; *afin que*, in order that; *de sorte que*, in order that; *sans que*, without. Again, if the subjects of both clauses are the same, you *may* be able to use a preposition which takes an infinitive: *avant de* instead of *avant que*, for example:

Il est venu avant de partir.
NOT **Il est venu avant qu'il parte.**
   He came before he left/leaving.

Compound tenses (past indefinite, past perfect, future perfect and conditional perfect) are formed as in English with an auxiliary and the past participle of the verb. *Avoir*, to have, is the auxiliary most commonly used, for all transitive verbs and for most others. *Être*, to be, is the auxiliary used for *all reflexive verbs* and for certain other verbs which express movement or change of state. Non-reflexive verbs conjugated with *être* are marked in the dictionary (*Aux:* ÊTRE).

In verbs conjugated with *être* the past participle agrees in number and gender with the *subject* of the verb. If the auxiliary is *avoir*, the participle agrees only with a *preceding direct object* (object pronoun, but not *en*, or relative pronoun). Otherwise the participle keeps the masculine singular form.

Jean est allé en ville. John went to town. (Subject is m. sing.)

Marie est allée en ville. Mary went to town. (Subject is f. sing.)

Jean a pris des chemises. John took some shirts. (Object follows)

Il les a prises. He took them. (Object precedes)

les chemises qu'il a prises. the shirts he took. (Object precedes)

The passive voice is formed as in English, but it is used much less frequently.

Sentence Structure

An affirmative sentence generally follows the same pattern as in English, except that most adjectives follow the noun. Adverbs usually follow the verb, and in a compound tense a short adverb is usually found between the auxiliary and the participle: *Elle a bien lu*, She read well. Pronoun objects precede the verb (or the auxiliary, which is the main verb grammatically speaking — the conjugated verb). Prepositional phrases go where they do in English.

● To form a *question* you have a choice:

1. You can begin the sentence with *Est-ce que*, Is it that . . . , and use normal word order:

Vous avez des pommes. You have apples.

Est-ce que vous avez des pommes? Do you have apples?

2. You can invert the pronoun subject and verb (auxiliary in compound tenses) and join them with a hyphen:

Vous avez des pommes. **Avez-vous des pommes?**

If the sentence has a noun subject, it remains where it is, and the corresponding subject pronoun is added after the verb:

Votre frère est venu. Your brother came.

Votre frère est-il venu? Did your brother come?

In the third person singular a *t* sound is needed between verb and subject. If the verb doesn't already end in *d* or *t*, add a *t*: *parle-t-il?* — just because it sounds better.

Est-ce que is easier; inversion is more elegant. You might use inversion for verbs you know well, *Est-ce que* for anything complex.

● French *negations* have two parts: *ne* before the verb and another negative word after it. *Ne . . . pas* (not) is most frequent. Others are:

ne . . . **plus**	no longer	ne . . . **rien**	nothing
ne . . . **que**	only	ne . . . **aucun**	no
ne . . . **personne**	nobody	ne . . . **ni . . . ni**	neither . . .
ne . . . **jamais**	never	ni . . . ni . . . **ne**	nor
ne . . . **guère**	hardly		

Examples:

Je vais en ville. Je ne vais pas en ville. I am (not) going to town.

Il a lu ce livre. Il n'a pas lu ce livre. He read/did not read this book.

Il a de l'argent. Il n'a plus d'argent. He has (no more) money.

(Remember that indefinite articles and partitives become *de* in a negation.) *Ne* precedes any pronouns that come before the verb:

Je ne les lui ai pas donnés. I didn't give them to him.

Il ne m'en a pas donné. He didn't give me any.

In compound tenses the second part of the negation usually follows the auxiliary. *Personne*, *que*, *ni . . . ni*, and *aucun* follow the participle. If *rien*, *personne*, or *aucun* is the subject of the sentence, it is in the normal subject position:

Personne n'est venu. Nobody came.

To make a negative imperative, form the negative sentence and omit the subject.

(vous) Ne faites pas ça! Don't do that.

● Remember that no auxiliary is used in French questions or negations, no equivalent of *do*. This can cause problems. Take for example, "*I want a beer. Do you?*" The first part is easy: *Je voudrais une bière*. But you can't say *Faites-vous? Faire* is never used this way. You can say *Et vous?*, And you?, or *En voulez-vous une?*, Do you want one? This principle is quite general: you cannot use an auxiliary, even in a compound tense, to avoid repeating the main verb: you cannot say "He had come." "Had he?" Either repeat the verb or find another expression. Often *Oui* or *Non* may be enough.

Conjugating Verbs

A French verb has two parts — the stem, which changes from verb to verb, and the ending, which changes according to person, number and tense. Conjugating a verb is a matter of finding the right stem and adding the proper ending: *chant-e*, *chant-ions*, etc. A regular verb keeps the same stem, while an irregular verb may have several. The endings remain basically the same.

There are three groups of regular verbs which you will recognize by the ending of the infinitive:
1. Verbs in *-er* (*chanter*, to sing). Nine tenths of all verbs.
2. Verbs in *-ir* (*finir*, to finish). About 300 verbs.
3. Verbs in *-re* (*vendre*, to sell). Only 20–30 verbs.

In addition to a verb from each group, the table shows the conjugation of a reflexive verb, *se laver*, to get washed. Not all reflexive verbs are from the first group!

We give three basic forms for each verb: infinitive, present participle, and past participle. The way to find the stem for each tense is explained just before the conjugation of that tense for -er verbs. The stem precedes the hyphen. The endings which follow it must be added to the stem of the verb you are using. The pronunciation of some endings is given.

-ER VERBS

INF.   chant-er

PRES. PART.   chant-ant

PAST PART.   chant-é(e)

PRESENT: For the singular, use the stem of the infinitive; for the plural, the stem of the present participle. This is the only tense where different groups have different endings.

je	chant-e	nous	chant-ons
tu	chant-es	vous	chant-ez
il, elle	chant-e	ils, elles	chant-ent

IMPERFECT: Use the stem of the present participle.

je	chant-ais	nous	chant-ions
tu	chant-ais	vous	chant-iez
il	chant-ait	ils	chant-aient

FUTURE: Use the infinitive without -r (-re for -re verbs).

je	chante-rai	nous	chante-rons
tu	chante-ras	vous	chante-rez
il	chante-ra	ils	chante-rent

CONDITIONAL: The conditional stem is *always* the same as the future stem.

je	chante-rais	nous	chante-rions
tu	chante-rais	vous	chante-riez
il	chante-rait	ils	chante-raient

SUBJUNCTIVE: For *nous* and *vous*, use the *nous* and *vous* forms of the *imperfect* tense. For the other forms, use the stem of the third person plural of the *present* tense (chantent, finissent, vendent, lavent). Here the two stems are the same, but this rule will help for irregular verbs.

que je	chant-e	que nous	chant-ions
que tu	chant-es	que vous	chant-iez
qu'il	chant-e	qu'ils	chant-ent

For the compound tenses, use the proper form of *avoir* and *être* with the past participle. See page 358 for the conjugation of *avoir* and *être*. The (e) is to remind you that the participle can change to agree with its subject or object. See page 350.

PAST INDEFINITE: Use the present tense form of the auxiliary verb with the past participle.

j'ai	chanté(e)	nous avons	chanté(e)
tu as	chanté(e)	vous avez	chanté(e)
il a	chanté(e)	ils ont	chanté(e)

PAST PERFECT: Use the imperfect tense form of the auxiliary verb with the past participle.

j'avais   chanté(e), etc.

FUTURE PERFECT: Use the future tense form of the auxiliary
                   verb with the past participle.
                   j'aurais chanté(e), etc.

CONDITIONAL PERFECT: Use the conditional tense form of
                     the auxiliary verb with the past
                     participle.
                     j'aurais chanté(e), etc.

IMPERATIVE: Use the second person singular, without -s,
             first and second person plural of present tense.
             First person plural translates: Let's sing!
             Chante!
             Chantons!
             Chantez!

-IR VERBS

TENSE FORMATION: See under -ER VERBS.

INF.   fin-ir

PRES. PART. finiss-ant

PAST PART. fini(e)

PRESENT:	je	fin-is	nous	finiss-ons
	tu	fin-is	vous	finiss-ez
	il, elle	fin-it	ils, elles	finiss-ent

IMPERFECT:	je	finiss-ais	nous	finiss-ions
	tu	finiss-ais	vous	finiss-iez
	il	finiss-ait	ils	finiss-aient

FUTURE:	je	fini-rai	nous	fini-rons
	tu	fini-ras	vous	fini-rez
	il	fini-ra	ils	fini-ront

CONDITIONAL:	je	fini-rais	nous	fini-rions
	tu	fini-rais	vous	fini-riez
	il	fini-rait	ils	fini-raient

SUBJUNCTIVE:	que je	finiss-e	que nous	finiss-ions
	que tu	finiss-es	que vous	finiss-iez
	qu'il	finiss-e	qu'ils	finiss-ent

PAST INDEFINITE:	j'ai	fini(e)	nous avons	fini(e)
	tu as	fini(e)	vous avez	fini(e)
	il a	fini(e)	ils ont	fini(e)

PAST PERFECT: j'avais fini(e), etc.
FUTURE PERFECT: j'aurai fini(e), etc.
CONDITIONAL PERFECT: j'aurais fini(e), etc.
IMPERATIVE: Finis!
            Finissons!
            Finissez!

-RE VERBS

TENSE FORMATION: See under -ER VERBS.

INF.   ven-dre
PRES. PART.   ven-dant
PAST PART.   vend-u(e)

PRESENT:	je	vend-s	nous	vend-ons
	tu	vend-s	vous	vend-ez
	il, elle	vend (add *t* if	ils, elles	vend-ent
		ending not *d* or *t*)		

IMPERFECT:	je	vend-ais	nous	vend-ions
	tu	vend-ais	vous	vend-iez
	il	vend-ait	ils	vend-aient

FUTURE:	je	vend-rai	nous	vend-rons
	tu	vend-ras	vous	vend-rez
	il	vend-ra	ils	vend-ront

CONDITIONAL:	je	vend-rais	nous	vend-rions
	tu	vend-rais	vous	vend-riez
	il	vend-rait	ils	vend-raient

SUBJUNCTIVE:	que je	vend-e	que nous	vend-ions
	que tu	vend-es	que vous	vend-iez
	qu'il	vend-e	qu'ils	vend-ent

PAST INDEFINITE:	j'ai	vendu(e)	nous avons	vendu(e)
	tu as	vendu(e)	vous avez	vendu(e)
	il a	vendu(e)	ils ont	vendu(e)

PAST PERFECT: j'avais vendu(e), etc.
FUTURE PERFECT: j'aurai vendu(e), etc.
CONDITIONAL PERFECT: j'aurais vendu(e), etc.
IMPERATIVE: Vends!
            Vendons!
            Vendez!

REFLEXIVE VERBS

INF.   se lav-er

PRES. PART.   lav-ant

PAST PART.   lav-é(e)

PRESENT

je me	lav-e	nous nous	lav-ons
tu te	lav-es	vous vous	lav-ez
il se	lav-e	ils se	lav-ent

IMPERFECT:

je me	lav-ais	nous nous	lav-ions
tu te	lav-ais	vous vous	lav-iez
il se	lav-ait	ils se	lav-aient

FUTURE:

je me	lave-rai	nous nous	lave-rons
tu te	lave-ras	vous vous	lave-rez
il se	lave-ra	ils se	lave-ront

CONDITIONAL:

je me	lave-rais	nous nous	lave-rions
tu te	lave-rais	vous vous	lave-riez
il se	lave-rait	ils se	lave-raient

SUBJUNCTIVE:

que je me	lav-e	que nous nous	lav-ions
que tu te	lav-es	que vous vous	lav-iez
qu'il se	lav-e	qu'ils se	lav-ent

PAST INDEFINITE:

je me suis	lavé(e)	nous nous sommes	lavés (lavées)
tu t'es	lavé(e)	vous vous êtes	lavés (lavées)
il s'est	lavé(e)	ils se sont	lavés (lavées)

PAST PERFECT:
je m'étais   lavé(e), etc.

FUTURE PERFECT:
je me serai   lavé(e), etc.

CONDITIONAL PERFECT:
je me serais   lavé(e), etc.

IMPERATIVE:
  Lave-toi! Lavons-nous! Lavez-vous!

Irregular Verbs

Most important are *avoir* and *être*.

                           AVOIR, to have

INF.   avoir
PRES. PART.   ayant
PAST PART.   eu(e) [*ii*]

PRESENT: I have
  j'ai   nous avons
  tu as   vous avez
  il a   ils ont

IMPERFECT:
  j'avais   nous avions
  tu avais   vous aviez
  il avait   ils avaient

FUTURE:
  j'aurai   nous aurons
  tu auras   vous aurez
  il aura   ils auront

CONDITIONAL:
  j'aurais   nous aurions
  tu aurais   vous auriez
  il aurait   ils auraient

The auxiliary for the compound tenses is *avoir* itself.

PAST INDEFINITE: I ~~was~~ had
  j'ai   eu(e)   nous avons eu(e)
  tu as eu(e)   vous avez   eu(e)
  il a   eu(e)   ils ont   eu(e)

PAST PERFECT:
  j'avais eu(e), etc.

FUTURE PERFECT:
  j'aurai eu(e), etc.

CONDITIONAL PERFECT:
  j'aurais eu(e), etc.

SUBJUNCTIVE:

que j'aie [*eh*]	que nous	ayons
que tu aies	que vous	ayez
qu'il ait	qu'ils	aient

IMPERATIVE:
  Aie.
  Ayons.
  Ayez.

ÊTRE, to be

INF.   être

PRES. PART.   étant

PAST PART.   été

PRESENT:

je suis	nous	sommes
tu es	vous	êtes
il est	ils	sont

IMPERFECT: *I was*

j'étais	nous	étions
tu étais	vous	étiez
il était	ils	étaient

FUTURE:

je serai	nous	serons
tu seras	vous	serez
il sera	ils	seront

CONDITIONAL:

je serais	nous	serions
tu serais	vous	seriez
il serait	ils	seraient

The auxiliary for the compound tenses is *avoir*.

PAST INDEFINITE:

j'ai été	nous avons	été
tu as été	vous avez	été
il a été	ils ont	été

PAST PERFECT:
  j'avais été, etc.

FUTURE PERFECT:
  j'aurai été, etc.

CONDITIONAL PERFECT:
  j'aurais été, etc.

SUBJUNCTIVE:

que je	sois [*swah*]	que nous	soyons
que tu	sois	que vous	soyez
qu'il	soit	qu'ils	soient

IMPERATIVE:
  Sois.
  Soyons.
  Soyez.

For all other irregular verbs, we give here the three basic forms: infinitive, present participle, and past participle. For some verbs this is enough to derive all tenses (the derivation of each tense is explained above before the regular conjugation of that tense). We list only forms you cannot find in this way. Most verbs are irregular in the present. (Remember that the imperative is always the same as the present, and that the third person plural of the present is used to form most of the subjunctive. If the present is irregular, these forms follow the same irregularities, and we won't mention them.) The stem of the future, too, is often irregular. (Remember that the conditional always has the same stem as the future.) Many verbs refer you to another that is conjugated in the same way. For compound verbs, see the basic verb, *venir* for *prévenir*, for example.

s'abstenir abstain *See* VENIR
acheter buy

  present participle achetant
  past participle acheté
  present achète, achètes, achète, achetons, achetez, achètent
  future achèterai

accueillir welcome *See* CUEILLIR
acquérir acquire

  present participle acquérant
  past participle acquis
  present acquiers, acquiers, acquiert, acquérons,
    acquérez, acquièrent
  future acquerrai

aller go

  present participle allant
  past participle allé
  present vais, vas, va, allons, allez, vont
  future irai
  subjunctive aille, ailles, aille, allions, alliez, aillent

apercevoir see *See* DEVOIR
apparaître appear *See* CONNAÎTRE
appartenir belong *See* VENIR
apprendre learn *See* PRENDRE
appeler call

  present participle appelant
  past participle appelé
  present appelle, appelles, appelle, appelons, appelez,
    appellent
  future appellerai

s'asseoir sit down

  present participle asseyant
  past participle assis
  present assieds, assieds, assied, asseyons, asseyez,
    asseyent
  future assoirai

atteindre attain *See* CRAINDRE
battre beat

  present participle battant
  past participle battu
  present bats, bats, bat, battons, battez, battent

boire drink

  presem participle buvant

past participle bu
present bois, bois, boit, buvons, buvez, boivent

bouillir boil

present participle bouillant
past participle bouilli
present bous, bous, bout, bouillons, bouillez, bouillent

céder yield *See* PRÉFÉRER
comprendre understand *See* PRENDRE
concevoir conceive *See* DEVOIR
conclure conclude

present participle concluant
past participle conclu

conduire lead

present participle conduisant
past participle conduit
present conduis, conduis, conduit, conduisons,
conduisez, conduisent

connaître know

present participle connaissant
past participle connu
present connais, connais, connaît, connaissons,
connaissez, connaissent

conquérir conquer *See* ACQUÉRIR
consentir consent *See* SORTIR
construire build *See* CONDUIRE
coudre sew

present participle cousant
past participle cousu
present couds, couds, coud, cousons, cousez, cousent

courir run

present participle courant
past participle couru
future courrai

couvrir cover *See* OUVRIR
craindre fear

present participle craignant

past participle craint
present crains, crains, craint, craignons, craignez, craignent

croire believe

present participle croyant
past participle cru
present crois, crois, croit, croyons, croyez, croient

croître grow

present participle croissant
past participle crû
present croîs, croîs, croît, croissons, croissez, croissent

cueillir pick

present participle cueillant
past participle cueilli
present cueille, cueilles, cueille, cueillons, cueillez, cueillent
future cueillerai

cuire cook *See* CONDUIRE
décevoir deceive *See* DEVOIR
découvrir discover *See* OUVRIR
décrire describe *See* ÉCRIRE
défaire undo *See* FAIRE
démentir deny *See* SORTIR
déteindre fade *See* CRAINDRE
détruire destroy *See* CONDUIRE
devoir owe, be obliged to

present participle devant
past participle dû
present dois, dois, doit, devons, devez, doivent
future devrai

dire say

present participle disant
past participle dit
present dis, dis, dit, disons, dites, disent

dissoudre dissolve

present participle dissolvant

past participle dissout
present dissous, dissous, dissout, dissolvons, dissolvez,
   dissolvent

dormir sleep

present participle dormant
past participle dormi
present dors, dors, dort, dormons, dormez, dorment

écrire write

present participle écrivant
past participle écrit
present écris, écris, écrit, écrivons, écrivez, écrivent

élire elect *See* LIRE

émouvoir move (feelings)

present participle émouvant
past participle ému
present émeus, émeus, émeut, émouvons, émouvez,
   émeuvent
future None

envoyer send

present participle envoyant
past participle envoyé
present envoie, envoies, envoie, envoyons, envoyez,
   envoient
future enverrai

espérer hope *See* PRÉFÉRER
éteindre extinguish *See* CRAINDRE
extraire extract *See* CROIRE
faire do, make

present participle faisant
past participle fait
present fais, fais, fait, faisons, faites, font
future ferai
present subjunctive fasse, fasses, fasse, fassions, fassiez,
   fassent

falloir be necessary *See* VALOIR

[Only third person singular forms are used.]

fuir flee

  present participle fuyant
  past participle fui
  present fuis, fuis, fuit, fuyons, fuyez, fuient

haïr hate

  present participle haïssant
  past participle haï
  present hais, hais, hait, haïssons, haïssez, haïssent

inclure include *See* CONCLURE
inscrire register *See* ÉCRIRE
instruire instruct *See* CONDUIRE
introduire introduce *See* CONDUIRE
jeter throw *See* APPELER
joindre join *See* CRAINDRE
lire read

  present participle lisant
  past participle lu
  present lis, lis, lit, lisons, lisez, lisent

mentir lie, tell an untruth *See* SORTIR
mettre put

  present participle mettant
  past participle mis
  present mets, mets, met, mettons, mettez, mettent

moudre grind *See* RÉSOUDRE
mourir die

  present participle mourant
  past participle mort
  present meurs, meurs, meurt, mourons, mourez, meurent
  future mourrai

naître be born

  present participle naissant
  past participle né
  present nais, nais, nait, naissons, naissez, naissent

offrir offer *See* OUVRIR
ouvrir open

  present participle ouvrant

past participle ouvert
present ouvre, ouvres, ouvre, ouvrons, ouvrez, ouvrent

paraître appear *See* CONNAÎTRE
partir leave *See* SORTIR
peindre paint *See* CRAINDRE
plaindre complain *See* CRAINDRE
plaire please

present participle plaisant
past participle plu
present plais, plais, plaît, plaisons, plaisez, plaisent

pleuvoir rain

present participle pleuvant
past participle plu
present pleut [Third person singular only.]
future pleuvra [Third person singular only.]
subjunctive pleuve [Third person singular only.]

pouvoir be able

present participle pouvant
past participle pu
present peux, peux, peut, pouvons, pouvez, peuvent
future pourrai
subjunctive puisse, puisses, puisse, puissions, puissiez, puissent

prendre take

present participle prenant
past participle pris
present prends, prends, prend, prenons, prenez, prennent

produire produce *See* CONDUIRE
recevoir receive *See* DEVOIR
réduire reduce *See* CONDUIRE
renvoyer send back *See* ENVOYER
résoudre resolve

present participle résolvant
past participle résolu
present résous, résous, résout, résolvons, résolvez, résolvent

rire laugh
  present participle riant
  past participle ri

savoir know
  present participle sachant
  past participle su
  present sais, sais, sait, savons, savez, savent
  imperfect savais, savais, savait, savions, saviez, savaient
  future saurai
  subjunctive sache, saches, sache, sachions, sachiez, sachent
  imperative sache, sachons, sachez

séduire seduce *See* CONDUIRE
sentir feel *See* SORTIR
servir serve
  present participle servant
  past participle servi
  present sers, sers, sert, servons, servez, servent

sortir leave
  present participle sortant
  past participle sorti
  present sors, sors, sort, sortons, sortez, sortent

souffrir suffer *See* OUVRIR
sourire smile *See* RIRE
suffire suffice
  present participle suffisant
  past participle suffit
  present suffis, suffis, suffit, suffisons, suffisez, suffisent

suivre follow
  present participle suivant
  past participle suivi
  present suis, suis, suit, suivons, suivez, suivent

taire be silent *See* PLAIRE
teindre dye *See* CRAINDRE
tenir hold *See* VENIR

traduire translate *See* CONDUIRE

vaincre conquer

  present participle vainquant
  past participle vaincu
  present vaincs, vaincs, vainc, vainquons, vainquez,
    vainquent

valoir be worth

  present participle valant
  past participle valu
  present vaux, vaux, vaut, valons, valez, valent
  future vaudrai
  subjunctive vaille, vailles, vaille, valions, valiez, vaillent

venir come

  present participle venant
  past participle venu
  present viens, viens, vient, venons, venez, viennent
  future viendrai

vivre live

  present participle vivant
  past participle vécu
  present vis, vis, vit, vivons, vivez, vivent

voir see

  present participle voyant
  past participle vu
  present vois, vois, voit, voyons, voyez, voient
  future verrai

vouloir want

  present participle voulant
  past participle voulu
  present veux, veux, veut, voulons, voulez, veulent
  future voudrai
  subjunctive veuille, veuilles, veuille, voulions, vouliez,
    veuillent
  imperative veuille, veuillions, veuillez